The Life and World of Francis Rodd, Lord Rennell (1895–1978)

The Life and World of Francis Rodd, Lord Rennell (1895–1978)

Geography, Money and War

Philip Boobbyer

ANTHEM PRESS

Anthem Press
An imprint of Wimbledon Publishing Company
www.anthempress.com

This edition first published in UK and USA 2022
by ANTHEM PRESS
75–76 Blackfriars Road, London SE1 8HA, UK
or PO Box 9779, London SW19 7ZG, UK
and
244 Madison Ave #116, New York, NY 10016, USA

First published in the UK and USA by Anthem Press in 2021

Copyright © Philip Boobbyer 2022

The author asserts the moral right to be identified as the author of this work.

All rights reserved. Without limiting the rights under copyright reserved above,
no part of this publication may be reproduced, stored or introduced into
a retrieval system, or transmitted, in any form or by any means
(electronic, mechanical, photocopying, recording or otherwise),
without the prior written permission of both the copyright
owner and the above publisher of this book.

British Library Cataloguing-in-Publication Data
A catalogue record for this book is available from the British Library.

ISBN-13: 978-1-83998-562-1 (Pbk)
ISBN-10: 1-83998-562-3 (Pbk)

Cover photo: Rodd in Sicily, 1943. Imperial War Museum.

This title is also available as an e-book.

To
Rodd's grandchildren and great grandchildren

CONTENTS

List of Figures — ix
List of Abbreviations — xi
A Note on Names — xiii
Acknowledgements — xv
A Personal Note — xvii

Introduction		1
Chapter One	Family and Youth	7
Chapter Two	The First World War	23
Chapter Three	Into the Sahara	45
Chapter Four	International Banker	75
Chapter Five	Negotiating with Italy	101
Chapter Six	West Africa, 1940	119
Chapter Seven	East Africa in Transition	137
Chapter Eight	AMGOT (Allied Military Government of Occupied Territories)	163
Chapter Nine	'Jack of Many Trades'	187
Conclusion		213

Sources and Bibliography — 221
Index — 237

FIGURES

1.1	James Rennell Rodd, c. 1920	14
1.2	Lilias Rodd (née Guthrie). Lithograph, 1894	15
1.3	Balliol College second eight, 1914	20
2.1	Rodd as a soldier in the Royal Field Artillery	25
3.1	Rodd with T'ekhmedin, 1922	52
3.2	Extract from a map of Aïr made in 1910 by Captain Cortier	55
3.3	Map of the trade roads of the Sahara, designed by Rodd	56
3.4	Agellal village and mountains	60
3.5	Peter Rodd, Augustine Courtauld and Francis Rodd	63
4.1	Francis and Mary's wedding, 3 August 1928	88
5.1	The Rodd	116
6.1	Rodd on Charles de Gaulle, extract from letter to Mary	133
7.1	Rodd sitting alongside Philip Mitchell, Nairobi, c. 1941	142
8.1	British soldiers in Catania, 5 August 1943	168
9.1	Evelyn Emmet, 1958	193
9.2	Rodd speaking at the Douglas Aircraft Company, Santa Monica, California, November 1956	198
9.3	Rodd, c. late 1950s	206
9.4	The Boy Jesus and the Shepherd, 1974. Etching in Chinese ink by Mary Rodd/Rennell	209
C.1	Rodd's gravestone, designed by David Kindersley	214

ABBREVIATIONS

ACC	Allied Control Commission
AFHQ	Allied Force Headquarters
AMGOT	Allied Military Government of Occupied Territories
ANB	Austrian National Bank
BIS	Bank for International Settlements
BOAC	British Overseas Airways Corporation
BUF	British Union of Fascists
CA	Credit-Anstalt
CCAO	chief civil affairs officer
CFA	controller of finance and accounts
CORB	Children's Overseas Reception Board
CPO	chief political officer
DCA	Directorate of Civil Affairs
DMI	director of military intelligence
EEF	Egyptian Expeditionary Force
GHQ	general headquarters
GOC	general officer commanding
G(R)	sub-branch of MI(R)
IAI	International African Institute
KBE	Knight Commander of the British Empire
LRDG	Long Range Desert Group
MEW	Ministry of Economic Warfare
MGS	Military Government Section
MI(R)	Military Intelligence (Research)
MRA	Moral Re-Armament
OETA	Occupied Enemy Territory Administration
OG	Oxford Group
OTA	Occupied Territory Administration
RAF	Royal Air Force
RFA	Royal Field Artillery
RGS	Royal Geographical Society
SCAO	senior civil affairs officer
SHAEF	Supreme Headquarters Allied Expeditionary Force
SOE	Special Operations Executive

A NOTE ON NAMES

The subject of this book was known as Francis Rodd until he was nearly 46 years old. His full name was Francis James Rennell Rodd. His father, who was called James Rennell Rodd, was given a peerage in 1933, and he took the title Lord Rennell of Rodd. He died in July 1941, and the title then passed to Francis. From then on, Francis was known as Lord Rennell or Francis Rennell. In the main text of this book, I have referred to Francis as 'Rodd' throughout, for reasons of clarity. In the references, I have adopted a different approach. Most sources of an official or public character authored by Rodd from late 1941 onwards are cited under the authorship of Lord Rennell. But with sources of a more informal or personal nature, Rodd is often retained as the designated author, even after 1941. In the text, Rodd's father is generally referred to as 'Rennell Rodd'. Rodd's mother, Lilias, and wife, Mary, along with some other family members and friends, are referred to by their first names.

ACKNOWLEDGEMENTS

The School of History at the University of Kent, where I have been based since 1995, has been an excellent place for working on this book. Stefan Goebel and Gaynor Johnson read the text in manuscript and made many thoughtful suggestions about how to improve it. I turned to Timothy Bowman and Mark Connelly whenever I needed advice about British military history. Andrew Cohen, Karen Jones, Aparaijta Mukhopadhyay and Juliette Pattinson shared insights on a number of issues. I feel very lucky to have had such expertise around me. From beyond Kent, I am indebted to Charles Withers for reading a draft of the manuscript and stressing the importance of seeing Rodd in a wide enough context. Saul Kelly's knowledge of the British exploration of the Sahara proved helpful, while Henrietta Butler was a source of knowledge about Tuareg culture. Martin Horn checked the chapter on Rodd's life as a banker. In addition to those mentioned, I would like to thank James Bruce, Peter Clarke, John Dickie, Edward Flint, Erik Goldstein, Richard Hammond, Catherine McIlwaine, Nan Miller, Helyn Parr, John Pollard, Phyllis Rodd, Charles Spicer and Jane Wellesley for helping me with various details or providing assistance. Thanks are also due to photographer David King for his help in preparing some of the illustrations. I also benefitted from talking with members of my family, particularly my mother, Juliet Boobbyer, and my aunt, Mary Daniell: they were a precious source of information about the history of Rodd's family. My cousins Joseph Blythe, Francis Dunne and Jemima Lord offered thoughts and help. I would also like to thank Roddy Edwards for prompting me to think about the nature of Britain's legacy in the world, and Ken Noble for his encouragement. Finally, I must express gratitude to my wife, Laura, for putting up with my moments of uncertainty about bringing this work to completion and for her enduring care and support.

A PERSONAL NOTE

For an academic work, this book is unusual in the sense that I have a personal relationship to the subject. Francis Rodd was my grandfather. Until recently, Russian history and twentieth-century religion were the main areas of my research. But I have long been aware that there were topics closer to home, in my own family, which would be of great interest to a historian such as myself. For many years, Rodd remained a relatively obscure figure to me. My knowledge of his career was limited to what could be gleaned from obituaries, short summaries of his life or family anecdotes. A chance discovery changed everything. Poking around my mother's house one day, I stumbled upon a file containing Rodd's wartime correspondence with his wife, Mary. I have always found letters intriguing, and this collection was no exception – it opened up a story largely unknown to the family. As I did further research into Rodd's life, his career and character came into sight like a submerged ship being raised out of the water. It turned out that Rodd was close to the action during a number of big events during the past century, and a worthy subject for a book.

I knew Rodd personally but not well. He died in 1978 when I was 14. I met him during family holidays at his home in Herefordshire. My memory of him is largely confined to personal, essentially trivial details – like the fact that he blew his nose loudly, came down to breakfast late and read the paper, and sometimes got angry at the barking of my grandmother's dogs. I was occasionally asked to mix him a pink gin – he liked a drink and took snuff. Then there was the large saddle of roast beef served on Sundays, and the fact that meals were cooked and served by employees from the locality – this was a milieu with a clearly defined class structure. In the family he was sometimes called 'Bompa' – one of his grandchildren once called him 'Bompa' instead of 'Grandpa' and the name stuck. My older cousins remember him for being interesting, affectionate and good company. The man I knew was declining in energy and not so easy to relate to. But to all of us, he appeared 'important'. We knew that he had had a big role in the war. Moreover, he was a 'Lord': he inherited a peerage in 1941.

Inevitably, the writing of this book has been personally interesting for me. While looking at Rodd from an academic perspective, I often found another pair of eyes – the eyes of a grandson – watching in the wings. In a sense, researching the book involved the two of us going on a journey together, in which he – through the medium of primary sources – introduced me to his life and world. In this process, at an imaginative level, I came to know him in a way I had never done in life. In spite of these things, this is meant to be a scholarly work. We know that no one in life is just an observer. This is certainly true in the case of people writing about their relatives, although the point could equally apply to anybody working on the recent history of their own country. Moreover, there is always a creative, literary dimension to the writing of history. For all that, there is value in trying to maintain a sense of critical distance, to stand back from the material and arrive at a more detached perspective. That has been my approach here. I hope Rodd, himself an admirer of the ideal of the unprejudiced study of life and nature, would have approved.

Canterbury, September 2020

INTRODUCTION

Fierce, restless and with a rich portfolio of interests, Francis Rodd was always looking for a new project to feed an insatiable curiosity for life. Different worlds intersected in a career packed with activity, sometimes combining easily and at other times jostling with one another for attention. The two world wars in a variety of ways gave shape and purpose to his life, with military intelligence and military government being important areas of focus. In between the conflicts, and after the Second World War, much of his time was devoted to geography and banking. Along the way, he made friends with Lawrence of Arabia, talked with Benito Mussolini, spent time with Charles de Gaulle and fell out with Anthony Eden. He inhabited that privileged echelon of British society satirised by novelist Nancy Mitford – his sister-in-law. The high point of his career came in 1943 when he was given the task of heading the first military government in Allied-occupied Europe – he was chief civil affairs officer in the organisation known as AMGOT (Allied Military Government of Occupied Territories). He proved a controversial figure. He had obvious leadership skills and a good knowledge of Italy, but some thought him difficult or eccentric, and there were those on the left who feared that his pre-war business activities had brought him too close to the Italian regime. Nowadays, he is little known. This book is a study of his life, with particular reference to his involvement in geography, banking, intelligence and military government, and his political convictions and religious beliefs.

Rodd first came to public attention for his travels to the south-central Sahara in the 1920s. He had been at Eton and Oxford before the outbreak of the First World War, after which he spent a year on the Western Front. Wartime duties in Italy, North Africa and the Middle East followed. An interest in the desert was awakened in these years, which then found expression in expeditions he made to the Aïr mountains in the French colony of Niger in 1922 and 1927. An outcome of the first of these was a study of the culture and history of the Tuareg, *People of the Veil* (1926), his most influential work. For his journeys and publications, he was awarded the Founder's Medal of the Royal Geographical Society (RGS) in 1929. After the Second World War, he was president of the RGS (1945–48). In this role, he worked to popularise geography and demonstrate its importance to education. Geography, in both its academic and romantic guises, was one of his enduring loves – perhaps the most consistent of them. Rodd's life in geography, hitherto unrevealed in any detail, deserves attention for what it tells us about both the British penetration of the Sahara and the revitalisation of the RGS after 1945.

Rodd's love of geography was often connected with an attachment to particular places, notably Aïr, Western Australia and the English–Welsh border. The first two were characterised by a combination of remoteness and relative emptiness, the latter also by a remote quality but in the more congested setting of Britain. Something connected with either the size or the solitude of these places appealed to him and stirred in him existential reflections. This was the experience of many British explorers encountering lonely and little-known parts of the world. Rodd was also aware of how natural history is shaped by the impact of human migration and settlement. He knew – as contemporary geographers point out – that places are not just containers.[1] The natural environment elicited from him a scholarly response: an aspiration to calculate, contextualise and historicise. In the case of the Sahara, there was also a more overtly political dimension to his interest. Knowledge of geography has always been indispensable to the conduct of war. But the First World War made geographers more aware than ever of the military relevance of their discipline, particularly by demonstrating the importance of maps for addressing battlefield questions. Rodd was fascinated by the caravan routes of the Sahara and quickly saw their relevance in the event of a new military conflict in North Africa arising. In seeing and reporting on desert road systems from a military point of view, his thinking fed into what has been called the 'militarisation' of the desert.[2]

Rodd grew up in a diplomatic milieu. His father, James Rennell Rodd, was a senior diplomat who served as ambassador to Italy during the First World War. Rodd followed him into the Foreign Office in 1919, but left after five years to become a stockbroker. In 1929, he moved again, this time to the Bank of England to work as an advisor to its chairman, Montagu Norman. In career terms, banking would become Rodd's core activity. In 1930–31, he was seconded to the newly formed Bank for International Settlements (BIS) in Basle. This meant that he was at the epicentre of events during the Austrian banking crisis of May–June 1931. He got on well with Norman and shared his vision of an international capitalist system free of nationalist influence. But in 1933, he moved to the British investment bank Morgan Grenfell & Co.[3] There was a family connection here: in 1928, Rodd had married Mary Smith, a daughter of one of the senior partners at Morgan Grenfell. From the vantage point of the Morgan banks, Rodd watched the collapse of the European order in the 1930s. After the German annexation of Austria in March 1938 (the *Anschluss*), he worked with others to maintain a transatlantic approach to dealing with Austrian debt, instead of allowing individual countries to make their own deals with Germany. But in the end, the Bank of England decided to approach the issue unilaterally.

As the Second World War approached, a new phase in Rodd's career opened up. In summer 1939, he joined the newly created Ministry of Economic Warfare (MEW). For

---

1. Doreen Massey and Nigel Thrift, 'A Passion for Place', in Ron Johnson and Michael Williams (eds), *A Century of British Geography* (Oxford: Oxford University Press, 2003), 292.
2. Isla Forsyth, 'Desert Journeys: From Exploration to Covert Operations', *Geographical Journal* 182, no. 3 (2016): 228. Michael Heffernan, 'Cartography and Military Intelligence: The Royal Geographical Society and the First World War', *Transactions of the Institute of British Geographers* 21, no. 3 (1996): 505.
3. The main work on Morgan Grenfell is Kathleen Burk, *Morgan Grenfell, 1838–1988: The Biography of a Merchant Bank* (Oxford: Oxford University Press, 1989).

roughly nine months during 1939–40, he represented the MEW in its dealings with Italy, pursuing a policy of using economic incentives to bolster Anglo–Italian relations and woo Mussolini. Whether or not the contentious term 'appeasement' is the right word to describe this approach, it was certainly one based on the assumption that the Italian leader was a man who could be negotiated with. The MEW has received considerable attention from historians, but no account of these negotiations has been written from Rodd's point of view. When the MEW's strategy failed, and Mussolini joined the war on Hitler's side, Rodd headed for West Africa with a position in Military Intelligence (Research) – 'MI(R)'. He set up an intelligence-gathering operation in Nigeria, with a remit to assess the allegiances of the French colonies and make plans for a possible invasion by Axis forces from the North. Although MI(R)'s work in sponsoring irregular warfare in East Africa at this time is well known, its work in West Africa, exemplified by Rodd, has received little attention.[4]

Rodd's work for MI(R) illuminates his connection with Ralph Bagnold, pioneer of the use of motorised transport in the desert and, in 1940, founder of the Long Range Desert Group (LRDG). Rodd was not personally involved in the LRDG, but he had input into its origins: he saw the military possibilities inherent in Bagnold's ideas and encouraged him to develop them. This book contains hitherto unknown details about Rodd's input into the LRDG's ground-breaking raid on Murzuk in southern Libya in January 1941. Here he was like many other geographers in finding that his expertise had a use in the Second World War.[5] For him the desert war also had a psychological appeal. It spoke to his notions of what constituted a life of adventure: discovery, courage and danger – here his conceptions of heroism were typical of many British soldiers.[6]

Rodd would have loved to make the desert war his priority. But his skillset meant that he was drawn instead into the sphere of military administration. Following a Free French coup in French Equatorial Africa in August 1940, he became financial advisor to the new government in Brazzaville. Experience in this role meant that in early 1941, as the Italian empire began to fall to the British, he was well placed to assist with the takeover of the newly conquered territories – a task assigned to the War Office and run from Cairo and Nairobi. First as controller of finance and accounts (1941–42) and then as chief political officer in East Africa command (1942–43), he was a key player in managing what was initially called the Occupied Enemy Territory Administration (OETA). Importantly, he was chief military administrator of Madagascar for September–October 1942. He found all this work challenging and exciting, but also frustrating, especially when there were departmental tensions. In

---

4. On MI(R) in East Africa, especially Ethiopia, see Simon Anglim, *Orde Wingate and the British Army 1922–44* (London: Routledge, 2010), 102, 105–12.
5. For a wider perspective on this, see W. G. V. Balchin, 'United Kingdom Geographers in the Second World War: A Report', *Geographical Journal* 153, no. 2 (1987): 159–80; Trevor J. Barnes, 'American Geographers and World War II: Spies Teachers and Occupiers', *Annals of the American Association of Geographers* 106, no. 3 (2016): 543–50.
6. See Graham Dawson, *Soldier Heroes: British Adventure, Empire and the Imagining of Masculinities* (London: Routledge, 1994), ch. 1.

Ethiopia, Emperor Haile Selassie was eager for power to be transferred to himself swiftly, following the end of Italian rule. Likewise, there was pressure for a quick transfer of power from the British to the Free French in Madagascar, following the success of Operation Ironclad in 1942. In these situations, the Foreign Office – eager to deflect charges of colonial intent – was keen to see a quick end to British rule, while the War Office was more cautious.[7] Rodd's insights into these situations demonstrate the extent of the departmental differences.

Rodd's involvement first with OETA and then with AMGOT sheds light onto the way in which the British applied the doctrine of 'indirect rule' to military government. The idea of indirect rule – popular in the interwar period – seemed to offer a way of protecting African traditions from the inroads of Western modernity, and it could easily be adapted to local conditions. But by the 1940s, the paternalistic concept of 'trusteeship', which gave it legitimacy, was under threat from the idea of 'partnership'.[8] The war gave indirect rule a renewed relevance. The Allies did not want to get bogged down in micromanaging conquered territories. Indirect rule gave them a rationale for leaving some existing structures in place, even while changing the people at the top. Historians of empire writing about indirect rule normally overlook the legacy of the doctrine in military government. Rodd's thinking – its origins and application – brings this into focus. His advocacy of indirect rule and the pragmatic outlook of which it was a part help to explain key aspects of AMGOT policy. In preparing for Operation Husky – the invasion of Sicily – the Americans promoted the idea of replacing prominent fascist leaders with Allied soldiers. But British planners, Rodd in particular, thought the Allies lacked the personnel to rule southern Italy directly. Rodd played a key role in persuading Harold Alexander, the general in charge of Operation Husky, and Dwight Eisenhower, the supreme commander, to embrace a gradualist approach to this issue.[9]

One of the architects of the policy of indirect rule, British imperialist and colonial administrator Lord Frederick Lugard, famously argued that it was possible for Britain to work for 'progress' in the colonies while at the same time using the empire for its own economic benefit. He termed this combination of commitments the 'dual mandate'.[10] His vision had something in common with that of US geographer Isaiah Bowman, a

---

7. See Richard Frost, *Enigmatic Proconsul: Sir Philip Mitchell and the Twilight of Empire* (London: Radcliffe Press, 1992), ch. 10; Martin Thomas, *The French Empire at War* (Manchester: Manchester University Press, 1998), 148–49; Edward Flint, 'The Development of British Civil Affairs and Its Employment in the British Sector of Allied Military Operations during the Battle of Normandy, June to August 1944', PhD thesis, Cranfield University, 2008, 110.
8. On indirect rule, see John Cell, 'Colonial Rule', in J. D. Brown and W. R. Louis (eds), *The Oxford History of the British Empire*, vol. 4 (Oxford: Oxford University Press, 1999), 237–43; Robert D. Pearce, *The Turning Point in Africa: British Colonial Policy 1938–48* (London, 1982), chs 1 and 2.
9. See on this Philip Boobbyer, 'Lord Rennell, Chief of AMGOT: A Study of His Approach to Politics and Military Government (c. 1940–1943)', *War in History* 25, no. 3 (2018): 304–27.
10. F. D. Lugard, *The Dual Mandate in Tropical Africa* (Edinburgh: William Blackwood and Sons, 1922), 617.

key advisor to the American president Woodrow Wilson at the Paris Peace Conference (1919–20): Bowman tended to identify the global good with American interests.[11] Rodd was like Lugard and Bowman in having an international outlook, yet also being a servant of the nation-state; the need to defend British interests was always present in his mind. Yet, while he was a pragmatist eager to expand or consolidate British influence, he was often critical of British policy. He was also an idealist ready to attach himself to political causes. His advocacy of indirect rule partly arose because of a certain localism in his thinking, fed by his upbringing and exposure to African cultures. He had a high-minded vision for the task of administration itself. Under AMGOT, when the Mafia started to re-establish itself in Italy – a topic of controversy to this day – he tried to take a principled stand against organised crime.

Publicly, Rodd was a confident person with an often brusque manner. Privately, he was self-reflective and sometimes uncertain of himself. This difference is intriguing. There are plenty of good sources available for building up a picture of his inner life. He wrote diaries or summaries of his activities during both world wars; hence, it is possible to construct a detailed picture of what he was doing and thinking. In 1950, in the course of discussions about the nature of religion with Mary, he wrote out a narrative of his life in some detail, which tells us a lot about his aspirations and insecurities.[12] Another rich source is his correspondence. He was a prolific letter writer. A large number of his letters to his parents and Mary survive. Historians have rightly noted that subjectivity is best understood as emerging from connection rather than detachment; human beings generally experience themselves through their relationships, and the character of those relationships changes over time, as does personal identity.[13] Rodd's personal life illustrates this. His thinking was always in dialogue with others. He was sometimes worried about how others saw him and, particularly after 1945, about how his career had evolved. His eagerness to put his private thoughts on paper was in some ways reflective of a person whose thoughts crystalised as he wrote them down.

One of the advantages of biography is that it can enable us to see a person in the round. Institutional histories or works built around one issue can miss seeing the full complexity of people's lives. This book is structured around a number of key themes. This allows us to get a picture of the range of Rodd's activities and how they were intertwined.[14] A potential weakness in biography is that it can exaggerate human agency or the importance of its subject. Western culture, thankfully, takes the view that human beings should be answerable for their actions – our systems of law depend on that idea. But Rodd's importance should not be overstated. He left an imprint in the worlds of geography and military government in particular but, even there, he can be

---

11. Neil Smith, *American Empire: Roosevelt's Geographer and the Prelude to Globalization* (Berkeley: University of California Press, 2004), xi.
12. Rodd, 'Life and Reflections', 1950, Rodd Family Papers, AC.
13. Mary Fulbrook and Ulinka Rublack, 'In Relation: The "Social Self" and Ego-Documents', *German History* 28, no. 3 (2010): 269.
14. For a good example of this kind of study, see Jay Bergman, *Meeting the Demands of Reason: The Life and Thought of Andrei Sakharov* (Ithaca: Cornell University Press, 2009).

seen as a person caught up in processes beyond his control. In many ways, he reflected the values of time. That need not deter us; it means that this book can serve to help us understand British society at a time of great change. But Rodd's life is not only of historical interest. He grappled with many of the issues we confront today: traditional societies threatened by modernisation; conflicts between the great powers; a global financial system facing upheaval; the relationship of armies with local populations; and the dialogue between religion, science and the humanities. All this makes him an intriguing subject for a book.

Chapter One
FAMILY AND YOUTH

Rodd was born on 25 October 1895, at 10 Curzon Street, London. He came from a family shaped by empire. He was very conscious of this – he was always proud of his ancestral lineage. Importantly, from a geographical point of view, he was descended from James Rennell (1742–1830) – he was Rennell's great, great grandson. A cartographer who became surveyor-general of the East India Company, Rennell was responsible for creating a number of early maps of India. He also knew Africa well. He was elected an honorary member of the African Association in 1792 after he had compiled a map of the northern part of the continent, and he later produced maps of the routes taken in Africa by the Scottish explorer Mungo Park. Like Rodd, he had an interest in camels – he wrote an article on the rate of travelling as performed by camels.[1] He was also an early pioneer of the discipline of oceanography. Although he died before the founding of the RGS, he helped to promote its idea, and he was recognised in 1930 as one of its founders. Clements Markham – president of the RGS (1893–1905) and an influential promoter of geography – called him the 'first great English geographer'; he also emphasised the breadth of his qualifications, in the context of the fact that geographers had to be 'many-sided' in their abilities.[2] Rodd was always proud of Rennell's legacy and, like Markham, thought of geography as a multifaceted discipline.

Empire and exploration were also evident on Rodd's mother's side of the family. His mother was Lilias Georgina Guthrie (1864–1951), a daughter of James Alexander Guthrie, the fourth Baron of Craigie. Her grandfather on her mother's side was James Stirling (1791–1865), a Scottish naval officer who was the first governor of Western Australia; he was the founder of the Swan River colony and the settlements of Perth and Fremantle.[3]

---

1. James Rennell, 'On the Rate of Travelling as Performed by Camels', *Philosophical Transactions*, March 1791; RGS Papers, 331411.
2. C. R. Markham, *Major James Rennell and the Rise of Modern English Geography* (London: Cassell, 1895), 9–11. J. N. L. Baker, *The History of Geography* (New York: Barnes & Noble, 1963), 130–57. Andrew S. Cook, 'Rennell, James (1742–1830)', *Oxford Dictionary of National Biography* (Oxford: Oxford University Press, 2004). A. M. Johnson, 'The Rennell Collection', *Geographical Journal* 148, no. 1 (1982): 38. For Rodd's comments on Mungo Park's journey, see 'Rennell's Comments on the Journeys of Park and Laing to the Niger', *Geographical Journal* 86, no. 1 (1935): 28–31. Based on Park's testimony, Rennell erroneously concluded that the Niger River emptied into an inland lake; see Charles W. J. Withers, 'Mapping the Niger, 1798–1832: Trust, Testimony and "Ocular Demonstration" in the Late Enlightenment', *Imago Mundi* 56, no. 2 (2004): 172–75.
3. Pamela Statham-Drew, *James Stirling: Admiral and Founding Governor of Western Australia* (Crawley: University of Western Australia Press, 2003).

One of his brothers, Edward Stirling (1797–1873), a civil servant with the East India Company, was one of the first Europeans to explore northern Afghanistan. The Guthries had strong army connections. One of Lilias's sisters, Violet, married Edward Montagu-Stuart-Wortley, an officer who rose to the rank of major-general and was, in 1915, general officer commanding (GOC) of the 46th Division at the Battle of Loos; they lived at Highcliffe Castle on the Dorset coast. Another sister, Rose, married the future major-general, Cecil Edward Bingham, commander of the Cavalry Corps in 1915–16.

Rodd's father (1855–1941) was the only son of a Cornishman, Major James Rennell Rodd, who served in the duke of Cornwall's Light Infantry and lived at Trebartha Hall near Launceston in Cornwall – a mansion pulled down in 1949. Early in his life, his parents took him on an 18-month journey around Europe. Experiences of travel, he later recalled, helped to liberate him from the 'conventions and prejudices' which were still strong in the latter half of the Victorian era; it gave him a glimpse of a 'wider world'. In part it was the discovery of other cultures that excited him. But it was also the encounter with nature he had while travelling in France and Switzerland. 'I have a vivid recollection of the emotion inspired by the mountains, real mountains with snow-covered peaks and dark zones of fir, haunted by the dread of being lost in the pathless woods', he wrote.[4]

It is worth going into some detail on Rodd's father – henceforth 'Rennell Rodd' – because he passed on many of his interests to Francis. He was educated at Haileybury, a school founded by the East India Company to train civil servants. From there, he went to Balliol College, Oxford, at a time when the famous educationalist Benjamin Jowett was master. According to Rennell Rodd, a characteristic feature of the college at that time was its 'universality'; it included men of 'all sorts and conditions'. While at Oxford, Rennell Rodd won the University's Newdigate prize for a poem about the Elizabethan courtier and explorer Walter Raleigh. This was a eulogy written in a patriotic tone – '[Raleigh] set free / for English sails the highways of the sea'. He later wrote a biography of Raleigh, which came out in the 'English Men of Action' series, published by Macmillan.[5] After graduation, he got involved in the milieu of bohemian London, associated with Edward Burne-Jones, John Whistler and Oscar Wilde. To cite writer Harold Acton, there was a 'cosmopolitan-romantic' quality about him.[6] Rennell Rodd then went into the Foreign Office. His first post was at Berlin where Edward Malet was the ambassador. While at Berlin, he got to know Crown Prince Frederick, who was briefly emperor in 1888 and about whom Rennell Rodd published a book after the Crown Prince's death.[7] After further jobs in Athens, Rome and Paris, he was assigned to the British agency in Zanzibar.

The origins of what became in Rennell Rodd a strong attachment to empire were to be found in his time in Zanzibar. He arrived in the city in late December 1892,

---

4. James Rennell Rodd, *Social and Diplomatic Memories, 1884–1893* (London: Edward Arnold, 1922), 2, 5.
5. Rennell Rodd, *Newdigate Prize Poem: Raleigh* (Oxford: T. Shrimpton and Son, 1880), 17; *Sir Walter Raleigh* (London: Macmillan, 1904).
6. Harold Acton, *Nancy Mitford: A Memoir* (London: Gibson Square, 2004), 48.
7. Rennell Rodd, *Social and Diplomatic Memories, 1884–1893*, 12, 95. Rennell Rodd, *Frederick, Crown Prince and Emperor: A Biographical Sketch Dedicated to His Memory* (London: D. Stott, 1888).

having travelled out with Roddy Owen, a Grand National horse race champion, and Raymond Portal, a Balliol contemporary. His predecessor in the role of agent and consul-general was Raymond's brother, Gerald. Another who joined them on the voyage from Aden was Frank Rhodes – the brother of Cecil Rhodes – who was subsequently war correspondent of the *Times* during Kitchener's Nile expedition of 1898. The chief minister in Zanzibar at the time was General Lloyd Mathews, a true 'apostle of empire', according to Lord Rosebery. Before Rennell Rodd established himself in Zanzibar, this group travelled to Mombasa in preparation for the forthcoming expedition to Uganda – which led to its annexation. It was a moment etched in Rennell Rodd's memory; he later described the members of the group as 'knight-errants of adventure'.[8] He was upset when first Raymond (in May 1893) and then Gerald (in January 1894) died. After Gerald's death, he wrote a poem expressing his sadness, which concluded with the lines: 'Henceforth whenever skies are red / I may think my own heart bleeds.'[9] Back in Britain after his posting in Zanzibar, he helped to complete Gerald's book, *The British Mission to Uganda* (1894), adding a memoir of his own to the text.[10] One of his tasks in Zanzibar was to prevent the slave trade still operating along the coast. He was also responsible for relations with the sultan, Seyyid Ali, and then, after the latter's death, managing the installation of his successor, Hamed bin Thwain, his own choice for the role.[11]

Like Francis, Rennell Rodd experienced a number of African journeys. In the summer of 1893, he was in charge of British involvement in the second Witu expedition, supported by Lloyd Mathews. The Witu region, on the Kenyan coast roughly a hundred miles north of Mombasa, had passed from being a German protectorate to British oversight in 1890. When unrest broke out there in May 1893, following the decision of the British East Africa Company to withdraw from the region, Rennell Rodd was instructed to restore order. He was tasked with putting Witu under the formal authority of the Sultan of Zanzibar, while in practice incorporating it into the British protectorate there. The conflict came to be focused around the struggle for two stockaded villages, Pumwani and Jongeni, used by forest-dwellers for selling slaves to the Somalis. The battle for Pumwani was Rennell Rodd's first experience of being under fire, as he recalled: 'Bullets pinged into the soft banana skins round us or plunked into the earth […] For an hour or so while I had no definite duties to perform I reflected, as I smoked my pipe, that I had a pretty heavy responsibility on my shoulders.'[12]

---

8. Rennell Rodd, *Social and Diplomatic Memories, 1902–1919* (London: Edward Arnold, 1925), 72, 277–84, 289.
9. Rennell Rodd, *Ballads of the Fleet and Other Poems* (London: Edward Arnold, 1897), 195.
10. Rennell Rodd, 'Memoir', in Sir Gerald Portal, *The British Mission to Uganda in 1893* (London, 1894), xxv–xlvi.
11. Rennell Rodd, *Social and Diplomatic Memories, 1884–1893*, 280, 292, 303–7.
12. Rennell Rodd, *Social and Diplomatic Memories, 1884–1893*, 317–18, 327; *Social and Diplomatic Memories, 1902–1919*, 22. On the background to the Witu Sultanate, see Marguerite Yivisaker, 'On the Origins and Development of the Witu Sultanate', *International Journal of African Historical Studies* 11, no. 4 (1978): 669–88.

Rennell Rodd was soon transferred to the embassy in Cairo, where he worked for eight years. For much of the time, he acted as an assistant to British consul-general Lord Cromer, a figure he came to admire. In the second volume of his memoirs, published in 1923, he set aside a number of pages to describe Cromer's character. In this, his aim was to respond to Lytton Strachey's portrayal of Cromer in his book *Eminent Victorians*, which appeared in 1918. In a chapter on General Gordon, Strachey had suggested that the East meant little to Cromer save as something to be looked after and a convenient vehicle for his own talents. Rennell Rodd described this as 'altogether unfair'; some of Strachey's remarks were accurate, he said, but the overall picture was a distortion. Instead, Rennell Rodd commended Cromer for being a clear-sighted person lacking personal ambition and being immune to the pressures of either approval or criticism. But he acknowledged that Cromer had an 'autocratic' tendency, while also suggesting that his outlook was 'too convincedly logical and Western' in character. Rennell Rodd's thinking contained some of the characteristics of what Edward Said has identified as 'Orientalism' – a world view assuming British superiority and justifying British power in the region: Rennell Rodd thought the 'Oriental mind' and the 'Arab mind' to be unstraightforward in character. The presence in Rennell Rodd's outlook of an 'orientalist' streak was tempered by a respect for the mentality of the region: he criticised Cromer for seeing the Oriental mind as an obstacle to be overcome rather than studied with 'sympathetic appreciation'.[13]

In 1897, Rennell Rodd was assigned the task of leading an expedition to negotiate an agreement with Menelik, emperor of Ethiopia. This episode was prompted by British fears of an Ethiopian expansion into areas of Somaliland within the British protectorate as defined by the Anglo–Italian Protocol of 1894, as well as concerns about potential French influence in the area. Ever since leaving Zanzibar, Rodd had felt a sense of 'haunting nostalgia' for Africa, so he was excited when this 'path of adventure' opened up.[14] The British delegation included Cecil Edward Bingham; Reginald Wingate, then head of military intelligence in the Egyptian Army; and Lord Edward Cecil, the fourth son of the prime minister. Getting to Addis Ababa was in itself demanding: it was roughly 500 miles each way from the Somaliland coastal village of Zeila to the Ethiopian capital. Among the many helpers, there were 80 camel drivers: for the first part of the journey, they took 191 camels and 30 mules.[15] The mission gave plenty of opportunities for nature tourism: Rennell Rodd loved the bird and plant life and the scenery. The expedition pretended to include a scientific dimension. Cecil was its official botanist, ornithologist and entomologist; unfortunately, most of the bugs and insects he collected shook to pieces on the journey back. In Addis Ababa, Rennell Rodd was given a mule covered with silk and gold embroideries to take

---

13. Rennell Rodd, *Social and Diplomatic Memories, 1894–1901* (London: Edward Arnold, 1923), 4, 16–19, 39. Edward Said, *Orientalism* (New York: Vintage, 2003), 36–41. Lytton Strachey, *Eminent Victorians* (Oxford: Oxford University Press, 2003), ch. 4.
14. Harold G. Markus, 'The Rodd Mission of 1897', *Journal of Ethiopian Studies* 3, no. 2 (1965): 25. Rennell Rodd, *Social and Diplomatic Memories, 1894–1901*, 123.
15. Count Gleichen, *With the Mission to Menelik* (London: Edward Arnold, 1898), 7–8. Rennell Rodd, *Social and Diplomatic Memories, 1894–1901*, 125, 144.

him to his first meeting with Menelik, and his entourage was preceded by horn and flute players.[16]

The negotiations themselves led to a treaty agreeing a permanent British presence at the court of the emperor, a most-favoured-nation trade agreement and a British veto on armaments passing through the country to the Mahdists. There was also much discussion over the final frontiers of the country to the North and to the East. The task of addressing this difficult issue was passed to Ras Makonnen. The problem lay in the fact that Ethiopians had encroached into areas perceived as belonging to the Somali protectorate in the region between Harar and Gildessa. Rennell Rodd and Makonnen finally agreed to Ethiopian jurisdiction over an area previously claimed by the Somali protectorate where Ethiopian outposts had, for a while, been established. But Makonnen, according to Rennell Rodd, had had much larger ambitions; he acknowledged that he had made certain concessions, but argued that it would have been impossible to dislodge the Ethiopians without resorting to arms.[17] The total area ceded to Ethiopia was 13,500 square miles of Somali territory, roughly one-third of what Menelik had claimed. The way in which the agreement was arrived at reflected a process that was typical of imperial border delineation. Borders artificially imposed by the British were extraneous to the peoples living in them. But indigenous populations also made significant inputs into the process.[18] The deal was mired in controversy thereafter, with some arguing that Rennell Rodd gave away too much. Others thought he had had no choice but to do what he did.[19]

Rennell Rodd remained committed to empire throughout his life. In a tribute to the British imperialist and statesman Lord Curzon at the end of his memoirs, he expressed a hope that the imperial instincts and values of his generation would survive, even if in a different way:

> [Service of the empire] was an ambition which in the late seventies and early eighties inspired a number of our contemporaries at Balliol [...] Their numbers are much reduced today. But with us of the older generation that are left the confidence remains that, in spite of different methods of application appropriate to the advancement of time, the same high sense of duty to the empire will prevail among the younger men.[20]

The empire, he also suggested, was a product of sacrifice; he lamented that many failed to show 'adequate reverence' for the empire, not realising the 'goodly lives by whose sacrifice [Britain's] African dominion grew'.[21] The idea that the imperial project contained

---

16. Rennell Rodd, *Social and Diplomatic Memories, 1894–1901*, 130–41; Gleichen, *With the Mission to Menelik*, 25, 125, 144.
17. Rennell Rodd, *Social and Diplomatic Memories, 1894–1901*, 182. Percy Loraine and Alan Campbell, 'James Rennell Rodd 1858–1941, Diplomatist and Classical Scholar', *Oxford Dictionary of National Biography* (Oxford: Oxford University Press, 2004).
18. On this, see Daniel Foliard, *Dislocating the Orient: British Maps and the Making of the Middle East 1854–1921* (Chicago: Chicago University Press, 2017), 267–68.
19. Markus, 'The Rodd Mission of 1897', 32–34.
20. Rennell Rodd, *Social and Diplomatic Memories, 1902–1919*, 393–94.
21. Ibid., 72.

within it a motive of service was clearly present in Rennell Rodd's mind. His vocabulary here contained echoes of a Christian conception of empire, even if his articulation of an ethic of self-sacrifice was not so obviously religious.

Alongside the idealism in Rennell Rodd's outlook, there was an underlying pragmatism. He had high regard for the qualities of 'common sense' and 'balance'. He once called businessman and politician W. H. Smith a typical exponent of 'well-balanced common sense' in British political life. He also thought that in the case of some African explorers, the 'hard life' of adventure they had experienced had strained their 'mental balance' and 'quality of mercy'. He was conscious that putting ideals into practice was not always easy. 'It is an easy matter to issue ordinances. To enforce their observance is another story', he recalled.[22] Connected with this, there was an anti-intellectualism in his outlook, or at least a suspicion of dogmatism and abstract principles which was not unusual in the English upper classes. Some decades later, he told the conservative historian Charles Petrie: 'Let me give you a word of advice as an old man to a young one. When Germans talk about things that end in "*ismus*", and French men about things that end in "*ologie*", it is wisest for an Englishman to retire to the bar.'[23]

Rennell Rodd was always a strong advocate of the principle of the balance of power. But, alongside that, he placed great emphasis on trying to understand others. Writing about diplomacy after he had left the Foreign Office, he observed that understanding the mentality of other nations required 'imagination, tolerance, elimination of prejudice, and most of all experience'.[24] Rennell Rodd also emphasised the importance of establishing good personal relations with people. He learned something of this from Edward Malet in Berlin. Malet, he once said, insisted on the 'human relation' in official life; he 'deprecated the superior answer and the bureaucratic manner'.[25] Rennell Rodd seems to have been an easy person for others to get on with; he once called himself 'practically quarrel-proof'. The fact that he was able to establish a good rapport with Emperor Menelik was one reason for the success of the 1897 visit to Ethiopia. 'I was glad when I saw your face at our first meeting, because there was no anger in it', Menelik told him.[26] Rennell Rodd was adept at finding the right words for saying things; Petrie commented that he was an outstanding exponent of the *discours d'occasion* – the ability to talk fluently in a public setting on a relevant issue.[27]

While some warmed to Rennell Rodd's genial character and adaptability, others were less impressed. These included Francis Bertie, Britain's ambassador in Rome from 1903 to 1905 – a man Rennell Rodd called a 'master in the art of quarrelling'[28] – and

---

22. Rennell Rodd, *Social and Diplomatic Memories, 1884–1893*, 260, 338, 342.
23. Charles Petrie, *A Historian Looks at His World* (London: Sidgwick and Jackson, 1972), 136. Luisa Passerini, *Europe in Love and Love in Europe: Imagination and Politics in Britain between the Wars* (London: I. B. Tauris, 1999), 71.
24. Rennell Rodd, *Diplomacy* (London: Ernest Benn, 1929), 68.
25. Rennell Rodd, *Social and Diplomatic Memories, 1884–1893*, 12.
26. Rennell Rodd, *Social and Diplomatic Memories, 1894–1901*, 163; *Social and Diplomatic Memories, 1902–1919*, 41.
27. Petrie, *Historian Looks at His World*, 120.
28. Rennell Rodd, *Social and Diplomatic Memories, 1902–1919*, 41.

his cousin, Charles Hardinge, from 1903 one of the permanent undersecretaries at the Foreign Office. Bertie and Hardinge, who were allies in trying to give the Foreign Office greater stature and influence, thought Rennell Rodd too soft. When, in the summer of 1905, Rennell Rodd was mentioned as a candidate for the newly vacated role of ambassador in St Petersburg, Bertie told Hardinge that it would be a mistake to send Rodd and his wife. 'To ingratiate himself to the Government to which he is accredited, [Rennell Rodd] would give way in everything', he said of him.[29] According to Thomas Otte, Rennell Rodd and his wife were sometimes imprudently ambitious. On one occasion, Lilias reportedly described Rennell Rodd as her 'husband and slave', outlining a career trajectory that would see him installed first as ambassador in Rome and then Paris. In the end, Rennell Rodd left Rome for the role of minister in the British Legation in Stockholm. He was based there from 1905 to 1908. During these years, he got to know Swedish geographer Sven Hedin. It was reluctantly that Hardinge made him ambassador in Italy in 1908.[30]

Rennell Rodd played a significant, if discreet, role in facilitating Italy's entry into the war on the Allied side in 1915. The *Berliner Tageblatt* claimed that Italian Prime Minister Antonio Salandra was under his control. This was, of course, an exaggeration. But he had a good relationship with certain key figures, particularly King Victor Emmanuel III and the Foreign Minister Sidney Sonnino.[31] As he subsequently explained, his part had been to try to help the British understand the Italian temperament. In the negotiations leading to the Treaty of London in April 1915, he advised the foreign secretary, Edward Grey, to accept Italy's demand for the annexation of the northern half of the Dalmatian coast, on the grounds that it would help Salandra's government persuade people of the merits of joining the Triple Entente. 'We must look to our own interests first [...] If we can close the ring round Germany and Austria, the end is in sight', Rennell Rodd emphasised. When, on 13 May 1915, the Salandra government resigned, under pressure from the forces demanding neutrality – spearheaded by the leading liberal politician Giovanni Giolitti – Rennell Rodd called it one of the 'grimmest moments' of his life. But when three days later after popular pressure it was restored, he was correspondingly elated, stating that this was a victory for king, government and people. After Italy came into the war, Grey thanked him for his 'courage and steadfastness' during a time of exceptional strain and recommended him for the distinguished Order of St Michael and St George.[32]

Rodd's mother was tough-minded and unsentimental. She was sometimes called 'Tiger Lil' on this account and also 'Black Lil' for her readiness to intrigue behind the scenes in favour of her husband. In England, the family home – known as 'Ardath' – was

---

29. Bertie to Hardinge, 27 August 1905, Charles Hardinge Papers, Mss 7, CUL.
30. Thomas Otte, *The Foreign Office Mind: The Making of British Foreign Policy 1865–1914* (Cambridge: Cambridge University Press, 2011), 24, 255–57, 319.
31. Rennell Rodd, *Social and Diplomatic Memories, 1902–1919*, 258–59.
32. Christopher Seton-Watson, 'Britain and Italy 1914–1915: The Role of Sir Rennell Rodd', in *Diplomazia e Storia delle Relazioni Internazionali* (Milan: Giuffrè, 1991), 222–29. Rennell Rodd, *Social and Diplomatic Memories 1902–1919*, 217, 229.

Figure 1.1 James Rennell Rodd, c. 1920. Photograph by Walter Stoneman. National Portrait Gallery.

in Godalming, Surrey. But the focus for the social life of the family was often the embassies or legations where they were based. Lilias was like her husband in thinking of diplomatic life in cultural as well as political terms. She was an energetic society hostess, often organising parties that developed the social life of an embassy. This sometimes involved amateur dramatics. For example, in February 1903, Rodd played the part of Puck in an adaptation of Shakespeare's *The Tempest* at the Palazzo Brancaccio. From 1910, family holidays were often spent at Posillipo in the Bay of Naples, at a villa given to the British government by Lord Rosebery. An impressive property, with three separate houses, it had once belonged to the count of Aquila, an uncle of the last king of Naples. It was an ideal location for a society family keen on entertaining. In August each year, Lilias organised an annual *festa* for the 'gardeners, boatmen and humbler neighbours', which included swimming races and other competitions and dancing.[33]

The parties thrown by Lilias were often used for building political relationships. After Rennell Rodd became ambassador, she arranged a party in the garden at Porta Pia, with supper tables dispersed under umbrella tents over the lawns, which was attended by the Italian prime minister. A few years later, in April 1913, she organised a 'pageant of the ages', in which guests were expected to appear in fancy dress. She herself came as the goddess Juno, while Rennell Rodd appeared as an Elizabethan ambassador in a

---

33. Programme for 'Oberon and Titania', 14 February 1903, Rennell of Rodd Papers, BD, Box 120. Rennell Rodd, *Social and Diplomatic Memories, 1902–1919*, 125–26, 144, 154.

Figure 1.2 Lilias Rodd (née Guthrie). Lithograph, 1894. National Portrait Gallery.

costume copied from a suit of Walter Raleigh's. Rodd dressed up as Mercury, while his cousin, Louise Stuart-Wortley, came as a Greek maiden. Figures in Italian public life came representing figures from Italian history. After the war, Rennell Rodd nostalgically recalled the event as marking the end of an era: 'For me personally that historic ball, which was one of the last great social events before the break-up of the old order, has [...] always seemed to have a certain analogy with the famous ball at Brussels on the eve of Waterloo.'[34] Lilias's activities complemented the fact that Rennell Rodd's brand of diplomacy was as much cultural as political. When he was ambassador in Rome, he set up the Keats–Shelley Association, which involved purchasing the house where John Keats died and inaugurating there a museum and library dedicated to the memory of the two poets. He also helped to set up the British School of Archaeology and the Arts.[35]

Rodd was the oldest of six children. He had three brothers: Christopher (who died at birth), Peter ('Prod') and Gustaf ('Taffy') – named after Gustav V of Sweden, who was his godfather; and two sisters, Evelyn and Gloria. For the first few years of Rodd's life, the family was based in Cairo. Reputedly, Rodd drank from the waters of the Nile when he

---

34. Rennell Rodd, *Social and Diplomatic Memories, 1902–1919*, 112, 174.
35. Ibid., 14, 121.

was only six weeks old. His father recalled an episode involving Rodd and Lord Cromer that took place in 1898 when Cromer and some others came to visit over Christmas:

> My wife persuaded Cromer to come [...] But we dreaded the moment of his arrival and the first words to be said on such an occasion. Then my wife had a brilliant inspiration. Our little boy Francis was now three and a half years old and an extraordinarily winning child of whom Cromer was very fond. Instead of being put to bed at the normal hour he was left sitting in the armchair alone in the drawing room till their arrival, dressed in his pink pyjamas. The rest of us were all in the plot to be rather late and allow the child to receive him. When we all came in a minute later we found Cromer quite content with the boy sitting on his knee [...] The ice was broken.[36]

For his early schooling, Rodd was educated by governesses. He later recalled this somewhat bitterly: 'I was largely brought up by governesses, except for formal production as an exhibition piece after meals to recite poetry and be doing turns as a "bright child".'[37] He then went to St Aubyn's Preparatory School in Rottingdean, East Sussex. This had been founded in 1895 by its headmaster and owner Charles Stanford. Rodd stood out as one of the brighter boys in the school – to the obvious pleasure of his parents. After a good school report in April 1907, his father wrote to him: 'As far as I can make out [...] you will soon be top of the school and then we shall be very proud of you.' He had high expectations of his son. 'I feel sure you will always do well and that you have the right ambition', he told him. His mother wanted him to get a scholarship to Eton and, for this, pressed on him the importance of concentration while also warning him of the 'very careless mistakes' he was making in his letters home.[38] The experience of travelling back and forth to school in Britain helped to engender in Rodd a spirit of self-reliance.

Rodd's time at St Aubyn's was interrupted in February 1906, when he became seriously ill with appendicitis, followed by pneumonia. His parents, then in Stockholm, came home immediately. His life hung in the balance for some days before his health improved. It was a big ordeal for Rodd, and the way he dealt with it impressed his father. In recalling the episode in his memoirs, Rennell Rodd wrote fondly of 'the pluck of that gallant little life which, hanging so long upon a thread, never allowed us to see his courage flinch through three severe operations'. It was a revealing remark. Rodd's father clearly accepted the 'code of the stiff-upper-lip' so much admired in Edwardian culture.[39] Rodd inherited this. In his subsequent life, he sometimes concealed his emotions from those around him, even though there was a strong emotional streak to his character. Rennell

---

36. Lord Rennell, 17 December 1953, House of Lords, Hansard. Rennell Rodd, *Social and Diplomatic Memories, 1894–1901*, 245–46.
37. Rodd, 'Life and Reflections', 1950, Section 2, 1, Rodd Family Papers, AC.
38. Eton School Clerk's Record, 1907–24, 288, Eton College Archives. Rennell Rodd to Rodd, 30 April and 26 May 1907; Lilias to Rodd, 22 March 1907, Rennell of Rodd Papers, BD, Box 123/1.
39. On British 'stiff-upper-lip' culture, see Thomas Dixon, *Weeping Britannia: Portrait of a Nation in Tears* (Oxford: Oxford University Press, 2015), 199–214.

Rodd was on friendly terms with King Edward VII, and this was evident during this episode; the king 'repeatedly' enquired after Rodd's health during these weeks. Rodd's doctors were Sir Alfred Fripp – surgeon to Edward VII – and his brother-in-law Hale White. The royal connection was evident again a few years later when, in spring 1909, Rodd and his parents were invited by the king for lunch on the royal yacht, Victoria and Albert.[40]

In January 1908, Rodd went to Eton – without a scholarship. The headmaster at the time was Edward Lyttelton, a man with strong Christian convictions and a reputation for promoting fads relating to hygiene and well-being, such as sleeping in the open air. He was put into the house of R. P. L. Booker, a popular teacher with an interest in English antiquity and archaeology. He later remembered Booker with affection, noting that he gained the reputation of being a 'Prince among housemasters'. But Rodd was not happy at the school. The effects of his earlier ill-health meant that he was not allowed to play certain games. Since games played a central role in Eton's life, this contributed to a feeling of isolation: 'I hated Eton like poison. I suppose I went there too young; I was only 12 and three months. I wasn't allowed to play games owing to my illness when I was nine. I was very much thrown back into myself for this reason and also because of my upbringing abroad.' Even when Rodd's parents were in England, he did not see much of them: 'My parents practically never came down to see me. Once when I was very ill with measles and pneumonia they sent the butler down to find out how I really was.'[41]

Rodd's school reports present a less negative picture of his time at Eton. In 1909, his teacher of classics – which was the preeminent subject in the curriculum – recorded that, while he was no scholar, he was teachable and pleasant and had a good sense of humour. Rodd won a physics prize in the same year – perhaps an early sign of what would later become an admiration for the natural and social sciences. In 1910, Booker noted that Rodd was 'interested and intelligent in everything' but 'solid in nothing'. Although not allowed to play some games, Rodd did get involved in rowing. He also became an active member of the House Debate Society; election to Debate was often an important step up in the social hierarchy of a House. There were contradictory elements in his character. Writing in 1910, Booker said that Rodd and his friends had formed 'an admirable bulwark of gentleness and decorum' against some of the more aggressive boys in the House. Yet, if there was a soft side to Rodd's character, it was combined with a strong will. Booker noted in Rodd a tendency to 'lay down the law' with some of his peers. He also noticed that he was very certain of his opinions: 'It is a strange thing about him that he should be so decided, and so capricious about what he likes and dislikes, and what he will work for and what he won't.'[42]

---

40. Rennell Rodd, *Social and Diplomatic Memories, 1902–1919*, 74–75, 112.
41. Rodd, 'Life and Reflections', 1950, Section 2, 1–3, Rodd Family Papers, AC.
42. Reports by L. P. Booker, 1909, 28 July 1909, 5 April and 30 July 1910, Rennell of Rodd Papers, BD, Box 64.. Tim Card, *Eton Renewed: A History from 1860 to the Present Day* (London: John Murray, 1994), 105, 123.

In spring 1911, Rodd's parents decided to take him out of Eton early, in order to give him private tuition abroad. Booker told Rennell Rodd this was a mistake:

> [Rodd] likes privacy and has to live in an atmosphere of noise and bustle. And he likes to follow his own way, and he has to conform to the ways of others. But I think these constraints are the very things he wants, and to give him his head before he reaches his sixteenth birthday is a proceeding I cannot think is wise.[43]

Booker thought that boys benefitted from the experience of taking responsibility which came with staying longer at the school, and that Rodd would ultimately lose out if he missed this.[44] These were perceptive remarks: throughout his life, Rodd liked to forge his own path.

While he was at Eton, around 1910, Rodd first encountered religion in a serious sense. Under the influence of Booker – whom Rodd called 'non-dogmatic' and 'sensible' in his approach to faith – he decided to be confirmed in the Anglican Church. If, in intellectual circles, Christianity was increasingly contested in Europe, it was still a central part of British social life.[45] Rodd's own upbringing had been non-religious, with his parents attending church only for ceremonial reasons. His father had some spiritual feelings, but of an undefined kind. But he was an admirer of the Franciscan tradition; he once called himself a 'constant and devout pilgrim' to Assisi – here he was influenced by the Franciscan scholar Paul Sabatier.[46] Rodd's mother was essentially anti-religious. When Rodd decided to be confirmed, she indicated that she thought this rather silly. Rodd's turn to faith had a considerable impact on him. He said in later life that, from this point on, he was always 'a Christian with a personal God in spite of everything'. He used to attend the early Sunday service at school. He also read some of the Christian classics, including Augustine's *Confessions*, Thomas à Kempis's *The Imitation of Christ* and *The Little Flowers of St Francis*. His choice of reading was probably typical. Harold Macmillan, another Etonian who went up to Balliol a year ahead of Rodd, included *Confessions* and *The Imitation of Christ* in his library of reading on the Western Front.[47] The culture among his peers did not always conform to a Christian outlook. Rodd recalled that he was 'shocked and shy' by some of the immorality going on around him in the school. 'I prayed hard and with full awareness and I prayed for all sorts of things good and bad', he wrote. If Rodd's religious thinking was to some extent reflective of contemporary culture, it also owed much to his own initiative. He summarised his faith on the eve of the First World War as a form of 'self-created Christianity'.[48]

---

43. Report by L. P. Booker, April 1911, Rennell of Rodd Papers, BD, Box 64.
44. Reports by L. P. Booker, 28 July 1909, 5 April 1910, Rennell of Rodd Papers, BD, Box 64.
45. Adrian Gregory, 'Beliefs and Religion', in Jay Winter (ed), *The Cambridge History of the First World War*, vol. 3 (Cambridge: Cambridge University, 2014), 418.
46. Rennell Rodd, *Social and Diplomatic Memories, 1902–1919*, 11, 393.
47. Alistair Horne, *Macmillan: 1894–1956* (London: Macmillan, 1988), 34–35.
48. Rodd, 'Life and Reflections', 1950, Sections 2, 3 and 8, & 3, 10, Rodd Family Papers, AC.

Rodd left Eton at the end of the Christmas term, 1911, soon after he turned 16. His parents obviously wanted him to have a kind of international, European education, because he was sent to live with a German family in Weimar for a year, with the idea of preparing him for his Oxford entrance exams and learning some German. The same process was then repeated in Geneva, where he worked on his French – this time for just six months. When he went up to Oxford in autumn 1913, he was already fluent in German, French and Italian. During these years in Weimar and Geneva, he advanced his knowledge of classics and acquired some interest in scholarly work. In Geneva, he met the British Japanologist Basil Chamberlain – who gave him the run of his library – and read some archaeology, French poetry and eastern texts from the Confucian, Buddhist and Taoist traditions.[49]

In autumn 1913 – when he was not yet 18 – Rodd followed his father by going to Balliol, just missing out on a scholarship. He had a 'wonderful' year there, he said later. He enjoyed his studies – his chosen subject was the course on classical history and thought known as 'Greats'. Greats, he recalled, taught him to look for 'honesty and scholarship', and he started to think about 'honesty of purpose'. He rowed in the college second eight and foursomes, in the position of bow, although it is doubtful he was too ambitious about it. He also attended services in the college chapel and the cathedral. Although he had been to school in England, he had hitherto not developed a sense of attachment to his own country, partly because he did not get to know English boys outside school. At Oxford, this somewhat solitary existence changed significantly:

> I became for the first time part of an English society of contemporaries of the Edwardian era. We had enough money to enjoy ourselves at Oxford and in London in the spacious easy cultivated world of the days before the First World War. We were, I suppose consciously, members of the English aristocracy of birth, money and intellect. And it was very pleasant. We talked about all the things that young men ought to talk about. We discussed God and Love and Humanity and Philosophy.[50]

One group Rodd joined was what he termed in a wartime diary the 'Balliol Roundtable'. This was possibly an affiliate of the Ralegh Club founded in 1912 by Lionel Curtis and Reginald Coupland as a debating society on imperial subjects. Inspired by Lord Milner, Curtis had in 1909 launched the periodical and discussion group known as the 'Round Table', devoted to securing the future of the British empire by turning it into a federation representing its constituent parts. From Rodd's year group at Balliol, the writer Aldous Huxley – who had also been at Eton with him – was another member of the Balliol Roundtable. He and Huxley remained in contact during the First World War.[51]

---

49. Rodd, 'Life and Reflections', 1950, Section 2, 6, Rodd Family Papers, AC.
50. Rodd, 'Life and Reflections', 1950, Section 2, 6, Rodd Family Papers, AC. Balliol Rowing Club Records, 1913–1914, Archives of Balliol College, Oxford.
51. Alex May, 'Lionel Curtis 1872–1955', *Oxford Dictionary of National Biography* (Oxford: Oxford University Press, 2004). Rodd, 17 October 1918, Diary for May 1917–January 1919, Rennell of Rodd Papers, BD, Box 125. Huxley to Rodd, 30 January 1916, Rennell of Rodd Papers, BD, Box 59/1.

Figure 1.3 Balliol College second eight, 1914. Rodd is on the top row, second from right. With permission of the master and fellows of Balliol College, University of Oxford.

An important detail from these years was that Rodd fell in love at the ages of 14 and 16 with two women who were a little older than him. One of them, Irene Lawley, was from a distinguished Yorkshire family. The social life of the embassy in Rome – young people, relatives and other guests were regular visitors – helped to foster their friendship. In summer 1913, Irene appeared as 'Nausicaa', a character in Homer's *Odyssey*, in Lilias's 'pageant of the ages'. The other, Dorothy ('Dottie') Ashton, who was from a society family living in Cheshire, also visited the embassy in Rome. Dottie later became known for her poetry – her work was much praised by W. B. Yeats. In April 1914, she married diplomat Gerald Wellesley, later the duke of Wellington, who was based at the Rome embassy for some years. Rodd corresponded regularly with both women. He later said that through these relationships he experienced the 'pain and joy of love, unfulfilled but unforgotten', and he also referred to having felt 'deep emotions of adolescence'.[52] Booker's suggestion that he was very self-willed is supported by evidence from Dottie's letters to him. 'Your manners are not good', she told him, noting that others had observed the same thing. She

---

52. Rodd, 'Life and Reflections', 1950, Section 2, 8, Rodd Family Papers, AC.

evidently thought he lacked graciousness when talking to older people, for she said: 'You stand up too much to the elders.'[53]

Rodd's upbringing gave him a feel for the world beyond Britain – it laid the foundations for the broadly international outlook that characterised his later life. It was a privileged upbringing, if at the same time limited in terms of exposure to different social classes and groups. It was also solitary, although that began to change while he was at Oxford. At times Rodd saw little of his own family. This was the experience of many children of the empire, attending boarding schools at home. In this sense, his education was typical of boys of his background. The sense of independence which was a feature of his later life had its roots in these years. In summarising his outlook on the eve of the First World War, Rodd remarked on how the nature of his education threw him back on his own resources. He had, he recalled, a 'lonely liberal education on very broad lines'; he had 'every opportunity to form [his] own mind and not much guidance in doing so'.[54]

---

53. 'Dottie' to Rodd, 15 April 1913, Rennell of Rodd Papers, BD, Box 123.
54. Rodd, 'Life and Reflections', 1950, Section 2, 8, Rodd Family Papers, AC.

Chapter Two

THE FIRST WORLD WAR

When the First World War broke out on 4 August 1914, Rodd immediately wanted to enlist – although his mother was not enthusiastic. Three days later, he applied for a commission in the Royal Field Artillery (RFA) through the Officers' Training Corps at Oxford and was accepted. In the period 4–8 August, over eight thousand men enlisted, while over a hundred thousand had joined up by 22 August. Why exactly Rodd wanted to enlist, after only a year at Balliol, is not clear. But his wish to enlist immediately indicates, if not necessarily support for the war in an abstract sense, a strong wish to be involved in it. Patriotic instincts seem a good explanation for this.[1] But there were probably other factors at work too. It may be that he simply did not want to stand aside while his peers were suffering and dying. An alternative explanation is that he thought war meant adventure; he always wanted to have a full experience of what life had to offer. There is also evidence to suggest that he wanted to enhance his profile among his contemporaries. In March 1915, he wrote to Jeanne Malcolm – daughter of the actress Lily Langtry and a good family friend: 'It will be a grand thing to come home with a war to your credit especially at my age.'[2]

Rodd's first task was to do a three-week gunnery course at Shoeburyness. This experience exposed him to a different social circle from the one he was used to. He found a sense of camaraderie there among the new soldiers that remained with him long afterwards: 'Those days were some of the most wonderful. We who knew nothing about soldiering were set down to train men who knew even less.' It was a matter of pride for Rodd that he had been among the first one hundred thousand to enlist: 'We were the first Hundred Thousand and knew it […] Officers and men are now trained under less romantic conditions though they cannot be keener or have more Esprit de Corps than we had.' Rodd was soon plunged into a position of leadership in 48th Brigade, 14th Division. A few weeks after starting, he reported to his father: 'So far I have got on very well. I am the sole officer in charge of the ammunition column to the brigade. I have about 150 men under me but as yet no horses.' He gained a reputation for being a gunnery expert: he was required to explain gunnery practices to the whole battery – 156th Battery. The only negative aspect was having to get up early in the morning: 'When I think of the prospect of getting up every morning at 6.00 until the war ends I am appalled!'[3]

---

1. See on this theme Adrian Gregory, *The Last Great War: British Society and the First World War* (Cambridge: Cambridge University Press, 2008), ch. 1.
2. Rodd to Jeanne Malcolm, 4 March 1915, Rennell of Rodd Papers, BD, Box 64.
3. Rodd to his father, 3 and 8 October, 26 November 1914, Rennell of Rodd Papers, BD, Box 64; beige notebook, summary dated January 1917, Rennell of Rodd Papers, BD, Box 58.

Rodd was billeted in a private home in Godalming. One evening, he was told to be ready to leave immediately for duties abroad and instructed to report to Fort Rownal, Gosport. This was unexpected, for he was not the next in line for such a mission. But the order stood, and he soon departed with a feeling of excitement:

> My battery cheered me when I said goodbye [...] [I] went out into the night with a feeling of wonder all over me. I was not really frightened but felt a feeling of wonderment come over me at the prospect of going out all alone to life[,] a new life so different from everything before. I wished someone could have come with me.[4]

Starting for the front, he wrote to his father: 'I am so happy to be out at last that I don't know what to say.' The assignment involved accompanying 60 garrison gunners from Southampton to Le Havre. Departure for France was emotional: 'The ship drew out amid cheers from the men on board and on shore. The former sang "Tipperary" to prevent themselves getting sad, the latter sent cheer on cheer over the water as we drew down.' Christmas when it came had a sense of novelty about it: '[It was] the oddest [Christmas] I shall ever spend but not the least enjoyable.' Here again Rodd enjoyed the sense of camaraderie he experienced: 'I made some punch over the brazier which was a great success. Drank some wine in the commandant's tent where we had gone to invite them over. Capital men. Went to bed about 11. Very happy.' As with many joining the army at the beginning of the war, there was an innocence in Rodd about what lay ahead.[5]

On 14 January, Rodd was made brigade orderly officer in 41st Brigade, 2nd Division. This brigade, which had been formed in August 1914, had already seen action at Mons and the Marne. When Rodd joined, it was located in or near the village of Le Touret, north-east of Bethune and under the command of Lieutenant-Colonel F. T. Ravenhill, an experienced soldier who had joined the army in 1887. Rodd liked Ravenhill, but sensed that he was prejudiced against him because he was not a professional soldier. He was pleased when Ravenhill began utilising his skills, even if it was just his facility in French.[6]

Rodd's work often involved assisting the adjutant D. C. Stephenson – another former Etonian, who was killed at the end of the war. One of his tasks was censoring staff letters. He was also involved in informing next-of-kin about the death of their loved ones. In September 1915, he was made adjutant in succession to Stephenson, and then the following month a lieutenant. His work as adjutant involved updating the war diary or intelligence summary of the activities of different batteries within 41st Brigade. Most of his entries in the war diary were one-line descriptions, but occasionally he provided more detail. 41st Brigade was involved in the Battle of Loos, which took place from 25 September to 13 October 1915 and was part of the wider Artois–Loos offensive of

---

4. Rodd, 21 December 1914, beige notebook, Rennell of Rodd Papers, BD, Box 58.
5. Rodd to his father, 21 and 25 December 1914, Rennell of Rodd Papers, BD, Box 58. Rennell Rodd, *Social and Diplomatic Memories, 1902–1919*, 231. Paul Fussell, *The Great War and Modern Memory* (New York: Oxford University Press, 2013), 30.
6. Rodd to his mother, 13 April 1915, Rennell of Rodd Papers, BD, Box 64.

Figure 2.1 Rodd as a soldier in the Royal Field Artillery. Rodd Family Papers.

autumn 1915. In April 1915, the Germans used gas for the first time, at the Second Battle of Ypres. The British followed this precedent at Loos – both sides were increasingly using extreme methods. In his summary of the activities of the 9th Battery for 24–27 September 1915, Rodd suggested that the British use of gas was not having much influence on the enemy: 'Wire cutting continued for four days. Assault took place at 6.30 am after forty minutes of bombardment and treatment of German trenches by gas. The Germans were not affected by gas – having lit fires and used sprayers. The assault failed.'[7] Loos was a 'bloody disaster', in the words of one historian; British casualties at the battle were close to 50,000.[8]

For many officers, the Western Front created opportunities to get to know their working-class compatriots. For example, Macmillan, who served for a time in the Grenadier Guards, gained insights into working-class lives through reading soldiers' letters home; he wrote back to his mother of the 'wonderful simplicity' he found in the letters of some of the older guardsmen.[9] For Rodd, the front also meant mixing with people from other backgrounds. He was not always impressed by the soldiers he met. In February 1915, he described the average British 'Tommy' as a 'dirty creature'. An outgoing brigade had left its quarters in an 'unspeakable condition', he told his father.

---

7. Rodd to his father, 16 February and 18 May 1915, Rennell of Rodd Papers, BD, Box 64. For Rodd's reports for September 2015, see WO 95/1326/4. Stéphane Audoin-Rouzeau, '1915: Stalemate', in Jay Winter (ed.), *The Cambridge History of the First World War* (Cambridge: Cambridge University Press, 2014), 69–70.
8. Gregory, *The Last Great War*, 83.
9. Horne, *Macmillan*, 36.

But he made a concerted effort to establish a rapport with the men he was in charge of, especially through sharing manual tasks. In August, he explained to Irene that he always made a point of 'digging and working' with the men under him. To his father, he said: 'I am a believer in the officer in charge working as hard if not harder than the men.' The physical work itself appealed to him; he told his father that he had never felt so fit in his life and that he came home after tea 'divinely weary'. These experiences were probably one reason why, a couple of years later, Rodd suggested that an 'amalgamation of classes' was taking place in British society.[10]

If Rodd had arrived on the Western Front with an idealised view of war, it was gone by May 1915. He summarised his experience of battle to his father:

> I know what a battle is like now father[,] it is hell [...] The day before yesterday was peculiarly impressive. We had to go up under heavy fire. Awful noise and not a breath of air. All the fumes from the high explosive hung in the air in yellow black clouds smelling very bad and choking one. The light through this was like the eclipsed sun.[11]

Rodd recounted the sense of strain and chaos he experienced when passing along trenches under fire:

> You stumble along behind a breastwork marked by shellfire ducking repeatedly behind a traverse [...] Every now and then you come across a wounded man[.] Mainly they are only slightly wounded but you trip up over a stretcher sometimes too. Everyone who can walk if he is wounded has to. They hobble along as long as they can hobble and help each other. The worst thing to see was the visible nerve strain on the men up there.[12]

In August, he told his father that he was now a different person from the youth who used to visit Posillipo before the war; the days of his grown-up youth had been replaced by a 'cynical old age'. 'I have seen unutterable things', he later reported to Irene.[13]

Rodd's letters home often contained references to moments of personal physical danger. In mid-February, he mentioned an occasion when a bullet whizzed past. A month later, a stray bullet came close to him and 'spat' into the ground.[14] He then had a brush with death in September, when he was laying a wire: 'A shell burst at the muzzle and the bits were whizzing all about. You should have seen me get into the ditch[.] It would have won a record at any Olympic games.' On the same occasion, he was nearly hit by fallout from the German heavy shells known as 'woollies' – named for their apparent likeness to woolly bears: 'On my way home [...] my zeal made me stop and mend someone else's

---

10. Rodd to his father, 1 February and 24 August 1915, Rennell of Rodd Papers, BD, Box 64. Rodd to Irene Lawley, 24 August 1915 and 12 December 1917, Irene Forbes Adam Papers, HUA.
11. Rodd to his father, 24 May 1915, Rennell of Rodd Papers, BD, Box 64.
12. Ibid
13. Rodd to his father, 24 August 1915, Rennell of Rodd Papers, BD, Box 64. Rodd to Irene Lawley, 3 January 1916, Irene Forbes Adam Papers, HUA.
14. Rodd, beige notebook, 17 February 1915, Rennell of Rodd Papers, BD, Box 58. Rodd to his mother, 16 March 1915, Rennell of Rodd Papers, Box 64.

telephone wire and of course two "woollies" came over just then. I don't know to this day where the pieces went.'[15] Rodd was in fact wounded by a fragment from a shell just after Christmas 1915. It was a mild injury, for he managed to avoid the shell's worst effects by throwing himself on the ground. 'I got off with a graze over my left eye', he told Irene. But Rodd was listed as wounded in the War Office's casualty list.[16]

There was a lot of self-evaluation in Rodd's letters and diary entries. Like many of his contemporaries, he monitored his responses to fear. In mid-January 1915, after coming under fire for the first time, he wrote in his notebook: 'I was a little nervous but felt no inclination to run.' He reported to his father the absence of fear at the actual moment of explosion: 'It was a funny sensation to be sure. The burst looked so nice and woolly that I was very interested. I was only perturbed afterwards when it was all over.' He thought of himself as lacking in courage – he had absorbed the idea that courage in the face of danger was a quality to aspire after. 'I go in constant fear and trembling because really I am an awful coward', he told his father.[17] The sense that he did not measure up in terms of bravery remained with him afterwards. In 1950, he recalled: 'My contemporaries who were all very brave thought I wasn't any use because I never looked for danger which they all seemed to enjoy as really exciting.' He sometimes turned to prayer when he was scared, and this set a pattern for later life: 'Thereafter for many years I said my prayers when frightened.'[18]

Rodd did not find the Western Front unremittingly grim. If he was often full of fear, he was also afraid of missing out on the danger. In April, after returning to the Front from a period of leave, he explained to his father that he would be disappointed if his experience of the war ended up by being limited to a low intensity form of trench warfare:

> When I was in England I was sorely frightened lest the war should cease before I got out. All I wanted was to get out and then I should be satisfied. Now I am rather afraid that for some reason I shall get home before the fighting begins. I should hate to have to own that all the fighting I saw [was] this siege warfare.[19]

Life at the Front also gave him a sense of purpose and the experience of being part of a community. Returning to his brigade in November from another period of leave, he explained to his mother that he was 'very pleased' to be back again: 'I like the place and job.' Life would be bearable, he said, because luxuries such as waders for the trenches were being supplied. 'I have rigged up a mess for the men and a bathing establishment with a furnace', he added. But conditions remained dreadful. 'The mud is awful. The trenches are such that you can no longer go along them', he reported in early December.[20]

---

15. Rodd to his father, 12 September 1915, Rennell of Rodd Papers, BD, Box 64.
16. Rodd to Irene Lawley, 3 January 1916, Irene Forbes Adam Papers, HUA. Record Details for F. J. R. Rodd, Forces War Records, Army.
17. Rodd, beige notebook, 15 January 1915, Rennell of Rodd Papers, Box 58. Rodd to his father, 18 January and 1 February 1915, Rennell of Rodd Papers, BD, Box 64.
18. Rodd, 'Reflections', 1950, Sections 2, 8 and 3, 1–2, Rodd Family papers, AC.
19. Rodd to his father, 8 April 1915, Rennell of Rodd Papers, Box 64.
20. Rodd to his mother, 22 November and 5 December 1915, Rennell of Rodd Papers, Box 64.

The Front threw up opportunities for Rodd to enjoy the outdoor life. In May, he reported to his parents:

> We are bivouacking in an orchard. The colonel sleeps in a dugout and we all sleep out of doors. The vet, the doctor and myself all in a row. We have not been shelled here at all so far though we are just behind a battery in action. Our horses are elsewhere. It is a grand life. You sleep and eat in the open entirely.[21]

But he added: 'It would be so much more delightful if there were no war on.'[22] Connected with this love of the outdoors, Rodd's wartime letters contain glimpses of the interest in landscape that would become a feature of his career in geography. In August 1915, in a letter to Irene, he reported his impressions from a ride he had had with a friend in a nearby forest: 'The lovely evening made the place very good to behold. My chief delight was seeing wet places under trees; you know how water runs across paths under a covering of trees and wets the fallen leaves.'[23] This kind of rural interest was not exclusive to Rodd; many accounts of life on the Western Front contained pastoral references alongside stories of the violence. The beauty of the natural world was a well-established trope in English culture.[24]

The summer of 1915 found Rodd reading books by Emile Zola and Thomas Hardy: there was plenty of free time.[25] There was space to indulge in speculation about when the war would end. In February, he told his mother he expected it to end soon, mainly because the military situation seemed to be going Britain's way: 'We have the offensive in our hands. We can attack more or less where and when we want with success which the Germans cannot.' Later in the year, he told his father of his hopes that the war would end in the winter: 'I am certain the Germans do not want to go on.'[26] There was sometimes a strange combination of death and ordinary life going on at the same time. In April, Rodd wrote in his notebook of the deadly impact of a German shell on the local population, at the same time as commenting on the good weather: 'They killed a woman and one boy and injured 13 other children. Today was lovely especially the evening. It is hard to realize we are at war when the weather is like this[,] still harder to realize one may be killed at any moment and hardest of all [to] realize death as a generality.'[27]

From May 1915 onwards, Rodd was looking for a way of leaving the Western Front. He pressed his father to lobby for this – here he could use family connections in a way others could not. Exactly why he wanted to move is unclear. It is possible that he realised he was in a dangerous place and wished to get out of it. But if that was true, it was

---

21. Rodd to his parents, 12 May 1915, Rennell of Rodd Papers, BD, Box 64.
22. Ibid.
23. Rodd to Irene Lawley, 19 August 1915, Irene Forbes Adam Papers, HUA.
24. Fussell, *Great War and Modern Memory*, 251–58.
25. Rodd to Irene Lawley, 13 October 1915, Irene Forbes Adam Papers, HUA.
26. Rodd to his mother, 13 February 1915; Rodd to his father, 27 April and 8 November 1915, Rennell of Rodd Papers, BD, Box 64.
27. Rodd, beige notebook, 15 April 1915, Rennell of Rodd Papers, BD, Box 58.

certainly not the only factor in his mind. More likely he was looking for some kind of career move or a new experience. In May, he wrote to his father, asking him to get him transferred onto the general staff in Italy. 'I should like nothing better', he declared.[28] A couple of weeks later, he told his mother he wanted to move to Italy, in any capacity. But he indicated a preference to work under Brigadier-General Charles Delmé-Radcliffe, the former military attaché in Rome, who was heading the military mission at Italian GHQ. Alternatively, he mentioned the possibility of his becoming an aide-de-camp (ADC) to a divisional general.[29] A week later, he raised with his father the option of his working with Delmé-Radcliffe. As an argument for his transfer, he advised his father to stress that since he had already done a stint of six months in western France, a move to Italy did not need to be considered a way of getting out of the Front. 'Try that', he concluded.[30] When the possibility of this transfer to Italy became a real possibility, he told his father that he needed to stress that it was 'essential' that he should go.[31] The tactics were successful: in January 1916, Rodd moved to the military mission in Italy.

In moving to Italy, Rodd was coming to a country where his parents were well known. In May 1915 – a week before Italy's formal declaration of war on Austria–Hungary – the king confirmed Salandra's government in office, thereby signalling his support for the Entente. When at this point a large crowd came to the British embassy in Porta Pia, Rennell Rodd himself insisted on remaining silent, but Lilias threw 'armfuls of flowers' onto the crowd from the embassy balcony. A week later, after war had been declared, Italian and British flags were hung side by side at the embassy entrance, and Rennell Rodd gave a supportive speech from the front door. Just under a year later, he hosted prime minister Herbert Asquith on a visit to Rome, when another large crowd came to the embassy. Once war was declared, Lilias got involved in caring for the Italian wounded, which led to her receiving a gold medal for service after the war.[32]

At the military mission, Rodd was assigned work in a section under intelligence officer Edmund Vivian Gabriel. Unfortunately, this turned into an unhappy experience: Gabriel was a demanding boss who criticised Rodd for asking questions outside his remit and failing to keep on top of his correspondence. The two of them did not get on well. In November 1916, Rodd requested a return to his regiment in France and then had a minor breakdown from overwork and worry. He was given two weeks' medical leave.[33] In his memoirs, Rodd's father delicately suggested that all had not been well with the military mission, observing that it tended to act in competition rather than cooperation with the diplomatic establishment.[34] In his unpublished reminiscences, Rodd himself was less

---

28. Rodd to his father, 27 May 1915, Rennell of Rodd Papers, BD, Box 64.
29. Rodd to his mother, 12 June 1915, Rennell of Rodd Papers, BD, Box 64.
30. Rodd to his father, 18 June 1915, Rennell of Rodd Papers, BD, Box 64,
31. Rodd to his father, 16 January 1916, Rennell of Rodd Papers, BD, Box 64.
32. Rennell Rodd, *Social and Diplomatic Memories, 1902–1919*, 253–56, 289, 315.
33. Gabriel to Rodd, 12 August 1916, Rennell of Rodd Papers, BD, Box 59/1, Folder 5. Rodd to Gabriel, 22 November 1916; Gabriel message, 30 December 1916, Rennell of Rodd Papers, BD, Box 59/1, Folder 2.
34. Rennell Rodd, *Social and Diplomatic Memories, 1902–1919*, 260–61.

inhibited; he said he had worked in Italy under two men who were 'crooks' and, in doing so, had his first insight into 'knavery' in the public service. The details remain unclear, but Gabriel was one of the men he had in mind. A friend who helped him get through this experience was fellow intelligence officer William ('Bill') Haslam. Haslam was to be a life-long friend.[35]

Rodd remained with the military mission until January 1917. As he was preparing to leave his job there, his father was approached by Reginald Wingate, British high commissioner in Cairo, for help in finding an Italian interpreter to work with the British mission in Libya. This was known as the 'Talbot mission' after its leader Colonel Milo Talbot. Its main work was conducting negotiations with the fundamentalist Sufi sect known as the Sanusi. Rodd's proficiency in Italian made him an ideal candidate, and he got the job. One of his duties at the military mission in Rome involved gathering information about the Italian presence in Cyrenaica, so he was already conversant with the situation in Libya.[36] The possibility of Rodd working on the Talbot mission had first arisen the previous summer, when the negotiations had started. Rennell Rodd had been in a position to arrange for Rodd's involvement, but he decided against the idea, and the job passed elsewhere. In explaining himself to his son, Rennell Rodd cited a preference for letting 'Providence' take its course, rather than trying to press for a particular outcome:

> My principle is to rather leave these things to Providence. If one has to do a thing one does it. That is always another matter than asking for it which in my case would have involved a tremendous responsibility if anything had happened. So I did not urge one thing or another [...] I followed the course I have always followed of leaving the dispositions of Providence alone.[37]

Rodd was always more inclined than his father to channel events in a particular direction. But he would arrive at a similar philosophy during the Second World War.

The Sanusi originated in a Sufi brotherhood founded in the nineteenth century by the Algerian Arab Muhammad Ibn Ali el Sanusi; el Sanusi preached a puritanical message that spread widely among the Bedouin tribes of Cyrenaica. They are best seen not as a racial group but as a kind of sect originating in one family – one with a strong interest in political questions and, over time, an increasingly nationalist outlook. Their power was felt as far south as the Kufra oasis in south-eastern Cyrenaica, and their ideas also spread into Tripolitania and the Fezzan.[38] When Italy entered the First World War in 1915, it

---

35. Haslam was one of two friends who helped Rodd get through this experience. The other was J. A. Spranger. Rodd, 'Life and Reflections', 1950, Section 3, 3, Family Papers, AC. Nicky Haslam, *Redeeming Features: A Memoir* (London: Cape, 2009), 14.
36. Rodd to William Haslam, 12 October and 21 December 1916, Rennell of Rodd Papers, BD, Box 59/1.
37. Rodd's father to Rodd, 6 July 1916, Rennell of Rodd Papers, BD, Box 123/1.
38. Saul Kelly, *The Hunt for Zerzura: The Lost Oasis and the Desert War* (London: John Murray, 2002), 3. Lord Rennell, *British Military Administration of Occupied Territories in Africa, 1941–47* (London: HMSO, 1948), 32–33.

affected their position in North Africa, for they were required to re-deploy some of their forces from the interior. The nominal head of the Sanusi, Sayyid Ahmed, initially took the Turco–German side in the war. With his headquarters at Jaghbub in north-eastern Libya, he tried to take advantage of the situation by invading Egypt, but was thwarted by British forces under General William Peyton. With this failure, his cousin, Sayyid Idris, became the dominant Sanusi figure in Cyrenaica. The British were keen to come to an agreement with both Italy – which had declared sovereignty over Libya in 1911 – and Idris, in order to transfer troops away from the area. At the end of the initial discussions, in July 1916, the British and the Italians came to an agreement to collaborate in future negotiations with the Sanusi and recognise Sayyid Idris as the Sanusi spiritual leader – if not its autonomous ruler. Yet, the situation remained problematic, and for this reason Talbot returned to the area in March 1917.

Talbot took Haslam with him on his first trip, as well as the young Egyptian Ahmed Hassanein. Rodd knew Hassanein from his year at Oxford; Hassanein had been in his final year as a student at Balliol in 1913–14, and the two of them had remained in touch afterwards. Rodd replaced Haslam on the second trip, but Hassanein remained part of the team. For Rodd, this meant becoming involved with a set of issues his father had been monitoring for a number of years. Rennell Rodd had a tendency to become an advocate for the countries to which he was accredited. On the eve of the First World War, he had had talks about Italy's East African interests with Giacomo Agnesa, director general of political affairs in the Ministry of Colonies, talks from which Agnesa concluded that he sympathised with the Italian cause.[39] Rennell Rodd thought there might be political advantage in supporting some of Italy's African ventures. In March 1915, he suggested to Gilbert Clayton, director of military intelligence in Cairo, that Britain recognise Italian control of Libya. An agreement over that, he said, might encourage Italy to come into the war on the Entente side.[40] In a general sense, the Italians saw the Sanusi as rebels, while the British saw them as being independent. Idris broadly trusted the British but not the Italians, while the Italians were suspicious of British intentions and wished to delay decisions about the area until after the war. Idris had a tendency to use delaying tactics when he did not like an idea. His links with the Turks strengthened his hand: he wanted to see an independent Amirate for the Sanusi, and it was hard for the British to oppose this because they had encouraged all Arabs to rebel against the Turks. The Italians were keen for Idris to recognise their sovereignty. But he resisted this, and the British did not press for it, as it would have lost him a lot of support.[41]

The Talbot mission was an exciting opportunity for Rodd. It was to be his first direct experience of political negotiations. It brought with it the chance to consult the main

---

39. See R. J. B. Bosworth, *Italy, the Least of the Great Powers: Italian Foreign Policy before the First World War* (London: Cambridge University Press, 1979), 270.
40. Robert L. Hess, 'Italy and Africa: Colonial Ambitions in the First World War', *Journal of African History* 4, no.1 (1963): 106–7. Letter from Rennell Rodd to the Foreign Office, 24 March 1915, cited in Timothy J. Paris, *In Defence of Britain's Middle Eastern Empire: A Life of Sir Gilbert Clayton* (Brighton: Sussex Academic Press, 2016), 166–67.
41. E. E. Evans-Pritchard, *The Sanusi of Cyrenaica* (Oxford: Oxford University Press, 1954), 134–38.

figures overseeing the Sanusi problem in Rome: ahead of the journey, he met Agnesa, as well as Gaspare Colosimo, Italian minister of the colonies.[42] It also threw up new travel opportunities. Passing through Sicily en route to Libya, Rodd was much impressed with Syracuse: 'I wish I could paint in words the glory of what Syracuse must have been in the days of the war with Athens', he wrote to Irene. His destination was Tobruk, where the Allied mission was based. Visiting Tripoli on the way there, he was welcomed by the governor – in deference to his father's role in Rome; and he was taken into the desert to see a fort. This was his first encounter with the desert, and it had an immediate impact on him. As he explained to Irene: 'The desert thrilled me. The sand round there was blowing and the dunes continually shifting. Except for the moderately green base quite close to the fort you could see nothing but sand.'[43]

On 13 March, Talbot, Rodd and Hassanein had a meeting with Idris. The visit took place not at Idris's base at Akrama, south-west of Tobruk, but at Beri Akrama, two-and-a-half hours away into the desert by car. The journey was uncomfortable: '[The] absence of road made our going very bumpy and the dust and high wind added to our discomfort.'[44] But the lunch laid on for the Westerners was, in Rodd's words, 'uniformly excellent' – for him, there was an element of culinary tourism in the visit. The first course included couscous and various ragouts in small dishes, while the second was roast sheep with steamed rice and peas. The dessert consisted of a cream made of camels' milk and ground rice with a sauce of raisins.[45] Rodd found it intriguing to eat with his hands, as he reported to his father: 'When we reached the roast mutton and rice (or peas) course I discarded the so called benefits of civilisation and used my fingers. We were only allowed to smoke afterwards as a great concession.'[46]

The March meeting led to a final agreement signed the following month. According to this, all British, Allied and Egyptian subjects had to be handed over by the Sanusi, while all Turkish and other enemy agents similarly handed over or sent out of Africa. Furthermore, no armed Sanusi were to be permitted on Egyptian territory. On Talbot's recommendation, the British blockade of the strategic town of Sollum came to an end; Sollum was opened up for trade, but with the Alexandria–Sollum route designated the only route for goods to come into Cyrenaica from Egypt. This settled affairs between the Sanusi and the British. The Italians remained in those parts where they had established themselves, with the Sanusi retaining control inland. The issue of sovereignty remained unresolved.[47] In his final report – which Rodd helped to draft – Talbot included a note

---

42. Rodd, Diary January–May 1917, Rennell of Rodd Papers, BD, Box 126.
43. Rodd to Irene Lawley, 4 and 8 February 1917, Irene Forbes Adam Papers, HUA. Rodd, Diary for January–May 1917, Rennell of Rodd Papers, BD, Box 126.
44. Rodd to his father, 18 March 1917, Rennell of Rodd Papers, BD, Box 64. See also Colonel Milo G. Talbot, 'Libya in the Last War: The Talbot Mission and the Agreements of 1917', *Journal of the Royal African Society* 40 (1941): 128–31. Michael Haag, 'Introduction', in Ahmed Mohammed Hassanein (ed.), *The Lost Oases* (Cairo: America University Press, 2006).
45. Rodd, 13 March 1917, Diary January–May 1917, Rennell of Rodd Papers, BD, Box 126.
46. Rodd to his father, 18 March 1917, Rennell of Rodd Papers, BD, Box 64.
47. Evans-Pritchard, *Sanusi of Cyrenaica*, 134–45.

commending Rodd's contribution, especially his feel for the Italian perspective: 'But for [Rodd's help], my difficulties would have been much greater and I should have been less successful in maintaining good relations at a time when my scruples must have been a cause of considerable irritation to the Italian delegates.'[48]

Signs of Rodd's emerging instinct for political questions were evident in some of his diary entries at this time. For example, he said that an early draft of the Anglo–Italian agreement, in which Idris's political power was not recognised, lacked coherence: 'We both agree to deny all recognition of temporal power to Idris and in the same breath accept a guarantee from him to stop all acts of war. The things are not consistent.' He was increasingly sceptical of the Italians. While acknowledging their contribution to road construction and railway building in Libya, he thought they deployed a 'divide and rule' policy which meant that local tribes were encouraged to fight among themselves. He reported in his diary a comment made by Agnesa to his father to the effect that the Italians were 'delightful' in Europe, but 'impossible' in Africa. As regards Idris, he stressed his status-conscious nature: 'He is continually afraid of making a fool of himself or of not behaving himself with the dignity befitting his position.'[49]

During the trip, Rodd produced papers on the Italian presence in Libya and the uprising in Tripolitania during the First World War.[50] He also wrote reports on some of the cities and ports of Libya: Tripoli, Derna, Benghazi, Tobruk and Bardia. His impressions of Bardia – a port in eastern Libya not far from Sollum – are a good example of how an awareness of geography fed into his work for military intelligence. The British, anxious to suppress Arab opposition north of Sollum, were considering asking the Italians to cede Bardia to them or to allow them to station troops there; another possibility was to expand the Egyptian border west to include it – that is, to occupy it. Rodd's report, written to inform discussion on this, included a lot of details likely to interest military planners; he covered the anchorage possibilities, the location of the cliffs over the sea and the ravines running through them, the town's defences and the make-up of the Italian garrison. Wingate was sufficiently impressed to send it on to foreign secretary A. J. Balfour.[51] Yet, Rodd was also interested in the natural history of the area. In a letter to his father, it was the geological features of Bardia that he emphasised: 'The sides of the cliffs are of yellow rock, a marine formation consisting of hardened sand and quantities of shells: the formation being geologically speaking recent [...] The whole effect is very magnificent.'[52]

As the work of the Talbot mission came to an end, Rodd thought of returning to the Western Front. But an alternative opened up. Conservative politician Mark Sykes – a

---

48. Milo Talbot, cover note to report, 28 April 1917, FO 141/653. Rodd, 24 April 1917, Diary for January–May 1917, Rennell of Rodd Papers, BD, Box 126.
49. Rodd, 5 and 13 March 1917, Diary for January–May 1917, Rennell of Rodd Papers, BD, Box 126.
50. See documents in The Rodd Collection, RGS, Box 15/1.
51. Rodd's report on Bardia, and Wingate's letter to Balfour, 30 April 1917, WO 106/675. See also Wingate to Rennell Rodd, 2 May 1917, Rennell of Rodd Papers, BD, Box 64.
52. Rodd to his father, 23 March 1917, Rennell of Rodd Papers, BD, Box 64.

friend of his father – passed through Rome en route to Egypt in early 1917. Knowing that a liaison officer was required for the Italian contingent assigned to take part in the Palestine campaign, Sykes suggested Rodd for the post because of his knowledge of languages. Rodd warmed to the idea and, with this as a possibility, went on to Cairo with Talbot and Hassanein rather than return to France. In relocating from the Western Front to Italy, Rodd had already benefitted from the patronage of his father. Here again, an important step in his career came about because of his father's position. They went first to Alexandria, on a two-day car journey across the northern coast. Rodd was inspired by the city. The grass, trees and water of Alexandria were like the 'Elysian fields' after the desert and the months in Tobruk, he told Irene.[53]

Rodd found Cairo stimulating. Initially, he and Talbot lived with Wingate at the Residency. Soon after their arrival, Rodd was present at a dinner attended by the French travellers Colonel Hilaire and Sub-Lieutenant Mercier, who had just completed an extended journey to the Egyptian capital from Wadai via Darfur – the first time this route had been accomplished by Europeans. At the end of April, he and Talbot visited the Egyptian Sultan Hussein Kamel; Kamel made a 'very good impression', Rodd recorded in his diary. He and Talbot also went to Hassanein's home for dinner. After Hassanein was killed in a motorcycle accident in 1946, Rodd recalled that some of his best memories of the First World War were dinners at the Hassanein family home in Bulaq, where his Circassian cook produced 'exquisite food under a moonlit palm tree'. Hassanein took Rodd to see the tombs of the caliphs and the mosque of Sultan Hassan. While awaiting transfer to his new duties, Rodd was given the job of indexing a handbook on Palestine, probably the *Military Handbook on Palestine* produced by the Arab Bureau.[54]

In the middle of May 1917, Rodd took up his new role as liaison officer in the Italian Palestine Detachment. For this, he was made a staff lieutenant (second class). The Detachment, which consisted of 456 soldiers, including 11 officers, was led by Major Francesco D'Agostino. Following its arrival on 19 May, it was based in Port Said. Just under a month later, Rodd accompanied a section of the Detachment when it moved to the front at Rafah, south of the city of Gaza. His work was often mundane: 'The day of their arrival I established myself as one of their own officers [and I] put up latrines, rode the mules down to water and detailed working parties.' Rodd was required to write a weekly report to GHQ and also to do correspondence. But he eventually came to play a central role in managing the Detachment, acting as adjutant and quartermaster. He was accountable to the department of intelligence in Cairo, where he came under the oversight of colonel-in-chief of political intelligence Wyndham Deedes and topographical specialist Walter

---

53. Rennell Rodd, *Social and Diplomatic Memories, 1902–1919*, 335. Rodd, 8 and 18 April 1917, Diary for January–May 1917, Rennell of Rodd Papers, BD, Box 126. Rodd to Irene Lawley, 22 April 1917, Irene Forbes Adam Papers, HUA.
54. R. A. Savile, 'Notes on the Account of Commandant Tilho's Journey', *Geographical Journal* 52, no. 6 (1918): 401. Rodd, 14, 28 and 30 April, 15 May 1917, Diary for January–May 1917, Rennell of Rodd Papers, BD, Box 126. Rodd, obituary of Hassanein, *Geographical Journal* 107, no. 1/2 (1946), 78. Yigal Sheffy, *British Military Intelligence in the Palestine Campaign, 1914–1918* (London: Frank Cass, 1998), 135.

Nugent. Commander-in-chief of the Egyptian Expeditionary Force (EEF), General Archibald Murray, visited the Detachment in early June. Murray's reputation had been dented by a couple of failed attacks on Gaza in March and April. Rodd found him pessimistic: he wrote in his diary that he was a 'very nice gentle and soft man unless he loses his temper', but also a 'depressed' person who saw 'no gleam for the future'. Here Rodd's views support the idea that there was a morale crisis under Murray's leadership.[55]

Rodd worked in the morning and then rode or walked about for the rest of the day. Once again, he relished the outdoor life. As he wrote to his father: 'I love the place as I ride about in my short sleeves all day and glory in a feeling of absolute fitness and health.' During this time, he got to know Major Maurice Portal, an officer in the Remounts Service and cousin of Raymond and Gerald Portal. He and Portal talked about the origins of the empire in the 1890s: 'We talked of the early days in East Africa for two hours and made great friends.' It suggests that his father's experience and understanding of the empire had left a mark on his thinking. He also learned to ride a camel at this time.[56]

The desert continued to stir Rodd's imagination. It seems that the physical feel of the sand was itself important to him, for many years later he recalled that, when he had been in Sinai, he had begun to live 'in sand, on sand and with sand'.[57] At times, he waxed lyrical about the natural environment. Writing to a friend Teresa Hulton – the future Lady Berwick who was then working for the Red Cross and British intelligence – he explained:

> The desert out south is my real joy. Miles and miles of gently sloping plain covered with prairie grass and dotted over with gardens of big trees [...] To sit in front of your tent and watch the sun set as it only can in Africa over white sand dunes and over the sea, that is worth having and feeling greater by far than the most interesting or important document you can hammer out of a typewriter.[58]

The night-time atmosphere of Cairo also appealed to him. A year later, he wrote again to Hulton, from the Savoy Hotel, stating that Cairo nights were 'more enchanting' than anything he had ever seen, mentioning the 'soft feel' of the air and the 'velvet blue' colour when there was no moon.[59]

While Rodd found the natural environment appealing, he was less taken with expatriot British society – he found it stifling at times. The class consciousness that had

---

55. Rodd to his father, 23 June 1917, Rennell of Rodd Papers, BD, Box 64. Walter Nugent to Rodd, 26 June 1917, Rennell of Rodd Papers, BD, Box 125. Rodd, 4 and 17 June, 2 July 1917, Diary of May 1917–January 1919, Rennell of Rodd Papers, BD, Box 125. Sheffy, *British Military Intelligence in the Palestine Campaign*, 123. James E. Kitchen, *The British Imperial Army in the Middle East: Morale and Military Identity in the Sinai and Palestine Campaigns, 1916–18* (London: Bloomsbury Academic, 2014), 108.
56. Rodd to his father, 23 June 1917, Rennell of Rodd Papers, BD, Box 64. Rodd, 21 May, 17 June 1917, Diary of May 1917–January 1919, Rennell of Rodd Papers, BD, Box 125.
57. Rodd, 'Life and Reflections', 1950, Section 3, 4, Rodd Family Papers, AC.
58. Rodd to Teresa Hulton, 25 July 1917, Papers of Lady Berwick, SCA.
59. Rodd to Teresa Hulton, 3 June 1918, Papers of Lady Berwick, SCA.

been evident in his letters from the Western Front was now evident in a different setting. A friend of his, John de Vere Loder – the future Baron Wakehurst and governor of New South Wales – was also working for British intelligence in Sinai. Rodd and Loder made a point of trying to break out of the social circle they were in. Writing in his diary for May 1917, Rodd complained: 'There is something all wrong with a social order like ours that professes to consider it "not done" to sit with a man who sells clothes or boots.' A year later, he returned to his criticisms of the English in a letter to his father: 'The people I hardly know at all are the English. They leave me rather cold as they are so silly abroad, thinking that the limitations of Cairo are imposed by the boundary of the Sporting Club.' 'Everyone gossips and speaks evil of everyone else', he added.[60]

At the end of July 1917, Rodd joined a reconnaissance expedition to the Ottoman railway base of El-Auja Hafir in eastern Sinai, a place linked by railway to the town of Beersheba in the Negev desert. His diary entries on this indicate a strong interest in strategic questions. Rodd was sceptical about aspects of the British military strategy, especially the destruction of wells; he thought the tactics being used limited the options available to British forces:

> The policy of blowing up wells [...] is still advocated so the same may be done at Auja. All of us think it is a great mistake. We are terrified of the Turks on our right flank and destroy resources which would enable us to attack his left at Beersheba. We could have connected up with his railway and relaid the track.[61]

A connected problem was that British tactics were alienating the local population: 'The wanton destruction of water can only have the effect of turning all native sentiment against us.'[62] These insights were evidence of a practical mind: Rodd was conscious of the need to stay in tune with local opinion, while wary of destroying the regional infrastructure.

On his return from the trip, Rodd was called to GHQ to discuss tensions in the Italian Detachment arising out of the fact that he and D'Agostino had a difficult working relationship. As early as 8 July, Rodd had warned General Edmund Allenby – who had replaced Murray – that the Italian Detachment lacked discipline.[63] While he was away on the reconnaissance expedition, D'Agostino had complained about Rodd to Arthur Lynden-Bell, chief of the general staff of the EEF. D'Agostino charged Rodd with spreading false rumours about him, spying on him, being anti-Italian and getting involved in political conversations. Rodd thought the problem arose because D'Agostino had come across some of his draft reports, which had not been complimentary about him; D'Agostino was trying to get rid of him as a result. Rodd was so upset by the episode

---

60. Rodd, 21 and 27 May 1917, Diary of May 1917–January 1919, Rennell of Rodd Papers, BD, Box 125. Rodd to his father, 31 May 1918, Rennell of Rodd Papers, BD, Box 64.
61. Ibid.
62. Rodd, 1 August 1917, Diary of May 1917–January 1919, Rennell of Rodd Papers, BD, Box 125.
63. Rodd, 12 July 1917, Diary of May 1917–January 1919, Rennell of Rodd Papers, BD, Box 125.

that he requested a return to his regiment in France. But Allenby defended him. Rodd remembered this with great appreciation:

> [Allenby] taught me the first lesson I had in command. He heard my story and my application to return to Gunners [in France]. He said that he sympathised but in no circumstances would he agree to my removal or my return to my regiment: that I had been right: that his information bore out my contentions: and that however much I wanted to go, I would stay with his support.[64]

But Rodd was also warned about getting drawn into political discussions – perhaps a rebuke about his often-opinionated manner.[65] Rodd eventually developed a tolerable working relationship with D'Agostino.

With Allenby's encouragement, Rodd soon recovered his confidence. A few days after talking with Allenby, he noted in his diary that he was in good standing with his superiors: 'Even the great ones at GHQ seem pleased to see me.' In a remark indicative of an underlying insecurity about how others saw him, he also noted: 'I have never before known what it is to be liked.'[66] Rodd had a high regard for Allenby's qualities as a strategist. A few months later, in December, he wrote to his father: 'Without doubt the two finest phases of the campaign as regards strategy are that Allenby made the Turks leave Gaza without a frontal attack and he made them evacuate Jerusalem without a gun or rifle being fired.' But he was less sure of Allenby's political instincts:

> Allenby's policy is obvious and well known. He declines to have anything to do with politics and is attempting to withdraw himself from this as much as possible. It certainly is sound as far as he is concerned but it is apt to draw him into a more serious situation and lays him open to the charge that he is allowing the person with most cheek to do what he pleases.[67]

During the August 1917 visit to GHQ, Rodd met the intelligence officer Richard Meinertzhagen, who had replaced Nugent. They got on well, and Rodd was disappointed when Meinertzhagen was moved to the War Office some months later. His departure left military intelligence without someone who was 'sufficiently simpatico' for him to talk to, he observed. Meinertzhagen's army diaries, published in 1960, cover this period, but do not mention Rodd. In any case, the diaries are regarded as unreliable; Meinertzhagen has since achieved notoriety for misrepresenting his activities in Palestine, as well as in the sphere of ornithology where he was renowned for his expertise.[68]

---

64. Rodd, 'Life and Reflections', 1950, Section 3, 3, Family Papers, AC.
65. Rodd, 12 August 1917, Diary of May 1917–January 1919, Rennell of Rodd Papers, BD, Box 125.
66. Rodd, 14 August 1917, Diary for May 1917–January 1919, Rennell of Rodd Papers, BD, Box 125.
67. Rodd to his father, 16 December 1917, Rennell of Rodd Papers, BD, Box 64. Rodd, 31 December 1917, Diary for May 1917–January 1919, Rennell of Rodd Papers, BD, Box 125.
68. Rodd, 14 January 1918, Diary for May 1917–January 1919, Rennell of Rodd Papers, BD, Box 125. Kitchen, *The British Imperial Army in the Middle East*, 104–5. Richard Meinertzhagen, *Army Diary: 1899–1926* (Edinburgh: Oliver and Boyd, 1960).

In late September, Rodd moved with the Italian Detachment to join the Composite Force at a point beyond Belah. Later in the autumn, it was based for a while in the village of Mendur, on the bank of the Wadi esh Sheria, while also occupying the port of Mendur for several days. But the only action the Detachment was involved in was the attack on Gaza in November. Rodd was always eager to be at the centre of the action, hence it was a 'great disappointment' to him when he was not involved in the Allied entry into Jerusalem on 11 December – unlike D'Agostino, whose position as head of the Italian Detachment required his presence, and Colonel de Piépape, commander of the French military contingent.[69] But Rodd was in Jerusalem with D'Agostino over Christmas, from 23 to 31 December, staying in a pilgrim's cell at the Franciscan hospice of Terra Santa. The hospice was full of intrigue over the question of who would accompany the father custodian of Terra Santa to Bethlehem for the Christmas mass. D'Agostino was annoyed to discover that this role, which he had expected to fall to an Italian, had been assigned to the French high commissioner François Georges Picot. The Italians were worried that a French–British axis could deprive them of having any influence. Rodd was sympathetic to their concerns: he recorded in his diary that Picot was trying to bring all religious orders under his protection.[70]

Over the next few months, Rodd spent a lot of time riding around the Judaean hills and the coastal plain between Gaza and Haifa on horse and camel.[71] He also did the 'Via Sacra' on a number of occasions; this was a walk going back at least to the Middle Ages, in which pilgrims visited some of the sacred sites of Jerusalem. In Jerusalem again for Easter, he noticed the politicisation of the atmosphere. He attended an early-morning high mass at the Church of the Holy Sepulchre, sitting in the front row opposite a large French contingent. At the service, 25 Italian carabinieri received communion at the High Altar, to the 'pained surprise' of Picot; Picot's permission had not been given. Rodd recalled, ironically, that the 'elect' – which included him and another British officer – were given candles to hold, and that Picot's candle was 'three calibres larger' than anyone else's. He was not impressed. He contrasted the Christian church unfavourably with the mosque of Omar (also known as the Dome of the Rock). He thought the silence and beauty of the mosque 'awe-inspiring', quite the 'reverse' of the Holy Sepulchre. The mosque was much admired by soldiers in the EEF.[72]

---

69. Rodd, 13 October, 7 November, 31 December 1917, Diary for May 1917–January 1919, Rennell of Rodd Papers, BD, Box 125. Nir Arielli, 'Hopes and Jealousies: Rome's Ambitions in the Middle East and the Italian Contingent in Palestine, 1915–1020', in Haim Goren et al. (eds), *Palestine and World War 1: Grand Strategy, Military Tactics and Culture in War* (London: I.B. Tauris, 2014), 46.
70. From Jerusalem, Rodd and D'Agostino went to the city of Beit Hanun, north-east of Gaza. Rodd, 31 December 1917, Diary for May 1917–January 1919, Rennell of Rodd Papers, BD, Box 125. For another account of Christmas in Jerusalem, see Ronald Storrs, *The Memoirs of Sir Ronald Storrs* (New York: G. P. Putnam's Sons, 1937), 297–98.
71. Rodd, 'Life and Reflections', 1950, Section 3, Family Papers, AC.
72. Rodd, 15 April 1918, Diary for May 1917–January 1919, Rennell of Rodd Papers, BD, Box 125. Rodd, 'Life and Reflections', 1950, Section 3, Family Papers, AC. Kitchen, *The British Imperial Army in the Middle East*, 93.

By early 1918, Rodd was looking for a different role. Deedes promised him an appointment in intelligence work at GHQ. This came through in April when he was made an officer of the Intelligence Corps. He was assigned work in the office dealing with Intelligence 'E' – cryptanalysis – where code-breaking was a key part of the work. His knowledge of German was doubtless useful in this. His office colleagues included two Etonians, Gerard Clauson and Hugh Wethered, alongside Major Rowland Raven-Hart.[73] Rodd initially lived at Shepheard's Hotel – the leading Cairo hotel – while taking his meals at the Italian Club. But in September, he moved out of the hotel to share rooms with Clauson, with whom he had become friends. The two of them explored parts of Cairo together, including the mosques of El Moyyad and El Akhmar.[74] Clauson, an expert on Turkish languages who devoted much of his time to translating Turkish sources, was later assistant undersecretary at the Colonial Office (1940–51).

Rodd's responsibilities involved his being head of section in some capacity. He loved the intensity of the work. He reported to his father:

> I enjoy hard work as always, and here there is the additional satisfaction of working in one's own way and being in charge of a very important section. I think this section gets through more work than any other in the country. I have been down here a fortnight and have not had one afternoon off yet. Nine hours a day.[75]

He was already at this stage aware of the fact that he had been jumping from one job to another during the war. But, writing in his diary in October 1918, he defended this:

> I have tried to do my job during the war in such a way to derive the greatest possible benefit from it. I have had many jobs and it might well be objected that I have not stuck long enough to one to do any good. I have therefore not had promotion or decorations as others have but I have not looked for them either.[76]

He also observed that his persistence in pushing his ideas often paid off: 'I have learned to deal with all sorts and conditions and have till now always ended up getting my own way in all I set out to get.'[77]

Rodd was fascinated by the work itself. 'The work is about the most interesting there is', he told his father.[78] A possible reason for this was that the role gave him a connection

---

73. Rodd was made a second-class agent and temporary lieutenant, although he was graded a first-class staff lieutenant. Rodd, 5 February 1918, Diary for May 1917–January 1919, Rennell of Rodd Papers BD, Box 125. Rodd to his father, 28 February 1918, Rennell of Rodd Papers, BD, Box 64. GHQ Cairo telephone directory, 18 September 1918, 7–8, Mediterranean Expeditionary Force/3–2 (K. 47299), IWM. WO 330/20364.
74. Rodd to his father, 31 May and 19, 21 and 24 September 1918, Rennell of Rodd Papers, BD, Box 64.
75. Rodd to his father, 31 May 1918, Rennell of Rodd Papers, BD, Box 64.
76. Rodd, 17 October, Diary for May 1917–January 1919, Rennell of Rodd Papers, BD, Box 125.
77. Ibid.
78. Rodd to his father, 18 May 1918, Rennell of Rodd Papers, BD, Box 64.

with T. E. Lawrence's activities; according to one summary of his life, part of his work at this time involved maintaining contact with Lawrence during his campaign against the Turks.[79] Later in life, he recalled that he had 'passionately wanted to go with Lawrence and his men' – an indication of Lawrence's appeal to young men like him.[80] Exactly when the two men first met is not clear. But the beginning of their friendship can be dated to the second week of October 1918 when, following the capture of Damascus on 1 October, Lawrence passed through Cairo on his way back to Britain. At this time, they had a number of conversations. One subject they discussed was the Sykes–Picot Agreement, signed secretly in 1916, in which the British and French agreed to divide the Ottoman empire into separate spheres of influence. This had been reissued on 30 September 1918 as a modus vivendi establishing three OETA territories, one under the British in south Palestine, a second under the French on the Mediterranean coast and a third temporarily under Arab control.[81] Lawrence disliked the Sykes–Picot Agreement, as Rodd noted in his diary: 'Lawrence is fed up and vows he will not return until the Sykes–Picot agreement is torn up. He refuses to run the country through a French liaison officer as every Arab in the place will come to him and all his sympathies are with them.' The two men established a good rapport. 'I had several long talks with [Lawrence] and I think he likes me for being natural and not a soldier', Rodd remarked.[82]

In late October, Rodd moved to the Arab Bureau. This involved relocating to Damascus, as well as an institutional shift out of intelligence work, since the Arab Bureau was answerable to the Foreign Office. On his birthday, en route for the Syrian capital, he took some time out to go hunting jackals. He also met with Gilbert Clayton – who had played an important role overseeing Lawrence's activities – to whom he was now accountable as a staff captain. On reaching Damascus three days later, he had dinner with director of the Arab Bureau, Kinahan Cornwallis, and W. F. Stirling, who had played a role as general staff officer under Lawrence earlier in the year.[83] Soon after his arrival, he was introduced to King Faysal. In his diary, he called Faysal 'a handsome man with a strong face full of fun and laughter'. Unlike most Arabs, he was 'absolutely straight', he said – here echoing views about the Arab personality held by Cromer and his father. He noted Faysal's desire to avoid accepting French policy at any price.[84]

---

79. Daphne Pollen, 'Mary Rennell', *Paintings and Drawings of Mary Rennell* (Leominster: Fowler-Wright/Cassell, 1976), 15.
80. Rodd, 'Life and Reflections', 1950, Section 3, 4, Family Papers, AC.
81. See J. C. Hurewitz, *The Middle East and Africa in World Politics: A Documentary Record–British–French Supremacy 1914–1945* (New Haven: Yale University Press, 1979), 118–27.
82. Rodd, 15 October 1918, Diary for May 1917–January 1919, Rennell of Rodd Papers, BD, Box 125.
83. Rodd, 31 October and 8 November 1918, Diary for May 1917–January 1919, Rennell of Rodd Papers, BD, Box 125.
84. Rodd, 8 November 1918, Diary for May 1917–January 1919, Rennell of Rodd Papers, BD, Box 125.

On arrival in the Syrian capital, Rodd was immediately plunged into ongoing debates about the Sykes–Picot Agreement – about which he himself was sceptical. His doubts about British policy in the region had preceded his conversations with Lawrence. Writing in his diary on 27 September, he declared that British occupation of Syria would give rise to 'endless difficulties'. He saw contradictions in making one set of promises to the Arabs while separately agreeing the Sykes–Picot Agreement with France. This, he suggested, meant Britain committing to two 'diametrically opposite' policies.[85] This scepticism was now reinforced by what he learned in Damascus. In his diary, he suggested that the British were now pledged not just to two but three 'diametrically opposite' policies: they had promised the Arabs independence and autonomy, committed themselves in the Sykes–Picot Agreement to divide up Syria between France and Britain, and offered Palestine to the Jews as a national home. He described the second of these as an 'egoistic partition of a country', about which the inhabitants of the country had not been consulted. As regards the third, he noted that the Arabs, who were in the majority in Palestine, resented the thought that the country would go to the Jews. As with Lawrence, he was uncomfortable with the plan from an Arab point of view: 'We have always advocated self-determination […] and propose putting the Arabs in Palestine under the Jews without asking them and those in Syria mainly under the French also without consulting them.'[86]

Rodd had doubts about Sykes himself – in this he was like his father. Sykes came to Damascus in November as head of a small mission representing the British government in the region.[87] Rodd talked with him in late November and was left unconvinced by his position: 'He cannot but see the mess he has made of things but being a man of considerable personality he carries most men in front of him.' A few days later, he added: '[He] is a superficial gentleman with ambitious propensities[,] most amusing and excellent company but devoid of any real knowledge of this country […] He seems to betray also a lack of geographical knowledge.' Rodd obviously believed that in-depth knowledge of a locality was a prerequisite for sound policy-making. He added that Cornwallis endorsed his view of Sykes while also citing the influential Arabist Gertrude Bell in support of his views. Rodd soon got involved in helping Cornwallis on political matters, which he enjoyed: 'My situation is really very satisfactory now. Cornwallis uses me for his odd jobs rather than others and I am passed the political work to see.' Yet, during the next few weeks, he became less confident about Cornwallis and Stirling; the former he thought lacking in 'savoir faire', and the latter 'haphazard'. He also worked on improving his Arabic and made preparations for despatching Turkish women and children to Istanbul.[88]

---

85. Rodd, 'Life and Reflections', 1950, Section 3, 4, Family Papers, AC.
86. Rodd, 8 November 1918, Diary for May 1917–January 1919, Rennell of Rodd Papers, BD, Box 125.
87. See Michael D. Berdine, *Redrawing the Middle East: Sir Mark Sykes, Imperialism and the Sykes–Picot Agreement* (London: I.B. Tauris, 2018), ch. 12.
88. Rodd, 21 and 24 November, 23 December 1918, Diary for May 1917–January 1919, Rennell of Rodd Papers, BD, Box 125.

In early January 1919, Rodd left Damascus, returning to Britain with his eye on joining the Foreign Office. Just before leaving, he wrote out a summary of his views for one of his superiors, in which he warned that the British would have 'eternal cause to regret' its policy of bringing the French into Syria against the wishes of the Arab population; the Arabs, he said, would have preferred an Arab government under British protection. 'If we allow the French to come in here we shall have lost a very great defeat', he declared, adding that he thought the British would have been 'just' and that under the British the natives would have benefitted at the expense of the European – which was 'only fair'. He also emphasised the value of having local knowledge: 'Time and again in our history the man on the spot with the knowledge has found it necessary to act and his action has eventually been approved at home though their views and policies were different.'[89] Finding fault with government, or with London, in some form, was to be repeated again in a number of episodes in his life.

Rodd returned home as staff captain in the Hijaz operation. At the same time, he was awarded the Italian Order of St Maurice and Lazarus. He was also mentioned in despatches in January 1919.[90] Back in London, he fell victim to influenza – which was deadly that winter. But he was still able to take the exams for entering the Foreign Office. With his father's reputation high and his connection to Balliol – so closely associated with the Colonial and Diplomatic Service – he was obviously an appealing candidate. His background fitted the culture of an institution still dominated by the public schools.[91] His application was successful – he came fourth out of the first batch of 24 applicants – and he was officially demobilised in February 1919.

Rodd was conscious of the fatalities caused by the war. The loss of life was particularly evident in his year-group at Balliol. Of the 62 undergraduates in the 1913 intake, 13 were killed or died in the war.[92] One of them, Rupert Fellowes, who was killed at Moyenville in August 1918, had been with him in the same boat in the Balliol Rowing Club and also a member of the Balliol Roundtable. When Fellowes died, Rodd noted in his diary that his passing meant that only a few members of the Roundtable group remained alive.[93] Rodd's own family had also been affected – one of his cousins, David Cecil Bingham, had been killed in action in September 1914. What did Rodd feel about

---

89. Rodd, Letter to 'Colonel', 5 January 1919, Diary for May 1917–January 1919, Rennell of Rodd Papers, BD, Box 125.
90. Rodd, 5 January 1919, Diary for May 1917–January 1919, Rennell of Rodd Papers, BD, Box 125. Army Form B.103, 19 January 1919, WO 339/20364.
91. See Alan Sharp, 'Adapting to a New World? British Foreign Policy in the 1920s', in Gaynor Johnson (ed.), *Foreign Policy and British Diplomacy in the Twentieth Century* (London: Routledge, 2005), 77.
92. Ivo Elliott (ed.), *The Balliol College Register 1900–1950* (3rd edition) (Oxford: Charles Batey at the University Press, 1953), 163–70.
93. Rodd, 17 October 1918, Diary for May 1917–January 1919, Rennell of Rodd Papers, BD, Box 125. Those members who remained live were Constantine Benson, Aldous Huxley, Harcourt Johnstone and Geoffrey Madan; Rupert Fellowes, Andrew Henderson, Geoffrey Jackson and Eric Lubbock had been killed.

all this? Some decades later, he wrote wistfully of the 'great souls who were killed during the war which cut short our full lives'.[94] There is no sense, however, that he carried some kind of trauma with him into the post-war era. Wade Davis has argued that a desire for 'imperial redemption' helped to drive the post-war assault on Everest by George Mallory and Andrew Irvine.[95] Rodd's post-war expeditions to the Sahara were not driven by this kind of motive. To some extent, they were an outcome of his travels during the war itself; they were a continuation of what he did during the war, rather than a reaction to it. The desert landscapes he encountered in 1917–18 left a mark on his imagination no less – perhaps even more – than his career on the Western Front. This should be seen in the context of a wider process. In becoming interested in the desert, Rodd was joining a network of enthusiasts with the same passion. Figures like Gertrude Bell and T. E. Lawrence had already made the desert appear 'mysterious and exotic' in the popular British imagination.[96]

War gave impetus to Rodd's geographical interests. There was a wider story here as well. The First World War left a significant impact on the world of geography. In Britain, geographers took advantage of the conflict to promote the relevance of their discipline to the battlefield. The Royal Geographical Society (RGS) played a central role in providing technical and cartographical assistance to the War Office. Arthur Hinks, who was made secretary of the RGS in 1915, was influential in this. Another important figure in wartime cartography was the director general of the Ordnance Survey, Charles Close, a member of the RGS Council and former director general of the Geographical Section of the general staff. The Ordnance Survey produced 32 million large-scale battlefield maps during the war.[97] American geography also emerged from the conflict with an enhanced reputation. The American Geographical Society prepared material, often in the form of maps, for the US delegation at the Paris Peace Conference. Its director, Isaiah Bowman, was chief territorial specialist for the United States during the negotiations.[98] Coming out of the war, the relevance of geography to political and military questions could not have been clearer.

---

94. Rodd, 'Life and Reflections', 1950, Section 2, Family Papers, AC.
95. Wade Davis, *The Great War, Mallory and the Conquest of Everest* (London: Vintage, 2012), 95–96.
96. Forsyth, 'Desert Journeys', 227.
97. Michael Heffernan, 'Cartography and Military Intelligence', 505, 509–11, 521.
98. Smith, *American Empire*, 113–80. On wartime French geography, see Michael Heffernan, 'The Spoils of War: The Société de Géographie de Paris and the French Empire, 1914–1919', in M. Bell, R. Butlin and M. Heffernan (eds), *Geography and Imperialism 1820–1940* (Manchester: Manchester University Press, 1995), 221–64.

Chapter Three
INTO THE SAHARA

While waiting for the result of his Foreign Office exams, Rodd visited Trebartha Hall in Cornwall and went walking on the local moors. He wrote to Irene of the impact they had on him, indicating that earlier holidays in Cornwall had inspired his love of nature:

> This afternoon on my beloved moors when it rained nearly the whole time I was very wet and happy [...] [The Cornish and Devon moors] are covered with stone circles and barrows and remains which I love as they were once my chiefest hobby and study. They are wet and rough as the granite comes out everywhere. They are wild and cold and no one but the hardiest can live on them and I love them.[1]

This suggests that while the desert had begun to stir Rodd's imagination, it also reinforced in him feelings about the outdoor life that had existed before 1914. In having a common love of the Sahara and south-west England, Rodd was similar to Ralph Bagnold. Bagnold was drawn to the landscapes of both Dartmoor and Egypt, as he explained in his memoirs: 'Egypt fascinated me from the start, just as Dartmoor had done when I was a boy. Both had the strange aura induced by the physical presence of the remote past and also great, bare, trackless expanses where the careless might well get lost.'[2]

When Rodd joined the Foreign Office, Hardinge was permanent undersecretary. He was succeeded in November 1920 by the tough-minded Eyre Crowe, a German specialist who had organised the blockade against Germany during the First World War. Rodd's first position was chargé d'affairs in Rome – a posting that he called a 'compliment' to his father. It was a role that consolidated his interest in North Africa, for the remit of his work involved monitoring Libya. The summer of 1919 found him reading about the nomads of Tripolitania.[3] During the following year, he worked on the section of the embassy's annual report on the Italian colonies, which covered developments in Tripolitania and Cyrenaica. He visited Tunis and Tripoli in January 1920 and then returned the following month, this time taking in the main coastal cities of Libya and venturing south to some of the towns of the interior. Out of this, he produced reports on naval matters and trade conditions. He also acquired a complete set of data on all landing grounds, including

---

1. Rodd to Irene Lawley, 22 February 1919, Irene Forbes Adam Papers, HUA.
2. Ralph Bagnold, *Sand, Wind and War: Memoirs of a Desert Explorer* (Tucson: University of Arizona Press, 1990), 51.
3. F. Stroppa, *Nomadismo i nomadi della Tripolitania* (Rome, 1915); Johnson, 'The Rennell Collection', 41.

air photographs. Aerial photography had become increasingly used for reconnaissance during the First World War. All this indicates that there was an intelligence purpose behind the trip.[4] In these years, Rodd also acquired a detailed knowledge of the recent history of Tripolitania. In late 1921 – after he had left the Rome embassy – he wrote to Howard Kennard, British counsellor in Rome, warning that Tripolitania was a potential source of unrest in the area. While he did not think opposition to Italian rule in Tripolitania hugely important in itself, he explained that if unrest there turned into a larger movement, it would become impossible to ignore.[5]

Sometime in 1919, Rodd met the traveller Rosita Forbes. Forbes had acquired a reputation for being an adventurer after making an extended journey to Asia in 1917–18, in the company of Amorei Meinertzhagen, wife of Richard Meinertzhagen. The expedition was written up in Forbes's book *Unconducted Wanderers* (1919). Rodd and Forbes began to correspond and to consider the possibility of making a journey together into the North African interior. He told Irene in October 1919: 'I keep hearing from my lady of the desert: The one I hope to go to Timbuctoo with one way or another.' This was undoubtedly Forbes.[6] The two met again when Rodd was in Libya in February 1920 – he reported to Irene: 'I have gotten one very good friend in the person of Miss Forbes.' Returning to Tripoli for Easter some weeks later, he joined Forbes and two other English visitors for a trip along the coast to Alexandria and some 200 kilometres to the south of Tripoli. He was 'bitten' with the East, he told Irene.[7] It is possible that there was a romantic element in the relationship between Rodd and Forbes.[8] If so, it was not long-lasting and left little mark on Rodd. Forbes was never part of Rodd's inner circle of friends, even if they remained on good terms thereafter.

During his visit to Libya with Talbot in 1916, Hassanein had conceived the idea of making a journey to Kufra. He and Rodd then discussed the possibility a year later while they were in Tobruk. The idea remained in Rodd's mind over the next year. In January 1918 he noted in his diary: 'We are contemplating a motor car reconnaissance to Kufra.'[9] The expedition to Kufra eventually materialised in 1920–21, but without Rodd, who was occupied with his Foreign Office work. Instead, Hassanein was joined by Forbes, following an introduction by Rodd. After the trip, Forbes reported back to Rodd with much enthusiasm: 'Oh, Francis, it was so much more difficult than we thought.' She stressed that if Rodd intended to do a similar trip, it was imperative that he learn Arabic properly and get to know the religion of the area.[10] Forbes acquired the reputation for being a

---

4. Draft for the 'Rome: Annual Report for 1920', and report of visit to Libya dated 13 February 1920, The Rodd Collection, RGS, Box 15/1. On aerial photography, see Peter Collier, 'Aerial Photography in Geography and Exploration', in Fraser Macdonald and Charles W. J. Withers (eds), *Geography, Technology and Instruments of Exploration* (Abingdon: Routledge, 2016), 179–98.
5. Rodd to Kennard, 16 November 1921, The Rodd Collection, RGS, Box 15/1.
6. Rodd to Irene Lawley, 24 October 1919, Irene Forbes Adam Papers, HUA.
7. Rodd to Irene Lawley, 16 February, Easter 1920, Irene Forbes Adam Papers, HUA.
8. Kamila Shamsie, *Daily Telegraph*, 22 April 2014.
9. Rodd, 14 January 1918, Diary of May 1917–January 1919, Rennell of Rodd Papers, BD, Box 125.
10. Rosita Forbes to Rodd, 22 April 1921, The Rodd Collection, RGS, Box 14/5.1.

self-publicist. There was even a discussion in the *Times* on the subject of whether she had exaggerated her role in the expedition.[11] She was certainly quick off the mark in publishing her account of the journey, *The Secret of the Sahara, Kufara*, which appeared one month after she returned from the expedition. Hassanein, on the other hand, returned to the area in December 1922 for a journey from Tripoli to Darfur. This resulted in his widely acclaimed book, *The Lost Oases* (1925), published with an introduction by Rodd's father. It was the first crossing of the Libyan desert that could be plotted accurately from a map. One of Hassanein's achievements was to determine the altitudes of the oases of Jalo, Zighen and Kufra.[12]

Hassanein wrote to Rodd in October 1923, following Rodd's expedition of 1922, regretting he could not meet him that year: 'I was looking forward to smoking a few pipes with you over many diverse subjects, including your trip and mine.' But he alerted him to a visit to London he was planning for May 1924. The two men obviously enjoyed discussing the technology of Saharan exploration, for he also told Rodd that the theodolite observations he had taken on his recent trip were a success, and that his chronometer watch had worked well.[13] Hassanein's 1924 visit to London was a great success. He gave a talk at the RGS, which awarded him its Gold Medal.[14] He also spoke at the Aeolian Hall in London about his journeys to Kufra. Rodd wrote it up in glowing terms for *The Field*, emphasising Hassanein's English education and the fact that he could be considered a 'gentleman':

> We cannot claim Hassanein Bey as an Englishman, but we can claim to have been instrumental in the courageous, tactful and persevering explorer which he has shown himself to be, for he completed his education at Balliol, Oxford [...] We can but hope that Egypt will use him as he deserves, and that a sportsman and gentleman of this type will be allowed to play a great part in the next few years of Egyptian history, for men like him are needed badly in the world just now.[15]

Here was an example of a tendency by the British to project onto the subjects of empire their own social categories. As David Cannadine has noted, the British empire was often constructed around the discovery of apparent sameness rather than difference in the social structures of overseas realms.[16] In ascribing gentlemanly status to Hassanein, Rodd was emphasising his Egyptian friend's similarity to himself and thereby

---

11. D. G. Hogarth, *Times*, 9 December 1921, 6. Edward Gleichen, *Times*, 20 December 1921, 11; 22 December 1921, 6.
12. Kelly, *Hunt for Zerzura*, 9–11. A. M. Hassanein Bey, *The Lost Oases*, with an introduction by Sir Rennell Rodd (London: Butterworth, 1925).
13. Hassanein to Rodd, 12 October 1923, Rennell of Rodd Papers, BD, Box 66.
14. Hassanein's talk on 19 May 1924 was reproduced in *Geographical Journal* 64, no. 4: 273–91; and 64, no. 5: 353–63. For the discussion that followed, see Arthur McGrath et al., 'From Kufra to Darfur: A Discussion', *Geographical Journal* 64, no. 5 (1924): 363–66.
15. Rodd, 'Across the Libyan Desert', *Field*, May 1924.
16. David Cannadine, *Ornamentalism: How the British Saw Their Empire* (Oxford: Oxford University Press, 2002), 4.

his trustworthiness. There was a long-standing tradition of British aristocratic and gentleman hero-adventurers. Doubtless, Rodd saw himself as belonging to that. Here he was inviting the idea that Hassanein was an Egyptian representative of this kind of tradition.[17]

The conversations between Rodd and Lawrence in October 1918 led to an enduring friendship between the two men in the years that followed. In spring 1919, Lawrence was on a flight from Paris to Cairo that crash-landed near Rome, and Rodd, who was staying at the British embassy at the time, went to see him in hospital. Realising that he was not injured to any serious degree, he invited him to stay at the embassy, and he remained there for a few days – with Arabian affairs a central topic of conversation.[18] Rodd clearly enjoyed the visit because he reported to Irene: 'There are few people in this wide world I have greater admiration for than Lawrence and I like him very well besides.'[19] Rodd's father's impressions of Lawrence from the visit were less favourable. In his memoirs, he suggested that while Lawrence had rendered 'invaluable service' to his country, he must have been a 'difficult problem' for the British authorities to deal with. He portrayed Lawrence as inflexible, intolerant and 'rigidly tenacious' in his opinions, if also sincere.[20] After his visit to Tunis and Tripoli in early 1920, Rodd wrote to Lawrence, explaining how it would be possible to do a journey from Tunisia into the Fezzan and then to go as far south as Aïr and Kano. Later in the year, he invited Lawrence to join him on a trip to either Tripoli or Tunis, but nothing came of it.[21]

In subsequent years, Lawrence was a regular visitor to a flat Rodd had in London's Brook Street.[22] After one visit, in early 1926, he wrote to Rodd, complimenting him on the quietness of the place: 'I've got to thank you for four exceedingly good nights in London […] The place so quiet, so absolutely mine, and the door locked downstairs, so that it was really mine.' Writing in 1928 to writer Robert Graves, Lawrence suggested that Rodd was a 'modern incarnation of Cesare Borgia' and a 'first-rate fellow'. He had been in the Foreign Office and 'knows a great deal', he said enthusiastically.[23]

Lawrence's *Seven Pillars of Wisdom* made its first appearance in 1922, but only in a manuscript edition. A condensed 'subscriber's edition' came out in 1926 in a print run of two hundred copies – the same year as *People of the Veil* was published. Lawrence, who was then based at the RAF cadet college in Cranwell, Lincolnshire, wrote to Rodd to

---

17. Mark Connolly and David R. Wilcox, 'Are You Tough Enough? The Image of the Special Forces in British Popular Culture, 1939–2004', *Historical Journal of Film, Radio and Television* 25, no. 1 (2005): 4.
18. John E. Mack, *A Prince of Our Disorder: The Life of T. E. Lawrence* (London: Weidenfeld and Nicolson, 1976): 270–71.
19. Rodd to Irene Lawley, 27 May 1919, Irene Forbes Adam Papers, HUA.
20. Rennell Rodd, *Social and Diplomatic Memories*, 383.
21. Rodd to Lawrence, 23 January and 27 November 1920, T. E. Lawrence Papers, BD, Ms. Eng. d. 3341.
22. *Sunday Times*, 23 June 1968, 45.
23. Lawrence to Rodd, 28 January 1926; Lawrence to Robert Graves, 28 June 1927, downloaded from T. E. Lawrence Studies (http://www.telstudies.org/) on 19 February 2019.

tell him not to bother buying his book on the grounds that it was too expensive: 'You don't really want one, you know. Thirty guineas is an absurd price. Wash out the idea.'[24] Rodd eventually acquired a signed first edition, although whether as a gift or a purchase is not clear. It was not until 1935 that the book was published for the first time in an edition intended for the general public. In 1934, Rodd was the conduit for an invitation to Lawrence by Montagu Norman to be secretary of the Bank of England. When Norman mooted Lawrence for the role, Rodd protested that he had no business experience. Norman countered by saying that a person who was good at one thing would be good at another – he called this an 'Elizabethan' principle. Rodd duly approached Lawrence, who turned the offer down. He explained to Rodd the sentiments he wanted to express to Norman on his behalf: 'Please say No, for me, but not a plain No. Make it a coloured No [...] It is heartening and I am more than grateful.'[25] Rodd was very upset when Lawrence died in 1935. One source suggests that it was a 'personal tragedy' for him, but that he resisted approaches to write an obituary of him because of a wish to respect his desire for privacy.[26]

Rodd was at the Rome embassy from April 1919 to May 1920, at which point he was transferred to the Legation in Sofia, Bulgaria, where his initial boss as minister was Herbert Dering. But his mind was increasingly drawn into the 'lore of N. Africa'.[27] His desire to get back to the desert came to a head in early 1922 when he teamed up with explorer Angus Buchanan for a journey to the mountains of Aïr. It was to be a landmark moment in his life, for it give impetus to many of his subsequent geographical interests. He was absent from the Foreign Office from February 1922 until February 1923. Technically, he did not 'obtain leave' for the trip, but the Foreign Office chose to 'release' him.[28] Buchanan had already visited Aïr and written up his journey in *Out of the World – North of Nigeria* (1921). In late 1921, Rodd approached him with a request to join him on a new expedition he was preparing. Buchanan agreed on condition that Rodd paid his own way and made a £500 contribution to the cinematic side of the trip – the two of them were to be joined on the journey by cinematographer T. A. Glover.[29] Rodd was hugely excited at the prospect of the journey. 'The great adventure has begun', he wrote in his diary as they were setting off from London. On the boat trip out, there was a fancy dress ball, in which he went dressed as a North African Arab, with Buchanan appearing as a Tuareg.[30] Seen from a wider perspective, he had now become one of those

---

24. Cited in John Pateman, *T. E. Lawrence in Lincolnshire* (Sleaford: Pateran Press, 2012), 90.
25. Andrew Boyle, *Montagu Norman: A Biography* (London: Cassell, 1967), 296–97. Mack, *Prince of Our Disorder*, 402. *Times*, 6 December 1950, 6. Lawrence to Rodd, 23 November 1934, downloaded from T. E. Lawrence Studies (http://www.telstudies.org/) on 12 December 2019.
26. Pollen, 'Mary Rennell', 15.
27. Rodd, 'Life and Reflections', 1950, Section 3, 7, Rodd Family Papers, AC.
28. Rodd, 'A Journey in Aïr', *Geographical Journal* 62, no. 2 (1923): 101.
29. Buchanan to Rodd, 3 December 1921 and 25 January 1922, Rennell of Rodd Papers, BD, Box 66.
30. Rodd, Diary for Saharan Expedition 1922, 8 and 15 March 1922, The Rodd Collection, RGS, Box 15/3.

representing the link between exploration and geography, in the words of Felix Driver, a 'foot-soldier of geography's empire'.[31]

European knowledge of the region had been much influenced by the works of German explorer Heinrich Barth, in particular his *Travels and Discoveries in North and Central Africa* (1857). Barth had travelled into Aïr in 1850–51 with a German colleague Adolf Overweg and the British traveller James Richardson – Buchanan was the first Englishman to visit Aïr since Richardson. Rodd was a particular admirer of Barth. The German traveller was a role model for him of how to combine an interest in discovery with a commitment to detailed research. He said of him that there had never been a 'more courageous or meticulously accurate explorer'.[32] Another who shaped European understanding of the Tuareg was French explorer Henri Duveyrier. His book *Exploration du Sahara: Les Touareg du Nord* (1864) was based on his journeys in the Ahaggar and Ajjer regions of Algeria and the Fezzan in Libya. What had changed since the mid-nineteenth century was French occupation of the area, which Rodd dated to 1899. It was in that year that the Foureau–Lamy mission had entered the borders of Aïr, and the French flag been hoisted at the city of Agadez. As a result, it was recognised that the region lay within the French sphere of influence. In a practical sense, Rodd dated French rule to 1904 when the French established a post at Agadez under Lieutenant C. Jean. Jean wrote a book on the Tuareg, which was one of the sources for Rodd's text – although Rodd thought it inferior to Barth's work. In 1904, the population of the Tuareg was roughly 50,000–60,000.[33]

Rodd and his companions travelled into Aïr by the same route Barth, Overweg and Richardson had taken, but in reverse. Leaving Kano in northern Nigeria in late April, they reached Katsina after seven days and then, three days later, the frontier of what were then known as the 'Niger Territories'. From there, they journeyed to the town of Tanut, the administrative capital of Damergu – a region of the Sahel – while also taking in the then capital of Niger Territories, Zinder.[34] At Tanut, Rodd left Buchanan and Glover for a 560-mile detour, in which he accompanied a French Camel Corps patrol on a journey to inspect the wells in the Termit mountains. He rejoined his party in the foothills of Aïr. They then travelled on to Agadez, and beyond that to Auderas, where they spent the rainy season. Famous for having an impressive grove of date palms, Auderas was a group of three villages that functioned as a regional capital. During the subsequent months, Rodd explored widely around Auderas. The three men sometimes travelled separately. In early August, Rodd took a party of 8 men and 26 camels into central Aïr, while

---

31. Felix Driver, *Geography Militant: Cultures of Exploration in the Age of Empire* (Oxford: Blackwell, 2001), 3, 39–40.
32. Francis Rennell Rodd, *People of the Veil: Being an Account of the Habits, Organisation and History of the Wandering Tuareg Tribes Which Inhabit the Mountains of Air or Asben in the Central Sahara* (London: Macmillan, 1926), 22. Heinrich Barth, *Travels and Discoveries in North and Central Africa* (London: Longman, 1857).
33. C. Jean, *Les Touareg du Sud-Est: L'Air* (1909). Rodd, *People of the Veil*, 27–28, 402.
34. Niger was known as 'Niger Territories' until October 1922, when it was renamed the 'Niger-Chad Colony'. It was headed by a lieutenant-general, answer to a governor-general in French West Africa. Zinder was capital from 1922 to 1926. Rodd, *People of the Veil*, 41n.

Buchanan and Glover headed in the opposite direction in search of a lion – lions being still present in the region but very rare.[35]

For Rodd, one of the most memorable aspects of the expedition was the friendships formed through it. For example, writing of Buchanan in his introduction to *People of the Veil*, he expressed hope that one day the two of them would be able to renew their 'companionship of the road'. He made a similar comment about one of the French officers he met, Henri Gramain, the officer in charge of the fort at Agadez. When on one occasion news was received about an imminent raid coming from the North, he was invited by Gramain to lead a group of Tuareg on a reconnaissance party. He later said that he owed Gramain 'the most perfect companionship' he had ever had the fortune to experience. He enjoyed the camaraderie with other French soldiers too. After the journey he made with the Camel Corps to the Termit mountains, he was made an honorary sergeant of the patrol – which went by the name of 'Peloton Méhariste de Guré'.[36]

Perhaps even more important to Rodd were the friendships with some of the Tuareg, particularly those of higher social standing. Auderas was ruled by a nobleman called Ahodu, a man with a record of mediating between the French and the Tuareg. He and Rodd got on well, talking mainly in Arabic; Rodd subsequently called him 'one of my fastest friends whose memory I shall always hold dear'. He also made close friends with one of the most famous guides of Aïr, T'ekhmedin, another man of noble birth who came from a village outside Auderas. No more than 40 years old, he was reputed to have done the 400-mile journey from Aïr to Ghat in south-western Libya some 80 times. He was one of the few Tuareg men Rodd saw without the veil. Rodd's link with the local people was enhanced by his learning the local language of Tamasheq to the level of being able to travel around with a guide, talking only in that language. At the conclusion of *People of the Veil*, he emphasised how much he appreciated his friendships with the Tuareg: 'They were my very good friends, and I was very pleased to live with them, for they were very agreeable. Perhaps we shall meet again and travel together once more.'[37] Rodd had something in common with Barth in his emphasis on the humanity of the Tuareg – one of Barth's legacies had been to humanise peoples seen as uncivilised in the age of imperial expansion.[38]

Like many travellers, Rodd took photographs during the expedition – for this he took the advice of Glover – many of which were reproduced in *People of the Veil*; the book contained more than fifty plates as well as some maps. Some of Rodd's pictures were intended to record aspects of Tuareg culture. These reflected a well-established tradition in imperial photography, in which photographers sought to keep a visual record of peoples seemingly threatened with extinction. The book also contained a photo of Rodd

---

35. Rodd, 'A Journey in Aïr', 84; *People of the Veil*, 81, 119, 446–51.
36. Rodd, *People of the Veil*, vii, 7.
37. Rodd, 'A journey in Aïr', 91; *People of the Veil*, 154, 421. Rodd spelt Tamasheq 'Temajegh'.
38. Steve Kemper, *A Labyrinth of Kingdoms: 10,000 Miles through Islamic Africa* (New York: W.W. Norton, 2012), 256.

Figure 3.1 Rodd (right) with T'ekhmedin, 1922. From *People of the Veil*, 178.

and T'ekhmedin standing alongside each other, prepared by Rodd himself (Figure 3.1). By including this in the book, Rodd surely intended to illustrate his friendship with the Tuareg guide while also presenting him as a person capable of standing alongside him on equal terms.[39]

Notwithstanding the human connection with T'ekhmedin, Rodd could not but help also looking at his Tuareg friend through an ethnographic lens – T'ekhmedin's very physiognomy was an object of curiosity. Speaking about the trip after his return home, Rodd described his features in some detail: '[He has] small hands, wrists, feet, and ankles typical of all Tuareg [...]. Slender thighs and a thin neck. No visible muscular development. Domed forehead joining the skull, which is rather high behind. He has the typical Berber indentation of the root of the nose, which is straight with rather broad nostrils.'[40] In making these comments, Rodd was trying to demonstrate an alertness to academic

---

39. Rodd, *People of the Veil*, plate 18. See on this James Ryan, *Picturing Empire: Photography and the Visualisation of the British Empire* (London: Reaktion, 1997), ch. 5.
40. Rodd, 'A Journey in Aïr', 93.

debates about race and racial origins. There was perhaps a duality or tension in Rodd's attitudes here – a duality confronting many explorers: T'ekhmedin was for Rodd a friend at the same time as being a kind of object to be studied. Rodd was sufficiently interested in head measurements to be the owner of a craniometer. This he donated to the RGS in February 1928, following his second expedition to Aïr. In a talk he gave at the RGS a couple of years earlier, he made a brief reference to controversies among anthropologists surrounding the merits of craniometry, but gave no indication as to his own views on the matter.[41]

An unexpected way in which Rodd established a connection with the local population was through attempts to help people with health problems. There was a tradition here: it was not unusual for European travellers in Africa to establish a rapport with native peoples through offering medical help. Rodd acquired a reputation for having medical skills after he helped heal a child with a severe abscess in its right ear. The child had previously been treated by having its orifice blocked with a paste made out of fresh camel dung, wood ash and the leaf of the Abisgi bush; when this was cleared out and the ear washed, the pain ceased. T'ekhmedin was another person Rodd helped: he 'nursed him back to health' after a bad bout of fever. Another vehicle for establishing a rapport was humour. On one occasion in Auderas, Rodd dressed up in such a way as to look like a Tuareg. This was not difficult because he had grown a dark beard and was sunburnt on his arms and legs. He then created a stir by riding into the village on a large white camel via a circuitous route. As he recalled: 'The people were puzzled about my identity, and some, as I was later told, decided from the colour of my limbs that I came from the Igdalen tribe. It was typical of the Tuareg that they eventually recognised not me, but my camel, and so guessed who I was.'[42]

Rodd described his visit to Aïr as the happiest year he had ever spent. The friendships he formed during this time were doubtless one reason for this. But there were other reasons why he found the expedition exciting and satisfying. One of these seems to have been that, on a number of occasions, he had to overcome physical challenges or get out of difficult situations. The expedition functioned as an opportunity for testing himself in an adverse environment. For example, in June 1922, he and his companions arrived at a well at Milen, to the south-east of Agadez, to water their camels. But in trying to water the last of their camels, their two-gallon bucket broke from the rope and plunged into the well, and it took some time for them to create another rope by untying their baggage – all in a scorching temperature. On another occasion, they arrived at what was supposed to be a watering place on the south side of the Tim'ia massif, but failed to find water. The following day they pressed on to the Tebernit valley, by which time their supply of water had run out. They were left awaiting the return of a group searching for water elsewhere.

---

41. Eugene Rae, Catherine Souch and Charles W. J. Withers, 'The Life and Liveliness of Instruments of British Geographical Exploration, c. 1860–1930', in Fraser Macdonald and Charles W. J. Withers (eds), *Geography, Technology and Instruments of Exploration* (Abingdon: Routledge, 2016), 152. Rodd, 'The Origin of the Tuareg', 135.
42. Rodd, *People of the Veil*, 82, 162.

At this point, Rodd began to search for water himself in the form of an 'Ers' – a waterscrape in the sand. Seeing a place where a ridge of rock crossed the bed of the valley, and noting an old village site nearby, he began to dig and found water about two feet down. The place became known to the expedition as 'Rodd's Ers'.[43]

During the expedition, Rodd made detailed geological and meteorological calculations of the area. He also made modifications to local maps. A map of the Aïr mountains had been produced in 1910 by the Cortier geographical mission, based on 33 astronomically determined coordinates, supplementing five that had been produced by the Foureau–Lamy mission.[44] Rodd thought Cortier's map reasonably complete, but misleading on the layout of the mountains around Auderas.[45] More generally, he was fascinated by the road systems of the Sahara. There were three Central Saharan trade roads coming south from the Mediterranean coast. One of them passed through the western Fezzan into Aïr on its way to Nigeria. Rodd set as one of his tasks for the journey tracing the actual tracks through Aïr of the people who used this road.[46] While this was an important trade route, Rodd was conscious of the fact that it had also been used by invaders coming from the North: the Romans had got at least as far south as the Fezzan and probably had had ambitions to press further south into Aïr; and the seventh-century Arab general Oqba ibn Nafi had got as far south as the Kawar cliffs in north-eastern Niger.[47]

Rodd was worried that, in the twentieth century, British territories could also be threatened by forces coming from the North. There was an immediate precedent for this. In 1916–17, there had been an uprising against the French occupation of Aïr headed by the Tuareg clan leader Kaocen Ag Muhammad. During the rebellion, the Sanusi, who had German and Turkish advisors, sent aid to Kaocen. Rodd was concerned that unrest of this kind might reoccur. He saw French West Africa as a kind of buffer. In his view, the resistance of French soldiers to the Tuareg uprising had had the indirect effect of protecting British rule in Nigeria: 'Their efforts in Air saved a British colony from facing a situation which might have become serious owing to the general depletion of forces there.'[48] Rodd was interested not only in the locations of the roads but also in the best way of travelling along them in desert conditions. For example, he noted that the size of armed groups moving across the desert was limited by the capacity of wells, observing that the French took to organising Camel Corps patrols of relatively small size and great mobility to deal with raiders in southern Algeria.[49] Rodd's eye for the military significance of the roads of the Sahara would prove significant in 1940, when his ideas helped shape planning for the desert war in North Africa.

Iferuan, the last permanently inhabited place in northern Aïr, where the French had established a fort in 1921, was as far north as Rodd got. He was much impressed there

---

43. Ibid., vii, 72–73, 213n, 243.
44. Ibid., 27.
45. Rodd, 'A Journey in Aïr', 92.
46. Ibid., 81–82.
47. Rodd, *People of the Veil*, 322–33.
48. Ibid., 85. 93. On the Tuareg uprising, see Finn Fuglestad, *A History of Niger, 1850–1960* (Cambridge: Cambridge University Press, 1983), 95–99.
49. Ibid., 11.

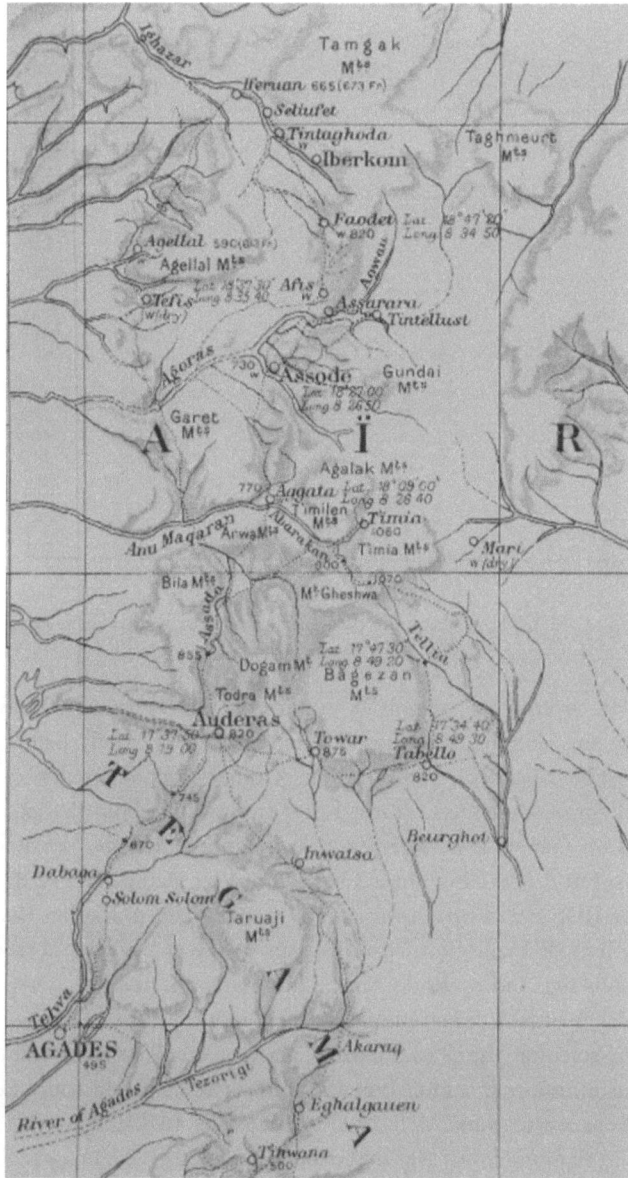

Figure 3.2 Extract from a map of Aïr made in 1910 by Captain Cortier. From *People of the Veil*, at end.

by the gardens and palm tree groves as well as the cool climate. He was also intrigued by Iferuan's strategic position as a place where several important Saharan roads met. The original plan for the expedition had been to travel from Nigeria to the Mediterranean coast. But there was a delay in receiving permission from the French authorities to go north of Aïr. In late November, with time too short to reach the Mediterranean, Rodd

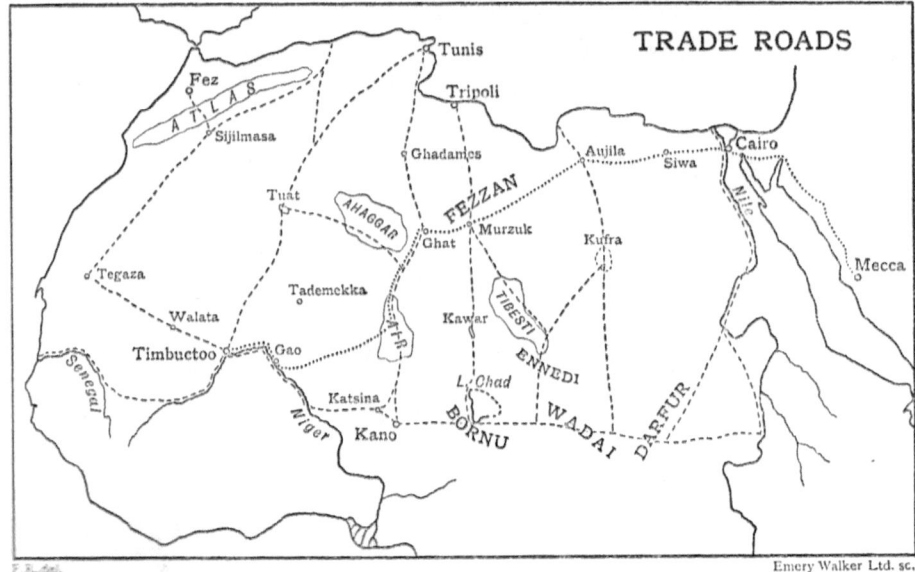

Figure 3.3 Map of the trade roads of the Sahara, designed by Rodd. From *People of the Veil*, 5.

turned back. He covered the roughly 550 miles back to Kano in 29 days – even the Tuareg thought this was fast travelling. He lingered there briefly before returning to Britain and what he called the 'dreary routine of office work in London'.[50]

A couple of months after his return, Rodd gave a talk about the expedition at the RGS. This was his first effort at organising his thoughts.[51] He also donated a collection of objects to the Pitt Rivers Museum in Oxford, then curated by Henry Balfour – later a president of the RGS (1935–38). It was a good year for gifts to the Pitt Rivers Museum; donations also included collections from Assam, Sarawak and the northern Amazon. Most of the items donated by Rodd came from Damergu and Aïr. They included two ornamental leather bags, a camel saddle, a shield made of wet raw hide, a cross-hilted sword, traps for catching giraffe and gazelle, armlets, a collection of written charms, a nutshell used as an ink-pot, a snuff box and a black veil.[52] Rodd could talk eloquently about the provenance of some of the objects. He later told Balfour that much of the ornate leather work found in Aïr was probably not of Tuareg origin and could have been introduced to the region after the Songhai conquest of Agadez (c. 1500).[53] There were 146 items in the collection given by Rodd. He subsequently made further donations, mostly in 1938 and 1945, to bring the total up to 177. If geography is seen as a set of

---

50. Ibid., 317, 419; Rodd, 'A Journey in Aïr', 101.
51. This talk came out as 'A Journey in Aïr'.
52. 'Report of the Pitt Rivers Museum, 1923', 1, 12–13, *Annual Reports 1911–1940* (Pitt Rivers Museum, University of Oxford).
53. Rodd to Balfour, 13 September 1932, Rennell of Rodd Papers, Box 146/4.

practices, with 'collecting' being one of them, he was doing all the things expected of a serious geographer.[54]

Rodd's journey had a political as well as an anthropological dimension. While still in Kano, he wrote a report for the governor of Nigeria, Hugh Clifford, covering the political, financial and judicial situation in Niger.[55] More significantly, 18 months later – just before leaving the Foreign Office – he wrote a memorandum on developments in North Africa, including in relation to the Tuareg. This was a synthesis of his thinking about the Sahara going back to the Talbot mission. It was a good example of his Foreign Office 'voice': the way he expressed himself to a Foreign Office audience. Rodd warned that an Islamic movement connected with a 'rapidly growing spirit of nationalism' was emerging, with the Nilotic Sudan, the Fezzan and Morocco possible sources of trouble. He also argued that the French were sitting on a 'live volcano' that was a potential threat to British rule in West Africa. The paper contained a justification for Rodd's preoccupation with the Tuareg: Rodd stressed that, historically, the nomadic peoples of the area tended to provide the 'spirit and motive power' of the sedentary peoples of the coast. According to Rodd, Murzuk – rather than Ghat – was increasingly the centre of trouble in the Fezzan and was conveniently situated for contact with the Sanusi. The Sanusi and the Wahabi were similar in their respect for Puritanism, he warned, while noting that the Tuareg would work with the Sanusi in the event of unrest. The paper contained evidence for a 'divide-and-rule' instinct. Rodd argued that, if there was an anti-European uprising in the Fezzan, the divisions between the Arabs and the Berbers could be 'turned to good account'.[56] The British national interest was a priority here. The memorandum was well received. John Murray, head of the Egyptian Department of the Foreign Office, arranged for it to be sent to British consulates and embassies in the Middle East and North Africa, alerting them to be on the lookout for local unrest. Rodd and Murray remained in contact well into the 1930s.[57]

Rodd's main intellectual focus at this time was turning his interest in the Tuareg into a book. Here his aim was to produce something that was academic rather than political in character; he wanted to be taken seriously as a scholar and was dismissive of writers whose methods he thought amateurish. This was exemplified in 1925, when he wrote a critical review of W. Harding King's *Mysteries of the Libyan Desert*, a book in which the author presented the results of his travels before the First World War. Rodd was unimpressed and concluded his review by saying the book was 'not productive of sensational results'.[58] This resulted in a robust exchange between Rodd and Harding King, in which the two men tried to iron out some of their differences. Rodd's main criticism was that

---

54. Driver, *Geography Militant*, 12.
55. Report to Sir Hugh Clifford, 15 January 1923, The Rodd Collection, RGS, Box 15/2.
56. Rodd, 'Memorandum on the Political Situation in North Africa', 21 June 1924, 1, 4–6, FO 371/10067 E5421. For an earlier unpublished paper on this theme, see 'Africa and Arabia', The Rodd Collection, RGS, Box 15/2.
57. Handwritten note by Murray on 2 July 1924, FO 371/10067 E5421. Rodd to Lamont, 4 September 1935, Thomas Lamont Papers, BK, Box 6.
58. Rodd, review of Harding King's book, *Geographical Journal* 65, no. 6 (1925): 539.

Harding King presented his work as a contribution to science and knowledge, whereas in reality it was more of a travelogue. 'I am as convinced that the book is superficial as he is that my review is superficial', he told Arthur Hinks.[59]

In making these comments about Harding King, Rodd was – consciously or unconsciously – evoking a discussion going back at least to the eighteenth century about the differences between serious academic research and popular travel literature.[60] He wanted his work on the Sahara to fall in the former category. Ironically, *People of the Veil* was originally intended to be a book of travel itself. But it expanded into a more ambitious study of the origins and nature of the Tuareg tribes. Its remit was explained in its subtitle: 'Being an Account of the Habits, Organisation and History of the Wandering Tuareg Tribes which inhabit the Mountains of Air or Asben in the Central Sahara'.[61] To turn the experience of his journey into a book of this ambition required from Rodd a lot of additional reading. This was reflected in a series of reviews he did in the mid-1920s for the *Geographical Journal*. He also did some more focused historical research: in 1925 he published an article on the seventh-century Berber queen Kahena.[62] In 1950 he said that between his Saharan journeys of 1922 and 1927, he worked harder than he had ever worked before or since: 'In writing my book I put in 2/3 hours daily at the British museum every weekday before going to the F.O. [I] dined out every night and went away every weekend for I was quite social and worked every night until 2–3 am after coming home.'[63]

People of the Veil was read in manuscript by D. G. Hogarth. Hogarth, keeper of the Ashmolean Museum in Oxford before and after the First World War, was a supporter of the ideas of Lionel Curtis. An influential figure on the RGS Council, with close links to the intelligence services, Hogarth had been associated during the First World War with the so-called Easterners, those who stressed the strategic importance of the war against the Ottoman empire – in contrast to the 'Westerners', who prioritised the Western Front. He worked and at times headed the Arab Bureau in Cairo in 1916–19. Like Lawrence, with whom he worked closely, he was suspicious of the Sykes–Picot Agreement and sympathetic to the Arab cause.[64] Rodd's connection with both Hogarth and Lawrence indicates that, socially and intellectually, he was involved in the same network as these men. From 1925 to 1927, Hogarth was president of the RGS. In November 1925, he was in the chair when Rodd gave a paper on the origins of the Tuareg. Admitting that

---

59. Nicola Thomas and Jude Hill, 'Explorations in the Libyan Desert: William J. Harding King', in Simon Naylor and James R. Ryan (eds), *New Spaces of Exploration; Geographies of Discovery in the Twentieth Century* (London: I.B. Tauris, 2010), 99–101.
60. Driver, *Geography Militant*, 1–2.
61. Rodd, *People of the Veil*, 216.
62. Rodd, 'Kahena, Queen of the Berbers: A Sketch of the Arab Invasion of Ifrikiya in the First Century of the Hijra', *Bulletin of the School of Oriental Studies* 3, no. 4 (1925): 729–46.
63. Rodd, 'Life and Reflections', 1950, Section 3, 8, Rodd Family Papers, AC.
64. Michael Heffernan, 'Cartography and Military Intelligence', 511–14. See also Philip Knightly and Colin Simpson, *The Secret Lives of Lawrence of Arabia* (London: Nelson, 1969), 21–29; Deborah Lavin, *From Empire to International Commonwealth: A Biography of Lionel Curtis* (Oxford: Clarendon Press, 1995), 256–59.

his arguments were speculative, Rodd suggested that the Tuareg should be differentiated from the more sedentary peoples of Libya, even if there was some merging of the two groups through intermarriage and that their origins could be traced to a southward migration of Nordic peoples into North Africa. In the discussion afterwards, Hogarth picked up on possible links between Libyan and Minoan culture.[65]

People of the Veil gave Rodd the opportunity to test out some of his ideas. One of his arguments was that Tuareg culture was not rooted solely in Islam, as had been generally accepted. For example, he thought the 'patience' and sense of 'honour' evident in the Tuareg character were attributable to something older than Islam. Tuareg people were not fatalistic but took the 'long view' of life and held to an 'optimistic school of thought', he explained.[66] Rodd was drawn to the view, associated with Duveyrier, that the Tuareg were originally Christian before they converted to Islam, this in spite of arguments to the contrary by American archaeologist Oric Bates and the views of the French monk and Tuareg expert Charles de Foucauld. Rodd thought that the presence of the cross in Tuareg decoration was a probable sign of this, as well as the existence in Tamasheq of certain words associated with Christianity. In his view, the 'cumulative evidence' for a Christian influence ran counter to Bates's argument that cross imagery reflected a tradition of sun worship originating in Libya.[67]

Another historical question exercising Rodd was whether Roman civilisation had stretched as far south as Aïr. Rodd had been excited to discover a rock drawing in a valley to the west of Mount Arwa in the likeness of an ox cart or chariot. This, he ventured, could have been evidence to support the idea.[68] The Tuareg veil, famously worn only by men rather than women, also interested him. With there being no single name uniting the Tuareg tribes, it was their common use of the veil that gave them a collective identity. Rodd talked with humour on the veil: 'Almost all Tuareg, unless they have become denationalised, would as soon walk unveiled as an English man would walk down Bond Street with his trousers falling down.'[69] *People of the Veil* also demonstrated a keen eye for material detail. On water-skins, Rodd wrote: 'A new skin recently greased with goat or sheep fat is abominable, as the water becomes strongly impregnated with the reek of goat. But water from a good old skin can be almost tasteless, though such skins are hard to come by.'[70] Rodd was also alert to the historical importance of documents. On one occasion, he transported a 'whole camel-load' of papers from the mosque at Assode – once the most important town in Aïr after Agadez – for safe-keeping in Iferuan. These

---

65. Rodd, 'The Origin of the Tuareg', *Geographical Journal* 67, no. 1 (1926): 37, 46. Hogarth, 'The Origin of the Tuareg: Discussion', *Geographical Journal* 67, no. 1 (1926): 47, 51–52.
66. Rodd, *People of the Veil*, 296.
67. Ibid., 275–78. See Oric Bates, *The Eastern Libyans* (London: Macmillan, 1914).
68. Rodd, *People of the Veil*, 321.
69. Ibid., 14–15, 286–90. See also Rodd, 'The Origin of the Tuareg', 31; 'A Second Journey among the Southern Tuareg', 17–18. Rodd thought the veil emerged between the fourth century AD and the time when Arab writers started to call the Tuareg 'veiled people'; in H. R. Palmer, 'The Tuareg Veil', *Geographical Journal* 68, no. 5 (1926): 418.
70. Cited in Kemper, *Labyrinth of Kingdoms*, 169.

Figure 3.4 Agellal village and mountains. Photograph by Rodd. From *People of the Veil*, frontispiece.

were the remains of the private library of a nineteenth-century collector El Haj Suliman of Agellal.[71]

People of the Veil also contained reflections of a social and political nature. Rodd was scathing about French policy in the region. After the Tuareg uprising of 1916–17 had been suppressed, the French adopted a policy of depopulating Aïr and resettling the Tuareg in the lands of Damergu and the Sudan geographical expanse. As many as 30,000 people left Aïr at this time, many settling in Kano and Katsina. Rodd thought this strongly decreased the chances of the French getting an economic return from this part of the Sahara. He welcomed the reversal of this policy in 1922, but wondered if it had not been already too late by then to reverse the damage. For the Tuareg, he thought the events of 1917–18 had proved so 'calamitous' that it had required them to change many of their habits and 'scattered' their traditions. Here the expedition gave impetus to Rodd's thinking on questions connected to government and empire. It instilled in him a respect for some of Lord Lugard's ideas on indirect rule; in *People of the Veil*, he wrote of the system 'so successfully instituted' by Lugard in Nigeria, contrasting it with the direct French approach.[72]

In Rodd's view, there was a strong emphasis on the principle of consent in the Tuareg approach to government. Noting, ironically, that the works of John Stuart Mill and Jean-Jacques Rousseau were not current in Aïr, he stressed that the principles of consent were observed there in a way that was often lacking in Europe. However, the pragmatist in him made him sceptical about the long-term future of Tuareg culture. In his mind, camel-borne trade, in the form of caravans and long-distance desert transport or even a trans-Saharan railway, would never be able to compete with seaborne traffic. But he was of the view that aircraft might one day facilitate a revival of the old camel roads, because the watering points along the routes might make for convenient stopping places.[73] Rodd

---

71. Rodd, *People of the Veil*, 302.
72. Ibid., 42, 361, 362.
73. Ibid., 38, 108.

was impressed with the Tuareg readiness to resist French rule. But he commended Ahodu for realising that resistance to the European advance could only end in disaster. He was much impressed with the courage and resilience of the Tuareg:

> They have an indomitable spirit and for that reason will perhaps survive [...] They may have patience after all to wait for the fulfilment of their fate and not throw themselves fruitlessly again on rifles and machine-guns [...] You have fought well you people. You would not bow your necks, so they have been broken, but perhaps your day will come again.[74]

Rodd loved the sense of pride he saw in the Tuareg. 'The men are born to walk and move as kings, they stride along swiftly and easily, like Princes of the Earth, fearing no man, cringing before none, and consciously superior to other men', he observed.[75]

Rodd thought Islam lagged behind Europe and America in its treatment of women. But Tuareg culture, he noted, was matriarchal and hence quite different, even if the Tuareg adhered to Islam. For one thing, Rodd saw monogamy rather than polygamy as the norm – on this, his thinking differed from the French soldier Jean. Rodd praised Tuareg women for being 'strong-minded, gifted and intelligent', as well as courageous in battle while remarking on their right to own property and participate in public life. The respectful treatment of women, he noted, had earned the Tuareg the epithet 'Knights-Errant of the Desert Roads'.[76]

People of the Veil was widely reviewed when it came out in 1926. The *Daily Telegraph* called it 'fascinating' and remarked on Rodd's 'captivating literary style'.[77] The *Guardian* praised the fact that every judgement in the book was based on a 'wealth of evidence'.[78] But the *Christian Science Monitor* felt that it was too intricate to appeal to the general reader and called for Rodd to produce a more popular volume.[79] This was a perceptive comment. Rodd was a fine chronicler of detail, but he sometimes found it hard to see the wood for the trees. The academic press was also positive. The French geographer E. F. Gautier – in Rodd's words the 'greatest living authority on the Sahara'[80] – applauded Rodd for his coverage of the Tuareg themselves. On matters relating to the Tuareg people – society, political organisation, mode of life and implements – Rodd had gathered 'very complete data' forming a 'well-balanced' picture, Gautier explained. But he felt Rodd lacked expertise in physical geography. He also thought him less assured when discussing the origins of the Tuareg. Similarly, another reviewer remarked that the book did not resolve debates about the ethnology of the Tuareg.[81] Rodd himself was not completely satisfied

---

74. Ibid., 420–21.
75. Ibid., 163. See also Rodd, 'The Forgotten of God: The Veiled Tuareg of the Sahara', *Geographical Magazine* 2, November 1935, 28.
76. Rodd, *People of the Veil*, 168.
77. *Daily Telegraph*, 24 December 1926.
78. *Guardian*, 19 November 1927, 7.
79. *Christian Science Monitor*, 2 March 1927.
80. Rodd's review of E. F. Gautier's *La Sahara*, *Geographical Journal* 66, no. 3 (1925): 268.
81. E. F. Gautier, review of *People of the Veil*, *Geographical Review* 18, no. 3 (1928): 478–81. E. N. F., *Geography* 14, no. 78 (1927): 158.

with the book. Significantly, he felt he had not been able to communicate the emotions the 1922 expedition aroused in him. 'I was never able to say in that book what I really felt. I tried to several times but I hated the "purple patches" that resulted', he recalled.[82] There seems to have been some tension in his mind between what he thought was expected of a scholarly book and communicating the real experience of the expedition. Whatever its weaknesses, *People of the Veil* was an impressive achievement. It brought the Tuareg to the attention of interwar Britain while also appealing to specialists.

In 1927, Rodd returned to Niger for a second expedition lasting a total of ten months. For this he obtained the permission of the French government and the local French authorities. On this second journey, he took with him his brother Peter and the future Arctic explorer Augustine Courtauld. He prepared meticulously for the trip: he did all the staff work for it and prepared himself by studying field astronomy and topography. The three men left Euston railway station in London in late April, seen off by Rodd's sister Gloria, her husband, society painter Simon Elwes and Lord Faringdon. They headed for Liverpool, where they took ship for Lagos, with some 80 pieces of baggage. The RGS lent them for the trip a number of instruments for doing meteorological measurements, including a whirling hydrometer, thermometers, barometers, a barograph, a thermograph, a rain gauge and an air meter. They also took with them a sand-proof Marconi radio, which they tested in the ship's wireless room on the way out and donated to the RGS on return. They also did an hour's strenuous exercise on-board ship every day.[83]

In Lagos, the party stayed at Government House before taking the train to Kano and driving on to Katsina. There they bought camels and supplies, as well as hiring helpers, before heading for Auderas. Throughout the trip, Rodd's caravan normally numbered between 12 and 15 people. In addition to the three Englishmen, it was made up of servants and camel men. It also included a Tuareg orderly of noble background named 'Arab', who had been lent to Rodd by H. R. Palmer, lieutenant-governor of Northern Nigeria. Palmer, who helped with some of the preliminary arrangements for the expedition, was another man with scholarly interests in the Tuareg. Rodd was most impressed with 'Arab', comparing him in 'quality of brain and manner' to Hassanein. They never travelled with fewer than 32 camels – which they took great care of. In a subsequent talk to the RGS, Rodd emphasised the importance of this: 'We took constant care of our beasts and devoted adequate periods to pasturage and reconditioning.' Respect for the camel, Rodd suggested, was a way of showing respect for Tuareg culture:

> I insisted on one of us three always attending the watering of the herd, not because we could do anything but follow the advice of T'ekhmedin or Arab, but because when the Tuareg

---

82. Rodd, 'Life and Reflections', 1950, Section 3, 8, Rodd Family Papers, AC.
83. For details of the equipment lent by the RGS, see Rodd, *Meteorological Results of Journeys in the Southern Sahara in 1922 and 1927* (London: HMSO, 1929), 7. Rodd, 26 April 1927, Diary for 1927 Expedition, The Rodd Collection, RGS, Box 4. Rodd to his father, 1 May 1927, The Rodd Collection, RGS, Box 7. Rodd to Hinks, 11 February 1928, The Rodd Collection, RGS, Box 14/5.

Figure 3.5 From left to right: Peter Rodd, Augustine Courtauld and Francis Rodd. From Augustine Courtauld, *Man the Ropes*, 49.

camelman once sees that his owner is really keen, he takes immense trouble to do his best for the charges in which every one of his race is by nature intensely interested.'[84]

Rodd added that the camel was a 'great subject', wryly suggesting that the truest thing ever said of the camel was that 'Providence manufactured him in a fit of abstraction'.[85]

Courtauld was impressed by Rodd's care for the camels, as well as his rapport with ordinary people: 'It was Rodd who stayed up all night watering camels at the almost dry well of Tagedufat [valley], and again who brought us successfully through a general strike of our camel staff. There are many of the simple people there who count the days to his return.'[86] More generally, Courtauld was impressed by Rodd's capacity to lead; in his memoirs, he stated that his 'leadership' had inspired his life.[87] Rodd came to be regarded in RGS circles as an authority on camels. Some years later, in 1935, he wrote the entry on camels for the RGS's *Hints to Travellers*. This influential advice manual, which had first come out in 1854, was then edited by cartographer E. A. Reeves. In his article, Rodd reiterated his belief in the importance of looking after camels: 'Let it be a

---

84. Rodd, 'A Second Journey among the Southern Tuareg', *Geographical Journal* 73, no. 1 (1929): 10.
85. Ibid., 15.
86. Augustine Courtauld, 'A Second Journey among the Southern Tuareg: Discussion', *Geographical Journal* 73, no. 1 (1929): 19.
87. Augustine Courtauld, *Man the Ropes* (London: Hodder and Stoughton, 1957), 5.

good rule, where the traveller owns his own camels or any other sort of animal transport, always to attend when the beasts are being watered, and to go the rounds frequently to deal with sores, sickness, etc.'[88]

T'ekhmedin, who was still alive, gave Rodd valuable assistance during the trip. On hearing of Rodd's return to the area, he walked 150 miles to Auderas to see him and for a time worked as head camel man for the expedition. As in 1922, this personal link with the Tuareg was important to Rodd. It is possible that he and his companions identified with their Tuareg companions at a psychological level. A biographer of Courtauld thought that the three upper-class Englishmen and the Tuareg had in common the fact that they belonged to social groups threatened by social change, and that Rodd and his companions may have subconsciously realised this: 'Perhaps, to three such Englishmen, the Tuareg were an elite who stirred sympathies deeper than they would admit. Perhaps, in the courage and courtesy and fierce disdain of that desert tribe, they recognised something – a quality of anachronism, even a hint of doom – that touched them sharply.'[89]

The expedition had several scholarly purposes. These included examining rock drawings and measuring rainfall. Map-making was also a priority. Since his first expedition, Rodd had kept abreast of new French maps appearing on the Central Sahara. He and his companions now mapped 400 square miles of unknown country. In Auderas, they hung their instruments in a tree under a shelter composed of two sun-proof canvas roof covers, with loosely hanging sides. While travelling, whenever the party stopped for the night, the instrument cases were opened, the radio, batteries and aerial connected up and the theodolite stand set up. From his trip in 1922, Rodd had concluded that it was possible to make accurate measurements by focusing on a small number of carefully chosen stars. Guided by this principle, they followed the same routine every night measuring the positions of a northern and southern star at between 25° and 50° in altitude, and east and west stars at similar altitudes. It was hard work, for measurements were taken nearly every two minutes, with Courtauld doing the time work, Peter the recording and Rodd himself the theodolite measurements. As Rodd explained to Hinks, tropical daylight made the theodolite hard to use during the day; but at night, it was easier, when electric lamps were also used.[90] Hinks had been secretary of the Royal Astronomical Society before the First World War, so he would have understood the challenges. Sometimes the task took them as little as one-and-a-half hours, but at other times they were up until midnight. Their astronomical calculations resulted in the whole of Aïr being moved two to five miles further east on the map from where it had been fixed by previous French calculation.[91]

---

88. Rodd, 'Camels', in E. A. Reeves (ed.), *Hints to Travellers*, vol. 2 (London: Royal Geographical Society, 1935), 147.
89. Nicholas Wollaston, *The Man on the Ice Cap: The Life of August Courtauld* (London: Constable, 1980), 75.
90. See Rodd, 'Three Maps of the Sahara', *Geographical Journal 67*, no. 3 (1926): 252–53. Rodd, *Meteorological Results of Journeys*, 7. Rodd to Hinks, 16 June 1927, CB9 (Francis Rodd), RGS.
91. Rodd, 'A Second Journey among the Southern Tuareg', 13.

Rodd's parents were worried about Peter. Born in 1904, he was a clever but unconventional figure. Like his brother he attended Balliol College, Oxford, but he was forced to leave ahead of completing his degree because of misbehaviour. The character of Basil Seal in Evelyn Waugh's satirical novels *Black Mischief* (1932) and *Put Out More Flags* (1942) was partly based on him. Bad with money, he found it hard to hold down a job for any period of time.[92] Rodd's parents hoped that the trip to the Sahara would do him good. In May, Rodd wrote reassuringly to his mother: 'Peter is behaving very well. He is neither unduly aggressive nor tactless and does exactly what he is told.' But a few months later, on reading some of Peter's diary entries about what they were doing on the expedition, he wrote: 'The trouble about Peter is that he cannot tell the truth.' There was a lively quality to some of Peter's descriptions of the weather and locality in central Aïr: 'A full moon and racing clouds, some black with the menace of rain, and some all silver [...] There were several ghosts in the ruined houses of the village [...] [Next day] we saw some mutton (potential) and converted it into mutton (actual).' During this trip, Rodd acquired the nickname 'Babban Bature' – a phrase meaning 'great white man' in Hausa. This was doubtless a light-hearted reference to his strong and authoritative personality. For the rest of his life, Peter started all his letters to Rodd, 'Dear B B'.[93]

From Auderas, Rodd and his companions travelled further north to Iferuan. From there they did a favour for the French authorities. Every autumn a large camel caravan travelled to the Kawar cliffs region to collect dates and salt. That year the French were lacking in people to do security patrols to protect this from the threat of raiders. Rodd and his friends offered to help. The result was a 150-mile journey to the Tarazit mountains, with members of Tuareg bands accompanying them. After returning to Iferuan, they decided to go back to Europe via Timbuktu – since the hoped-for permission to travel on to the Mediterranean never came. On the 500-mile journey west, they were accompanied by another old friend of Rodd's, Ahmed, a wealthy figure who owned a herd of goats; Ahmed and his servant Ewad joined Rodd and his party to do the journey to Timbuktu at just ten minutes' notice. 'We remember him as one of the greatest gentlemen it has ever been our good fortune to meet in any land', Rodd said of Ahmed. Here again Rodd was identifying one of his African friends as a gentleman. They travelled through some difficult terrains before reaching the French post of Burem on the River Niger, where they sold their camels, and going on to Timbuktu by boat. After four days there during the Christmas season, they joined a river steamer for the eight-day journey to Dakar in Senegal, where the smart clothes that they had taken with them in their luggage were brought out for social events.[94]

The Sahara left a strong mark on Rodd's mind. A number of photographs in *People of the Veil* were of large landscapes unencumbered by people, animals or dwellings.

---

92. On Peter Rodd, see Selina Hastings, *Nancy Mitford* (London: Hamish Hamilton, 1985), ch. 4.
93. Rodd to his mother, 6 May 1927, The Rodd Collection, RGS, Box 7. Rodd, 21 August 1927, Diary for 1927 Expedition, The Rodd Collection, RGS, Box 4. Rodd, 'A Second Journey among the Southern Tuareg', 5. F.R./P.R. journal, 1 September 1927, The Rodd Collection, RGS, Box 12.
94. Rodd, 'A Second Journey among the Southern Tuareg', 6–8, 16.

This suggests that the very emptiness of the landscape appealed to his imagination. He once called his two journeys a 'retreat into the Wilderness', comparing the impact the desert had on him to the experience of Charles de Foucauld.[95] Rodd's interest in spiritual questions had been boosted in 1919, when he was at the embassy in Rome: sometime after taking up his post there, he had visited Assisi and been inspired by Franciscan ideals. His expeditions to the Sahara gave further impetus to this. The remoteness of the environment prompted religious feelings in him. As he later explained to Mary: 'The Wilderness produced the result it usually does, the sense of the omnipresence of God. Father de Foucauld said after [his time in] Morocco that it seemed to him [that] in the East everyone prayed to God – except the Christians. He did and I followed his example. My Moslem companions wholly approved: they understood that.' However, Rodd thought Islam lacked a sense of a personal God: 'I accepted the [Islamic] conception of omnipresence but [God] remained personal. I never could then, or have since been able to see the difficulty of the undergraduate of Balliol whom Jowett reproved for not attending chapel because he couldn't find a personal God, on pain of going down. I know the Moslem conception of God but [for me] He remains personal as well as omnipresent.'[96]

It is not surprising that Rodd was an admirer of Foucauld. As well as being an exponent of a mystical form of Catholicism, he was a prodigious researcher on Tuareg culture. One of his legacies was a four-volume dictionary of the Ahaggar dialect of the Tuareg language. In *People of the Veil*, Rodd had been anxious to correct what he saw as some misstatements about Foucauld's death in December 1916 at the hands of tribal raiders. He stressed that the killing of Foucauld was understandable from the local, radical point of view. Foucauld had been a source of information for French Intelligence and helped persuade the people of Ahaggar against rising against the French. The attack on him could thus be considered a 'justifiable act of war'. Furthermore, Rodd noted that the attack on him did not come from people in his own locality; Foucauld's attackers were a mixed band of Arabs and Tuareg from another part of the Sahara.[97]

Rodd was far from alone in responding to the Sahara at a spiritual or existential level. Lawrence was another who found the desert psychologically appealing. In *Seven Pillars of Wisdom*, he wrote: 'The abstraction of the desert landscape cleansed me, and rendered my mind vacant with its superfluous greatness: a greatness achieved not by the addition of thought to its emptiness but by its subtraction.'[98] Another North African explorer Bill Kennedy Shaw, who was later involved in the Long Range Desert Group, was attracted by the desert because it was 'clean of people, quiet and beautiful', although he also wondered if it invited a kind of escapism.[99] It was not just the Saharan expanse that had

---

95. Rodd, *People of the Veil*, 11. See also Rodd's review of René Bazin, *Charles de Foucauld*, Geographical Journal 63, no. 1 (1924): 78–79.
96. Rodd, 'Life and Reflections', 1950, Section 3, 7–9 and 5, 4, Rodd Family Papers, AC.
97. Rodd, *People of the Veil*, 12–14. Henrietta Butler (ed.), *The Tuareg or Kel Tamasheq and a History of the Sahara*, introduction by Robin Hanbury-Tenison (London: Unicorn Press, 2015), 114.
98. T. E. Lawrence, *Seven Pillars of Wisdom* (Global Grey, [1926] 2018), 511.
99. Kelly, *Hunt for Zerzura*, 65.

this kind of effect on explorers. During the British Arctic air route expedition of 1930–31, Courtauld had a spiritual experience similar to that of an 'ascetic meditating in the desert', according to a fellow explorer.[100]

Part of the appeal was aesthetic. Barth had written of the beauty of the mountains around Agadez.[101] Rodd responded to the area in the same way. From his first expedition, he recalled one view in central Aïr as having a beauty about it he would 'never forget': 'The rocks shone blue-black with their feet in a carpet of green that seemed too vivid to be real.' He had a similar feeling in 1927, when watching a sunset over Mount Todra: 'That evening was the most lovely thing I have ever seen. After a day of clear, fresh breezes with silver clouds in small masses chasing each other across the sky, [there was a] sunset in a glory of crimson lighting up for a moment the whole of Todra till it blazed brick red.'[102] There is a sense in which Rodd's expeditions were in some way validated by these special or out-of-the-ordinary experiences. There was a tradition here. Looking back at Lhasa in Tibet, after it was annexed in 1904, Francis Younghusband – president of the RGS (1919–22) – noted the 'mysteriously purple haze' enveloping the city and found his feelings in sympathy with the scenery. For him, such fleeting experiences were 'real life', in contrast to the ephemeral and the insubstantial.[103]

Rodd also liked the desert because of the freedom he experienced there. During the 1927 expedition, he wrote to his future wife, Mary, from near Iferuan: 'The real joy of the country and life is that one is not bound to go in any direction or to any place: one can go where the spirit moves one.'[104] In general, the Sahara provoked in him feelings similar to those experienced by Wilfred Thesiger – another former Etonian, 15 years younger than Rodd – on crossing the 'Empty Quarter' in what is now Saudi Arabia in 1946–47; Thesiger found there a 'freedom unattainable in civilisation'; a 'life unhampered by possessions'; a 'comradeship inherent in the circumstances'; and a 'belief that tranquillity was to be found there'.[105] Clearly, for some people, geography and contemplation of various kinds – of nature, beauty, freedom, God – went together. But, if the Sahara evoked in Rodd a sense of freedom and wonder at the nature of the world, it remained for him also a place peopled by local tribes and containing traces of invaders and explorers; it provided a landscape against which individuals could be imagined, often solitary but sometimes in groups. Rodd brought his own 'shaping perception' and historical imagination to the desert.[106]

---

100. Lancelot Fleming, cited in Linda Parker, *Ice, Steel and Fire: British Explorers in Peace and War, 1921–45* (Solihull: Helion, 2013), ch. 10.
101. Kemper, *Labyrinth of Kingdoms*, 90.
102. Rodd, *People of the Veil*, 126. Rodd, 12 August 1927, Diary for 1927 Expedition, The Rodd Collection, RGS, Box 4.
103. Francis Younghusband, *India and Tibet* (London: John Murray, 2010), 279.
104. Rodd to Mary, 17 October 1927, Rodd Family Papers, AC.
105. Wilfred Thesiger, *Arabian Sands* (Oxford: Penguin, 2007), 37.
106. See Simon Schama, *Landscape and Memory* (London: HarperCollins, 1995), 10.

The Saharan expeditions and *People of the Veil* established Rodd as an important figure in British geography. He had become a fellow of the RGS in 1921. He was then elected to the RGS Council in 1927 and, in the same year, awarded the Cuthbert Peek Medal. Then, in 1929, following the second expedition, he was awarded the Society's prestigious Founder's Medal. In giving Rodd the award, Charles Close – now president of the RGS – remarked on the thoroughness of his work, declaring that no traveller in recent times had brought back his records in better order.[107] Rodd would have welcomed Close's remarks – they signified that he was being taken seriously as a scholar. In reporting on the 1927 expedition to the RGS in April 1928, he emphasised that he wished to avoid anything that could be called 'unsubstantiated speculation'. Paraphrasing philosopher Baruch Spinoza, he stressed the importance of trying to understand objectively the nature of other cultures: 'The part of travellers is neither to deride nor praise nor blame, but to try and understand the people who live in other places.'[108] He obviously identified with the quest for impartial, objective knowledge associated with the Enlightenment. Barth would have approved of such an approach.[109] But it would be wrong not to observe that in serving geography, Rodd was also, to some degree, promoting the reputation of his own family. In March 1930, he was present for the laying of a wreath at Westminster Abbey to mark the centenary of James Rennell's death.[110]

The Sahara continued to play a role in Rodd's life throughout the 1930s. He did not get back to Africa until the end of the decade, apart from making a trip to Gambia in the spring of 1932 to visit H. R. Palmer.[111] Intellectually, however, his North African interests remained very much alive. In 1933 he published a book on William Eaton, the nineteenth-century US general who during the First Barbary War (1801–5) had manoeuvred to put a local prince, Hamet Karamnelli, on the throne of Tripoli. Rodd regretted Eaton's failure – he described his plan as 'feasible'. This suggests he was sympathetic to a kind of western internationalism.[112] The *Times* welcomed the book, calling it a 'labour of love' on Rodd's part and comparing Eaton to T. E. Lawrence.[113] The subtitle of the book was 'the failure of an idea'. This pointed to a conviction that Rodd held, which he would reiterate in the Second World War, that history is often driven by ideas.

Rodd played a significant part in cementing links between British and French specialists on the Sahara – many of Europe's main Tuareg specialists were French. A key institution in popularising the French Sahara was the Musée d'Ethnographie du Trocadéro, a museum which, under the leadership of Paul Rivet and Georges Henri Rivière, had assigned itself the task of being both scientific and popular. In 1933, the

---

107. 'Meetings: Session 1928–29', *Geographical Journal* 74, no. 2 (1929): 196.
108. This paper was read on 28 April 1928; Rodd, 'A Second Journey among the Southern Tuareg', 2, 16.
109. Kemper, *Labyrinth of Kingdoms*, 184.
110. *Daily Telegraph*, 31 March 1930, 18.
111. See Rodd's diary for the trip, The Rodd Collection, RGS, Box 15/4.
112. Francis Rennell Rodd, *General William Eaton: The Failure of an Idea* (London: George Routledge and Sons), 154–55.
113. *Times*, 24 February 1933, 8.

museum played host to an exhibition of objects collected by French ethnographers on the Dakar–Djibouti expedition of 1931–33, a trip financed by the French government. It drew in a large body of visitors, demonstrating a public appetite for this kind of event. It was followed by a major exhibition on the Sahara, from May to October 1934, under the leadership of geologist Conrad Kilian. Rodd represented the RGS at the opening of this. Some items of Tuareg provenance belonged to him, including copies of some rock drawings he had found in 1927.[114] As Lisa Bernasek has observed, this was not an apolitical event; it demonstrated France's domination of the Sahara and the work its scientists and explorers had done in exploring it. The French minister of the colonies, Pierre Laval, officially opened the exhibition.[115]

A portion of the exhibition was subsequently transferred to London for showing in the Ambulatory. A set of items originally collected by James Rennell, which now belonged to Rodd, was part of this. It included an autographed letter by Friedrich Hornemann – one of the earliest Saharan travellers – written from Murzuk to the English explorer and naturalist Joseph Banks; a map of Hornemann's route prepared by Rennell; and a letter written by Alexander Gordon Laing, the first modern European to reach Timbuktu. The general aim of this exhibit was to demonstrate how much the opening up of the Sahara was due to British initiative.[116] Doubtless, there was a desire to counter French propaganda in this. Rodd was conscious of colonial competition in the way each country's achievements were displayed. In reporting back on the Paris exhibition to RGS president Percy Cox, he mentioned the fact that the British material in the cartographical part of the exhibition was the largest after the French, as well as being prominently displayed. He also noted that the British exhibition of early printed maps of Africa was the largest in the exhibition.[117]

On Rodd's instigation, Kilian was invited to give a talk at the RGS in May 1934, at the time of the Paris exhibition. Bagnold and Cox were among those in the audience, along with Rodd. In the discussion following the talk, Rodd credited Kilian with establishing more accurately the location of the watershed between the Niger river and lake Chad, as well as the lie of the plateau connecting the mountain ranges of Tibesti and Ahaggar; and he also drew attention to Kilian's readiness to endure the 'hardship of thirst' – Rodd was drawn to stories about human resilience against the odds.[118] A few years later, he published an article on rock drawings, about which he was in touch with Kilian; in his article, he used a couple of Kilian's photos of a leather Ahaggar robe, which had been

---

114. RGS Council Minutes, 11 June 1934, The Rodd Collection, RGS, Box 14/4. See also E. F. Gautier, *Exposition du Sahara* (Paris: Museé d'Homme, 1934).
115. Lisa Bernasek, 'Colonial, Popular and Scientific? The *Exposition du Sahara* (1934) and the Formation of the Musée de l'Homme', *Museum Anthropology* 42, no. 2 (2019): 89–92.
116. 'British Exploration of the Sahara', *Geographical Journal* 85, no. 3 (1935): 299.
117. Rodd to Cox, 4 June 1935, The Rodd Collection, 15/5, RGS. For a description of James Rennell's maps in Rodd's possession at the time of his death, see Andrew S. Cook, 'Maps by James Rennell in Lord Rennell's Bequest', *Geographical Journal* 144, no. 3 (1978): 515–17.
118. Rodd, cited in Percy Cox, Francis Rodd and R. A. Bagnold, 'Explorations Sahariennes: A Discussion', *Geographical Journal* 86, no. 1 (1935): 26.

on show at the 1934 exhibition.[119] Among French experts, Rodd also corresponded with Henri Lhote, an ethnographer and expert on cave art, and he arranged for the publication of two articles on the Sahara by naturalist and explorer Théodore Monod. Both Lhote and Monod had been on the organising committee for the Sahara exhibition. Rodd also corresponded with French explorer Jean Tilho about the altitude of the wells in the Termit mountains in Aïr; Tilho had led an expedition to Niger in 1899–1902 and, a few years later, was involved in delineating the border between Nigeria and Niger.[120]

In the 1930s, Rodd continued to be interested in the caravan tracks of the Sahara. In 1936, he reviewed a book by Emilio Scarin on the oases of the Fezzan, which linked European penetration of the region to the decline there of caravan traffic.[121] The history of how these tracks and roads had historically been used for military purposes remained another preoccupation. This was evident, again in 1936, when he co-published a couple of documents on a Fezzani military expedition of 1821 which had proceeded south into the states of Kanem and Bagirmi. Rodd was particularly struck by the fact that the expedition to Bagirmi had travelled along a little-known track in south-western Tibesti.[122] His collaborator in this was E. W. Bovill, author of *Caravans of the Old Sahara* (1933), an account of the history of that part of West Africa known as 'western Sudan'. Like Rodd, Bovill was a man who had a career combining business activities with a scholarly interest in Africa. Rodd was much impressed with Bovill's book at a general level; in a review for *Antiquity*, he called it the 'first standard work' on the subject. But in his book, Bovill had cited some of his ideas on the origins of the Tuareg. This Rodd was obviously slightly embarrassed by, for he observed that Bovill had accepted certain conclusions which Rodd now suspected were incorrect – although he did not explain which.[123]

It is important not to view Rodd's activities in isolation from the wider British interest in the Sahara. For example, his journey of 1927 followed another, more modest expedition into the same area by D. G. R. Cameron: leaving Kano in October 1926, Cameron had passed through Agadez en route to Ouarghla in Algeria. In 1927, Douglas Newbold, from the Sudan Political Service, and Kennedy Shaw completed an extended camel journey from Kordofan province in southern Sudan to Wadi Halfa on the Nile. Rodd and Newbold had previously been in touch over issues surrounding the origins of the Tuareg.[124]

---

119. Rodd, 'Some Rock Drawings from Aïr in the Southern Sahara', *Journal of the Royal Anthropological Institute of Great Britain and Ireland* 68 (January–June 1938): 99, n1.
120. Tilho to Rodd, 14 December 1934, Rodd to Tilho, 15 December 1934, The Rodd Collection, RGS, 14/1. Rodd, *People of the Veil*, 41.
121. See Rodd's review of *Le Oasi del Fezzàn*, *Geographical Journal* 88, no. 2 (1936): 175.
122. Rodd and E. W. Bovill, 'A Fezzani Military Expedition to Kanem and Bagirmi', *Journal* of *the Royal African Society* 35, no. 139 (1936): 153–68.
123. Rodd, *Antiquity* 9, no. 35 (1935): 377–78. E. W. Bovill, *Caravans of the Old Sahara: An Introduction to the History of Western Sudan* (London: Oxford University Press, 1933), 20, 24, 26, 90. On Bovill, see the obituary of him by Gilbert Laithwaite, *Geographical Journal* 133, no. 2 (1967): 280–81.
124. D. R. G. Cameron, 'A Journey across the Sahara from Kano to Ouarghla', *Geographical Journal* 71, no. 6 (1928): 538–59. Kelly, *Hunt for Zerzura*, 12. Rodd to H. A. Macmichael, 28 November 1926, and Newbold to Rodd, 25 April 1926, The Rodd Collection, RGS, Box 15/2.

Much of the energy of British exploration in the eastern Sahara was connected with the search for the so-called Zerzura oasis. A figure who played an important role in this was Robert Clayton East Clayton. In early 1932, Clayton teamed up with the Hungarian traveller Count L. E. Almasy on an expedition to the Libyan desert, which involved an aerial reconnaissance of the plateau on the southern border of Egypt and Libya, known as the Gilf Kebir. Unfortunately, Clayton died from polio a few weeks after his return. Rodd wrote up a short version of Clayton's visit to the Gilf Kebir, suggesting that Clayton was a substantial personality: 'The happy-go-lucky manner he affected concealed real organizing capacity.' A year later, Clayton's wife, Dorothy, became involved, joining another experienced North African explorer, Patrick ('Pat') Clayton, on a trip that Rodd had a hand in organising through the medium of Hassanein.[125]

Rodd also had links with Bagnold. In 1927, Bagnold went on a 400-mile car journey from Cairo to the Siwa oasis in western Egypt and followed this with further trips along the Sudan border and in the Libyan desert over the next three years. In 1932–33, he returned for a journey though the eastern Sahara, covering roughly 3,700 miles. There had originally been some talk of Rodd joining this expedition but, in the event, he was busy elsewhere. But he was peripherally involved in other ways. In the planning for the trip, Rodd and Newbold had been persuaded by Bagnold to approach the Sudan government and the British high commissioner in Cairo, Percy Loraine, to get permission for the travellers to enter the Sarra Triangle, a territory in the Kufra district of southern Libya.[126] During the expedition itself, Bagnold's party entered French territory on a couple of occasions, eliciting a mild protest from the French authorities. In unpacking what had happened, Rodd corresponded with head of the Egyptian Department of the Foreign Office, Maurice Peterson. At one point, Peterson called Bagnold Rodd's 'protégé'. Rodd suggested that since the French authorities had been forewarned of the expedition, the problem probably lay in a lack of communication and changes of personnel at the French end. Rodd had earlier been instrumental in sponsoring an expedition by T. A. Glover on a trip across Africa from west to east, which had also encountered difficulties, this time with the Italian authorities in Italian Somaliland and Eritrea.[127]

Bagnold described the 1932–33 expedition in his book *Libyan Sands* (1935). Prior to its publication, he sent a paper on the expedition to the RGS, which was read in his absence and followed by a discussion in which Rodd participated. In his remarks, Rodd noted that Bagnold and his friends had first learned their trade during the First World War, observing that cars and aeroplanes were now accomplishing what camels would probably never achieve. When RGS members were invited to recommend people for awards in

---

125. Rodd, 'A Reconnaissance of the Gilf Kebir by the Late Robert Clayton East Clayton', *Geographical Journal* 81, no. 3 (1933): 250. Kelly, *Hunt for Zerzura*, 86.
126. Cited in Kelly, *Hunt for Zerzura*, 65–66. Rodd to Bagnold, 11 July 1932, The Rodd Collection, RGS, Box 14/5. Loraine to Rodd, 15 April 1932, The Rodd Collection, RGS, Box 14/2.
127. Rodd to Peterson, 6 March 1933; Peterson to Rodd, 13 February and 13 March 1933; Rodd to Bagnold, 16 May 1933, The Rodd Collection, RGS, Box 14/2.

1934, Rodd picked out Pat Clayton for his many years of work in the Libyan desert while also recommending Bagnold as one deserving of recognition.[128] Bagnold was awarded the RGS's Founder's Medal that year, while Clayton was given it in 1941. Clayton played a leading role in the LRDG's raid on Murzuk in 1941. Clearly, the RGS played a vital role in holding together the network of people whose experiences of the Sahara subsequently fed into the desert war. This does not mean that the RGS was being driven by a conscious and systematic political-military agenda. Michael Heffernan has observed, writing about the RGS in the First World War, that we should avoid overstating the institutional cohesion and political influence of the RGS. The same could be said about the interwar era. There were specific military outcomes from the activities of explorers like Bagnold and Rodd, but advancing British power was not the sole motivation of these men.[129]

Rodd got to know Wilfred Thesiger in the mid-1930s. In April 1936, the two of them met for dinner to discuss Thesiger's growing interest in Tibesti and Aïr, and a couple of years later, Thesiger wrote to Rodd asking his advice ahead of a three-month journey he was planning from Darfur to Tibesti. One subject they discussed was a book by the Unitarian educator L. P. Jacks, *The Revolt against Mechanism*, based on Jacks's Hibbert Lectures of 1933.[130] Jacks's contention was that the modern mind had an unhealthy obsession with controlling everything, including nature. It was not surprising that Rodd found this interesting. In spite of his enthusiasm for modern technology, he felt a certain nostalgia for the premodern world, an indication of which was a preference he had for camels over cars. In a letter to Rodd, a friend of his who had crossed the Sahara by car in 1935, G. I. Jones of the Nigerian Police, quipped: 'Soon Haggar and Air will have become a health report' – Jones had in mind the impact of motorised transport on the region. Rodd had arrived in Agadez 'only just in time' to avoid that, Jones said. Rodd called Jones's picture of modern travel 'gruesome'; he was obviously worried that the machine age would end up by destroying the distinctive character of the Sahara.[131] On these matters, Rodd's instincts overlapped with Thesiger's. Thesiger was fond of camels and suspicious of mechanisation. In his post-war *Arabian Sands* (1959), he remarked that 'mechanised transport' would rob the world of its diversity. Bagnold, on the other hand, was more relaxed about this. The transition from camel to car could not be stopped, he wrote in *Libyan*

---

128. Bagnold, 'A Further Journey through the Libyan Desert', *Geographical Journal* 82, no. 2 (1933): 103–26. Rodd's contribution to the subsequent discussion, *Geographical Journal* 82, no. 2 (1933): 128. Rodd to Hinks, 27 February 1934, The Rodd Collection, RGS, Box 14/2. Heffernan, 'Geography, Cartography and Military Intelligence', 522.
129. David Syrett, *The Eyes of the Desert Rats: British Long Range Reconnaissance Operations in the North African Desert 1940–43* (Solihull: Helion, 2014), ch. 2.
130. Thesiger to Rodd, 16 March and 26 April 1936, The Rodd Collection, RGS, Box 14/1. Thesiger to Rodd, 10 March 1938, The Rodd Collection, RGS, Box 14/3. Thesiger's family home was Milebrook House, Powys. This was not far from Rodd's home in Herefordshire.
131. Jones to Rodd, 4 November 1935, Rodd to Henry Balfour, 10 March 1936, The Rodd Collection, RGS, Box 14/1.

Sands. For him the sense of romance in exploration was not destroyed by mechanical innovation.[132] In time, Rodd became wholly reconciled to mechanised transport. In particular, he came to love aviation.

While many of Rodd's geographical interests were intellectual in nature, he was also actively involved in helping the RGS administratively. For example, he served on the Expeditions and Instruments Committee. Here he was involved in creating a new system for insuring the organisation's instruments. He also served on the Finance Committee. In 1934, when there were financial difficulties surrounding the British Graham Land Expedition to the Antarctic, he was instrumental in bringing in Ralph Hamlyn, co-founder of the accountancy firm 'Binder, Hamlyn', to put the accounts in order. Hamlyn, a New Zealander, was a close friend of Rodd, who had joined him on the trip to Gambia. Rodd was thereafter eager to ensure that proper records were kept of expeditions that received grants from the RGS.[133] Rodd's organisational skills were also evident in an important initiative to popularise geography. In 1934 he brought to the RGS Council a concept for a magazine that would be analogous to *National Geographic* in the United States. Although previously mooted, the idea had foundered on administrative difficulties. Rodd's suggestion was that the president of the RGS should chair the trustees of the magazine, but that it would be financially independent of the RGS. The resulting *Geographical Magazine* was launched in May the following year, published by Chatto and Windus. Under its first editor, diplomat Michael Huxley, the magazine had a literary and aesthetic feel to it. Rodd contributed an article on the Tuareg to the November 1935 edition.[134]

Rodd wanted to be both a gentleman and a serious geographer. To a certain extent, he resembled the so-called gentlemanly specialists of the nineteenth century: men of high social standing who had the leisure and means to throw themselves into scholarly activity and paved the way for academic professionalisation.[135] He came from an upper-class background. Many opportunities came his way through the patronage of his father and the elite networks he grew up in. He had a lot of freedom to pursue his own interests. All this enabled him to become an important figure in European Tuareg studies. But the analogy with the 'gentlemanly specialist' goes only so far. Even if Rodd had a privileged upbringing, he still had to earn his living. He wanted to approach geography in a

---

132. Wilfred Thesiger, *Arabian Sands* (London: Penguin, 2007), 83–84, 278. Ralph Bagnold, *Libyan Sands: Travels in a Dead World* (London: Eland, 2010), 14. Isla Forsyth, 'Desert Journeys', 228.
133. See list of members of the Geographical Club, 1930 and 1932, Minutes of RGS Council, 5 December 1932, The Rodd Collection, RGS, Box 14/4.1. See also documents in Box 14/6, including summary of discussion with John Shuckburgh at the Colonial Office, 7 December 1934, and letter to William Goodenough, 22 November 1937. On Hamlyn, see Haslam, *Redeeming Features*, 24.
134. Minutes of the RGS Council, 11 June 1934, The Rodd Collection, RGS, Box 14/4. Driver, *Geography Militant*, 207. Rodd, 'The Forgotten of God: The Veiled Tuareg of the Sahara', 23–28.
135. See on this Martin Rudwick, *The Great Devonian Controversy* (Chicago: University of Chicago Press, 1985), 17; Ben Marsden and Crosbie Smith, *Engineering Empires: A Cultural History of Technology in Nineteenth-Century Britain* (London: Palgrave Macmillan, 2005), 8, 35, 38, 171.

systematic, professional way, but did not have the time or, probably, the inclination to turn that aspiration into a permanent feature of his career. The fact that he was able to devote so much energy to activities relating to geography, while he was also working for the Foreign Office and then in the stock exchange and in banking, suggests he was adept at compartmentalising his activities.

Chapter Four

INTERNATIONAL BANKER

While he was working at the Foreign Office between 1919 and 1924, Rodd showed an interest in economic questions. In 1920, when he was at the Legation in Bulgaria, he wrote the section of the annual report covering commercial, financial and economic affairs. A year later, he drafted the whole report, pending the appointment of a new minister in place of Dering. The material on commercial and financial matters from this report was then published in a slightly different form as a pamphlet for the Department of Overseas Trade.[1] The information in these reports was penned in a style that was to become characteristic of Rodd's later writings: comprehensive, detailed and essentially factual in character. This was typical of Foreign Office documents; it was expected that people would keep their own opinions from intruding into official reports and papers. Rodd was made second secretary in Sofia in December 1921. His sympathy for the Tuareg suggests he had an ability to empathise with subject peoples. By contrast, there was a more dismissive aspect to his attitude to Bulgaria. He reported to Harold Nicolson at the Foreign Office: 'From one point of view Bulgaria is of course entirely unimportant, except in so far as peace or war is concerned, in the same way as Czechoslovakia or Switzerland. They do not matter to the British Empire as a whole. Yet each of these funny little people might matter as much as Greece is conceived to matter.' Ironically, Rodd was trying to convey the idea that small nations like Bulgaria were significant. But his tone was patronising and arrogant.[2]

Rodd left the Foreign Office at the end of June 1924. The immediate reason seems to have been a change in policy in regard to promotions that meant Rodd went down the list in the queue for advancement. But he had also come to dislike the atmosphere. In a summary of his thinking written in 1923 for a friend, Maurice Ingram – who had entered the Foreign Office in the same year as he did – Rodd complained that the whole institution was like an elementary school or servant's hall where close loyalty of a 'rather pernicious variety' tended to protect inefficiency. He warned of people becoming 'robots' in the office, observing that a 'machine' would never make a man.[3] He was not alone in thinking the Foreign Office narrow and inflexible. A few years earlier, in October 1920,

---

1. *Bulgaria: Annual Report, 1920*, 3, FO 409/13. Rodd, *Report on the Commercial & Financial Situation in Bulgaria* (London: HMSO, 1922).
2. Rodd to Harold Nicholson (*sic*), 25 August 1921, cited in Erik Goldstein, 'Neville Chamberlain, the British Official Mind and the Munich Crisis', in Igor Lukes and Erik Goldstein (eds), *The Munich Crisis, 1938: Prelude to World War II* (London: Routledge, 1999), 282.
3. Rodd to E. M. B. I. (Maurice Ingram), 1923, The Rodd Collection, RGS, Box 15/2.

his friend John Loder, another 1919 entrant to the Foreign Office, left the service. In explaining his reasons to Rodd, he said: 'The system [in the Foreign Office] is deadening, kills initiative and aims at turning out animated telephones.' Laurence Grafftey-Smith, who worked under Rodd during the Second World War, remarked in his memoirs that in losing Rodd and Loder the Foreign Office lost 'first-class brains'.[4] It may be that Rodd was simply too independent of character and vocal in his opinions to fit comfortably into a civil service environment. But he did not leave the Foreign Office with a bad reputation. He was later told that it might be possible for him to return to a post there. Rodd's departure may also have been connected with a wish to go back to the Sahara. His friend, Dorothy Wellesley, welcomed his decision by saying, 'I am glad you have decided to go back to Africa'. She suggested that thoughtful and intelligent people should follow their 'urge', noting that there was a 'bit of the reformer' in Rodd's character.[5]

In 1926, Rodd turned to the world of finance and joined Buckmaster and Moore, a stockbroking firm which emphasised the importance of research and statistical analysis. The firm was led by Oswald Falk, who had been a member of John Maynard Keynes's Treasury team at the Paris Peace Conference, and was interested in the theory of currency and exchange. He was an advocate of 'active investment', the practice of encouraging investors to give their financial advisors maximum discretion over where to put their money.[6] Falk had also helped to initiate the dining society known as the Tuesday Club, which met monthly at the Café Royale and was an important focus for discussions on economic questions during the 1920s and beyond. Rodd sometimes attended. The Tuesday Club gatherings were often dominated by Keynes. Rodd was for a time a 'great personal friend' of Keynes and his wife, Lydia Lopokova.[7]

Rodd remained at Buckmaster and Moore until early 1929. He threw himself into the work and enjoyed it. But he found it demanding, as he explained to Mary in April 1928: 'I enjoy [the work] enormously and it has become lucrative despite my infinitesimally small share of the profits, but it is a dog's life. I don't seem to get away much before 7pm and [am] then so tired that I could drop if I did not have to dine out.' He also expressed a worry that the work was 'precarious', because it was so dependent on 'good times' in the market while insisting that it would have to be something very special to take him away from his partners.[8] Falk was a demanding figure with a sharp tongue,

---

4. Loder to Rodd, 4 and 20 August 1920, Rennell of Rodd Papers, BD, citation courtesy of Erik Goldstein. Laurence Grafftey-Smith, *Bright Levant* (London: John Murray, 1970), 68.
5. Dorothy Wellesley to Rodd, 24 May 1924, Rennell of Rodd Papers, BD, Box 66.
6. Judy Slinn, 'Falk, Oswald Toynbee (1879–1972)', *The Oxford Dictionary of National Biography* (Oxford: Oxford University Press, 2004). David Kynaston, *The City of London: Illusions of Gold 1914–1945*, vol. 3 (London: Pimlico, 2000), 304. Nicholas Davenport, *Memoirs of a City Radical* (London: Weidenfeld and Nicolson, 1974), 44–47.
7. Robert Skidelsky, *John Maynard Keynes: The Economist as Saviour 1920–1937* (London: Macmillan, 1992), 22. Frederick Leith-Ross, *Money Talks: Fifty Years of International Finance* (London: Hutchinson, 1968), 147–48. R. S. Sayers's interview with Rodd, 24 April 1969, BE, ADM 33/25, 3. For a brief exchange of letters between Keynes and Rodd in July and August 1931, see Rennell of Rodd Papers, BD, Box 151/4.
8. Rodd to Mary, 5 April 1928, Rodd Family Papers, AC.

and Rodd was aware of it. Falk's character was obviously something he had discussed with Mary, for when he wrote to her about the sense of liberty he felt in the desert, he remarked: 'I shall not again in my life [...] be as free and perhaps even Falk will not find it in him to blame me very much.'[9] In 1929, Rodd moved again, this time to work for the Bank of England. Buckmaster and Moore initially released him to address problems at the British–Italian Bank, and Rodd stayed on.

Rodd's involvement with Italy was unsurprising. His father remained closely involved with the country even after he ceased to be ambassador. Before leaving the embassy, he had purchased a vineyard over the small bay of Trentaremi near Naples; he built a house there that was completed in 1924 and was a regular visitor. The family also had a base in Rome, on the Via Giulia. Rennell Rodd was active in the world of cultural diplomacy. He was the first president of the Friends of Italy Association, founded in May 1923, which was supported by the Italian government and included senior Italian politicians and aristocrats.[10] He was also involved in the British–Italian League, a cultural organisation set up in 1916 when he was ambassador, which often functioned as a conduit for high-level links; he was chairman of the League in the early 1930s. To begin with at least, he did not have concerns about Italian fascism. When Mussolini came to power in October 1922 following the march on Rome, he praised fascism as a patriotic national movement which offered an alternative to the left-wing extremism paralysing Italy. A few years later, in the third volume of his memoirs, he went as far as to say that Mussolini had 'saved his country at a critical hour', suggesting that the Duce combined in himself qualities associated with the Machiavellian concept of *virtu*: vitality, courage, ability and will.[11] Rennell Rodd was well known in elite Italian circles. In 1932, he was one of the speakers at a conference on the nature of Europe organised by the Italian Royal Academy and the Foundation Alessandra Volta, which was opened by Mussolini himself.[12]

The British–Italian Bank, which was one of the five largest Italian commercial banks, was owned and managed by a British company, the British–Italian Banking Corporation. It included among its shareholders three of London's 'Big Five' banks, roughly a dozen other British banks and some insurance companies. In short, the London financial community was closely involved in the fate of the bank. Problems came to a head in early 1929: interest rates were rising globally and investors sought to withdraw their deposits from the bank. Montagu Norman put in place a rescue operation, offering some financial

---

9. Rodd to Mary, 17 October 1927, Rodd Family Papers, AC.
10. *Times*, 16 May 1923, 15. Claudia Baldoli, *Exporting Fascism: Italian Fascists and Britain's Italians in the 1930s* (Oxford: Berg, 2003), 22–23.
11. Rennell Rodd, 'Italy and the Fascisti', *Spectator*, 11 November 1922, 691–92; *Social and Diplomatic Memories*, vol. 3, 249–50. 'Virtu', not to be confused with the English term 'virtue', is discussed in Machiavelli's *The Prince*. Peter Rodd did a translation of this book: Niccolò Macchiavelli, *The Ruler*, trans. Peter Rodd (London: The Bodley Head, 1954).
12. Passerini, *Europe in Love, Love in Europe*, 72. Bernhard Dietz, *Neo-Tories: The Revolt of British Conservatives against Democracy and Political Modernity (1929–1939)* (London: Bloomsbury Academic, 2018), sec. 4.4.2. Rennell Rodd, *Social and Diplomatic Memories, 1902–1919*, 385. Rennell Rodd, *Trentaremi and Other Moods* (London: Edward Arnold, 1923). *Times*, 22 June 1927, 13.

support from the Bank of England and drawing both the Bank of Italy and Mussolini into attempts to solve the problem. Rodd became an important figure in this process. Working from Milan, he did much of the initial research work on the situation. He then became nominee director of the new holding company and remained in charge for some time.[13] The underlying problems in the bank were not fundamentally resolved, however, and the bank was taken over by an American consortium the following year.

In trying to sort out the situation at the British–Italian Bank, Rodd met Mussolini on a few occasions. Rodd was with two British colleagues when they first met in March 1929, at the Italian Foreign Office. But his easy command of Italian meant he ended up talking with Mussolini on his own on a number of occasions over subsequent months. These discussions took place at Mussolini's office in Palazzo Viminale. Mussolini gave Rodd the time because he was anxious to avoid the reputational damage to the Italian economy that would have accompanied the collapse of the bank. Rodd's account of these meetings comes from an unpublished interview he gave to the BBC in 1970, so his memory of them may have been affected by later events. He was impressed with Mussolini in some ways. He found him straightforward to deal with: 'He said either yes or no […] But he did not hedge.' Moreover, their conversations had none of the 'exaggerations and superlatives' so evident in Mussolini's speeches. The atmosphere was also relaxed: '[Mussolini] just sat there and asked questions while we talked […] we were […] on a basis of talking one man to another which was very much accentuated by the fact that he saw me alone and in plain clothes with nobody there.'[14]

While Rodd found Mussolini approachable, he found him touchy about an issue of corruption. He asked the Italian leader to help address a problem of fraud by one of the employees at the British–Italian Bank, to which he agreed. But Rodd went on to suggest that this employee was being protected by fascist politician Roberto Farinacci. Farinacci had been a ruthless secretary of the Fascist Party in 1925–26, before Mussolini replaced him and began bringing the party fully under state control. But he remained a member of the Chamber of Deputies. 'Can you get rid of Farinacci and stop him protecting this man?', Rodd asked Mussolini. The Duce protested that he could not do anything about this: 'Caro Rodd – No, I can't do that […] Even I can't do that, but I will tell him to stop interfering.' In summarising his impressions from these meetings, Rodd cited Tacitus's phrase 'Capax imperii nisi imperasset' (roughly meaning 'capable of ruling until he actually ruled') as applicable to Mussolini. The Italian leader had genuine leadership skills, Rodd thought, but they became corrupted: 'He could have remained a likeable man if he had not become a dictator and he could have governed Italy well if he had not become impatient.' Rodd sensed the Italian leader's anxiety about his standing and status and linked this to the country's subsequent push for colonies. In his view, he was not initially

---

13. R. S. Sayers, *The Bank of England 1891–1944* (London: Cambridge University Press, 1976), vol. 1, 259–61, 356: vol. 2, 622.
14. Transcript of BBC interview with Rennell, 2 December 1970, 1–9, Rennell of Rodd Papers, BD, Box 102.

a bloodthirsty dictator, nor was his political trajectory set in stone from the outset; the dictatorial side of his character evolved over time.[15]

The historian of the Bank of England, R. S. Sayers, observed that Norman often tried to deal with issues through 'privacy, speed, determination and reliance on a few able men at pivotal points'.[16] Rodd's involvement in addressing the crisis at the British–Italian Bank, as a kind of on-the-ground fixer, reflected this. It was also the kind of problem-solving activity he enjoyed. Following his return to London, he helped to build up the Bank of England's foreign relations, with a particular focus on Italy and Scandinavia. He was also part of Norman's advisory team, which operated slightly separately from the regular staff of the bank and often lunched with Norman and the other directors. This group included at various times Otto Niemeyer, later a director at the Bank of England; Henry Clay, warden of Nuffield College, Oxford, in the late 1940s; and financial advisors Harry Siepmann, Walter Stewart and R. N. Kershaw.[17]

Rodd soon found his work as a problem-solver replicated on a much bigger scale. In 1930–31, he was seconded to the newly formed Bank for International Settlements (BIS) in Basle. The BIS had been launched in May 1930 with the task of dealing with all money payable as reparations, including German debt repayments arising out of the Dawes plan (1924) and the Young plan (1929). It also had the aim of promoting cooperation between central banks; it was to be a 'central bank for central banks', free of political interference. To this end, it was decided that there would be no government current accounts at the BIS, and that the BIS itself would not give money to governments. This non-political vision for the BIS was strongly pushed by Norman and supported by president of the German Reichsbank, Hjalmar Schacht. But the BIS was never as apolitical as Norman had intended – to his frustration. This was partly because the reparations issue was inherently political. Another factor was that appointments to the key roles were to some extent made on the basis of nationality. The BIS's first president was the American Gates W. McGarrah, with his compatriot Leon Fraser acting as his alternate. Rodd thought McGarrah a weak person, but was more positive about Fraser.[18] Ernst Hülse, a German, was assistant general manager and responsible for banking. The Italian Rafaele Pilotti had charge of the General Secretariat, and Frenchman Pierre Quesnay was responsible for central banking. Rodd, along with Marcel von Zeeland from Belgium, was a manager in an executive capacity and a director in the Central Banking Department.[19]

Rodd was not first choice for the role. But the more natural candidate, Siepmann, who had played a role in setting up the BIS, did not wish to move to Switzerland. Rodd was having tea with Norman one day, when Norman complained that the BIS was, in practice, going to be run by the French. Rodd responded by saying that he was willing to

---

15. Ibid.
16. Sayers, *Bank of England*, vol. 1, 262–63.
17. A. S. G. Hoar, 'Bank of England Memories', unpublished manuscript.
18. Sayers's interview with Rodd, 24 April 1969, BE, ADM 33/25.
19. Gianni Toniolo (with Pierre Clement), *Central Bank Cooperation at the Bank for International Settlements* (Cambridge: Cambridge University Press, 2005), 63, 504 f.19.

go to Basle to help. Norman agreed, suggesting that a fortnight there would probably be adequate. But Rodd ended up staying for a year-and-a-half. He shared Norman's vision for the bank and conviction that treasuries needed to be independent.[20] When the bank was launched, he was eager to counter the impression – especially to the French – that the British were in some way 'sulking' and not supportive of it. He wrote to Robert Vansittart, permanent undersecretary at the Foreign Office: 'In spite of the atmosphere in which the organisation has started, we must make – and are making – every effort to get it running properly and on [the] right lines. No one can afford to see an integral part of the Young Plan, and an organisation that might contribute a great deal to international stability and relations, broken down.'[21]

Rodd's role meant he became closely involved in the Austrian banking crisis of 1931. This crisis had its roots in the fact that the world's major banks were pegged to the Gold Standard. This was a system that worked relatively well in times of prosperity, but gave central banks less room for manoeuvre in a crisis. The problem originated in 1929 when Austria's second largest bank, Boden-Credit-Anstalt, got into difficulties and was forced to merge with the larger Rothschild-owned Credit-Anstalt (CA). To compensate CA for its takeover of Boden-Credit-Anstalt, an elaborate and secretive system of cross-deposits was created, whereby the Austrian National Bank (ANB) deposited money in foreign banks which was then rechannelled back to CA – thus making it unnecessary for the bank to advertise a reduction in its reserves in published statements. A couple of years later, on 11 May 1931, CA itself collapsed, having lost most of its capital. The implications of this were far-reaching, since the influence of CA went well beyond Austria.[22]

Rodd's responsibilities in the BIS's Central Banking Department, alongside the fact that he was a liaison officer with the Bank of England, meant he became a central figure in trying to sort out the mess. On 11 May, he and his colleague Hans Simon were sent to Vienna to explore whether a central bank loan could help stabilise the situation. They lived at the Hotel Sacher in Philharmoniker Strasse, while working from an office inside the ANB itself. In the words of historian Per Hansen, Rodd was the 'sensemaker in chief' here; it was he who was tasked with establishing the facts according to which the BIS, the Bank of England and the Federal Reserve Bank in New York took their decisions.[23]

As an initial step, in late May, the BIS arranged for a 100-schilling loan to be advanced to the ANB.[24] At a subsequent BIS board meeting on 8 June, a decision was made to offer

---

20. Sayers's interview with Rodd, 24 April 1969, BE, ADM 33/25, 2. Sayers, *Bank of England*, vol. 1, 352–56.
21. Rodd to Robert Vansittart, 20 May 1930, FO 371/14346 C3974.
22. Iago Gil Aguado, 'The Creditanstalt Crisis of 1931 and the Failure of the Austro–German Customs Union Project', *Historical Journal* 44, no. 1 (2001): 201–17. Nathan Marcus, *Austrian Reconstruction and the Collapse of Global Finance* (Cambridge: Harvard University Press, 2018).
23. Per H. Hansen, 'Sensemaking and Financial Crises: Central Banks and the Austrian Financial Crisis of 1931', unpublished paper, 12.
24. See 'Memorandum of Agreement between the Austrian National Bank and the Bank of International Settlements', Basle/Vienna, 30 May 1931, BIS Archives, 7(18)2, MCG 1.3, vol. 1.

a further 100 million schilling credit. But on this occasion, the loan was made conditional on the ANB issuing a bond loan of 150 million schillings, which had to be available to foreign creditors. It was Rodd who briefed the BIS board meeting about the plan, while the Bank of England was represented at the meeting by Siepmann.[25] Unfortunately, during the following week, the ANB sustained massive losses in the foreign exchange markets; the possibility emerged of its declaring a moratorium on paying its debts – an outcome that would have undermined the financial stability of neighbouring countries as well as the Austrian currency. On 11 June, Rodd and Gijsbert Bruins, a representative of the BIS advising the ANB, met with Austrian chancellor Otto Ender to press him as to the urgency of concluding negotiations – with the French in particular. Ender was in no doubt as to the seriousness of the situation because, on 15 June, he told the cabinet that he feared a collapse of law and order in Austria. On 14 June, Rodd was joined in Vienna by Robert Kindersley, a director at the Bank of England; James Gannon, from the Federal Reserve in New York; and representatives of the International Creditors' Committee.

It was a tense situation. If, by the end of 16 June, the foreign loan had not been finalised, an ANB statement due the following day would have revealed such a weak position in its foreign currency reserves that investors would have taken fright. The problem was made more complicated by the fact that the French government wanted to extract political advantage from the situation. In March 1931, the Austrian and German governments had announced a plan to create an Austro–German Customs Union. Fearful of the emergence of a strong German-speaking power bloc in Central Europe, the French and Czechoslovak governments had reacted to this with alarm. On 16 June, the French government issued a note to the Austrian government making its support for the loan conditional on the Austrian government submitting its finances to a League of Nations enquiry, and suspending any policies that might affect Austria's political and economic relations – that is, the plan to create the customs union. In fact, already on 15 June, Ender had told the cabinet that the customs union would have to be abandoned. In spite of the intense pressure, the Austrian government rejected the French terms. The government also collapsed. A moratorium was only averted by a last-minute bailout – in the form of a seven-day renewable advance to the tune of 150 million schillings in sterling and dollars – from Montagu Norman, endorsed by the British Treasury and secured by the ANB's gold reserves in London. Rodd and Bruins were present for a meeting late on 16 June, which included Ender, the finance minister and the president of the ANB, where the details were explained.[26] On the same day, Rodd told McGarrah – using a maritime image – why he had not yet returned to Basle: 'We are doing our best to bring ship which is constantly springing new leaks into harbour and I am optimistic […] Until harbour lights in sight and pilots are on board and in charge I cannot properly leave.'[27]

---

25. See Rodd's preparatory notes for and the draft minutes of BIS Board of Directors meeting, 8 June 1931, BIS Archives, Rodd 7(18)9, Rodd, 1.1.b.
26. Rodd, 'Memorandum', 20 June 1931, BIS Archives, 7(18)2, MCG 1.3, vol. 2, 17. Marcus, *Austrian Reconstruction and the Collapse of Global Finance*, 314. Aguado, 'The Creditanstalt Crisis of 1931', 213. Toniolo, *Central Bank Cooperation*, 95–96.
27. Rodd to McGarrah, BIS Archives, telegram 16 June 1931, Rodd 7(18)9, Rodd, 1.1.a.

The situation remained unstable for a number of weeks until in the autumn the Austrian government introduced exchange controls.[28]

Some commentators have taken the view that the BIS could have acted more swiftly in confirming its June offer. According to this scenario, a more coordinated and clearer banking response would have helped restore order more quickly. It has also traditionally been argued that the financial crisis that hit Europe in summer 1931 was triggered by the fallout from the CA crisis. This has recently been contested by Nathan Marcus, arguing that the CA crisis did not cause the subsequent financial upheaval, even if it may have aggravated pre-existing problems.[29] Rodd's views on the episode were expressed in a memorandum presenting the CA crisis in terms of Austrian failure and French plotting as against British responsibility and competence. He placed part of the blame at the door of the Austrian government's 'dilatoriness' in guaranteeing CA's internal deposits. But the thrust of his account pointed the finger at the French for making the crisis worse. He indicated that the run on the Austrian currency that had taken place after 8 June had been artificially engendered by the withdrawal of funds from the ANB by banks with a connection to the French government. The clear implication was that the French had artificially aggravated the crisis in order to put political pressure on Austria. Rodd also thought the French ultimatum out of order: 'It seems doubtful whether any Government, Austrian or other could have accepted conditions presented in such a manner.'[30]

Rodd's memorandum also contained a hint that his BIS colleague Pierre Quesnay had played an unhelpful role in the situation; Rodd reported a remark made at a key moment in the train of events, attributed to Quesnay, to the effect that an Austrian government guarantee of internal schilling payments was not essential – which was completely at odds with BIS policy and Rodd's stabilisation strategy.[31] Rodd got on well with Quesnay, but he did not find him straightforward; in July he wrote to Norman highlighting what he saw as disingenuous behaviour by Quesnay and a tendency in him to prioritise French interests.[32] From the very origins of the bank, Quesney was regarded by some of the British as 'politically minded' and 'not over-scrupulous'.[33]

Rodd's sense that he had been witness to a moment of high drama was evident in a note he wrote accompanying his June memorandum, which he sent to a number of the key players:

> I enclose a copy of the note which I promised you regarding the events which occurred in Vienna and culminated with the Bank of England credit on Tuesday night. I am afraid the style is not quite appropriate to the facts. It should have been written in the manner of the

---

28. Toniolo, *Central Banking Cooperation*, 96.
29. Marcus, *Austrian Reconstruction and the Collapse of Global Finance*, 318, 339.
30. Rodd, 'Memorandum', 20 June 1931, BIS Archives, 7(18)2, MCG 1.3, vol. 2, 5–6, 11, 15. A copy of the memorandum with handwritten notes is also available at BIS Archives, 7(18)9, ROD, 1, 1a. See also on this Hanson, 'Sensemaking and Financial Crises', 7.
31. Rodd, 'Memorandum', 20 June 1931, BIS Archives, 7(18)2, MCG 1.3, vol. 2, 11.
32. Andrew Boyle, *Montagu Norman* (London: Cassell, 1967), 265.
33. See comments by E. H. Carr, 23 May 1930, FO 371/14346 C3974.

good 20th Century political spy or detective novels. The facts are certainly sufficiently in keeping with such novels to justify their being reedited in more appropriate language.[34]

Britain left the Gold Standard on 19 September 1931. This was a major embarrassment for Britain. As Siepmann observed to Rodd, it created the impression that the Bank of England had abandoned the principles of sound finance in favour of defending its own interests.[35] Rodd supported the decision, taking the line that the only way out of the economic crisis was for Britain and other European countries to leave the Gold Standard temporarily and then return to it at a lower level. He also tried to put a positive gloss on it. A few days after Britain's departure from Gold, he told Niemeyer that he was 'not at all pessimistic', even while stating that it was important for Britain to come up with a plan to deal with the situation. There was a 'reasonable chance' of getting half-a-dozen countries to peg themselves to a 'sterling standard', he explained. His position did not mean he was against the Gold Standard in an abstract sense. When, a year on from the Austrian financial crisis, he was asked to recommend two books on world banking and money, he singled out British economist R. G. Hawtrey's case for Gold, *The Gold Standard in Theory and Practice* (1927) as one, the other being political commentator Walter Bagehot's book on the Bank of England, *Lombard Street: A Description of the Money Market* (1873).[36]

In October 1931, Rodd was mooted for the role of advisor to the Hungarian National Bank. But he did not wish to take the job on a permanent basis, and the role passed elsewhere. He remained at the BIS until November 1931 and then returned to the Bank of England to work on liaison with the Bank of France. During the following year, he also helped to launch the League Loans Committee. In the mid-1920s, the Finance Committee of the League of Nations had played an important role in overseeing a range of reconstruction projects in countries that needed help, including Austria, Bulgaria, Greece and Hungary.[37] When, during the Great Depression, these countries got into financial difficulties, Norman suggested the creation in London of the League Loans Committee, funded by the Bank of England. He thought the original scheme a good experiment in international cooperation and wanted to maintain it. He was also wary of French motives and disappointed when the French, rather than the League of Nations, became involved in addressing financial problems in Romania.[38] The Committee was

---

34. Rodd to James Gannon, 22 June 1931, BIS Archives, 7.18(9), Rodd, 1, 1a.
35. Siepmann to Rodd, 20 October 1931, cited in Jack A. Seddon, 'Between Collapse and Decline: The Dissolution of International Monetary Systems in Comparative Historical Perspective', DPhil, Oxford University Press, 2015, 132.
36. Donald Moggridge, *Maynard Keynes: An Economist's Biography* (London: Routledge, 1992), 525. Rodd to Niemeyer, 23 September 1931, Rennell of Rodd Papers, BD, Box 151/4. Rodd to R. H. Hadow, 7 June 1932, cited in Hansen, 'Sensemaking and Financial Crises', 11. R. G. Hawtrey, *The Gold Standard in Theory and Practice* (London: Longmans, Green, 1927). William Bagehot, *Lombard Street: A Description of the Money Market* (London: Henry S. King, 1873).
37. Norman to McGarrah, 24 October 1931, BIS Archives, 7.18(2) MCG 1.21, vol. 1. Toniolo, *Central Bank Cooperation*, 63, 504, f.19. See also Margaret G. Myers, 'The League Loans', *Political Science Quarterly* 60, no. 4 (1945): 492–526.
38. *Times*, 14 June 1932, 14. Sayers's interview with Rodd, 24 April 1969, BE, ADM 33/25, 3.

given the authority to negotiate with debtor governments and assess what they could afford, as well as working out arrangements to give bondholders a reasonable percentage of what they were owed. Rodd was the first secretary to the committee. He helped to recruit its membership – which was initially all British and then widened to include representatives from other countries – and build links between the committee and the city. The committee's first chairman was former foreign secretary Austen Chamberlain. Rodd stepped down in autumn 1932, handing on the role to C. A. Gunston.[39]

In January 1933, Rodd moved from the Bank of England to become a partner in the investment bank Morgan Grenfell & Co. But he always retained an affection for Norman. Some decades later, he wrote an article for the *Sunday Times* defending him against charges of being arrogant and treating the Bank of England as his own personal empire. Norman was not arrogant, Rodd insisted; rather, he was kind and thoughtful and saw his work in terms of service to his country. He had a vision for the reconstruction of Europe and the world after 1918, which included an emphasis on the stability of money, the rehabilitation of Germany and the soundness of the United States. His weakness, Rodd suggested, was that, unlike Keynes, he was not good at explaining his ideas to those beyond his immediate circle. This was why some saw him as arrogant. Rodd, apparently, did not suffer from this problem. On one occasion, after Britain's departure from the Gold Standard, Rodd briefed a Treasury committee on the reactions of the BIS and France. Norman was so impressed that he said, 'I would give an eye or a limb to be able to explain as you did to the committee.' Rodd retrospectively said that Norman could and ought to have stopped the 'frenzied' lending of money to Germany. He described Norman as 'anti-Morgan', because Jack Morgan (J. P. Morgan Jr.), the ageing head of New York-based J. P. Morgan & Co., was anti-German – explaining that this was ultimately the reason why the Morgan banks did not participate in the 'Standstill' agreements designed to prevent sudden withdrawals of foreign credit from German banks.[40] Norman was sad to lose Rodd, for at one point he had thought of him as a possible next-but-one successor.[41]

Although Rodd left the Bank of England, he remained for a time a member of an internal Bank of England committee on organisation. He also continued to be a member of the Treasury delegation to the Preparatory Committee of the World Economic Conference which had its first meetings in Geneva in November 1932 and January 1933. The conference itself took place in London in June–July 1933, with its main focus being the breakdown of the Gold Standard and the possibility of encouraging floating currencies to return to it.[42] The Bank of England's policy for the World Economic Conference, as Rodd summarised it in November 1932, involved encouraging

---

39. League Loans Committee, First Annual Report, 1932, 1, 6–7. 29, T 260/731. Henry Clay, *Lord Norman* (London: Macmillan, 1957), 452. Hoar, 'Bank of England Memories'.
40. Rennell, 'The Obverse of the Coin', *Sunday Times*, 30 May 1965, 8. Sayers's interview with Rodd, 24 April 1969, Bank of England Papers, ADM 33/25. Sayers, *The Bank of England, 1891–1944*, vol. 2, 503–12. See also Ron Chernow, *The House of Morgan: An American Banking Dynasty and the Rise of Modern Finance* (New York: Simon and Schuster, 1990), 191.
41. Cable from 'Changeless', 4 November 1932, Rennell of Rodd Papers, BD, Box 59.
42. Patricia Clavin, '"The Fetishes of So-Called International Bankers": Central Bank Cooperation for the World Economic Conference, 1932–33', *Contemporary European History* 1,

a consistent exchange value for the pound, even if it was not accompanied by stabilisation, calling for a review of the technical operation of the Gold Standard and promoting the supply of cheap abundant money. The French position ran counter to this – France had always opposed Britain's departure from Gold and was hostile to cheap credit.[43] Rodd was gloomy about what the conference could achieve because there was no obvious immediate solution to currency problems: 'My difficulty is that I do not see what we are trying to do. [Prime Minister Ramsay] Macdonald is largely responsible for convening this World Economic Conference and so it ill becomes us merely to stonewall or deliberately to obstruct. But on stabilisation we must stonewall for the present, and stabilisation is like the Polish question here.' Privately, Rodd acted as a kind of spy for Norman, writing letters to him on the views of his Treasury colleagues and others. In the event, the conference's currency agenda was undermined in April 1933 by the United States' decision to come off Gold. But discussions at the conference paved the way for the subsequent Tripartite Agreement, in which the United States, Britain and France committed themselves to coordinate their currencies.[44]

Morgan Grenfell was part of an international network of private banks involved in corporate finance and international transactions. When Rodd joined Morgan Grenfell, the partners at J. P. Morgan and Co. were also partners in Morgan Grenfell. But in June 1934, Morgan Grenfell shifted from being a private unlimited company to a private limited company. This meant that the two banks became legally separated: the New York partners ceased to be partners in Morgan Grenfell. From this point onwards, partners were called managed directors. In spite of the legal separation, the London partners still felt emotionally close to the New York bank, while Jack Morgan continued as a director of the British bank.[45]

J. P. Morgan & Co. had a tradition of investing in war. Through its branches in London and Paris, it had helped to fund the Franco–Prussian and Boer wars, and it lent the Allies upwards of 1.5 billion dollars during the First World War. It also helped to create and sustain the interwar international system. For example, it was instrumental in the setting up of the BIS. When Britain came off Gold in September 1931, Edward Grenfell, one of the senior partners at Morgan Grenfell, acted as liaison between Ramsay Macdonald and American banks, including J. P. Morgan & Co. By the time Rodd joined Morgan Grenfell, Thomas W. Lamont was the most influential of the partners in J. P. Morgan & Co. Lamont was an excellent networker who was in some ways as much a diplomat as a banker. He had been an advisor to Woodrow Wilson during the Paris Peace Conference. In general, the Morgan banks were supportive of the Gold Standard and the internationalism

---

no. 3 (1992): 288–89. Sayers's interview with Rodd, 24 April 1969, BE, ADM 33/35. See also Siepmann to Rodd, Band of England Papers, OV 4/72.

43. Rodd to Norman, 28 November 1932, BE, OV 4/72. Clavin, 'The Fetishes of So-Called International Bankers', 290.

44. Rodd to Richard Hopkins, 3 November 1932, cited in Patricia Clavin, *The Failure of Economic Diplomacy* (London: Macmillan, 1996), 48. Rodd to Norman, 9 and 11 January 1933, Rennell of Rodd Papers, BD, Box 59/2. Leith-Ross, *Money Talks*, 168, 170.

45. Burk, *Morgan Grenfell, 1833–1988*, 158.

it implied. But inside J. P. Morgan & Co., there were different views about Britain's departure from Gold; Jack Morgan supported the British decision, while Lamont was opposed.[46]

To be a partner in a Morgan bank was a major accolade – as the *New York Times* observed, this was one of the 'most coveted partnerships' in the banking world.[47] The Morgan partners doubtless thought Rodd a major catch, for he offered an appealing mix of leadership skills, banking experience and social connections. On taking up his appointment, Rodd received an upbeat message from Jack Morgan reassuring him both about his suitability for the role and the global importance of the bank; it was, Morgan emphasised, a 'great business' which had for many years been carried on to the 'benefit of the world in general' as much as for the material benefit of the partners.[48] Lamont also wrote a letter of support to Rodd a couple of months later, saying he had heard about him 'for a long time past' and looked forward to their 'new association'.[49] Rodd's views were considered a helpful guide to contemporary events. 'Your views on so many matters of current interest are of real importance to us', Lamont assured him a couple of years later.[50] Rodd's connections meant that he could be a discreet medium for spreading Morgan influence. For example, shortly after he joined Morgan Grenfell, there was talk of setting up an international bankruptcy court. This alarmed the New York partners and indeed Rodd himself. Rodd wrote to Austen Chamberlain at the League Loans Committee – where he was still acting in an informal advisory role – suggesting that such a body might encourage debtors to default. In his view, negotiation rather than arbitration was the best way to deal with such issues.[51]

Rodd's opening at Morgan Grenfell came partly through developments in his personal life. Throughout the First World War and after, Rodd corresponded with Irene Lawley. He had probably hoped to marry her. He was heartbroken by the announcement in November 1920 of her engagement to Colin Forbes Adam, an old Etonian from a Yorkshire family who worked for the Indian civil service. There is even some suggestion that his plans to go to the desert were a reaction to this. In the mid-1920s, he once again became friendly with Dorothy Wellesley, who had separated from Gerald in 1922. This was not exactly an 'affair', Rodd later said, but it was a close relationship nonetheless.[52] It did not last. On 3 August 1928, Rodd married Mary Constance Vivian Smith (1901–81), an artist who had trained at the Slade School of Art under teacher Henry Tonks. Mary

---

46. Chernow, *House of Morgan*, 179, 195, 200, 206, 209, 228, 335. Martin Horn, 'J. P. Morgan and Co., the House of Morgan and Europe, 1933–39', *Contemporary European History* 14, no. 4 (2005): 523.
47. *New York Times*, 1 January 1933, N7.
48. Jack Morgan to Rodd, 11 December 1932, Rennell of Rodd Papers, BD, Box 68/1.
49. Lamont to Rodd, 10 February 1933, Thomas Lamont Papers, BK, Box 112, Folder 3.
50. Lamont to Rodd, 9 August 1935, Thomas Lamont Papers, BK, Box 112, Folder 6.
51. Rodd to Chamberlain, 16 March 1933, ARC 1214, Box 31, Foreign Loans and Financing, MP.
52. Rodd, 'Life and Reflections', 1950, Section 5, 5, Rodd Family Papers, AC. For more on Dorothy Wellesley, see Jane Wellesley, *Wellington: A Journey through My Family* (London: Weidenfeld and Nicolson, 2015), ch. 12.

was a daughter of Vivian Hugh Smith, a senior partner at Morgan Grenfell who had a record of involving the bank in advising and financing industry. He was also another Etonian; Etonians were well represented at the top of the City of London throughout the twentieth century.[53] His father, Hugh Colin Smith, had been a governor of the Bank of England, while his wife, Sybil, was the daughter of William McDonnell, the 6th Earl of Antrim, and Louisa Grey, a grand-daughter of Whig reformer Earl Grey. Sybil had been a suffragette: she was arrested and briefly jailed in November 1911 after participating in demonstrations protesting Prime Minister Herbert Asquith's failure to take suffragette demands seriously.[54]

In a social sense, then, Rodd was already part of the Morgan circle when he joined the bank. He was thus a safe appointment from a Morgan point of view. Morgan Grenfell was in many ways a family bank. Edward Grenfell and Vivian Hugh Smith were cousins. Hugh Smith's son, Randall Hugh Vivian Smith – known as 'Rufus' – was a partner in the bank. It was also a bank with a foothold in aristocratic circles. Many of its partners or directors were or became peers. Grenfell became Lord St Just in 1935, while Hugh Smith was made Lord Bicester in 1938. Another partner, William Harcourt, became a Viscount in 1922 while he was a pupil at Eton. Another colleague, the Scottish businessman Tom Catto, became a peer in 1936. At the heart of the bank, there seems to have been a slight unease about this. In April 1940, Catto became a director at the Bank of England and joined the Ministry of Supply as director general of equipment and stores; and the following year, he became a financial advisor at the Treasury. In August 1941, after Rodd inherited his father's title, Catto wrote to him: 'The number of peers who are partners is quite amusing, but this is not your and Bill [Harcourt's] fault for you have inherited your titles, whereas three of us have done the crowding by accepting titles of our own free will. In any case mine is now out of the list.'[55]

Shortly after Rodd joined Morgan Grenfell, Hitler became German chancellor. Rodd kept a close eye on events in Germany. He initially believed that fascism could be moderated. For example, in late January 1933, a day before Kurt von Schleicher's resignation as chancellor of Germany, he wrote a memorandum – unsent because it was taken over by events – envisaging the creation of a coalition government in Germany involving members of the Nazi and Centre parties. If this happened, he suggested, the Nazi party might well turn away from being a quasi-revolutionary or fascist movement: 'With its gradual transformation into a political party a programme becomes essential. Realisation of this necessity and the possibility of Schleicher creating a governmental or constitutional party have contributed to a revision of many views and opinions held by the leaders of the Nazis.' Rodd added that the Germans themselves were becoming more optimistic about their economic situation. But, he concluded, 'severe shocks' were still

---

53. Paul Thompson, 'The Pyrrhic Victory of Gentlemanly Capitalism: The Financial Elite of the City of London, 1945–90', *Journal of Contemporary History* 32, no. 3 (1997): 296.
54. On Sybil McDonnell, see E. Sylvia Pankhurst, *The Suffragette Movement* (London: Virago Press, 1972), 355, 393; Chernow, *House of Morgan*, 246.
55. Catto to Rodd, 25 August 1941, Morgan Grenfell Papers, DBBAR 001, File 006.00.

Figure 4.1 Francis and Mary's wedding, 3 August 1928. From left to right: Vere Smith, Peter Rodd, Mary Smith, Francis Rodd. Rodd Family Papers.

possible, and the country was not yet 'out of the woods'.[56] A year later, during visits to Paris in March and May 1934, Rodd picked up suggestions that a coup was a possibility in Germany, emanating from either the Right or the Reichswehr, perhaps coming after the harvest. He passed this on to Victor Wellesley, the man responsible for the Economic Relations Section of the Foreign Office.[57]

Although wary of the revolutionary aspects of fascism, Rodd accepted an invitation to be a founder member of the January Club when it was launched at a dinner in January 1934.[58] This was a discussion group on the far right of the political spectrum, which grew out of some dinners and functions organised in autumn 1933 by Robert

---

56. Draft letter on situation in Germany, January 1933, Morgan Grenfell Papers (Kathleen Burk), LMA, Box 4 (B12/030).
57. Rodd to Victor Wellesley, 12 July 1934, Rennell of Rodd Papers, BD, Box 59/2.
58. Rodd to Captain H. W. Luttman-Johnson, n.d., H. W. Luttman-Johnson Papers, IWM, H LJ/7, see also H LJ/8.

Forgan, a Scottish doctor whom was involved in the British Union of Fascists (BUF) led by Oswald Mosley. The club's stated aims included creating a platform for discussing fascist and 'corporate state' ideology, as well as for hearing from people who were not fascists. A number of its members were sympathetic to fascism, but many are better categorised as 'enquirers' after the ideology. Italophiles, Mosleyites and Conservatives were involved.[59] Exactly why Rodd joined the club is not clear, nor how many meetings of the club he attended. There is no evidence to suggest that he was drawn to fascist ideology, or that he found fascist economic ideas appealing. That being said, his father thought Mussolini had saved Italy from leftist extremism in 1922, and he himself had seen some positive qualities in the Duce during his discussions with him in 1929, even while he had also had reservations about him. He may have thought that there were some positive aspects to the Italian regime, even if he was not an adherent of fascism as such. It should be remembered that in 1934 Italy was still an ally of Britain and France in the task of containing Germany. One plausible explanation for his decision to join the club is financial. The Morgan banks were active in Italy. It is credible to think that Rodd was interested in discussing the nature of fascism for this reason. There was a similar incentive to be involved in discussions about Nazi Germany. The Morgan banks were not involved with Germany, except in relation to Dawes and Young loan repayments. But the Morgan partners were hopeful that the country could normalise. Schacht, German economics minister under Hitler, was well known to them. The fact that he was not a Nazi gave him the reputation of being slightly at a distance from the regime, and so a person whom they could work with.[60]

There is evidence from early 1934 suggesting that Rodd was dissatisfied with some aspects of western capitalism, but it points more in a left-wing than a right-wing direction. Just a month after the launch of the January Club, Rodd wrote to Mary with some positive comments about socialism: 'I find that the more I consider banking generally and private banking in particular, the more socialistically minded, or perhaps communistically minded I know I am.' He added that he was out of sympathy with the older generation for whom the pursuit of private profit was the main incentive.[61] This sympathy with socialism never took root.

Peter Rodd also joined the January Club at its launch. Unlike his brother, he was clearly aligned to fascism at this point. In December 1933, he had married Nancy Mitford, the eldest of the Mitford sisters, and the two of them were involved with the BUF for a significant part of 1934. They bought black shirts and attended meetings, including the mass rally at Olympia in June 1934 which ended in a confrontation with anti-fascist protestors. Peter's father, in spite of his earlier enthusiasm for Italian fascism, was uneasy. He wrote to Nancy expressing concern about Peter becoming publicly

---

59. *Times*, 22 March 1934, 11. Richard Griffiths, *Fellows Travellers of the Right: British Enthusiasts for Nazi Germany 1933–9* (London: Constable, 1980), 50–52. Martin Pugh, *Hurrah for the Blackshirts! Fascists and Fascism in Britain between the Wars* (London: Pimlico, 2006), 146.
60. Horn, 'J. P. Morgan and Co., the House of Morgan and Europe, 1933–39', 528.
61. Rodd to Mary, 8 February 1934, Rodd Family Papers, AC. This was written from Stockholm after driving through Berlin.

involved in fascist demonstrations and an anti-Semitic campaign; he warned that while there were elements in the movement that could be encouraged, things were 'taking a wrong direction'. Peter and Nancy's support for the fascist cause quickly dissipated, and they soon began to condemn the movement. In her novel, *Wigs on the Green* (1935), Nancy lampooned aspects of the BUF, while also implying that suffragette and fascist militancy had something in common. This caused upset in her family: the final version of the novel had been considerably toned down after pressure from her sisters, Diana and Unity. Diana married Oswald Mosley, founder of the BUF, in 1936, while Unity was a fervent admirer of Hitler.[62]

Any hopes Rodd (Francis) had for a swift change of mentality in the Nazi party were soon checked. On visiting Berlin in early 1935, ahead of a meeting with Karl Blessing in the Ministry of Economics, he told Mary that the place seemed like 'Alice's Wonderland'. There was 'improvisation' but also 'chaos' and the absence of any real plan, with events drifting towards a 'complete jam'.[63] A few months later, in July 1935, Lamont met with Schacht in Baden–Baden to discuss the servicing of the Dawes and Young plan loans; negotiations were difficult, and a full settlement was not achieved until the autumn through the involvement of the State Department.[64] In early 1936, Rodd was back in Germany for a visit which left him depressed about developments in the country. He wrote an official report of his trip to the Accepting Houses Committee, while privately giving Lamont a more detailed account of what he saw as Germany's deteriorating economy. The growth of the floating debt since the advent of the Nazi government he described as 'fantastic'. He reported that, according to his Reichsbank friends, increasing the debt by financing public works schemes would create serious problems. Overcentralisation was at the heart of the problem. Rodd feared the German economic structure becoming detached from the world of capital and private enterprise. In his view, the only stable elements in Germany were the army and Schacht. There was practically no one in the civil service milieu apart from Schacht who had the resilience to resist the 'wild and amateurish' party officials and their schemes. Moreover, the party's more respectable members had either resigned in disgust or been turned out. The party's anti-capitalist direction worried him: 'The Party itself, I regret to say, does not appear to be less powerful and is certainly more Left in the sense of being more anti-capitalist.'[65]

Rodd's approach to Germany's economic problems reflected his commitment to an international, capitalist system and, of course, the assumptions of the Morgan banks. His sobering analysis seems to have had some impact on Lamont. Lamont had always hoped that the Germans might come round to continuing with the Dawes and Young plans. But reading Rodd's account of the situation in Germany, Lamont wrote: 'It doesn't sound at all good to me. Dr Schacht may be a wizard, but there comes an end of wizardry after

---

62. Hastings, *Nancy Mitford*, 96–98. See also Julie V. Gottlieb, *Feminine Fascism: Women in Britain's Fascist Movement* (London: I.B. Tauris, 2003), 160, 220n.
63. Rodd to Mary, 21 January 1935, Rodd Family Papers, AC.
64. Horn, 'J. P. Morgan and Co., the House of Morgan and Europe, 1933–39', 528.
65. Rodd to Lamont, 6 February 1936, Morgan Grenfell Papers (Kathleen Burk), LMA, Box 4 (B12/030).

a time.'[66] Rodd's sense of foreboding about Germany was coupled with what can be seen, with hindsight at least, as a lack of realism about the possibility of war in Western Europe. Writing to Lamont after his 1936 visit, he suggested that war between Germany and Russia was much more likely than war in the West; the Germans had no intention of getting into trouble with the French or the British, unless they manufactured the colonial question into an excuse for war. He added that he was relaxed about the possible break-up of Spain, suggesting that that might be preferable to a communist or a fascist dictatorship.[67]

Rodd became more concerned about the Italian regime in the mid-1930s, with the invasion of Ethiopia a probable cause of this. In March 1937, at a dinner with Oliver Harvey, private secretary to Anthony Eden, Rodd said that Mussolini would have to be 'brought up short', or the British would have great trouble with him. On the same occasion, he expressed support for the recent appointment of Nevile Henderson as ambassador in Berlin. Henderson was thought to be a forceful character capable of establishing a rapport with strong leaders – Rodd probably had this in mind. But Henderson proved controversial in the role: some thought he got too close to his German hosts.[68] Rodd's father also attended this dinner – he and Rodd often attended the same functions. In May 1937, the two of them, along with Mary and Lilias, attended a reception given by Joachim von Ribbentrop, the German ambassador, on the day after the Coronation, an event attended by Neville Chamberlain, Winston Churchill, Eden and many others.[69]

One issue facing – and indeed, dividing – the Morgan banks in the late 1930s concerned Austrian debt repayments on a large loan the country had been granted in 1930. This became an important issue following the Nazi occupation of Austria in March 1938. What would happen to these debts now that the Nazis were in control? The British part of the loan had been serviced by a number of British banks, including Morgan Grenfell. In this context, the partners in J. P. Morgan & Co. were worried that Morgan Grenfell would put its own and British interests before the interests of the Morgan banks as a whole. This threw into sharp focus the tension felt by some of the banks between allegiance to their national governments and transatlantic cooperation between and among banks. Rodd was drawn into these affairs. In doing so, he tried to act as an informal go-between between the British and American governments, through the medium of the Morgan network – an example of his manoeuvring behind the scenes to resolve a problem. On 6 May 1938, following a visit to the Treasury, Rodd phoned Lamont to alert him to a planned visit by senior Treasury official Frederick Leith-Ross to Geneva and Berlin later in the month, telling him that it was vital that all governments involved in the 1930 loan make representations to Germany about loan repayments. He wanted Lamont to be in touch with the State Department about this as a matter of

---

66. Lamont to Rodd, 8 and 19 February, Thomas W. Lamont Papers, BK, Box 112/7.
67. Rodd to Lamont, 1 September 1936, Thomas W. Lamont Papers, BK, Box 112/7.
68. Oliver Harvey, in John Harvey (ed.), *The Diplomatic Diaries of Oliver Harvey 1937–40* (London: Collins, 1970), 33. Peter Neville, 'The Appointment of Sir Nevile Henderson, 1937 – Design or Blunder?', *Journal of Contemporary History* 33, no. 4 (1998): 611–12.
69. *Times*, 14 May 1937, 15.

urgency, prior to Leith-Ross's visits. His concern was that if the State Department did not get involved, then the British would end up discussing their own part of the debts. Rodd's approach to Lamont was unofficial – perhaps even a product of his own initiative – for, when Lamont suggested to Rodd that he send him a memorandum with some details, Rodd retorted that the British negotiations were confidential and he was himself not supposed to know about them. The two men touched on the events of 1934, when Britain had agreed its own terms with Germany in the form of the Anglo–German Payments Agreement. Rodd reassured Lamont that the 1934 situation was 'very present' in the minds of the Treasury.[70]

The stress on the need for international coordination was evident later in the month. A meeting of the clearing houses in London on 24 May resulted in their agreeing to have all tranches of the loan maintained 'on an international basis'. If this could not be achieved, they noted, they might have to work out arrangements in line with the Anglo–German Payments Agreement, but that was not their first objective. The clearing houses agreed to ask Morgan Grenfell to write to the BIS along these lines and be in touch with Leith-Ross as well.[71] Rodd duly wrote the letters. In his letter to the president of the BIS, J. W. Beyen, Rodd asked the BIS to approach the German government for an assurance that its payments of monthly remittances in foreign currencies would be made for all tranches of the 1930 loan. His letter to Leith-Ross, then staying at the British embassy in Berlin, contained a similar thought: 'We express the hope that every endeavour will continue to be made to secure that the service of the Austrian government loans, including the 1930 loan, will be maintained on an international basis.'[72]

In the event, the British did come to their own arrangement with the Germans – in July 1938. This provided for the transfer of Dawes and Young payments to British bondholders but not to others. It was, in other words, a separate agreement that ran directly counter to the principle of doing things on an international basis. Lamont was annoyed and wrote a letter of protest to Norman. He replied saying that circumstances had forced his hand: 'I regret as much as you do that these loans, which were issued on an international and financial basis, are now treated piecemeal on a national and political basis. This is indeed politics and not ethics but it has been the general trend of recent years and I do not think we can do more than regret it.' But Norman also suggested that the fault lay across the Atlantic; if the American government had taken a 'firm stand' alongside the creditor governments concerned, he suggested, an international approach might have worked.[73] In his frustration, Lamont wrote a robust letter to the Morgan partners in London in which he warned that in the event of war, Anglo–American cooperation could not be taken for granted. 'Must we accept that the high sanction of Great

---

70. Notes of a telephone conversation between Rodd and Lamont, 6 May 1938, Morgan Grenfell Papers (Kathleen Burk), LMA, Box 8 (B12/030).
71. Memorandum of meeting on Austrian Government International Loan 1930, 24 May 1938, Morgan Grenfell Papers (Kathleen Burk), LMA, Box 4 (B12/030).
72. Rodd to Beyen, 24 May 1936; Rodd to Leith-Ross, 24 May 1936, T 160/866.
73. Clay, *Lord Norman*, 453. See also Chernow, *House of Morgan*, 434.

Britain is to be given to the growing habit of ignoring international connections and the rights of property?', he asked.[74]

Rodd was worried by the implications of Lamont's letter, which he sent on to the Treasury. Rodd's closeness to Whitehall was understood by the American partners. A few months earlier, he had been the conduit for an invitation from Lamont to Anthony Eden to give a lecture in the United States.[75] But in this case Rodd acted without Lamont's permission, and Lamont was furious. He telephoned Rodd and followed this up with a letter stressing that the London partners ought to have communicated their concerns to the American partners first. He added that it had never occurred to them that Rodd would circulate the letter to the Treasury and the Bank of England: 'Our thought simply was that you would take some occasion in your own way to express such views.' He went on to say:

> There was of course no reason why you should not show in confidence a draft of our letter to Mr. Montagu Norman, but why, when you had these strong reserves in your own mind, adopt his suggestion of making the matter very formal to both authorities, rather than calling us up with your personal views which always have weight with us?[76]

Lamont wanted to address issues through informal, private influence; in his mind, the advantage of a 'private partnership' between the banks was that it allowed people to express their views honestly and to guard against 'hasty action'. In the times they were living in, he wanted to see the 'friendliest possible relations' existing between the two Morgan banks, as well as 'strong mutual confidence'.[77]

Lamont also reiterated his annoyance at the Anglo–German Clearing Agreement of 1934. He stated that because J. P. Morgan & Co. was the chief issuing house for the Dawes and Young loans and the Austrian loan of 1930, it had a responsibility to the entire American investment community. 'We are bound by our commitment to American investors not to permit such things again', he insisted, noting that unilateral behaviour by the British undermined 'goodwill' between the two countries. In another letter, Lamont spoke even more robustly: 'We have never thought of Morgan Grenfell & Co. as a post office for the transmission of our letters to the British Government.' Although Lamont was annoyed by what had happened, it did not damage his relationship with Rodd. Lamont told him that the partners at J. P. Morgan & Co. were not 'unduly exercised' by the matter while reassuring him as to the value of his advice: 'We have a feeling that you are particularly well informed and that while no one can make predictions with any degree of confidence, nevertheless, we all attach great importance to your own opinion.' In reply to Lamont's letters, Rodd wrote: 'I quite appreciate your point of view and will be guided in the future by what you

---

74. Lamont to Morgan Grenfell, July 1938, cited in Chernow, *House of Morgan*, 435.
75. Rodd to Eden, 26 May 1938, Morgan Grenfell Papers, DBBAR 001, File 006.00. Eden went on a lecture tour to the United States in December 1938. *Times*, 14 December 1938, 15.
76. Lamont to Rodd, 14 September 1938, Thomas W. Lamont Papers, BK, Box 112/10.
77. Ibid..

say.' Separately Jack Morgan spoke to Norman, with whom he had a good relationship, to smooth things over.[78]

These exchanges between Rodd and Lamont took place as the Munich crisis was coming to a head in September 1938. Here Lamont thought that the best that could be hoped for was for the crisis to fade away gradually. He and Jack Morgan were strong supporters of the Munich agreement, while Rodd's father-in-law, now Lord Bicester, was more sceptical. Lamont was a good friend of Lady Astor, who with her husband, Waldorf Astor, owned the Cliveden estate. The so-called Cliveden set has long been associated with a strongly pro-appeasement position. In reality, members of the group held to a greater diversity of views than their far-right image would suggest. But as a rule, they looked to find a negotiated settlement with Germany.[79] Lamont shared this outlook. His approach to the Italian regime was similar. Italy's relationship with the Western powers had looked to be in a healthy state in April 1935 when Mussolini agreed to join Britain and France in the 'Stresa Front' – a reaffirmation of the 1925 Treaty of Locarno and the principles of the Treaty of Versailles. But the solidity of the alliance was undermined by the Anglo–German Naval Agreement of June 1935 and then the Abyssinian crisis. The Italian invasion of Ethiopia significantly dented Mussolini's reputation. Lamont hoped that, with a discreet brand of personal diplomacy, the Italian leader's dictatorial tendencies could be tamed. In April 1937, at a meeting with Mussolini in Rome, he indicated that better economic relations with the United States could be an alternative to continued militarism.[80]

Rodd was also involved with Italy through his banking work. The agent for the Morgan banks in Rome was Giovanni Fummi. An Anglophile, Fummi's role among other things was to act as an advisor to the Vatican bank, the Special Administration of the Holy See. The bank had been set up in 1929 on the orders of Pope Pius XI, under the leadership of Bernardino Nogara. On the advice of Fummi, Nogara chose J. P. Morgan & Co. and Morgan Grenfell to be his main advisors on investments. On joining Morgan Grenfell, Rodd became the man at the bank responsible for managing the Vatican bank's portfolio, while Lamont was involved in giving advice from the American side. The Vatican bank offered the Morgan banks a back-channel for trying to influence Mussolini. In the spring of 1939, Fummi and Nogara were the conduits for a letter from Lamont to the Italian government, stating that the United States would strongly oppose German aggression. This was an implicit warning to Italy as well. A year later, Lamont sent another letter to Mussolini – cleared with Roosevelt and which Tom Catto showed to British foreign secretary Lord Halifax – in which he warned Mussolini not to count on the support of Italian Americans in the event of war. This letter was transmitted to Mussolini by Fummi through Nogara. After Italy entered the war, Fummi was arrested.[81]

---

78. Lamont to Rodd, 14 September 1938, Thomas Lamont Papers, BK, Box 112/10. Chernow, *House of Morgan*, 435.
79. See Norman Rose, *The Cliveden Set: Portrait of an Exclusive Fraternity* (London: Pimlico, 2001).
80. Horn, 'J. P. Morgan and Co., the House of Morgan and Europe, 1933–39', 532. Chernow, *House of Morgan*, 241, 277, 279, 405–6, 433, 436.
81. Chernow, *House of Morgan*, 285–86, 407, 454–56.

We can discern some of Rodd's thinking on the Vatican finances from a paper he wrote after the war for his colleagues at Morgan Grenfell. Although he had a high regard for Nogara, he had doubts about the church's wisdom in collaborating with the Italian regime: 'By accepting from Mussolini's government not only recognition of the Holy See as a temporal power, but much more so by receipt of a large sum of money under the Lateran Treaty [1929], the Vatican indubitably compromised itself with the Italian Government and inevitably became closely linked with the Italian currency system.' In Rodd's view, the consequence of temporal sovereignty should have been the setting up of a central treasury with a currency and centralised financial control, but this did not happen. During the Second World War, Rodd became suspicious about the financial activities of some Italian churchmen in Africa. He thought that as the Italian empire in Africa collapsed during the war, many Italian funds were transferred into ecclesiastical accounts, particularly ones associated with Apostolic delegates. In his view, many clerics had been unable to manage money properly, either through dishonesty or incompetence.[82]

Rodd acquired a certain public profile as an Italian expert. When, during the Munich crisis, the BBC arranged for radio bulletins of 'objective news' to be broadcast in Germany, France and Italy, he read the ones in Italian.[83] His reputation for having an in-depth understanding of Italy doubtless stemmed partly from his family's social connections with the country. They had close links with Italian high society; for example, in October 1938, Rodd joined his parents and Peter at a party given for the princess of Piedmont by his brother-in-law Simon Elwes.[84] Rodd's knowledge of Italian finance was another obvious reason why he was seen as an expert on Italy. Here his views were sought in the Foreign Office. In August 1938, on the recommendation of Maurice Ingram, the Foreign Office approached him for advice about an Italian businessman, one Signor Perrone, claiming close links with Mussolini, who wanted British and French support to try to oust a pro-German group in the Italian armaments industry. While it was accepted that German influence in Italy was increasingly strong, the Foreign Office thought Perrone's plans rather fantastic and wanted Rodd's mind on the matter. Rodd backed the Foreign Office view, sending a succinct reply: 'Spherical, in the plural (5 letters).'[85]

Rodd's father was made a peer in 1933.[86] Through speeches in the House of Lords and letters to the *Times*, he was a regular commentator on events in Europe over the next few years. He tended to adopt a non-confrontational approach to relations with Italy and Germany. During the Abyssinian crisis, he expressed disappointment at the failure of the League of Nations to respond to Ethiopian calls for help. But, although strongly

---

82. 'Memorandum on the Administration of Vatican Funds and on Their Nature', 4, 7, 20 and 27 September 1950, Rennell of Rodd Papers, BD, Box 102.
83. *Daily Telegraph*, 30 September 1938, 10.
84. *Times*, 29 October 1938, 15.
85. Rodd to P. B. Nicholls, 23 August 1938, FO 371/22425. Ingram was chargé d'affaires in Rome, 1935–37.
86. He was made Baron Rennell of Rodd in the county of Hereford.

opposed to the Italian invasion of Ethiopia, he did not support the policy of sanctions against Italy that followed the crisis; he thought giving way graciously would turn out to be more advantageous than prolonging 'ineffectual opposition'.[87] In 1935, he joined the newly formed Anglo–German Fellowship. This organisation has often been presented as providing a home for Nazi sympathisers. But recent work suggests that it occupied a more mainstream, pro-appeasement position than a pro-Nazi one; the number of openly pro-Nazi members was a small percentage of the total.[88] Rennell Rodd was not a Nazi sympathiser, but it took him some years to see the true nature of the Nazi regime. Visits to Germany in the mid-1930s left him with a positive impression of the state of the country. He told the House of Lords in April 1936 that there was a new spirit of confidence in Germany, and a few months later – after attending the Berlin Olympics – he wrote to the *Times* along the same lines. Following the Munich Agreement, he still seems to have been hopeful – at least publicly – for the future of Anglo–German relations. At an Anglo–German Fellowship dinner in October 1938, he toasted the German ambassador, Herbert von Dirksen, remarking that Britain and Germany had more in common to unite them than divide them.[89]

By the spring of 1939, however, Rennell Rodd's thinking had markedly shifted. The change can be attributed to 'Kristallnacht' in November 1938 and the German occupation of Czechoslovakia in March 1939. Speaking in the House of Lords in April 1939, Rennell Rodd warned of Germany's history of disregarding international ethics and using 'deliberate deception' to advance its aims. In this speech and a couple of subsequent letters to the *Times*, he cited Otto von Bismarck – whom he had met in Berlin over 50 years earlier – as setting a precedent for recent German behaviour.[90] It was a revealing remark. Rennell Rodd tended to interpret the tensions of the 1930s in the light of his own experience as a diplomat. And there certainly were continuities between the pre-1914 world and the 1930s. But, like many others, he found it hard to see that fascist movements, while having roots in the past, had within them a destructive dynamism differentiating them from what had come before. Although broadminded and honest, there was an enduring streak of naivety in his outlook.[91] After the outbreak of war in 1939, his long-held affection for the British empire was evident. In a poem published in the *Times*, 'The Voice of the Empire', he celebrated the way in which Britain's dominions had rallied to its support: 'With a single voice in a common cause we bid the challenger know / We stand with the Mother Country, and where she leads we go.' Some months

---

87. *Times*, 2 June 1936, 13.
88. For this perspective, see Charles Spicer, '"Ambulant Amateurs": The Rise and Fade of the Anglo–German Fellowship', PhD thesis, School of Advanced Study, University of London, 2018. See also Griffiths, *Fellow Travellers of the Right*, 184; Pugh, *Hurrah for the Blackshirts!*, 270.
89. Lord (James) Rennell, *Times*, 27 August 1936, 8; 20 October 1938, 16. Rennell, 8 April 1936, House of Lords, Hansard.
90. Lord (James) Rennell, 19 April 1939, House of Lords, Hansard. *Times*, 16 June 1939, 15; 30 June 1939, 16; 5 September 1939, 9.
91. This was evident already before the First World War; see Bosworth, *Italy, the Least of the Great Powers*, 270–71, 320.

later, he wrote a verse expressing his pride at the British people who had 'ventured all in freedom's name'.[92]

Clearly, in the run-up to the Second World War, the international banking system came under huge pressure. Lamont's concerns about the British approach to Austrian debt in 1938 reflected that. At the same time, Rodd had his own concerns about J. P. Morgan & Co. Although generally pro-American in outlook, he was concerned that the American bank lacked a commitment to the Morgan banks as a collective. This was evident in early 1940 when the French bank Morgan & Cie got into difficulties. Rodd had conversations with the French partners, Dean Jay and Alan Arragorn, about this. One way of resolving the problem might have been for Morgan & Cie to become a branch of J. P. Morgan & Co., but the French would not countenance this. In this context, Rodd, writing from Rome, where he was then working for the Ministry of Economic Warfare, suggested to Catto that an alternative solution would be for Morgan Grenfell to take a 50 per cent share in the French bank's capital, estimated to total £500,000. Rodd thought this 'perfectly logical and reasonable' in the light of economic developments between the two countries. But he thought that in the long term, Morgan Grenfell's own survival was at stake because J. P. Morgan & Co.'s commitment to it could not be assumed: 'If M & Cie goes for lack of interest we shall as sure as eggs is eggs have the New York partners in a year or two trying to liquidate their holding in M.G & Co. in an unwilling market.'[93]

Catto rebuffed Rodd for trying to act too quickly and without proper consultation, stating that only a full discussion could resolve such a big issue of principle: 'To try and rush it or for you to want to discuss it while you are engaged in your present important work is a grave mistake. One thing at a time old man!' Rodd followed up by indicating that the French were worried that the United States was becoming 'less and less Europe minded'. Catto promised Arragorn that he would consider the matter.[94] These interactions reinforce the idea, promoted by Martin Horn, that in the 1930s the Morgan banks remained committed to a kind of international transnational vision; but that at the start of the Phony War, the New York partners became more aligned to the position of the American government and resisted pressure from Morgan & Cie to advocate American intervention.[95]

Catto's response to Rodd's ideas suggests that Rodd had a reputation for being headstrong. That being said, Catto had a high opinion of him. When in April 1940 Edward Grenfell became too old to be a director at the Bank of England, Catto was approached to replace him. It is likely that Rodd was thought a possibility for this role. Ahead of accepting the post, Catto felt he needed to write to Rodd indicating that he had been offered the role and that he had mentioned him as a credible alternative

---

92. Lord (James) Rennell, *Times*, 4 October 1939, 11; *War Poems with Some Others* (London: Edward Arnold, 1940), 6.
93. Rodd to Catto, 1 February 1940, Morgan Grenfell Papers, DBBAR 001, File 006.00.
94. Catto to Rodd, 8 and 20 February 1940, Rodd to Catto, 15 February 1940, Morgan Grenfell Papers, DBBAR 001, File 006.00.
95. Horn, 'J. P. Morgan and Co., the House of Morgan and Europe, 1933–39', 538.

candidate: 'I suggested that the succession should fall to one of our younger partners and I told him there had always been a feeling that in such an event the succession should fall on you.'[96]

Although Rodd had no problem identifying publically with the Morgan banks, there is some evidence to suggest that, privately, he sometimes questioned whether he had made the right decision leaving the Bank of England. Mary, certainly, came to question his move to Morgan Grenfell. This was because of what she saw as flaws in Jack Morgan's character. She was particularly alarmed by a conversation she had with Jack in the United States in 1941, which she recounted in a letter to Rodd. Jack had told her that, after the First World War, Norman had suggested that the two of them work together for the reconstruction of Europe, but he had refused. Moreover, he boasted to her of how he had taken Rodd away from his work with Norman at the Bank of England. Mary was not impressed. 'I had never seen before how wide-reaching one man's holding on to personal prejudice can be', she declared. She suggested that the fact that Jack Morgan had 'ultimate power' in the company meant that Rodd had never been free to use his 'creativeness and imagination' properly; leaving the Bank of England had taken him away from the good work he had been doing with Norman. Joining Morgan Grenfell had been a 'mistake', she said. Unless the situation changed, it would 'not be right' for him to go back to working with the firm after the war. After the Second World War, she was still unconvinced that Morgan Grenfell was the right place for him to work.[97]

Rodd had some doubts about Jack Morgan himself. Jack was a Republican who was hostile to Roosevelt – even though he supported his decision to leave the Gold Standard in 1933. Writing to Rodd in July 1935, he called Roosevelt's government a 'dictatorship'. Rodd thought Jack himself was on the 'wrong track', even though Rodd was not sure about Roosevelt either.[98] Rodd believed Jack became a less creative person as he grew older. When Jack died in 1943, Rodd told Mary that he must have died a 'fairly unhappy man' and that he had 'stopped growing' at a certain time. But what he said about him altered according to his audience, for, at the same time, he told Lamont that he had been 'a great and good man and a true friend' to him.[99] He once compared Jack to the Swedish banker Markus Wallenburg. He thought there were similarities between the positions and roles of the two men in their respective countries.[100]

During the 1930s, Rodd also got involved with other enterprises and causes that made use of his financial and administrative talents. For example, in 1935, he became a director of the manufacturing company Courtaulds, a position he retained until 1944; its

---

96. Catto to Rodd, 29 February 1940, Morgan Grenfell Papers, DBBAR, File 006.00.
97. Mary to Rodd, 3 August 1941, Rodd Family Papers, AC. Mary to Rodd, 22 October 1945, Rennell of Rodd Papers, BD, Box 72/1.
98. Jack Morgan to Rodd, 3 July 1935, ARC 1214, Box 31/Foreign Loans and Financing, MP. Horn, 'J. P. Morgan and Co., the House of Morgan and Europe, 1933–39', 524–26. Rodd to Mary, 10 May 1935, Rodd Family Papers, AC.
99. Rodd to Mary, 27 March 1943, Rodd Family Papers, AC. Rodd to Lamont, 17 March 1943, Thomas Lamont Papers, BK, Box 127/8.
100. Rodd to Mary, 12 and 16 January 1936, Rodd Family Papers, AC.

director Samuel Courtauld was the father of Augustine Courtauld. He was also for a time treasurer of the London Child Guidance Clinic, and honorary treasurer of the British Institute in Paris.[101] In 1939, as war became more likely, he helped to found a group called the Association for Service and Reconstruction. This was dedicated to promoting the idea of national service and preparing the country for war or the threat of war, including economic warfare. In support of this, Rodd was in March 1939 co-signatory of a letter in the *Daily Telegraph* indicating support for a government of national unity. Intriguingly, the letter suggested that in order to command support from all sections of society, some restrictions on the flow of money, in the form of capital controls, might need to be introduced – an indication of a readiness on Rodd's part to accommodate some aspects of the socialist cause. This elicited a supportive letter to him from Nancy Mitford suggesting that while she believed in the country being governed by 'sensible men of ample means' – an allusion to a phrase associated with Walter Bagehot – some of these 'sensible men' were too afraid of 'losing their ample means'.[102]

---

101. *Observer*, 31 March 1935, 2. *Times*, 19 July 1934, 15; 22 January 1937, 10; 16 December 1938, 11; 5 July 1944, 9.
102. *Daily Telegraph*, 27 January 1939, 20; 21 March 1939. *Financial Times*, 10 February, 1939, 6. Nancy Mitford to Rodd, 23 March 1939, Rennell of Rodd Papers, BD, Box 66/67.

Chapter Five
NEGOTIATING WITH ITALY

Rodd's life in banking up until this point suggests a man who enjoyed working at the interface of finance and politics. At the end of the decade, an opportunity arose which gave him a further chance to work in this area, with particular reference to British relations with Italy. In summer 1939, he joined the Ministry of Economic Warfare (MEW), this while remaining a director at Morgan Grenfell. This ministry was formally established following the outbreak of war, with Ronald Cross as its first minister and Frederick Leith-Ross its first director general, and with a remit that had much in common with the Ministry of Blockade during the First World War. Its more immediate roots went back to the winter of 1929–30, when the Committee of Imperial Defence set up a small staff to study the economic preparedness of foreign countries to make war. Just over a year later, in 1931, the Industrial Intelligence Centre was set up, headed by Desmond Morton; Morton and his team shaped many of the ideas on which plans for economic warfare were developed, and they formed the nucleus of the Intelligence Department at the MEW. The culture of the Department was more 'pugnacious' than the Foreign Office, to which it was effectively subordinate. The foreign secretary, initially Lord Halifax, represented the MEW in the War Cabinet.[1]

Rodd's involvement with the MEW did not come out of the blue. One family friend recorded that already in 1938 he and some former colleagues from the Foreign Office had been part of a 'cadre' for a government department being planned for enforcing contraband control in the event of war.[2] Rodd was one of the earliest to join the MEW: he and four others were the first to move into its first premises.[3] Rodd was formally offered a role at the MEW on 14 July. He was assigned to the Intelligence Department, initially as a temporary assistant. To begin with, the Ministry sought to make use of his knowledge of Scandinavia – arising out of work he had done with the Nordic countries during his time at the Bank of England.[4] But, not surprisingly, in view of his knowledge of Italy, he was immediately drawn into issues connected with that country. After the war broke out, he became the MEW's chief negotiator with Italy.[5] There is a sense in which his involvement

---

1. W. N. Medlicott, *The Economic Blockade*, vol. 1 (London: HMSO and Longmans Green, 1952), 1, 13, 17, 64, 68, 69.
2. Pollen, 'Mary Rennell', 17.
3. Rennell of Rodd, 'Economic Warfare', 9 May 1944, House of Lords, Hansard.
4. Foreign Office letter to Rodd, 14 July 1939, Rennell of Rodd Papers, BD, Box 61.
5. Robert Mallett, *Mussolini and the Origins of the Second World War* (Basingstoke: Palgrave Macmillan, 2003), 212.

with Italy at this time followed on from the work of his father: just as Rennell Rodd had played a role in drawing Italy into the First World War on the Allied side, so Rodd was determined to keep Italy on good terms with Britain in the present conflict.

British leaders were conscious of the fact that in the previous war, Italy had eventually abandoned the Triple Alliance and joined the Allies. The Foreign Office hoped this would happen again; indeed, it remained a credible possibility at least until February 1940. But if this could not be achieved, the British government wanted to keep Italy neutral; keeping Italy out of German hands was seen as essential for protecting British interests in the Mediterranean. Economic measures were the obvious means for trying to achieve this. Anglo–Italian trade relations were regulated by a commercial agreement between the two countries in March 1938, revised a year later. Italy's main British import was coal, while the chief Allied imports from Italy were foodstuffs, fibres and wool yarns. In total, Italy relied on Germany for 20 per cent of its imports as opposed to 14 per cent from the Allies, with Germany taking 19 per cent of Italy's exports, and the Allies 14 per cent. German indebtedness to Italy was high – as much as £27 million – and Italy was anxious to reduce this.[6]

Rodd's ideas about how to deal with Italy were already evident in summer 1939. In late July, he wrote to Ingram – who had been seconded to the MEW from the Foreign Office – with information indicating that Mussolini had only unwillingly agreed to the 'Pact of Steel' with Hitler in May 1939. His source, a senior figure in Italian industry with links to Mussolini, suggested that the Italian leader would be open to a Europe-wide agreement diluting the Pact. Information of this kind made Rodd think that Italy could be lured away from Hitler. His first instinct was to deploy a strategy familiar to the Morgan banks – offering economic inducements to get political influence. He floated the idea with Ingram of trying to detach Mussolini from Germany by means of an Anglo–French loan. He used a tennis analogy: 'I am sure we should play into Mussolini's court and give him as many balls to return as possible.'[7] Other information coming into London reinforced what Rodd had been told. Deputy head of the Italian Railways, M. Giannini, who was in Britain in September, reported that Mussolini was angry about the German invasion of Poland; in this context, British purchases in Italy might be favoured over German ones.[8]

Policy towards Italy was discussed at a key meeting at the Foreign Office on 2 September 1939, the day before Britain declared war on Germany. Representing the MEW, Rodd proposed a plan to prevent Germany importing materials that contributed to their war industries. His idea was for Britain to try to gain leverage over Italy through becoming its main supplier of coal. The plan involved Britain buying products like aircraft engines and spare parts from Italy, and Italy using the profits to buy British coal in return. The wider context was the strategy of economic blockade against Germany, which meant that a measure of control over Italian trade was important.[9] The MEW's proposed

---

6. Medlicott, *Economic Blockade*, vol. 1, 282–84.
7. Ingram to Rodd, 31 July 1939; Rodd to Ingram 25 July and 1 August 1939, Rennell of Rodd Papers, BD, Box 61.
8. Medlicott, *Economic Blockade*, vol. 1, 283.
9. Robert Mallett, 'The Anglo–Italian War Trade Negotiations', *Diplomacy and Statecraft* 8, no. 1 (1997): 140–41.

strategy was endorsed by the War Cabinet on 8 September. Undermining Italy's relationship with the Axis powers was widely accepted as the right approach.[10] The man tasked with opening up negotiations on these matters on an informal basis was Percy Loraine, recently appointed British ambassador in Rome. Loraine had established a reputation for being ready to stand up to Mussolini, after he had a distinctly cool initial meeting with the Italian leader in late May. But he had also been a supporter of appeasement over the Munich Agreement.[11] The plan was for Rodd to operate alongside him.

Loraine was already known to Rodd. The two men had corresponded when Loraine was high commissioner in Egypt and Sudan, 1929–33. There was also a family connection. Loraine was married to Rodd's cousin, Louise Stuart-Wortley.[12] In subsequent months, whenever Rodd visited Rome for negotiations, he stayed with Loraine and Louise, which he greatly enjoyed. Visits to Rome reminded Rodd of the pre-war period; when he came to the embassy at the end of September, he was given a room in the same part of the building as his family had stayed in before the First World War. At the end of the year, he wrote to Loraine, saying: 'I cannot tell you how much it meant to me to live and work with you in the same house.'[13] Other key figures in the negotiating team were Edward Playfair from the Treasury and Richard Nosworthy, commercial councillor at the Rome embassy.

The initial prospects for a commercial agreement with Italy seemed good. In early October, Rodd was optimistic; he told Mary that there was no danger of Italy coming into the war on the German side unless Germany invaded Italy, although he observed that Italy was in a difficult situation militarily and economically.[14] A meeting took place on 7 October at the Ministry of Exchange between the British and Italian delegations. On the same day, Loraine and Rodd had discussions with Senator Amadeo Giannini, director of Italy's Commercial Affairs Department, at which Giannini signalled both an enthusiasm for the British proposals and a concurrent caution about anything that would alienate Germany.[15] Loraine was well aware of this problem. In early September he had advised extreme caution in applying measures to blockade Italy – for fear of pushing Mussolini into the hands of Germany.[16]

On his return to Britain, Rodd briefed Halifax about the situation. Privately, he told Mary that Halifax was one of the few people with a good understanding of what was going on.[17] He then wrote a report for the MEW – which Halifax circulated to the

---

10. Lord Hankey, cited in David W. Ellwood, *Italy 1943–1945* (Leicester: Leicester University Press, 1985), 19.
11. Adam Richardson, 'Sir Percy Loraine and British Relations with Italy, 1939–40', *Diplomacy & Statecraft* 31, no. 2 (2020): 260, 264.
12. Violet Stuart-Wortley, *Life without Theory: An Autobiography* (London: Hutchinson, 1946), 141.
13. Rodd to Mary, 5 October 1939, Rodd Family Papers, AC. Rodd to Loraine, 29 November 1939, FO 1011/206.
14. Rodd to Mary, 3 October 1939, Rodd Family Papers, AC.
15. Mallett, 'The Anglo–Italian War Trade Negotiations', 147–48.
16. Medlicott, *Economic Blockade*, vol. 1, 280.
17. Ingram to Loraine, 17 October 1939, FO 1011/206. Rodd to Mary, 9 November 1939, Rodd Family Papers, AC.

War Cabinet – in which he declared: 'Any purchase we can make of war material from the Italians, especially from existing stocks, even if we do not really want them, would be worth doing in order to ensure ourselves against the possibility of Italy coming in on the side of Germany.' But he warned that this should not be done to the extent of antagonising Germany: 'In putting pressure on the Italians, pressure should not go beyond the point at which the danger of German military reprisals is reached.' Italy was in a difficult position in regard to maintaining neutrality, he observed. A neutrality beneficial to Britain risked German reprisals, while a neutrality beneficial to Germany exposed Italy to possible Allied economic pressure. In the same memorandum, Rodd argued that a distinction needed to be drawn in the British press and public life between fascism and Nazism – which he felt could 'legitimately' be done.[18] In other words, the government needed to prepare public opinion for some kind of agreement with Italy. Rodd's remarks here indicate that he saw Italian fascism as more benign than Nazism. Some tolerance of Mussolini's regime needed to be considered for reasons of expediency.

At the meeting on 7 October, Giannini suggested to Rodd the setting up of an Anglo–Italian Joint Standing Committee along the lines of a similar French–Italian committee set up before the war. The plan was for it to have an executive function, but the British, while endorsing the idea, wanted something more consultative in character, and this was accepted. The committee was formalised on 27 October, with a petroleum sub-committee being set up a few days later. Rodd was made the first acting British chairman of the committee, with Playfair, Nosworthy and the British naval attaché P. Bowyer-Smith also members. In November, Rodd was replaced as the British chairman by Noel Charles – a future ambassador to Italy – before, in December, master of the rolls Wilfrid Greene took over as the committee's permanent chairman. On the Italian side, the committee was chaired by Amadeo Giannini and included M. Masi, general director of trade at the Ministry of Trade and Exchange. Its main areas of focus were contraband control and war trade issues.[19]

The committee was designed to be informal – because the Italians were anxious to avoid offending Germany.[20] Rodd's strategy placed a great emphasis on developing good relationships. As he explained in a 'Progress Report' in early November: '[Italian cooperation] takes a form which will not admit of official voluntary cooperation for fear of German reactions but will provide the reality which we seek even if not the form we might like.' He stressed that good relations with the Italians themselves – some of whom were unsympathetic to Germany – might pave the way for political cooperation. In his mind, it was important to deal with the Italians with 'as light a rein as possible'; he thought that once the Joint Standing Committee was well established, closer cooperation would naturally follow.[21] In early November, Rodd told Mary that 'patience and forbearance' were needed in the negotiations. He added that he was good – perhaps too

---

18. War Cabinet Memorandum, Italy, 24 October 1939, Rennell of Rodd Papers, BD, Box 102.
19. Medlicott, *Economic Blockade*, vol. 1, 284–85.
20. Mallett, 'The Anglo–Italian War Trade Negotiations', 152.
21. Francis Rodd, Progress Report dated 7 November 1939, section 13, FO 1011/206.

good – at seeing the other person's perspective: 'I am too prone to see the other chap's points of view and thinking that his argument is really better than mine! You may not believe it but it is so.'[22] The need for patience was perhaps an allusion to Giannini, whom Rodd found difficult. He came to the conclusion that Giannini's 'capacity for irrelevant argument' would make formal meetings 'otiose', and that informal sub-committees might work better.[23]

The Italians were sometimes irritated at a perceived British slowness. Not until 6 December did Britain put to the Italians a comprehensive plan for purchases of their goods. In the meantime, a surplus of hemp that could have gone to Britain went to Germany, because of the tardy arrival of hemp experts in Rome; and the French stepped in to buy aircraft ahead of the arrival of British representatives of the Air Ministry. This irritation was reinforced by recurring problems relating to the application of contraband control: establishing a modus vivendi on this was one of the main issues preoccupying the Joint Standing Committee. The British were eager to subject ships coming into Italian ports to investigation, while monitoring traffic in the Aegean and at the port of Trieste was also a concern. There were periodic reactions from the Italian side at what were perceived as slights to their national dignity, although, for the most part, the irritation seemed more about the application of contraband control than the principle itself. For example, the Italians were touchy about the examination of ships coming from the Eritrean port of Massawa on the grounds of national prestige. Italian foreign minister Galeazzo Ciano told Loraine at the end of November that Mussolini was 'on the verge of boiling point' on the issue of contraband control.[24]

Rodd thought that British bureaucracy was at times an impediment to the negotiations. As he explained to Ingram:

> I have asked the Italians to do certain things to facilitate control. They have agreed to a number of these suggestions and the effect is precisely nil. They were asked to give advice on the prospective arrival of ships and in many cases have done so, but where they have done so, the ships in question have been held up in precisely the same way as ships for which no advices have been given.[25]

The problem, he suggested, lay in 'administrative chaos' in the MEW and in a lack of staff at the embassy in Rome. He recognised that he was being rather outspoken, but insisted that his remarks were not an exaggeration. Privately he told Mary a similar story about the problems in the MEW. Writing from Rome in November, he said: 'I have been so rude about so many things that they may ask me to go away which would be splendid. As it is they have told me that I am virtually indispensable which provoked my violent

---

22. Rodd to Mary, 2 November 1939, Rodd Family Papers, AC.
23. Francis Rodd, Progress Report dated 7 November 1939, FO 1011/206. Michael John Budden, 'British Policy towards Fascist Italy in the Early Stages of the Second World War', PhD thesis, King's College London, 1999, 108.
24. Medlicott, *Economic Blockade*, vol. 1, 287–94.
25. Rodd to Ingram, 18 December 1939, FO 837/494.

retort that if I was it was only because they had a damn bad organisation and were incompetent themselves.'[26] In a statement on Italian policy some months later, Rodd returned to his criticism of British administrative structures, specifically blaming competition between ministries for the government's failure to implement its clearing policy in a coherent way.[27] Rodd's reaction may at times have reflected a tendency in him to be melodramatic. But the picture he painted was similar to that later made by the MEW's official historian W. N. Medlicott; Medlicott argued that in the winter of 1939–40, the MEW was characterised by 'feverish administrative activity' and a 'fallacious sense of achievement'.[28]

Rodd found some of the personality conflicts hard to deal with. For example, he was frustrated when, in November, Charles was made chairman of the Joint Standing Committee – in his view, Nosworthy, who was more up to speed with the progress of negotiations than Charles, was the more obvious candidate. Nosworthy was also disappointed. Rodd wrote to Loraine, stating that he found this type of issue difficult to deal with: 'How I hate these personal matters. It is such a pity to upset relations which seemed to me so good out here [...] But I suppose everyone has their peculiarities and is entitled to them in a society which we are striving to maintain against the opposition regimes who don't allow of individualities when they are inconvenient.'[29]

The messages coming from the Italian regime in December were not reassuring. A meeting of the Fascist Grand Council on 7 December reaffirmed Italy's non-belligerent position, while also reaffirming its commitment to the Pact of Steel. Just over a week later, Ciano suggested that the conflict in Europe had been caused by the Allies trying to encircle Germany. Rodd thought this demonstrated how far from each other Britain and Italy were, noting that it would be rash to count on Italy as 'friendly neutrals' for any indefinite period.[30] Loraine persisted in believing that differences over contraband issues were the primary cause of tension. On 22 December, he floated with Ciano the idea that the Italians might manage the whole matter themselves, and Rodd and Nosworthy had further discussions with Ciano the day after. On 24 December, Loraine appealed to London for a solution to the problem of a build-up of ships in Italian ports, associated with what was known as the Black Diamond system of inspection and release. A decision was made to release all cargoes held in ports destined for Italian consumers on receipt of appropriate guarantees. On returning to London, Rodd reported that this had helped to ease political tensions. Ciano was pleased with this outcome and promised to try to reassure Mussolini as to Britain's goodwill towards Italy.[31]

---

26. Rodd to Mary, 9 November 1939, Rodd Family Papers, AC.
27. Rodd, 'Italian Policy', 1 April 1940, FO 837/498, 5.
28. Medlicott, *The Economic Blockade*, vol. 1, 43–44. See also Gill Bennett, *Churchill's Man of Mystery: Desmond Morton and the World of Intelligence* (London: Routledge, 2007), 202.
29. Rodd to Loraine, 6 November 1940, FO 1011/206.
30. Rodd to Ingram, 18 December 1939, cited in Michael Budden, 'British Policy towards Fascist Italy in the Early Stages of the Second World War', 132.
31. Rodd, 'Second Progress Report on War Trade Negotiations with Italy', 25 February 1940, 4, FO 837/496. Medlicott, *Economic Blockade*, vol. 1, 296.

By the end of the year, a framework for further negotiations was emerging, which was intended to address the fact that the Italians needed sterling in order to buy British coal. A war trade agreement with Italy was envisaged, which would allow the Italian government greater autonomy. Greene went to Rome at the end of January with a two-pronged offer: to accept an Italian state guarantee not to re-export goods arriving in Italy to Germany – this was subject to French approval; and to make available 8.3 million tonnes of British coal to Italy while committing Britain to purchase Italian goods to the tune of at least £20 million. The list of envisaged purchases included £5 million of agricultural equipment and armaments, including the well-regarded Breda gun. Ciano welcomed the proposals, as did Giannini and the foreign ministry official responsible for economic warfare, Count Pietromarchi. But evidence that all was not well soon emerged around a proposed contract with the company Caproni for the supply of training aircraft to the UK. On 2 February, Mussolini seemed to have no problem with this, but on 8 February, he refused to allow it to go ahead. A few days later, on 13 February, Ciano told Loraine that Mussolini was now unwilling to sell armaments to Britain because of his relations with Germany.[32]

The collapse of these negotiations was a serious blow to the British strategy. But the team promoting it were not yet ready to give up. On 14 February, Loraine wrote to Halifax, with whom he had a good working relationship, urging him not to be too discouraged and suggesting that the extent of the setback should not be exaggerated. He acknowledged that Britain's proposals for an economic agreement had been politically unpalatable for Mussolini; signing up to them would have meant 'tacitly' taking a political decision of a 'far-reaching' character – it would have allied Italy with Britain and France against her German ally. While stating that it had not been the British intention to force Mussolini's hand, Loraine noted that if the British had succeeded, it would, in practice, have been a 'political success of considerable magnitude'. In his view, all was not yet lost; the fact that Italy would suffer economically from pulling out of negotiations might focus Mussolini's mind.[33] Rodd was struck by the fact that relations with the Italians had not broken down at a personal level. As he explained to Mary: 'We have had a complete breakdown of our negotiations but not of course of friendly relations and I must try to help take stock of things and see what is up when the curtain of fog lifts.'[34]

At the end of the month, Rodd wrote a second progress report on the negotiations with Italy, summarising his own thoughts on why what had seemed a promising strategy had gone wrong. In part, he blamed the British side for its slowness in bringing its proposals to a head. But he had also come to the conclusion that the British had overplayed their hand; in particular, he thought the decision to insist on the purchase of guns as part of the agreement had been a tactical mistake, because it resulted in the Germans putting

---

32. E. L. Woodward, *British Foreign Policy in the Second World War*, vol. 1 (London: HMSO, 1970), 148. Medlicott, *Economic Blockade*, vol. 1, 301. George Waterfield, *Professional Diplomat: Sir Percy Lorraine of Kirkharle Bt. 1880–1961* (London: John Murray, 1973), 254–55.
33. Loraine to Halifax, 14 February 1940, FO 1011/67. Richardson, 'Sir Percy Loraine and British Relations with Italy, 1939–40', 269.
34. Rodd to Mary, 15 February 1940, Rodd Family Papers, AC.

pressure on the Italians over the issue. Like Loraine, he thought the British had effectively tried to bring Italy down on Britain's side, and this had limited the Duce's freedom of action.[35] His thinking on this was probably shaped by a conversation that he and Playfair had had in Rome on 17 February with Masi, in which Masi stated that the British insistence on buying guns had created an unfavourable atmosphere.[36] Similarly, Rodd had had, a few days later, a conversation with Italian industrialist Alberto Pirelli – with whom he had a long-standing connection – in which Pirelli suggested that the negotiations had only collapsed because of the arms issue while warning him against Britain over-reacting and thereby provoking a dangerous situation.[37]

Like Loraine, Rodd tried to be optimistic. In the progress report, he argued that while Britain had not succeeded in pushing the Italians into the British camp – this was an ambition he called 'le grand coup', citing contacts in the French embassy in Rome – all was not yet lost: 'Apparently our relations have not deteriorated and therefore I am driven to the conclusion that if we have lost "le grand coup" we have still retained the position we have won since the beginning of the war.' Using an image from roulette, he insisted that Britain should not give up yet: 'Though we may have lost our stake on the number we have won our stakes on the colour more than once and have kept our winnings.' The solution was to adopt a more piecemeal approach; Britain should avoid trying to arrange a comprehensive agreement with Italy, but seek instead to restore 'gradually by approaches on individual points' its position on economic questions. Patience was needed: 'In other words: – "Softlee, softlee, catchee monkey".'[38] From a trip to Paris at the end of the month – where he was witness to French–Italian economic discussions – Rodd concluded that Italy was desperate to acquire enough sterling to pay for coal.[39] There seemed every reason to press on with negotiations.

Another factor in Rodd's thinking was the attitude of some of the Italians themselves. He sensed that some of the Italian negotiators were personally keen to come to an agreement. He also saw a growing Germanophobia in Italy. Here there were echoes of his father's experience. Rennell Rodd had a high regard for the natural instincts of the Italian people. In his view, popular opinion had played an important role in bringing about Italy's entry into the First World War. When, a couple of decades later, it was reported that poison gas was being used in Ethiopia, he said that it was 'absolutely inconceivable' that the Italian people themselves, humane and kindly as they were by nature, would countenance such actions.[40] Whether or not Rodd was influenced by his father, his outlook contained something of the same tendency. The goodwill of the people they were negotiating with was an encouragement. Unfortunately, pressure from Germany

---

35. Rodd, 'Second Progress Report on War Trade Negotiations with Italy', 25 February 1940, 8–14, FO 837/496.
36. Playfair Memorandum, 17 February 1940, FO 837/497.
37. Rodd to Ingram, 23 February 1940, FO 837/496.
38. Rodd, 'Second Progress Report on War Trade Negotiations with Italy', 25 February 1940, 14–16, FO 837/496.
39. Rodd to Waley, 29 February 1940, FO 837/496.
40. Lord (James) Rennell, 30 March 1936, House of Lords, Hansard.

trumped pro-British feeling. In mid-March, following a trip by Ribbentrop to Rome, there was an Italo–German agreement which involved Germany committing to provide Italy with a million tonnes of coal per month. A meeting between Hitler and Mussolini on 18 March at the Brenner Pass was a further indication of a growing closeness between the two countries. But, confusingly, when Playfair went to Rome some days later, he sensed an Anglo–Italian agreement was still possible.[41]

Rodd's personal reputation had not been diminished by the February events. His energy and knowledge of Italy meant that he had become a figure of considerable authority. At the end of March, Giovanni Bastianini, Italian ambassador in London, approached Leith-Ross with a request for Rodd to be sent to Rome for further discussions, while a similar request reached Leith-Ross through the medium of Fummi. This was a matter for the Foreign Office to decide. Leith-Ross supported the idea, noting that Rodd had in the eyes of the Italians now come to represent British policy towards Italy more generally:

> On our staff is Mr Rodd, who in view of his past activities in Rome (arising out of purely MEW work such as contraband control, but developing so as to cover a much wider field than the purely MEW field) has acquired a more than MEW status. Mr Rodd has come inevitably to be identified with the wider policy of His Majesty's Government in Italy.[42]

At this point, Rodd was still convinced that a deal was possible. At the beginning of April, he suggested that the government faced a choice: it needed either to pursue a policy of engagement with Italy more positively or take a harder line on the possible accumulation of stocks that could be used in war. He warned against a policy of drift. He continued to favour the positive approach, especially since the French were themselves seeking a rapprochement with Italy at the time. A proactive approach to preventing goods reaching Germany could, he thought, be combined with economic incentives that might be appealing to Italy. If the hard-line approach was adopted, it would involve a significant shift in how contraband control was exercised in relation to neutral countries. He wanted the full implications of that to be understood.[43]

The Foreign Office agreed to Leith-Ross's recommendation to send Rodd to Rome. But the planned visit was then put off when the War Cabinet ordered a review of Anglo–Italian economic relations, with reference to contraband control. But the review did not alter the strategy. Faced with the choice Rodd had outlined of continuing with negotiations or moving towards a tougher stance on contraband, the Cabinet on 24 April chose the former option. On 26 April, Halifax gave the Italian ambassador an aide-mémoire summarising the British position and suggesting Rodd return to Rome for negotiations. There were those who had by now come to the conclusion that economic incentives would not be enough to sway Mussolini. On a couple of occasions in April, the Foreign

---

41. Medlicott, *Economic Blockade*, vol. 1, 306.
42. Memorandum by Leith-Ross starting with 'Rome Telegram No. 260', 29 March 1940, FO 837/497.
43. Rodd, 'Italian Policy', 1 April 1940, 6–7, FO 837/498.

Office floated with Bastianini – informally – the possibility of Italy having some of its territorial claims recognised in the event of a German defeat in the war.[44] These discussions came to nothing. Rodd pressed ahead with his economic strategy. On 29 April, he wrote another paper for the MEW, in which he called for Britain to order 20 ships from Italy. He suggested that if Cesare Sacerdoti, a naval specialist selling Italian ships in Britain, could report such a purchase, it would have a big impact on Italian thinking:

> I think it is very necessary to place an order for 20 rather than 11 ships [...] The political effect throughout Italy of an order for 20 ships will be much greater than for 11 [...] I hold very strongly that matters should be so arranged that Sacerdoti can telegraph to Italy this week to say that he has secured an order for 20 ships.[45]

In the event, Rodd did not return to Italy at this time. But Greene went back to Rome on 20 May, along with Playfair and J. W. Nicholls – a Foreign Office representative – for further discussions. In an increasingly desperate situation, this was a final effort to keep Italy neutral. But on 28 May, the British negotiators were informed that Mussolini was no longer supportive of the discussions – to the apparent surprise of Giannini and Masi. If the Italians negotiating with the British were in good faith, they were ultimately undercut by their leader.[46] If Rodd's general interpretation of events was correct, it was Mussolini, rather than Italian officialdom, who blocked a deal; the Italian dictator was the key figure in determining the course of events. Here Rodd's perspective was similar to that of Loraine, who had always been of the view that Mussolini was the dominant figure in Italian politics.[47]

On 15 May, Cross was replaced at the MEW by Labour MP Hugh Dalton. Rodd did not welcome this and left the MEW; he thought Dalton was unsympathetic to businessmen like him from the City and observed that he had appointed as his immediate advisors all the left-wing members of staff.[48] Another factor was that Dalton was sceptical about the overall strategy towards Italy with which Rodd was identified. Dalton had played a central role in the 1930s in moving the Labour Party away from a semi-pacifist position to one of advocating re-armament. He had also helped to facilitate the cross-party alliance that brought in Churchill in place of Chamberlain – whose appeasement policy he fiercely opposed. He listened to Rodd's accounts of events. But he concluded, as he explained in a letter to Loraine, that not all of the MEW's decisions over the previous nine months had been 'wise'.[49] Privately, Dalton was more scathing. In a diary entry three

---

44. Woodward, *British Foreign Policy in the Second World War*, vol, 1, 152. Telegram to Loraine, 31 March 1940, FO 837/498. Budden, 'British Policy towards Fascist Italy in the Early Stages of the Second World War', 209, 249–50.
45. Rodd, Report to the MEW, 29 April 1940, Rennell of Rodd Papers, BD, Box 61. Andrea Doria, *Cento Uno Viaggi* (Milan: Hoepli, 2006), 272.
46. Medlicott, *Economic Blockade*, vol. 1, 310–11. *Spectator*, 23 May 1940, 2.
47. Richardson, 'Sir Percy Loraine and British Relations with Italy, 1939–40', 270.
48. Rodd, Diary 1940 (written in 1942), 3, Rennell of Rodd Papers, BD, Box 69/1. This 'diary' is a summary of Rodd's life in the second half of 1940 written in 1942. Rodd to Mary, 7 June 1942, Rodd Family Papers, AC.
49. Dalton to Loraine, 25 May 1940, FO 1011/211.

years later, he recorded an exchange he had had with diplomat Gladwyn Jebb, in which he suggested that Rodd's judgement was poor and that he was too close to certain Italian industrialists such as the former finance minister Giuseppe Volpi: 'Gladwyn agrees that Rodd has very bad judgment, and that there is a danger, if he has any real influence, of all sorts of undesirable Italians, e.g. Volpi, having a voice in the future.' He went on to suggest that Rodd's interpretation of Italian intentions had been 'incredible' and that Greene's mission to Rome in May 'fatuous'. Rodd obviously told Dalton that it had been a mistake to include the Breda gun in the proposed list of purchases in February 1940. Dalton summarised Rodd's thinking on this in a dismissive, sarcastic tone:

> I recalled [to Jebb] how [Rodd] had asserted that Mussolini would have sold us large quantities of arms for use against Germany, and might even have come in on our side, had the British Foreign Office not foolishly insisted on including in the list of items to be sold, some particular gun in which the Duce took a special interest.[50]

The discussion concluded with Jebb stating that he would in future try to diminish Rodd's potential for influence.[51] Ironically, Rodd belonged to the same social set as Gladwyn Jebb and his wife Cynthia.[52]

Rodd was later eager to counter any sense that the negotiations with Italy had been rooted in a policy of appeasement. When, in March 1942, Loraine produced a paper summarising relations with Italy in the run-up to Italy's entry into the war, Rodd criticised it for giving that impression: 'The major omission which I regret [in Loraine's paper] is the absence of reference to the specific instructions from H. M. G., and by the Chiefs of Staff in particular, to seek an agreement in order to keep the Mediterranean open as long as possible.' He thought Loraine's despatch would leave some people thinking that the effort to keep Italy out of the war was only a continuation of Chamberlain's appeasement policy. 'It was nothing of the sort', insisted Rodd; it was, rather, a 'military and naval desideratum' which amounted to a 'necessity' in the view of British and French Service staffs.[53]

Much here depends on how appeasement is defined. The difficulty with the concept is that it is hard to distinguish from any other form of negotiation involving compromise or concession. It has also acquired pejorative associations, making it hard to use as an analytical tool.[54] In one sense, Rodd was right. The Anglo–Italian war trade negotiations did not involve the kind of political concessions to Italy that Chamberlain made to Germany at Munich. But the use of sweeteners to try to placate Italy may in a looser sense be considered a form of appeasement, fitting into a British tradition of trying to

---

50. Ben Pimlott (ed.), *The Second World War Diary of Hugh Dalton 1940–45* (London: Jonathon Cape in Association with the London School of Economics, 1986), 622.
51. Ibid.
52. Haslam, *Redeeming Features*, 15.
53. Rodd cited in Waterfield, *Professional Diplomat*, 282.
54. Norrin M. Ripsman and Jack S. Levy, 'Wishful Thinking or Buying Time: The Logic of British Appeasement in the 1930s', *International Security* 33, no. 2 (2008): 153.

manage the Italian dictator through negotiation. The historian Robert Mallett suggested that a policy of appeasement was present in the very task of trying to keep Italy neutral as well as the in-war trade negotiations.[55] It is important to see these negotiations in a longer-term perspective, and not only in the context of 1930s appeasement. Anglo–Italian relations had for decades been intertwined with the wider challenge for Britain of managing German power in Europe. Rodd's own father had played a discreet but significant role in bringing Italy into the First World War on the Allied side. Perhaps the more important question is whether Britain would have been better served by adopting a more confrontational policy from the outset. Archibald Wavell, commander-in-chief in the Middle East (1939–41), was one who thought so: 'I am sure that a more robust attitude towards Italy during the period of waiting instead of our weak-kneed and apologist attempts at appeasement would not have increased the danger of war and might perhaps have lessened it.'[56] Wavell may have been right. But it is understandable that, on the basis of information coming from Italy and perceived strategic necessity, a more conciliatory approach was tried. Rodd himself loved trying to solve a problem. In the end, he and Loraine, and their superiors in government, overestimated the capacity for economic incentives to influence Mussolini.

Rodd resigned from the MEW on 3 June. He was in a patriotic frame of mind. Sometime in May or early June, he wrote an anonymous letter to the editor of the *Times*, Geoffrey Dawson. Rodd's missive contained language similar to that used by Churchill in his famous 'Dunkirk' speech in the House of Commons on 4 June. Writing a couple of years later, Rodd speculated as to whether his letter had been passed on to Churchill and had helped inform the speech:

> London was in turmoil when I left. Churchill had only recently come in. I wrote to the 'Times', among many, a letter which they never published saying that the Germans should know that we would fight them in England on the beaches, if they came, on the hills and in the sea. And if we were beaten, we would fight them from Canada and until the end of the world. Later I heard that he made a speech in that same theme. I wondered if Geoffrey Dawson had ever sent him that anonymous letter. I don't suppose so.[57]

Rodd's letter to Dawson has not been found. Moreover, the fact that this account was written at a later date may mean that Rodd did not recall these details exactly. Churchill's speeches did have input from others. As Richard Toye explains, Churchill was, in the days prior to the Dunkirk speech, being pressed to make a clear statement about Britain's readiness to fight Germany, whatever the cost, by a pro-British foreign news editor, William Philip Simms. Churchill may have been influenced by Simms.[58] It cannot be

---

55. Mallett, 'The Anglo–Italian War Trade Negotiations', 138. See also William C. Mills, 'The Nyon Conference: Neville Chamberlain, Anthony Eden and the Appeasement of Italy in 1937', *International History Review* 15, no. 1 (1993): 1–22.
56. John Connell, *Wavell: Scholar and Soldier* (London: Collins, 1964), 234–35.
57. Rodd, Diary 1940 (written in 1942), 10, Rennell of Rodd Papers, BD, Box 69/1.
58. Richard Toye, *The Roar of the Lion: The Untold Story of Churchill's World War II Speeches* (Oxford: Oxford University Press, 2013), 49.

ruled out that Rodd was another, anonymous influence. But his own instinct that the letter was not shown to Churchill is probably right.

The clash with Dalton was not the sole reason for Rodd's disaffection with the MEW. He had talked of leaving even prior to Dalton's appointment – the frustrations he had felt in the autumn had not gone away. In mid-April, he wrote to Mary: 'I hope I am allowed to leave MEW and become more human and less of a piece of machinery.'[59] A possibility at this point was for Rodd to move across the Atlantic: Leith-Ross floated the idea of his going to North America to set up a branch of the MEW in either the United States or Canada, so that there could be a nucleus of people to represent Britain if the country was occupied. But Rodd was not convinced by this suggestion, partly because he thought his links to J. P. Morgan & Co. might prove embarrassing. In March 1941, Dalton sent Noel Hall to the embassy in Washington for this purpose.[60]

Free from his MEW responsibilities, Rodd considered what to do next. Although still a leading figure in Morgan Grenfell, he did not want to limit himself to banking work. The bank had a diminished role during the war. Many of its operations were relocated from London to a country house near Berkhamstead, owned by one of Lord Bicester's sons. At the start of the war, its total staff numbered 100 men and 32 women. Of these, 50 men and three women were eventually called into some kind of national service.[61] Rodd wanted to do something directly connected to the war. Without breaking his links with the bank, he applied to be called up in the Officers' Emergency Reserve. He had in mind returning to Africa to do intelligence work. His application was accepted. This meant leaving his family behind, in a situation where there was a real threat of German invasion and occupation. Some of his time in June 1940 was spent talking with Mary about what should happen to his family in his absence. He joined a ship bound for Lagos on 19 June.

After their marriage, Rodd and Mary lived in London, although they based in Basle when Rodd worked at the BIS. Mary had a studio at home and was well connected to London's art world. Shortly after their wedding, Rodd reported to a friend that he was 'very happy'. Over the next few years, they had four daughters.[62] Socially and intellectually they had much in common. But differences emerged from the mid-1930s onwards, in their attitudes to religion and spirituality. In 1932, following an illness, Mary got involved in the Oxford Group (OG), a religious movement founded by American Lutheran pastor Frank Buchman. The OG, known from 1938 by the name 'Moral Re-Armament' (MRA), had considerable influence in interwar Britain. Drawing on a tradition of Anglo–American evangelical spirituality, Buchman and his network of supporters

---

59. Rodd to Mary, 16 April 1940, Rodd Family Papers, AC.
60. Rodd, Diary 1940 (written in 1942), 4, Rennell of Rodd Papers, BD, Box 69/1. *Times*, 20 March 1941, 2.
61. Burk, *Morgan Grenfell 1838–1988*, 166–69.
62. Rodd to Cynthia Noble, 18 November 1928, Papers of Cynthia Gladwyn, CCC, 1/2/1. They lived initially in Park Square, Regent's Park, before moving to 10 Holland Park. In September 1936, they found a place in Clymping, Sussex – 'Kent's House' – which became for a few years a home away from London. Their daughters were named Joanna, Juliet, Mary and Rachel.

encouraged people to seek for what was 'right' in any situation, citing the possibility of their getting 'guidance' from God about their lives. They also promoted the idea that global conflict could only be addressed by a change in people arising out of a deep religious experience. It was a message that resonated with people worried about the growing threat of war. In late 1938, Rodd's father, although not overtly religious, put his name to a letter in the *Times* supportive of MRA by the earl of Athlone. Controversy arose when, in the mid-1930s, the OG tried to spread its message of spiritual renewal in Nazi Germany. Some charged Buchman with being naïve and sympathetic to Hitler. By contrast, the Gestapo saw the OG as a 'dangerous opponent' and closed down its activities.[63]

Mary, who was an enthusiast by nature, threw herself into Buchman's work. Rodd also got slightly involved in the movement, but more cautiously. He helped host one OG house party in Holland Park and joined Mary in attending others in Oxford, Bournemouth and elsewhere. On his own, he was present at a gathering hosted by Conservative peer Lord Salisbury at Hatfield House in October 1936.[64] Tension arose because Mary wanted Rodd to embrace a life of faith more wholeheartedly, while he thought she could be overzealous and one-sided in her interests. They often tried to talk through their differences. In spring 1940, Rodd suggested that it was not so much Mary's convictions that he found a problem as a lack of balance in applying them. He used a metaphor to convey his thoughts: 'A wise horseman does not go all out always. He nurses his horse and his own strength. You are overstraining both.' He suggested that the two of them talk on the basis that 'both may be right and both may be wrong'.[65]

A further cause for anxiety in the family was Peter Rodd. Peter was reckless with money and prone to drink. He was also unfaithful to Nancy. Their marriage became complicated and unhappy – they eventually divorced in 1958. Rodd himself was sufficiently sceptical about Peter's behaviour that he once warned the BBC against employing him. Nancy was furious, writing to her friend, travel-writer Robert Byron: 'I have put [Francis's] name in a drawer, and *hope he dies*.'[66] Nancy never got close to the Rodds as a family. She caricatured them in her novels – as she did her own family. Rodd was portrayed as the pompous Luke Garfield – 'cold as a fish and a great bore' – in *Pigeon Pie* (1940).[67] There was something of Peter in the characters of Tony Kroesig and Christian in *The Pursuit of Love* (1945), and Rodd's parents were depicted as the eccentric Lord and Lady Montdore in *Love in a Cold Climate* (1949). The family sensed Nancy's distance. In 1943, on his way back to his wartime work in Africa, Rodd reported to Mary that he had seen her on a few occasions: 'Nancy I saw a few times; as ever, she is cordial and pleasant but cold and separate from all of us.'[68]

---

63. Philip Boobbyer, *The Spiritual Vision of Frank Buchman* (University Park: Pennsylvania State University Press, 2013), 33–55, 136–40. *Times*, 12 November 1938, 8.
64. Garth Lean, *Frank Buchman: A Life* (London: Constable, 1985), 250n; see also 276n.
65. Rodd to Mary, 16 April 1940, Rodd Family Papers, AC.
66. Cited in Hastings, *Nancy Mitford*, 115, emphasis in original.
67. Nancy Mitford, *Pigeon Pie* (London: Hamish Hamilton, 1976), 6. Bill Haslam's son Nicky – who was his godson – called Rodd 'somewhat humourless'; Haslam, *Redeeming Features*, 23.
68. Rodd to Mary, 11 January 1943, Rodd Family Papers, AC.

In 1938, Rodd acquired 'the Rodd' in Herefordshire, a large Elizabethan manor house near the Welsh border town of Presteigne, set in an estate of 480 acres. It was a place with strong family associations for him: the house and lands had been in the family up until the late seventeenth century. One of his ancestors was supposed to have set out from the Rodd on the Third Crusade and been knighted by Richard I for his contribution to the Ascalon campaign in 1191. Back in autumn 1906, Rodd's father had thought of buying it when it came on the market, but its price at auction proved too high. The family moved into the main house on the estate in January 1940. But only in May 1940, when Rodd was there for a two-week holiday, did he have the leisure to appreciate it. During the war, when he was away in Africa, he looked back on these weeks with much nostalgia: 'I enjoyed the county, the family and the life as I have never done anything before. I did a great deal of manual work of all sorts. Mary and I went out and called on neighbours and the family became re-established in the home of its ancestors to the delight of the neighbours and the children.' The house needed considerable work. This was funded by a loan from Tom Catto, which Rodd managed to pay off during the war.[69]

As Rodd was getting ready to leave for Africa, he got wind of the government's intention to launch a scheme for the evacuation of children to the dominions – this following an offer of hospitality from the four dominions on 31 May 1940. The scheme was publicly launched on 20 June, through the establishment of what was called the Children's Overseas Reception Board (CORB). It proved hugely popular: in just two weeks, it had 211,448 applications before the government grew alarmed at its success and suspended it.[70] Rodd was attracted by the idea of sending daughters abroad, because of what had happened during the First World War: 'I was afraid not of bombing or even of invasion but of semistarvation. I had known too much of what happened in Europe during our blockade during the last war.' He and Mary discussed it and agreed that evacuation made sense. Their idea, the details of which were still to be worked out when Rodd left for Africa, was for their daughters to go to North America, while Mary remained behind in Britain on her own. As Rodd later explained: 'It was a bad moment. [Mary] and I thought it was right [...] I left Euston [station] to a world of adventure again in Africa and she to loneliness in England with the children in strange hands in America or Canada.'[71]

Rodd's boat to Nigeria left from Liverpool. Ahead of embarkation, he wrote to Mary from the Adelphi hotel there expressing a range of feelings – including sadness at parting and pride in his children: 'I was sad at leaving you and wishing we could have these last happy weeks [again] [...] I am well pleased with the children – thanks to you they are

---

69. Pollen, 'Mary Rennell', 17. Lilias to Rodd, 28 October 1906, Rennell of Rodd Papers, BD, Box 123/2. Rodd, Diary 1940 (written in 1942), 1–2, Rennell of Rodd Papers, BD, Box 69/1. Rodd to Mary, 7 December 1941, Rodd Family Papers, AC. Rodd bought the house from Colonel Gilbert Drage, deputy lieutenant of Herefordshire. *Radnorshire Society Transactions* 22 (1952): 29.
70. Michel Fethney, *The Absurd and the Brave: CORB – The True Account of the British Government's Evacuation of Children Overseas* (Sussex: Book Guild, 1990), 37–43, 55.
71. Rodd, Diary 1940 (written in 1942), 9–10, Rennell of Rodd Papers, BD, Box 69/1.

Figure 5.1 The Rodd. Photograph by Philip Boobbyer.

good material.' He added that he felt he had treated her harshly at times: 'You must and I think will forgive me all my hardness and unfairness to you [...] You have been very patient with me and I appreciate it.' He also confided that he had 'too many fits of lack of confidence' – another example of the insecurity he sometimes felt.[72] After they had said their goodbyes in London, Mary was initially tearful. 'I am afraid I just howled, especially as I thought the children were going without me', she explained in a letter to Rodd. After she had come to terms with Rodd's departure, she sought spiritual inspiration about what to do with the family. As she explained: 'I've really been very calm & steady & cheerful, [...] the thing I find is not to be pushed hurriedly into doing the first thing that shows, because others are frightened and [...] anxious something should be settled, but to wait until clear direction [from God] comes.' She also said that in going to Africa, Rodd was doing the 'right job'.[73]

In the event, Mary joined her daughters in going to North America. They went to the United States and not Canada, and not as part of the CORB scheme – this following an offer by the J. P. Morgan & Co. partners, Lamont and Harry Davison, to provide a home for the family for the duration of the war. Mary made her own

---

72. Rodd to Mary, 18 June 1940, Rodd Family papers, AC.
73. Mary to Rodd, 25 June 1940, Rennell of Rodd Papers, BD, Box 71/1.

arrangements to cross the Atlantic. Rodd learned all this only after reaching Lagos, from a telegram from Mary announcing the family's safe arrival in the United States, along with a couple of nephews and some friends' children. He was delighted at the news. 'I danced for joy', he recalled. He felt liberated by it: 'That telegram was a great relief. It meant I was free from worry and free to do what I could or go where I wanted with the certainty that Mary and the children would always have enough to eat even if they had to stay in America 10 years or for ever.'[74] The family based initially on Long Island, in the home of Lamont's son Thomas S. Lamont, with the children attending a Quaker school, Friends Academy, in the small city of Glen Cove.

---

74. Rodd, Diary 1940 (written in 1942), 17, Rennell of Rodd Papers, BD, Box 69/1.

Chapter Six
WEST AFRICA, 1940

Rodd left for West Africa in June 1940 with a position in military intelligence. His active involvement in intelligence can be traced to November 1938 – at that time he was accepted into the Officers' Emergency Reserve and earmarked for intelligence duties. A few months later, he was called to the War Office for a chat with Gerald Templer, a lieutenant-colonel in military intelligence responsible for training the intelligence corps.[1] Templer was answerable to Major-General Frederick Beaumont-Nesbitt, deputy director of military intelligence from August 1938 to September 1939, and thereafter director until December 1940, following the division of the Directorate of Military Operations and Intelligence into two sections. Another former Etonian, Beaumont-Nesbitt had been married to one of Rodd's cousins, Cecilia Bingham. Templer, supported by Beaumont-Nesbitt, was eager to develop plans for irregular warfare. On this, he kept in close contact with MI(R), a unit within Section D of the Secret Service, based at Station XII at Aston House near Knebworth, also working on clandestine operations. From spring 1939, MI(R) was headed by Major J. C. F. Holland, a strong supporter of covert operations. It included Holland's friend Major Colin Gubbins, author of *The Art of Guerilla Warfare* (1939) and *The Partisan Leader's Handbook* (1939) – pamphlets with which Rodd was familiar – and subsequently a key figure in the Special Operations Executive (SOE) set up in July 1940 under the umbrella of the MEW. The history of the Arab revolt was influential in these circles. Holland put Lawrence's *Seven Pillars of Wisdom* on the essential reading list for all MI(R) personnel.[2]

Following the meeting with Templer, Rodd and Haslam went on a visit to West Africa, which included visits to the Gold Coast and Nigeria. In the Gold Coast, Rodd and Haslam were received at the highest level; on arrival in Accra, they lunched with the governor Arnold Hudson at Christiansborg Castle. They also visited Achimota College, a school for educating young Africans that impressed Rodd hugely. 'It is one of the really good pieces of work in Africa and makes up for a lot of the sordidness of colonial life especially

---

1. 'Slip', 26 November 1938, WO 339/20364. Templer to Rodd, 11 January 1939, Rennell of Rodd Papers, BD, Box 61.
2. Simon Anglim, 'MI(R), G(R) and British Covert Operations 1939–42', *Intelligence and National Security* 20, no. 4 (2005): 634–35. Anglim, *Orde Wingate and the British Army*, 53. John Cloake, *Templer, Tiger of Malaya: The Life of Field Marshall Sir Gerald Templer* (London: Harrap, 1985), 67–70. On Beaumont-Nesbitt, see Michael Goodman, *The Official History of the Joint Intelligence Committee. Vol 1: From the Approach of the Second World War to the Suez Crisis* (London: Routledge, 2014), 22–28. Peter Wilkinson and Joan Bright Astley, *Gubbins and SOE* (Barnsley: Pen and Sword Military, 2010), ch. 5.

among Europeans especially on the G. Coast', he reported to Mary. Evidently, African education was a matter of interest to Rodd before the war. During the journey, Rodd was reading Lionel Curtis's *Civitas Dei: The Commonwealth of God* (1938), a book arguing for the United States to rejoin the British Commonwealth and for the United States and Britain to collaborate in forming a world government. A central figure in the network associated with Cliveden, Curtis had long been critical of the Versailles Settlement and suspicious of nationalism. The fact that Rodd was reading his book suggests that his earlier involvement in the Balliol Roundtable had had an impact on his thinking. The book no doubt fed his belief in the importance of the transatlantic alliance.[3]

There may well have been an intelligence intent behind this visit to the Gold Coast, for Rodd came away concerned by what he saw as a lack of awareness in military circles of the possible threat to Nigeria from Italian and German motorised parties arriving from the Fezzan.[4] In April 1939, Rodd contacted Beaumont-Nesbitt about this, showing him some maps of the Sahara and drawing attention to the road system in southern Libya. His long-standing interest in the caravan routes of the Sahara was now assuming a new relevance. On Beaumont-Nesbitt's invitation, Rodd then gave a talk at the War Office on military developments in North Africa. The following month, he sent Beaumont-Nesbitt an outline for the establishment of a Nigerian Defence Force, explaining the potential threat from the North coming from Axis forces were war to break out:

> If the French do not hold Tibesti, the defence of N. E. Nigeria becomes extremely difficult and [...] you will probably have to consider moving Imperial troops into Nigeria, since I have no reason to suppose that the – what I call – African Axis will be content merely with a narrow neck of land east of Lake Chad [...] In my opinion a Mobile Defence Force must be ready by the time the rains are over in September.[5]

The idea of using mobile units in a desert environment was not new. The British had had experience of this during the Anglo–Sanusi conflict in the First World War, in particular through the so-called light car patrols.[6]

Rodd's ideas on irregular warfare remained in abeyance over the next year. But on leaving the MEW, he returned to the topic. He broached with Beaumont-Nesbitt the idea of mobilising the Fezzan against Italian rule. He was fortunate that his thinking slotted naturally into the MI(R) programme then being developed by Holland. This programme was given impetus by the evacuation of forces from Dunkirk between 26 May and 4 June 1940. After Dunkirk, there was a renewal of interest in covert operations, in view of the difficulty of defeating the Germans in battle. Rodd fitted the profile of people

---

3. Rodd to Mary, 29 January and 9 February 1939, Rodd Family Papers, AC. Lavin, *From Empire to Commonwealth*, 273. Rose, *Cliveden Set*, 185.
4. Rodd, Diary 1940 (written in 1942), 5, Rennell of Rodd Papers, BD, Box 69/1.
5. Rodd to Ingram, 27 April 1939; Rodd to Beaumont-Nesbitt, 15 April 1939 (postscript), 9 and 12 May 1939, Rennell of Rodd Papers, BD, Box 61. Rodd, *People of the Veil*, 32.
6. Syrett, *The Eyes of the Desert Rats*, ch. 2.

being recruited – Holland tended to avoid recruiting regular officers for MI(R), preferring instead to draw in people from the ranks or reserves or civilian life. MI(R) was active in promoting covert operations in the Middle East and Africa, through a sub-branch based in Cairo, called G(R), which was attached to the general staff at GHQ Middle East. The most famous of these was the one led by Orde Wingate in Gojjum, Ethiopia; Wingate inherited an already existing operation there applying Gubbins's ideas. It tended to attract independent, adventurous personalities. MI(R) was dissolved in October 1940, with some of its personnel being transferred to the SOE, while G(R) remained within GHQ Middle East.[7]

Impressed with Rodd's ideas, Beaumont-Nesbitt arranged for him to be given an appointment in MI(R), as GSO III in the Middle East, with the formal cover title of acting captain in the Royal Artillery. In the days before leaving for Africa, he read through the War Office files on irregular operations in Africa, noting that there was a lack of expertise concerning central North Africa and little contact between Middle East command and West Africa. Rodd's initial instructions were to go to the Middle East overland from Casablanca and report on the state of mind of the French in Morocco and French West Africa, passing through Nigeria on the way. He left with Cairo his intended final destination. He was due to report to the head of MI(R) there, Lieutenant-Colonel Adrian Simpson. But on the way out – reading Joseph Conrad and relearning Arabic – Rodd met Bernard Bourdillon, returning to his post as governor in Nigeria. A decisive, reform-minded figure, Bourdillon was to be an important figure in the evolution of Rodd's wartime career, both for his intellectual influence and for the way he encouraged Rodd's activities. They met the governors of Sierra Leone and the Gold Coast en route, before reaching Lagos on 7 July.[8]

On reaching Nigeria, Rodd's remit quickly evolved. A couple of days after his arrival, he reported to Holland on conversations he had had with the British governors in West Africa, as well as the commander-in-chief of the South Atlantic: 'There is plenty of scope for [an] M.I.R. section in Nigeria for intelligence and other purposes beyond Nigerian frontiers but officers must have a first class knowledge of French.'[9] Rodd offered to start an organisation in Nigeria. The Directorate of Military Intelligence agreed to this. He was told to stay on in Lagos pending further instructions, rather than travel to the Middle East. Rodd was thrilled. He reported to Mary: 'I have now had definite instructions to stay here to do exactly what I wanted for so many years to do.' With this development, his formal role changed; he was now made GSO III West Africa Forces, residing in Nigeria, with the remit to act as intelligence officer for Accra as well.[10] The War Office initially suggested Rodd become Bourdillon's advisor on paramilitary affairs, pending his taking

---

7. Anglim, 'MI(R), G(R) and British Covert Operations 1939–42', 635, 640. *Orde Wingate and the British Army*, 102, 107–12.
8. Rodd, Diary 1940 (written in 1942), 15, Rennell of Rodd Papers, BD, Box 69/1.
9. Governor to Secretary of State, Telegram 709, 9 July 1940, Rennell of Rodd Papers, BD, Box 69/1.
10. Rodd, Diary 1940 (written in 1942), 17, Rennell of Rodd Papers, BD, Box 69/1. Rodd to Mary, 19 July 1940, Rodd Family Papers, AC.

on the coordination of all such activities in West Africa. But Rodd told Holland that he did not think this practicable, because it ran counter to the necessity of maintaining a close contact between intelligence officers and the governors and officers commanding troops in each colony. While a liaison officer at GHQ could help with the distribution of equipment and information, immediate control of paramilitary operations needed to be localised in each colony.[11]

In a paper of 20 July titled 'Para-Military Activity', Rodd outlined the kind of intelligence service he had in mind for Nigeria. He distinguished between internal and external work. In regard to the former, he called for preparations for a possible enemy attack on Nigeria. Noting that instructions had already been sent out to create local defence units, he explained that he wanted to see small groups forming to create guerrilla activities or administer operations. In his *Art of Guerilla Warfare*, Gubbins had emphasised the importance of choosing leaders with standing in their locality and with the necessary qualities of personality.[12] There were echoes of this in Rodd's paper. He thought local Europeans already on the spot would be ideal, but some of them would need training: 'The sort of persons I have in mind would be men who like living in the bush, who have done a good deal of shooting and who like living with natives.' As regards external threats to Nigeria, he envisaged paramilitary activity being divided into two categories: operations and intelligence. The nature of the former would depend on events on the ground, he noted. But, in the meantime, intelligence work was essential. He suggested the creation of a 'trans-frontier intelligence service'. Here Rodd emphasised the potential value of his own contacts in the region. 'There are certain personal contacts that I wish to make and resume', he said, adding that he wanted to 'exert such political influence as may be possible'.[13]

There was some suspicion of Rodd's activities from General George Giffard, who arrived in West Africa at the same time as Rodd to take on the role of GOC West Africa Forces, with his base in Accra. Giffard was sceptical about the value of paramilitary activities, as he was also about the Free French movement. He was frustrated that Rodd, while formally a captain in the Royal Artillery, was in practice a civilian answerable to the Directorate of Military Intelligence and MI(R).[14] In some ways, the formal authority of the army presented the same problem for Rodd as did the Foreign Office – it confined him. Rodd acknowledged as such in a letter to Mary a couple of years later: 'I came [to Africa] as a Captain and left the Army soon afterwards. I should have had an almighty row had I remained [...] in the army and would probably still have been a Captain or court-martialled.'[15] Rodd's project for setting up an intelligence network went ahead

---

11. Secretary of State to governor (telegram), 11 July 1940, governor to Secretary of State (telegram), 19 July 1940, Rennell of Rodd Papers, BD, Box 69/1. Secretary of State for colonies to governor of Nigeria (telegram), 11 July 1940 (78), WO 208/52.
12. Colin Gubbins, *The Art of Guerilla Warfare* (London: MI(R), 1939), 7.
13. Rodd, 'Para-Military Activity', 20 July 1940, Rennell of Rodd Papers, BD, Box 69/1.
14. Robert Pearce, *Sir Bernard Bourdillon Biography of a Twentieth Century Colonialist* (Oxford: Kensal Press, 1987), 292. Rodd, Diary 1940 (written in 1942), 19, Rennell of Rodd Papers, BD, Box 69/1.
15. Rodd to Mary, 7 November 1942, Rodd Family Papers, AC.

in spite of Giffard's scepticism. After discussion between the Colonial Office and War Office, a sum of £1,000 was allocated to the work from the colonial government budget, charged to military expenditure.[16]

Rodd thought much depended on obtaining adequate equipment from Britain or the United States. He alerted Holland to the lack of equipment available. He sought to use his links forged through the Morgan network. Jack Morgan's son, Harry, had informed Rodd that he could send him sub-machine guns and revolvers. Rodd asked Holland to arrange the shipment, with the payment to be charged through Morgan Grenfell. Concurrently, he floated with Catto the idea of creating a direct supply system between the United States and the West African coast – noting that the United States was no further from West Africa than the UK.[17] In the event, it did not prove feasible to get the material from the United States. But in mid-July, the Directorate of Military Intelligence arranged for Rodd to get a tonne of high explosive and ancillary devices, with 300 pistols to follow.[18] He also got some money from G(R).[19]

Shortly after his arrival in Lagos, Bourdillon sent Rodd off to Porto Novo in Dahomey (now Benin), with Reginald Taylor from the Public Works Department, to discuss communications and economic matters with French Governor Armand Annet. It was a tense moment in British–French relations because the Vichy government had just broken off diplomatic relations with London, following the British attack on the French naval base at Mers-el-Kébir on 3 July. Rodd was depressed by the news, as he explained to Mary: 'When one starts shooting at one's allies one has got to near the end of all decencies.' But he added: 'I do not doubt that we were obliged to do so.'[20] The trip to Dahomey was essentially a fact-finding one, but it had as an undeclared aim research into the political allegiances of the colony. Rodd found Annet 'charming but non-committal', bristling at any hints of British threats to the French colonies while insisting that he was strongly opposed to Italian or German aggression. Privately some of Annet's officials talked of a possible coup d'état in favour of the British. As well as visiting Porto Novo, Rodd visited Badagri, the former slave-trading port, and then the capital, the commercial city of Cotonou, where he had an extended conversation with the president of the Chamber of Commerce.[21]

The intelligence organisation Rodd set up in Nigeria had a centre in Lagos to cover the Dahomey border from the south of Niger to the sea and the Spanish island of Fernando Po,

---

16. Secretary of State to governor, 22 July 1940, Rennell of Rodd Papers, BD, Box 69/1.
17. Governor to Secretary of State (telegram), 13 and 19 July 1940, Rennell of Rodd Papers, BD, Box 69/1. Rodd to Catto, 20 July 1940, Morgan Grenfell Papers, DBBAR 001, File 006.00.
18. London to Lagos, Telegram 82436, mid-July, Rennell of Rodd Papers, BD, Box 69/1.
19. Rodd, Diary 1940 (written in 1942), 17, Rennell of Rodd Papers, BD, Box 69/1. Anglim, 'MI(R), G(R) and British Covert Operations 1939–42', 635, 640.
20. Rodd to Mary, 6 July 1940, Rodd Family Papers, AC.
21. Rodd, Diary 1940 (written in 1942), 24–25, Rennell of Rodd Papers, BD, Box 69/1. Governor of Nigeria (Bourdillon), cypher telegram (88), 16 July 1940, WO 208/52. For Rodd's summary of the visit to Dahomey, see his letter to Bourdillon (governor), 16 July 1940, Rennell of Rodd Papers, BD, Box 69/1.

and a centre in Kano to monitor Nigeria's northern borders from Chad across to Niger and beyond. The Lagos centre was tasked with the coordination and dissemination of intelligence. In practice, this meant the distribution of a weekly intelligence summary.[22] The man responsible for the Kano operation was district officer Bryan Sharwood Smith, who in the post-war era became governor-general of Northern Nigeria. The Lagos centre was run by J. G. C. Allen, a district officer from eastern Nigeria; Allen was for a time chief of military intelligence in Nigeria before working for a year as liaison officer with the Free French general Philippe Leclerc.[23] On Sharwood Smith's suggestion, the base for the Kano operation was 'Gidan Shettima', a large two-storied house not far from the emir's palace, which had previously been used as a rest house by the British resident there and earlier as the base for the Bornu emissary at the Kano court. It was a place where northern agents could come and go without suspicion. Rodd had visited Kano in both 1922 and 1927, and he loved being back there. 'My goodness this is a lovely place', he wrote to Mary, noting that the walls, gables and houses of the city were of red earth – 'redder than Burnt Sienna, not as pink as Indian Red'.[24]

The coverage of the Kano office was vast; the border area it oversaw was close to 1,000 miles in length, to a depth of 200–500 miles. For 10 days or so each month, the Kano team toured the border areas. Part of their work was to evaluate Vichy opinion in Niger.[25] The whole project gave Rodd an opportunity to re-engage with his former connections and rediscover the area. He learned that T'ekhmedin was still alive. He brought in 'Arab', who had been with him on the 1927 expedition, to work at the Kano office. On one occasion, he went to see the emir of Katsina to ask for his help. In practice, he was travelling so much that he was rarely in Kano himself; but when he was there, he was drawn into propaganda work with French officers coming over from Zinder.[26]

Rodd's thinking was often directed towards the situation in Chad. The decision on 26 August 1940 by the governor of Chad, Felix Eboué, to come out in support of de Gaulle was an important moment in the North African war, because it sparked a series of uprisings in favour of the Free French. On 27 August, forces under Leclerc seized control of Cameroon. The following day in French Equatorial Africa, there was a Free French coup in Brazzaville under the leadership of General Edgard de Larminat. Free French forces also took control in Bangui, capital of the Oubangui–Chari region of the country (now known as Central African Republic) – although the allegiance of the French garrison there remained confused. At this point, momentum was moving towards the Free French. But the failed raid on Dakar, from 23 to 25 September, brought an end to that.[27]

---

22. Rodd to director of military intelligence, 3 October 1940, Rennell of Rodd Papers, BD, Box 69/1.
23. J. G. C. Allen, 'Nigerian Panorama', 156, J. G. C. Allen Papers, BD, Mss Afr. s. 1551.
24. Rodd to Mary, 10 August 1940, Rodd Family Papers, AC.
25. Bryan Sharwood Smith, *'But Always as Friends': Northern Nigeria and the Cameroons, 1921–1957* (London: George, Allen and Unwin, 1969), 132–35.
26. Rodd, Diary 1940 (written in 1942), 29, 37; Rodd to H. U. Richards, 14 August 1940, Rennell of Rodd Papers, BD, 69/1.
27. Rodd, Diary 1940 (written in 1942), 48, Rennell of Rodd Papers, BD, Box 69/1.

Rodd considered Chad of great importance. Shortly after Eboué had declared for de Gaulle, Rodd met the veteran imperial expert Lord Hailey passing through Lagos en route to Leopoldville (now Kinshasa). Hailey had been sent out with the agenda of identifying Belgian goods for purchase to keep the economy of the Belgian Congo going, as well as with the broader aim of keeping the colony on the Allied side.[28] At this point, Hailey recorded Rodd as 'pressing on all quarters the great strategic importance of Fort Lamy'.[29] Rodd got up to the Chadian capital himself on 16 September, keeping his agenda secret from Giffard. He was there for just under a week, meeting many of the main military and civil authorities in the colony, as well as all the military officers of the garrison. He was struck by the fact that not all the French were supportive of Eboué. While Rodd was in Fort Lamy, he concocted a plan for gathering intelligence in the Fezzan and set up a private code for communications between Sharwood Smith and Captain de Guillebon, an officer who was later Leclerc's chief of staff. Rodd envisaged working with de Guillebon on G(R) operations.[30]

Concurrently, Rodd was monitoring events in Niger, where there was also restiveness from late August. The office in Kano was at the centre of trying to organise a coup in the country – with preparations far advanced. 'At any time during the first fortnight in September a coup could have been achieved [in Niger]', he recalled. One suggestion on the British side was that, if the garrison at Zinder remained loyal to Vichy, other parts of Niger could be encouraged to rebel – in particular the region around the Kawar cliffs and the eastern city of N'Guigmi. It was thought that Agadez might follow their lead.[31] In Fort Lamy, Rodd sought backing for a coup among possible supporters, including the influential Corsican officer commanding troops, Colonel Camille d'Ornano. But he found a lack of initiative. By the third week of September, the 'psychological moment' had passed. The failure of the raid on Dakar then made a coup out of the question.[32] Rodd was scathing about the Dakar raid. Recalling the event a couple of years later, he described it as a 'shocking story of incompetence, intrigue and mismanagement' and a 'stunt' by Churchill and his friends, Desmond Morton and Edward Spears.[33]

Rodd came to the conclusion that momentum was a vital factor in the success or failure of any movement. Summarising events in the early autumn, he wrote: '[I said] of the Free French movement in Africa that unless it snowballed it would probably stop and die. In such a movement success breeds success. A failure can be retrieved by immediate

---

28. Bruce Fetter, 'Changing War Aims: Central Africa's Role, 1940–41, as Seen from Léopoldville', *African Affairs* 87, no. 348 (1988): 382. See also E. J. Joint, 'The First Year of the War: Summary of Events at Leopoldville/Brazzaville', 1 November 1940, 1–10, FO 371/26328 C186/7/4.
29. Lord Hailey, Diary, 31 August–1 September 1940, Lord Hailey Papers, BD, Mss, Afr. s. 73.
30. Rodd, 'September and October in AEF', handwritten; Diary 1940 (written in 1942), 43, Rennell of Rodd Papers, BD, Box 69/1.
31. Sharwood-Smith, points discussed with brigadier, 2/3 September 1940, Rennell of Rodd Papers, BD, Box 69/1.
32. Rodd, 'September and October in AEF', handwritten, 6–7. On plans for Niger, see S.S. to Rodd, 18 September 1940; Richards to Rodd, 17 September 1940; Rodd's note from Kano office, 13 September 1940, Rennell of Rodd Papers, BD, Box 69/1.
33. Rodd, Diary 1940 (written in 1942), 46, Rennell of Rodd Papers, BD, Box 69/1.

action and another success: the one fatal thing is inaction.' In his view, a better outcome would have been achieved if, following the coup in Brazzaville, the movement had adopted a more modest strategy – a policy that had been recommended by Bourdillon and Free French politician René Pleven: 'The extension of the movement from [French Equatorial Africa] outward as had been advocated by René Pleven and the Governor of Nigeria was the safer ground since each minor success made the next following one more certain.'[34] Rodd had himself joined Bourdillon in counselling caution; they suggested a step-by-step approach to encouraging Vichy defectors, akin to the 'tache d'huile' (oil stain) strategy deployed by French general and administrator Hubert Lyautey in his conquest of Morocco before 1914.[35] Lyautey's significance in French colonial history was well known in British geographical circles; hence, Rodd's reference to him is not a surprise. In 1921, Lyautey had been awarded honorary membership of the RGS, and ten years later, he visited the RGS in person. When he died in 1935, Percy Cox, president of the RGS, likened him to Lord Cromer.[36]

Rodd's long-standing connection with Bagnold became important during his visit to Fort Lamy. In early 1939, Rodd had prompted Bagnold to approach the War Office with the idea of applying the techniques of self-contained long-distance desert travel to meet the possible threat of Italian raids from Libya across French territory into Northern Nigeria.[37] Nothing came of it at that time. Bagnold was called into active service in August 1939. But en route to a posting in Kenya, he stopped in Egypt, where his presence came to the attention of Wavell, who had been long interested in mechanised guerrilla warfare. Wavell had Bagnold reassigned to 7th Armoured Division. Bagnold's ideas prompted Wavell first in November 1939 and then again in January 1940 to propose the idea forming small mobile units to operate inside Libya. Initially, there was nervousness about provoking the Italians. But after Italy came into the war, these ideas assumed renewed relevance.[38] The Long Range Patrol, which turned into the LRDG, began to take shape in summer 1940.

Simpson wrote to Rodd at the beginning of October 1940, alerting him to the emerging plan to deploy small motorised units.[39] Bagnold suggested a meeting in Fort Lamy between Rodd, representatives of GHQ Middle East and the Free French. He was conscious of Rodd's long-standing conviction that Kano was vulnerable to Italian forces coming from the Fezzan – even if they were on camels. According to Rodd, the camel raiders of the northern Tuareg were the finest raiders in North Africa, and their traditional raiding ground was in the direction of Nigeria.[40] The idea of using animal

---

34. Rodd, 'September and October in AEF', handwritten, 6–7, Rennell of Rodd Papers, BD, Box 69/1.
35. Rodd, Diary 1940 (written in 1942), 46, Rennell of Rodd Papers, BD, Box 69/1.
36. Percy Cox, Address at AGM, 24 June 1935, *Geographical Journal* 86, no. 2 (1935): 89.
37. R. A. Bagnold, C. 12: War Diary and Narrative LRDG, ch. 1, 'Formation of the Long Range Patrols', 1, Ralph Bagnold Papers, CCC.
38. Syrett, *Eyes of the Desert Rats*, ch. 3.
39. Simpson to Rodd, 1 September 1940, Rennell of Rodd Papers, BD, Box 69/1.
40. R. A. Bagnold, 'Occupation of Kufra', 14 October 1940, 1, 3, C.12, ch. 3, Appendix 5, Ralph Bagnold Papers, CCC. H. W. Wynter, 'The History of the Long Range Desert Group (June

transport in the desert was still taken seriously in some quarters. As late as the spring of 1940, a division of horsed cavalry was sent to the Middle East.[41]

Rodd was not able to go to Fort Lamy. But Bagnold flew to the city on 31 October, where he linked up with Eboué and d'Ornano. Together they talked through the details of what, if Rodd's accounts are correct, had originally been Rodd's own idea. Bagnold's plan involved attacking Italian forces in Gatrun and Murzuk in the Fezzan. A few months later, in January 1941, the raid on Murzuk took place, headed by Pat Clayton. At the time of the operation, Rodd wrote to Mary explaining that the initial plan had been his: 'My plan has been accepted and is in full execution. I am disappointed that I have not yet succeeded in seeing my own baby.'[42] A couple of years later, he wrote:

> The direct outcome of my conversations at Fort Lamy was the joint plan led by Bagnold[,] who came on a visit to Fort Lamy[,] of the raid on the Fezzan in January 1941 with his Long Range Desert Patrol. With a few French officers and supplies sent to the place I had proposed they raided Gatrun, Tedjerri and Murzuk itself.[43]

Rodd felt personally vindicated by what Bagnold had achieved: 'The raid proved what I had always maintained[,] that long range motor patrols were possible and extremely annoying to the enemy.'[44] All this suggests that Rodd played a significant role in conceptualising this important episode in the history of the LRDG.

In the run-up to the raid, Rodd was in regular touch with Simpson in Cairo. He supplied Simpson with details about the roads going south from Libya into Chad and Niger, north of the Tibesti mountains, including the route between Murzuk and the Tummo pass on the Libya–Niger border, which was the route the raiders took after leaving Murzuk.[45] He and Simpson also exchanged messages about how to mobilise Sanusi opinion, especially in Tripolitania; Sayyid Idris, now in Cairo, had remained loyal to the British, but many Arabs in Tripolitania had been influenced by the fact that they thought an Axis victory more likely. 'These Tripolitans will play but need stirring up', Rodd told Simpson.[46] In this context, Rodd sought to get the support of Ahmed Seif en Nasr – half-brother of the Cairo-based Abd el Galil en Nasr – for the struggle against the Italians; Abd el Galil en Nasr had been a key opponent of Graziani's takeover of Libya in the 1920s. Through Simpson, he arranged for letters of encouragement to be sent from Sayyid Idris and Abd el Galil en Nasr to mobilise Tripolitanian resistance.[47] Abd el Galil

---

1940–March 1943)', *Special Forces in the Desert War 1940–1943* (London: National Archives, 2008), 14–15, 30–31.
41. Syrett, *Eyes of the Desert Rats*, ch. 2.
42. Rodd to Mary, 19 January 1941, Rodd Family Papers, AC.
43. Rodd, Diary 1940 (written in 1942), 44, Rennell of Rodd Papers, BD, Box 69/1.
44. Ibid.
45. Rodd to Simpson, letter and attachments, 1 November 1940, Rennell of Rodd Papers, BD, Box 69/1.
46. Rodd to Simpson, 23 September 1940, Rennell of Rodd Papers, BD, Box 69/1.
47. Rodd, Diary 1940 (written in 1942), 43; Stephen Longrigg to Rodd, 22 October 1940, Rennell of Rodd Papers, BD, Box 69/1.

en Nasr took part in the Murzuk raid. Rodd was himself offered the services of Sayyid Idris's cousin, Safi al Din, as a guerrilla fighter.[48]

Rodd's trip to Fort Lamy turned out to be a turning point in his wartime career. At this moment, he could have gone to Tibesti to explore the possibility of fomenting unrest in the northern part of Niger. If he had done so, he would almost certainly have become more involved in guerrilla activities. But his career now took a different turn. On returning to Lagos, he got involved in discussions about how to help the new Free French government in French Equatorial Africa. After the coup in Brazzaville, de Larminat found himself in a difficult situation; he was particularly short of administrative support, since most of the French senior officers had left. In addition, many business people had not backed the coup, so economic advice was much needed. With Bourdillon's support, Rodd flew to Leopoldville on 27 September, bringing Pleven with him in his plane. Rodd knew Pleven from Tuesday Club dinners; Pleven had been a director of Anglo–Canadian Telephones before the war. Rodd then visited Brazzaville to assess the economic situation there, in the company of Frederick Pedler, assistant to Hailey.[49] He concluded that de Larminat needed his own economic advisor. de Larminat wanted to avoid any sense of being subservient to the interests of Leopoldville; so having his own advisor, even if the person was British, appealed to him. Rodd brought de Larminat back to Lagos for negotiations.

On the journey back to Lagos, de Larminat took the opportunity to review troops at Bangui, Fort Archambault and Fort Lamy – the Free French cause still needed careful shepherding. The route was chosen so as to avoid direct flights by the sea route and over Gabon because of concerns about fuel capacity, but it was a demanding journey. They encountered a major storm outside Bangui on the Ubangi river, where they were forced to fly along the river but under the cloud, with the result that they were 'skimming the tree tops'. 'It was very frightening as we only just ran out of the storm a few minutes before reaching Bangui', Rodd recalled.[50] It was an example of how the natural environment, always of great interest to Rodd, suddenly made itself felt in the midst of the business of war. The Congo swamp intrigued him. He told Mary it was 'the foulest, nastiest thing' he had ever seen; but he also found it 'rather fascinating'.[51]

Rodd and de Larminat arrived in Lagos to discover that de Gaulle was himself soon to arrive. Rodd was present for the first of the meetings between the two French generals and claimed credit for their encounter: 'Things worked out well because within an hour of our arrival in Lagos, an announcement of de Gaulle's arrival there two days later came. I had been largely instrumental in bringing about their first meeting at Gov't House Lagos with my friend the Governor as sponsor.'[52] The meetings proved difficult; Rodd

---

48. Telegram to DMI, 15 October 1940; Rodd to DMI, n.d., handwritten summary of message from Simpson to Rodd, Rennell of Rodd Papers, BD, 69/1.
49. Frederick Pedler, Diary, 29 September 1940, BD, Afr. s 1814/18. Eric Jennings, *Free French Africa in World War II* (Cambridge: Cambridge University Press, 2015), 21.
50. Rodd, 'Return Journey from Leopoldville to Lagos', Rennell of Rodd Papers, BD, Box 81.
51. Rodd to Mary, 9 November 1940, Rodd Family Papers, AC. Rodd, Diary 1940 (written in 1942), 61, Rennell of Rodd Papers, BD, Box 69/1.
52. Rodd to Mary, 9 November 1940, Rodd Family Papers, AC.

reported to Bourdillon that they were 'not very satisfactory', noting that the fact that de Larminat had succeeded in Brazzaville, while de Gaulle had failed at Dakar, made things awkward.[53] But a working relationship between the two men was established.

The obvious person to fulfil the role of advisor to de Larminat was Rodd himself. Whether he immediately saw himself in the role is not clear, but de Larminat certainly thought him credible. On 2 October, Bourdillon telegraphed London to explain that he thought Rodd could meet this need: 'De Larminat has asked that Rodd should be head of economic mission and wishes to take him back to Brazzaville day after tomorrow. [Giffard] is willing to spare Rodd and in fact agrees with me that his qualifications are largely wasted in his present job. I am therefore anticipating your approval and sending Rodd with de Larminat.'[54] Rodd's banking background meant there was an obvious logic to his taking on the role. His old friend, Gerard Clauson, working at the Colonial Office, had already suggested to him that he get involved in economic issues in Africa.[55] The upshot was that Rodd went back to Brazzaville with de Larminat, with the initial intention of his being there for six months.[56] Over the next few months, he did the round trip to Leopoldville five times: four on planes of various sorts – usually a Lockheed – and one by flying boat.[57]

This new role did not bring Rodd's MI(R) work to an end, even though the work of setting up an intelligence network in Nigeria was largely completed by early October. As he explained to Beaumont-Nesbitt, the economic aspect of the mission in French Equatorial Africa had the advantage of serving as 'cover' for his plans for MI(R) work in southern Libya. It also enabled him to keep an eye on the Free French in the colony.[58] But Rodd was ambivalent about the fact that the new role took him further away from the desert; he had flown to Chad in September to 'lay a trail for the desert', he reported to Mary.[59] In mid-October, he wrote to Bourdillon explaining why he did not want to stay in Lagos working with him. 'I would willingly work with you if life with you were not so safe and so comfortable', he said. He continued that if he went north – and thus became more involved in the desert war – he would have the opportunity of being 'hungry, thirsty and [...] scragged'. 'Scragged' was a slang expression meaning something like 'beaten or broken'.[60] This would suggest that war for Rodd functioned in some ways as a place for testing a kind of heroic self-image or ideal of masculinity. It came with an ideal of what constituted a courageous person; to be a man was to be exposed to physical danger.[61]

---

53. Rodd, 'Since I Wrote to You' and 'September and October in AEF', Rennell of Rodd Papers, BD, Box 69/1.
54. Bourdillon, cypher telegram, 2 October 1940, BE, OV100/12.
55. Clauson to Rodd, 20 August 1940, Rennell of Rodd Papers, BD, Box 69/1.
56. Hailey, Diary, 23 October, Lord Hailey Papers, Mss, Afr.s. 73, BD.
57. Rodd to Mary, 9 November 1940, Rodd Family Papers, AC.
58. Rodd to Beaumont-Nesbitt, 3 October 1940, Rennell of Rodd Papers, BD, Box 69/1.
59. Rodd to Mary, 9 November 1940, Rodd Family Papers, AC.
60. Rodd to Bourdillon, 14 October 1940, Rennell of Rodd Papers, BD, Box 69/1.
61. See on this theme Dawson, *Soldier Heroes*, ch. 1. Juliette Pattinson, 'Fantasies of the "Soldier Hero": Frustrations of the Jedburghs', in Linsey Robb and Juliette Pattinson (eds), *Men, Masculinities and Male Culture in the Second World War* (London: Palgrave Macmillan, 2018), 25–46.

Rodd was also worried that he was having an easy life by comparison with that of people back home. In September, a few days after the start of the German bombing campaign against Britain, his mother had written to him saying that civilians were being 'slaughtered by the thousand'. He was 'unhappy in his conscience' at being in no danger while Britain was being bombed, he told Mary.[62]

The central Sahara continued to have a deep emotional appeal for Rodd. This was evident from a couple of letters he wrote to Mary after he returned to London at the end of the year. There had been some discussion about his becoming involved in the follow-up to the raid on Murzuk. In mentioning this to Mary, he talked of the remote Sahara as the 'Land of Heart's Desire': 'Then came a request for me to go to the Land of Heart's Desire on the job which I had worked out to be done.' A few days later, he used the same phrase in the plural – 'Lands of Heart's Desire'.[63] In using these phrases, Rodd may have been alluding to the play by W. B. Yeats, *Land of Heart's Desire* (1894/1912), a work recounting the story of a new bride, Mary, lured away from her family and religion by fairies to a place apart. There was also a Hebridean song of that title associated with folklorist Marjory Kennedy-Fraser.[64] If the exact influence is hard to ascertain, it is reasonable to think that Rodd was in some way projecting onto the North African landscape and world images and feelings associated with Celtic culture. The precise location Rodd associated with this image is not clear, but it was probably some combination of Niger, southern Libya (perhaps the Fezzan) and Chad – including some places he had visited but also areas which for him were still tantalisingly out of reach.

American landscape writer J. B. Jackson found from his experience – he was involved in the Sicilian campaign – that armies tended to look at landscapes purely from the point of view of how they might help or hinder the achievement of military objectives.[65] Rodd's experience was different – perhaps partly for the reason that, after he left the Western Front in early 1916, he was never exposed to the heat of battle, and also because his wartime roles did not involve a direct engagement with the battlefield. Here we can see that even in planning MI(R) operations, the terrain he was thinking about appealed to him at a psychological level. It suggests that there was a strong emotional dimension to his politicomilitary activities which was not specific to the war itself. In the end, Rodd felt a moral duty calling him to the work with de Larminat. He told Mary that, while he had not gone to Africa to be involved in economics and finance, he had offered to do it because it was the 'right thing to do'.[66] Talking in terms of an ethical imperative would have appealed to Mary.

---

62. Lilias to Rodd, 11 September 1940, Rennell of Rodd Papers, BD, Box 71/1. Rodd to Mary, 22 November 1940, Rodd Family Papers, AC.
63. Rodd to Mary, 19 and 27 January 1941, Rodd Family Papers, AC.
64. See W. B. Yeats, *The Land of Heart's Desire; The Countess Cathleen* (London: T. Fisher Unwin, 1925). On Kennedy Fraser, see J. L. Campbell, 'Fraser, Marjory Kennedy (1857–1930), folklorist', *Oxford Dictionary of National Biography* (Oxford: Oxford University Press, 2004).
65. John Brinckerhoff Jackson, 'Landscape as Seen by the Military', *Discovering the Vernacular Landscape* (New Haven: Yale University Press, 1984), 133.
66. Rodd to Mary, 9 November 1940, Rodd Family Papers, AC.

In the following weeks, Rodd spent a lot of time in the company of de Larminat and Pleven, a fact which put him in a good position to monitor public opinion in French Equatorial Africa in the weeks before de Gaulle's arrival there on 24 October. He sometimes saw de Larminat several times a day. 'The more I see of him the better quality I think he is', he wrote of him. He indicated that de Larminat and Pleven were uncertain of what to make of de Gaulle and, at the same time, unsure as to British intentions towards the Free French; Pleven had even speculated as to whether Dakar had been a way of the British trying to get rid of de Gaulle.[67] In general, Rodd thought that the transition to Free French rule in Brazzaville was shakier than outsiders realised. His perspective coincides with the view of historian Eric Jennings that the Free French takeover of the colony was 'messier, less unanimous and less predetermined' than most testimonies allow.[68] Before de Gaulle's arrival, Rodd was gloomy. In a letter to Bourdillon in mid-October, he even declared that the Free French movement had failed. He was conscious of the effectiveness of the anti-British propaganda being put out by Pierre Boisson, the Pétainist governor-general of French West Africa.[69]

Rodd's relationship with de Gaulle is not known to historians.[70] His early impressions of the French general were not positive. He was present when de Gaulle flew into Brazzaville, and thought him rude when he refused to be introduced to the many French officials there to welcome him. Three days later, in a speech announcing the creation of the Committee for the Defence of a Free France, de Gaulle claimed legislative powers over French territories and the right to negotiate directly with the United States. Rodd, Hailey reports, was 'greatly concerned' on both points.[71] But Rodd warmed to the French leader in the following weeks. He had at least two serious conversations with him. The focus of these were Rodd's ideas for advancing the war into Libya from Chad. They had a discussion on 1 November, during which Rodd offered to get directly involved with the Free French movement. de Gaulle responded with some enthusiasm. Rodd reported to Simpson:

> I have had [de Gaulle's] permission to continue discussing these matters, and have further had his promise that as soon as H. M. G. will release me from financial and economic duties here, he will attach me to the O. C. Troops, Chad Territories for the work I have in mind. He went into some detail on ways and means, and was apparently delighted at the prospect of being able to use some of his mobile forces for this purpose.[72]

---

67. Rodd, 'Since I Wrote to You' and 'September and October in AEF', Rennell of Rodd Papers, BD, Box 69/1.
68. Jennings, *Free French Africa in World War II*, 18.
69. Rodd to Bourdillon, 14 October 1940; Rodd to Woolley, 11 October 1940, Rennell of Rodd Papers, BD, 69/1.
70. I mention their relationship in 'Lord Rennell, Chief of AMGOT', 308. But most of the detail here is new.
71. Hailey, Diary, 24 and 27 October 1940, Lord Hailey Papers, BD, Mss, Afr.s. 73. For De Gaulle's ordinances, see his *War Memoirs: The Call to Honour, 1940–42. Documents*, 1 (London: Collins, 1955), 46–48.
72. Rodd to Simpson, 1 November 1940, Rennell of Rodd Papers, BD, Box 69/1.

But Rodd went on to say that he doubted the readiness of French troops to do this; he argued that it would be better to use a combination of Camel Corps and some irregulars. He stressed that the recent meeting between Hitler and Pétain – the two men had met at Montoire on 24 October – gave these possibilities added relevance; Nigeria remained vulnerable to incursions from the North. His interest in camels came into play here; he remarked that some areas of potential activity were easily accessible only by camel.[73]

At a subsequent meeting on 13 November, de Gaulle was more circumspect, insisting that since Chad – the proposed base of operations – was under his authority, it could only become involved with the war in Libya through a direct approach from the British government. Rodd wrote to Bourdillon:

> All this is very odd and awkward. I think myself it represents the direct reaction of what some of us have foreseen in the man – the reaction against what he regards as tutelage. He is trying to establish in any way he can that he is an independent sovereign state whose alliances and cooperation can be enlisted, but who will not be ordered about; the more people tell him what to do the more strongly he reacts.[74]

He added, however, that he had the permission of both de Gaulle and de Larminat to join a French Camel Corps unit if he wished. Rodd's previous involvement with the Camel Corps, the méharistes, during his 1922 expedition seems to have persuaded de Gaulle of his suitability. As he explained separately to Beaumont-Nesbitt: 'I have secured de Gaulle's consent for joining a French unit as a French officer if necessary in the north [...] [This] was only given because I happen to be as you probably know an honorary corporal in the méharistes; also because I think he likes me personally.'[75]

Separately Rodd wrote to Mary explaining that he found de Gaulle articulate and interesting, if bad-mannered and lacking a sense of humour. The Gaullist vision attracted him. It appealed to the idealist in him. He saw in it an example of a movement driven by ideas: 'The Free French movement is interesting and worthwhile. De Gaulle is a remarkable man. I think the *idea* is gaining ground, and it is only ideas which are going to succeed in this world.' But he thought that ideological convictions needed to be genuine and not means to ends: 'If we do not [believe in our ideas], we risk resorting to expedient after expedient and people will not sacrifice themselves for expedients.'[76]

Rodd's relationship with de Gaulle was not lastingly smooth. Towards the end of his time in Brazzaville, Rodd had a seeming rebuff from him, in connection with his activities as an economic advisor. Already in November – as Hailey reports in his diary – de Gaulle had expressed a concern about whether British financial proposals for the Free French colonies might interfere with him 'as a sovereign state'. This issue came into focus again in December. Rodd had proposed that the British government purchase products from French Equatorial Africa – even some which it did not need – with the aim of

---

73. Ibid.
74. Rodd to Bourdillon, 14 November 1940, Rennell of Rodd Papers, BD, Box 69/1.
75. Ibid.; Rodd to Beaumont-Nesbitt, November 1940, Rennell of Rodd Papers, BD, Box 69/1.
76. Rodd to Mary, 9 November and 3 December 1940, Rodd Family Papers, AC.

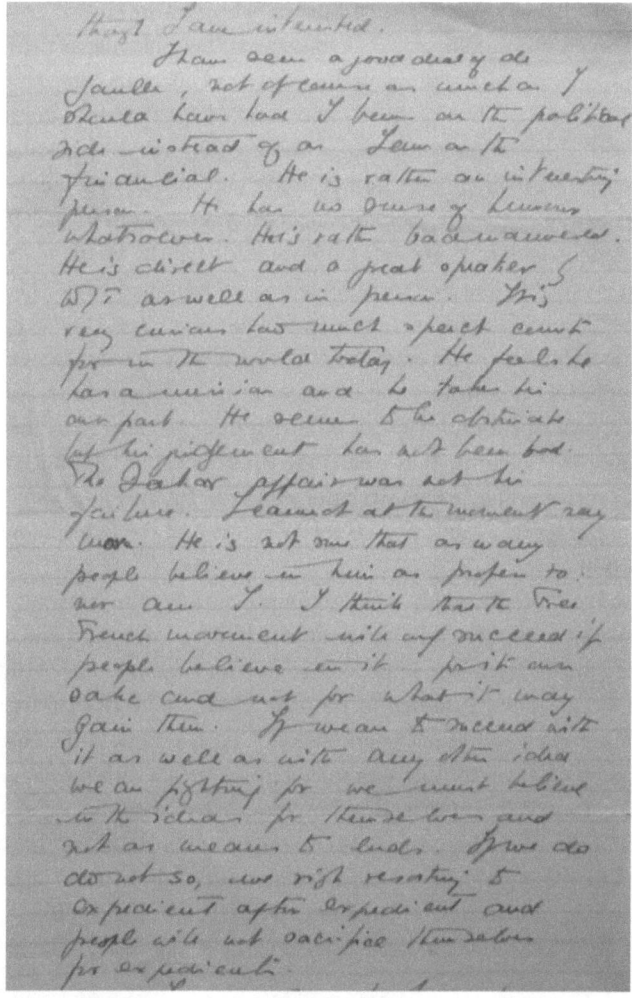

Figure 6.1 Rodd on Charles de Gaulle, extract from letter to Mary, 9 November 1940. Rodd Family Papers.

allowing the country to keep its own gold reserves intact as security for its currency. de Gaulle then intervened to stress that all negotiations of this kind had to be made between his own organisation and the British government, and that French Equatorial Africa could not enter into such negotiations on its own. This greatly annoyed de Larminat and Pleven. An underlying problem, Hailey explained in his diary, was that there had been an 'unpleasant slur' on Rodd to the effect that he had a 'private interest' in what was being proposed – which was that 'his' firm (Morgan Grenfell) might ultimately benefit from the agreement.[77]

---

77. Hailey, Diary, 8 November and 10 December 1940, Lord Hailey Papers, BD, Mss, Afr.s. 73.

The source of the slur was Edward Spears, who was in charge of British liaison with the Free French movement. Spears had come to Leopoldville as part of the British military mission to Brazzaville, following the failure at Dakar. In conversation with head of the mission, Colonel Williams, Spears had cited de Gaulle as saying that, in associating himself with the economic aspects of the Free French movement in Brazzaville, Rodd had been seeking to advantage himself and the firm with which he was connected. Rodd, who was extremely agitated by this suggestion, was annoyed that Spears had not discussed this directly with him. He wanted Bourdillon to take up the matter in London. Hailey thought it possible that Spears himself had undermined Rodd. Pleven suspected that this was so.[78] There was certainly some tension between Rodd and Spears. Rodd was suspicious of the military mission from the outset, probably because he was worried that the size of it might hint at a British ambition for control. Hailey was also sceptical about it, although in practice he found it less of a burden than he expected. This he attributed to the personality of Williams. It is clear that Rodd became involved in some of the internal politics surrounding Spears's relationship with the mission; Hailey reports that he became a 'useful lever' against Spears for Williams and the British consul-general in Brazzaville, Robert Parr.[79]

Lord Hailey rated Rodd highly. His first impression of him had not been positive; when they first met in August, Hailey described him as 'an intelligent man of rather queer manners'. But he found he improved greatly on acquaintance. Most of the time, Rodd lived in Leopoldville in order to be near Hailey. The two of them sometimes went for walks together and made good friends.[80] At the same time, Rodd sometimes felt lacking in people to talk to. Life was spiced up by meals with colleagues at the local pensione 'Paula'; in mid-November, Rodd hosted a party there for many of the British representatives in the city. There were also moments when Rodd was bored, in spite of his hectic schedule. Perhaps for this reason, he attempted a little trade of his own. He set up a business selling oysters from the coastal city of Pointe Noire. 'If everyone doesn't get poisoned I shall sell them for hard currency', he explained to David Waley at the Treasury.[81]

The British attempt to woo France's African territories by means of economic assistance had been well under way before Rodd even came to Brazzaville. Already on 4 August 1940 Churchill had given de Gaulle a promise of economic support for the French colonies, so long as they were in alliance with Britain. Throughout August,

---

78. Rodd, Secret and Personal, telegram to BE, sent by Bourdillon to Secretary of State, Rennell of Rodd Papers, BD, Box 69/1. Lord Hailey Diary, 10 December 1940, Lord Hailey Papers, BD, Mss, Afr.s. 73. Pedler, Diary, 17 December 1940, BD, Mss Afr.s 1814/18.
79. Rodd to Bourdillon, 14 October 1940, Rennell of Rodd Papers, BD, Box 69/1. Hailey, Diary, 7 and 19 December, Lord Hailey Papers, Mss Afr.s. 73, BD.
80. Hailey, Diary, 31 August–1 September, 12–13, Lord Hailey Papers, BD, MSS Afr. s 731. Rodd to parents, 22 November 1940, Rennell of Rodd Papers, BD, Box 32.
81. Pedler, Diary, 14 November 1940, BD, Mss Afr.s 1814/18. Rodd to 'Sigi' (David Waley), 22 November 1940, Rennell of Rodd Papers, BD, Box 69/1.

negotiations took place between Britain and Chad in the light of the possibility of Chad coming over to the British side. A particular challenge was to help the country acquire enough pounds sterling to purchase imports. In mid-August, the British promised to buy Chadian goods, through Nigerian banks, in pounds sterling. There is no doubt that all this fed into Eboué's decision to back the Free French. After the coup, the British government undertook to make every effort to purchase stocks of cotton and other goods from Chad.[82]

When Rodd became de Larminat's advisor, he set about trying to find money for the regime in Brazzaville. He had some success with this. Towards the end of September, 434,000 francs was secured on Hailey's personal guarantee. Rodd and Pedler often worked together. On 5 October, the two went over to Brazzaville with the news that £150,000 had been credited to the country through a local national bank, Banque Afrique Orientale. In the end, it was agreed that the British would make a monthly contribution of £200,000.[83] Rodd's responsibilities in Brazzaville also involved managing cotton purchases. He and Pleven worked out a scheme for financing the cotton crop by using government credit. Rodd took the view that French Equatorial Africa, rather than the British government, should buy unsold goods, because that would mean less in the way of profits being siphoned into private accounts. But, although the British government gave money to subsidise imports, importers were slow to react. At times, Rodd found communicating with London frustrating; in his diary, Pedler mentioned an occasion in mid-October when Rodd drafted a 'long telegraphic scream' to London on the subject of cotton stocks, which he and Hailey had to tone down.[84] One of the problems they faced was finding currency to pay for soldiers and administrators, in places with only a rudimentary banking service. Rodd and de Larminat decided to issue new bank notes of large denominations. In order to satisfy local banking regulations, these were kept in vaults, thus allowing smaller notes and change to be released for circulation.[85]

Rodd was aware of the fragility of the Free French movement and eager to avoid putting excessive pressure on the Brazzaville regime. This was one of the factors in his mind when discussions took place about turning the Banque Afrique Orientale into the Central Bank of the Free French African territories. This idea was backed by the Foreign Office. A proposal was drafted suggesting a board of directors, seven French and two British, under the authority of de Gaulle and his representative working alongside a smaller consultative committee in London with majority English participation. The challenge was to help the Free French establish themselves economically, without giving the impression

---

82. Jennings, *Free French Africa in World War II*, 23–24. Report on Negotiations for an Agreement between Chad and Britain, approved 31 August and 3 September, 1, Rennell of Rodd Papers, BD, Box 69/1.
83. Pedler, Diary, 5 October 1940, Frederick Pedler Papers, BD, Mss Afr.s 1814/18. Jennings, *Free French Africa in World War II*, 21.
84. Hailey, Diary, 19 and 30 October 1940, Lord Hailey Papers, BD, Mss, Afr.s. 73. Pedler, Diary, 21 and 29 October 1940, Frederick Pedler Papers, BD, Mss Afr.s 1814/18.
85. P. M. H. Bell, *Britain and the Fall of France* (Farnborough: Saxon House, 1974), 222–23.

that they were being controlled from London. While, in general, supportive of the idea, Rodd thought there was a lack of personnel available for such an important operation. Moreover, he thought that a new issue of notes known to be pegged to sterling, arising out of the formation of such a bank, could destabilise the economy.[86] Back in London in early 1941, he made similar arguments. He suggested that the time was not ripe for the centralisation of economic control of the Free French colonies in London in case the movement found itself developing under another French leader. The implication was that it would be better for French Equatorial Africa to retain control of its gold reserves, rather than make them available to the wider movement. For the time being, it was better to keep the affairs of each individual colony ad hoc.[87] For all of his support for de Gaulle, then, Rodd thought that it was not clear how events were going to unfold.

By late November, Rodd had come to the conclusion that his role as an advisor in French Equatorial Africa could be interpreted as indicating a British desire for control over the territory; he thought a more diplomatic form of rendering advice would be preferable.[88] Hailey had also concluded that his role needed a rethink; in his mind, too much depended on the good working relationship existing between him and Rodd: 'My personal relations with Rodd enable us to be of mutual assistance to each other in economic matters but this will continue only so long as we are both here.' His suggestion was for a more integrated system in which an ambassador was appointed to oversee both territories, with his own financial advisor, with consul-generals allocated separately to each.[89] By December, Rodd was eager to leave. His work with de Larminat meant that, from 11 November, he had been a representative of the Treasury and Bank of England in Brazzaville rather than under the authority of the army. Knowing this, Williams and Parr wrote to the Bank of England suggesting he have a 'roving commission' to the Free French movement: 'Rodd's abilities of judgment and known faith and enthusiasm for [the] cause should not be lost to the Free French movement at this stage.' He had the 'entire confidence' of everyone there, they declared.[90] Rodd himself had noticed how the people around him treated him with respect. In one letter to Mary, he commented that, although he was a captain surrounded by colonels and generals, the latter treated him as if he were senior in rank.[91] But nothing came of the idea of expanding his role. He returned to Britain to spend Christmas 1940 with his parents.

---

86. See FO telegram to Joint, 24 October 1940, and Rodd's note, No. 390, 2 November 1940, BE, OV 100/12.
87. Meeting at the Colonial Office, 3 January 1941; telegram to Parr, 6 January 1941, BE, OV 100/12.
88. Rodd, cited in Parr to Secretary of State, 22 November 1940, Rennell of Rodd Papers, BD, Box 69/1.
89. Hailey, 24 November 1940, BE, OV 100/12.
90. Telegram, 11 November 1940, Rennell of Rodd Papers, BD, Box 69/1. Williams to Bank of England, 10 December 1940, BE, OV 100/12.
91. Rodd to Mary, 9 November 1940, Rodd Family Papers, AC.

Chapter Seven

EAST AFRICA IN TRANSITION

The war in Africa saw some major developments in late 1940. Italy had joined the Axis powers with an ambition to dominate the Mediterranean. It seized British Somaliland in August 1940 and then invaded Egypt from Libya the following month. But, by the end of the year, the momentum had shifted. On 6 December 1940, Italian-run Cyrenaica fell to Wavell's forces. Wavell telegraphed the War Office asking for guidance on the administration of occupied Italian colonies. The fall of Eritrea and Ethiopia in April 1941 expanded the set of challenges confronting him. Initially, the British government considered the possibility of permitting the continuance of Italian rule in Eritrea and Somalia, and even thought of returning Eritrea to Italian rule after the war. But the rapid collapse of Italian rule in Cyrenaica and Italian East Africa meant that other plans had to be considered. For the time being, Wavell suggested that military government be established in the Italian colonies, with Cyrenaica, Eritrea and Somalia being administered on a 'care and maintenance basis' in line with the Hague Convention of 1907.[1] Ethiopia was a special case because of the return to the country of its emperor Haile Selassie.

Some of these questions were discussed at a meeting at the War Office on 30 January 1941. The meeting was chaired by Frederick Bovenschen, soon to be permanent undersecretary at the War Office, and attended by representatives of the Foreign, Colonial and India Offices. At the meeting and a War Cabinet meeting three weeks later, it was decided that the newly conquered territories should be administered by the War Office. The Foreign Office did not have experience of this kind of work, and to give responsibility to the Colonial Office would imply that the new territories might be incorporated into the empire. An interdepartmental committee was set up in March to give advice on these matters to the Secretary of State for War. The work itself was assigned to the Directorate of Military Operations – which was part of the general staff. The Directorate was designated MO11. The plan was to use the form of military government adopted by Allenby in Palestine during the First World War, which was for the commander-in-chief to govern through political officers especially appointed for the work.[2]

---

1. Saul Kelly, 'Desert Conquests: Early British Planning on the Future of the Italian Colonies, June 1940–September 1943', *Middle Eastern Studies* 50, no. 6 (2014): 1009.
2. Lord Rennell of Rodd, *British Military Administration of Occupied Territories in Africa During the Years 1941–47* (London: HMSO, 1948), 368. Interview with Rennell, 24 April 1969, BE, ADM 33/25. F. S. V. Donnison, *Civil Affairs and Military Government: Central Organization and Planning* (London: HMSO, 1966), 23–25. Frost, *Enigmatic Proconsul*, 118–19.

Following the War Office meeting, a political branch headquarters was set up in Cairo. The man to be appointed Wavell's chief political officer was Philip Mitchell, governor of Uganda and deputy chairman of the East African Governors' Conference. Mitchell was tasked with overseeing the whole structure, with deputy chief political officers being assigned to individual territories under him. The commander-in-chief, initially Wavell, delegated his authority to Mitchell in all matters relating to the administration of the territories. The idea was to appoint alongside Mitchell a controller of finance and accounts (CFA) and a chief legal officer. Rodd would find his next role here.

The structure that Mitchell ran was known initially as the Occupied Enemy Territory Administration (OETA). The word 'Enemy' was removed from this in summer 1941 to make the shorter Occupied Territory Administration (OTA). The change of name was because Ethiopia, although occupied, was friendly to the British, and British Somaliland, not an enemy territory, had been reconquered from the Italians. Mitchell envisaged OETA operating as a form of high commission for a group of territories. As Rodd explained, this meant that the organisation formed at headquarters came to resemble more the Indian than the colonial system of government. Mitchell's general approach was to leave all authority with the heads of local administrations while reserving certain matters for control from the headquarters. In early 1943, military administrations were renamed 'civil affairs administrations', with the word 'political' being replaced with the term 'civil affairs' to accommodate US thinking and planning. The terms 'chief political officer' and 'political branch' became 'chief civil affairs officer' and 'civil affairs branch'. But in Italy, following the Allied invasion, the term 'Allied military government' was used instead of 'civil affairs administration'.[3]

Following his return from West Africa, Rodd still hankered after an involvement in the desert war. There was an initial plan for him to fly out for work in this sphere on 17 January 1941. But his place on the plane was commandeered, and he stayed on in London for a few weeks. The result was that he was drawn back into finance and administration. Robert Haining, vice chief of the Imperial General Staff, saw him on at least a couple of occasions and steered him in this direction. Haining was dismissive of his desire to be involved in fighting the Italians. At a meeting on 7 February 1941, he mooted the idea of Rodd becoming financial advisor to Wavell, stating that he would be suitable for the role because he was familiar with the 'military point of view'. Rodd did not commit immediately. He left London for Cairo on 12 February, at which point there was still the possibility of his becoming involved in Wavell's advances west of Cyrenaica. Wavell wanted him to work as a liaison officer establishing links between a French Camel Corps group operating in Tibesti and the LRDG.[4] But, just before his departure, John Dill, chief of the Imperial General Staff, sent Wavell a telegram about the finance role

---

3. Rennell, *British Military Administration of Occupied Territories in Africa During the Years 1941–43* (London: HMSO, 1945), 4–5, 7, 312. Frost, *Enigmatic Proconsul*, 118–19.
4. Rodd to Catto, 9 February 1941, Morgan Grenfell Papers, DBBAR 001, File 006.00. G. McDonald to G. H. Thompson, 10 February 1941. Record Details for F. J. R. Rodd, Forces War Records, Army. Rennell, *British Military Administration in Africa 1941–47*, 347.

stating: 'Am advised most suitable man would be Rodd [...] but that he will certainly quarrel with Mitchell.' Wavell talked through the matter with Mitchell, explaining that Rodd was able and well qualified, but difficult. He knew Rodd from the previous war: he had met him while working for the EEF.[5] Mitchell agreed to take Rodd, on condition that he could show him the telegram – believing that this would start off their relationship on the right footing. Their first meeting took place on 22 February, and Mitchell was open with Rodd about how it came about. The conversation went well; Mitchell wrote in his diary: 'I have no doubt that we shall get on well if [Rodd] takes it.'[6] This he did, starting on 24 February, in the role of CFA and with the rank of colonel.

The structure of OETA underwent a number of changes over the next year. Cairo was its initial centre. The first military administration was set up in Cyrenaica, but then Cyrenaica was evacuated in April 1941. At the same time, the British occupation of Ethiopia, Eritrea and British Somaliland pushed the centre of gravity of its actions towards East Africa. To take this into account, Mitchell moved his office to Nairobi, where there was a stronger administrative infrastructure.[7] In autumn 1941, East Africa command became independent of Middle East command, but with Mitchell remaining chief political officer for the whole operation. From February 1942, a more formal division between Cairo and Nairobi took place. It was decided that there should be two political branches, in Cairo and Nairobi, with different chief political officers acting in the Libyan and East African areas through local military administrators. Rodd's rank had been raised to that of brigadier in October 1941, but when the functions of the CFA were divided in February 1942, the grading was again reduced to colonel. When the Cairo and Nairobi offices were divided, Rodd moved back to Cairo to be CFA north, formally accountable to Ralph Hone, the former attorney general of Uganda appointed chief political officer north. Eritrea was transferred from East Africa command to the responsibility of the Middle East in February 1942.[8]

There was huge pressure on Mitchell and his team, for their work meant bringing civil administration into large territories under military occupation at great speed. From the outset, Rodd was faced with building up a work from a very small base. A key challenge was shortage of personnel. Initially, he had no staff to work with, with the exception of one assistant. It was not until 19 April 1941 that the man appointed OETA's accountant general, P. W. Adshead, took up his post. It took a year for an adequate cohort of accounting officers to be established. In a report of September 1941, written for General Claude Auchinleck – who took over from Wavell at the end of June 1941 – Mitchell explained that Rodd had been practically single-handed at headquarters until the beginning of June, and that the way he had dealt with all the issues was 'beyond praise'. In mid-April 1941, the political branch of GHQ Middle East itself consisted of

---

5. See Rodd to his father, 9 September 1917, Rennell of Rodd Papers, BD, Box 64.
6. Philip Mitchell, *African Afterthoughts* (London: Hutchinson, 1954), 199. Philip Mitchell, Diary, 22 February 1941, Philip Mitchell Papers, BD, Mss Afr.r. 101.
7. Rennell, *British Military Administration in Africa 1941–47*, 1, 25, 57, 295.
8. Rennell, *British Military Administration in Africa 1941–47*, 37; *British Military Administration in Africa during the Years 1941–43*, 6.

only nine officers, plus three administrators of other ranks and six stenographers and clerks. In September 1941, the total number of staff available for the administration of Eritrea, Ethiopia, British Somaliland and Italian Somaliland was only 270.[9] Rodd often deputised for Mitchell when he was away. In these circumstances, as he explained to Lamont, he was effectively 'acting governor or high commissioner' for a 'parish' of 10–12 million native Africans and some 120,000 Italians and other prisoners of war.[10]

Rodd had a range of reactions to the challenges facing him. On the one hand, he was excited. He told Mary: 'I have got a job which is big enough for me to be all out.' But he also found it stretching work: 'I am appalled at the magnitude of the job I have and a terrible insufficiency in personnel to deal with it.'[11] The size of the task caused Bourdillon to write in September: 'I do not envy you your job, nor Mitchell his – making bricks without straw would be child's play in comparison.'[12] In the early stages, just ensuring adequate food supplies was difficult, and he was dependent for this on the army. In early June 1941, he wrote – with a sense of urgency – to General Alan Cunningham, who was responsible for Middle East command, asking: 'Will your force in Ethiopia be able to supply OETA relief foods, i.e. buy them, despatch them and carry them? [...] I haven't got the personnel. I haven't got the transport.' He and Cunningham established a good working relationship. When Cunningham was moved to a post in the 8th Army in August 1941, he wrote to Rodd saying his association with him would be 'outstanding and long-treasured'.[13]

OETA's tasks required a lot of improvisation. While there were existing principles to guide the British in their approach to military government, they had no textbook to tell them what to do. Each occupied country was different, and occupation itself went through different phases. In notes issued in 1942 under the authority of the commander-in-chief, Middle East command, which were based on the experience of 1941–42, it was observed that three phases were evident: the period of active military operations; the period of defence against aggression, external or internal; and the period in which government could be established permanently under a chief administrator.[14]

In this fluid environment, much depended on the good working relationship between individuals. As Mitchell had predicted, he and Rodd got on well. In September, Rodd told Mary that he 'liked' Mitchell and that they had not had 'one difference of opinion' over any issues. Together with Hone, they formed an effective triumvirate with – in Mitchell's words – an 'almost uncanny mutual understanding'.[15] As a kind of 'executive

---

9. Report of CPO (Mitchell) to Auchinleck, until 15 September 1941, 15, CAB 106/356. Rennell, *British Military Administration in Africa 1941–47*, 39, 354.
10. Rodd to Lamont, 17 September 1941, Thomas Lamont Papers, BK, Box 112/12.
11. Rodd to Mary, 11 and 29 July 1941, Rodd Family Papers, AC.
12. Bourdillon to Rodd, 10 September 1941, Rennell of Rodd Papers, BD, Box 69/2.
13. Rodd to Cunningham, 5 June 1941; Cunningham to Rodd, 27 August 1941, Rennell of Rodd Papers, BD, Box 69/2.
14. Rennell, *British Military Administration in Africa 1941–43*, 3–4; *British Military Administration in Africa 1941–47*, 566.
15. Rodd to Mary, 24 July 1940, Rodd Family Papers, AC. Mitchell, *African Afterthoughts*, 199.

council', they oversaw all branches of government between them. Rodd's remit came to involve not only finance, currency and banking affairs, but also economic matters, supply, commerce, public works, transport, agriculture and public health. Good personal relations sometimes compensated for structural weaknesses. In a report that Rodd wrote in 1943 for Lieutenant-General William Platt – who was in charge of East Africa command – he suggested that the division of the OTA structure in February 1942 had been a mistake, but that the situation had been ameliorated by the good working relationship between Mitchell, Hone and himself.[16] In April 1943, Rodd observed: 'With administrations such as we have built up there is a very large personal element in the absence of tradition. That personal element surrounded the originators Philip Mitchell, Ralph Hone and myself.'[17] The fluidity of the wartime situation, coupled with the fact that major responsibilities were devolved onto a few people, meant that Rodd had a lot of power – which he enjoyed. '[The folks in London] leave me very much alone and have never done anything but support what I have advocated', he told Mary in September 1941.[18]

In January 1945, an article appeared in *The Times* claiming that the British had not lost their 'genius for government', paying tribute to the way in which Mitchell, Rodd and Hone had been able to adapt military government to local circumstances. Exactly who wrote this – and indeed whether or not any one of Mitchell, Rodd and Hone had input into the article – is not clear. But the emphasis on the importance of adapting to circumstances accurately reflected the pragmatic culture of OETA/OTA. Rodd told Mary he was proud of what they achieved: 'We had no precedent to work on and builded [sic] empirically. But we builded [sic] well with scarce human material and have achieved the aims that were set without famine[,] distress or disorder.'[19]

Rodd's role meant that he was financial advisor to Mitchell and other members of the commander-in-chief's staff for all financial questions relating to the occupied territories, excluding military matters. The accounts of the occupied territories, alongside the administration of the territories and the organisation at general headquarters, came within his sphere of responsibility. In each territory, a deputy CFA was appointed, answerable to the deputy CPO. Once military operations came to an end, these deputies were appointed military administrators with additional delegated powers. To begin with, some of Rodd's funds came from the chief paymasters of the commands, but it was intended, as far as possible, to keep the financial side of civil administration separate from the finances of the military. Once the structure was operating properly, it was overseen by an accounting officer within the War Office. Budgets were prepared in the different territories and then submitted through Rodd to the War Office for its approval.

---

16. Rennell to Platt, report for 1 May–31 December 1942, 30, Maurice Lush Papers, IWM, Box 2/5.2. Rennell, *British Military Administration in Africa 1941–43*, 7; *British Military Administration in Africa 1941–47*, 312.
17. Rodd to Mary, 13 April 1943, Rodd Family Papers, AC.
18. Rodd to Mary, 2 September 1941, Rodd Family Papers, AC.
19. 'African Achievement', *Times*, 31 January 1945, 5. Rodd to Mary, 31 March 1943, Rodd Family Papers, AC.

Figure 7.1 Rodd (front left) sitting alongside Philip Mitchell, Nairobi, c. 1941. From Bodleian Library, Rennell of Rodd Papers.

Accounts were internally audited by the chief accountant within OETA/OTA and also subject to external audit by the officer in charge of the Exchequer and Audit Department in Cairo.[20]

Currency policy was one of the biggest issues facing Rodd. This had been on the agenda of the War Office meeting on 30 January – which Rodd attended, along with other staff from the Bank of England and the Treasury, including Keynes. The idea emerging out of the meeting, which Rodd supported, was that Britain would not fix or raise the Italian lira, but let it deteriorate. Here, as Rodd subsequently explained, British thinking was influenced by what had happened in Palestine and Mesopotamia during the previous war. Funds which had then been paid out by the British administration had come to replace the Turkish currency, without the resort to an exchange of currencies or the formal withdrawal of the Turkish currency. It was hoped that a similar process might work in Italian Africa.[21] Rodd summarised the British approach to the lira as follows:

---

20. Rennell, *British Military Administration in Africa 1941–47*, 355.
21. Report of CFA (Rennell) to Auchinleck, until 15 September 1941, 1, 4, CAB 106/357. Rodd, draft letter to Stephen Longrigg, May 1942, Rennell of Rodd Papers, BD, Box 73. Rennell, *British Military Administration in Africa 1941–47*, ch. 15.

To refuse to stand behind the Italian lira and make it exchangeable in terms of our money: to let it depreciate if it wanted to, to vanishing point, but only to let that happen slowly so as not to hit too many people [...]: to substitute our own currency as we wanted to spend money and use it for commerce between the occupied territories and the outside world: to keep people and the territories going at as small a cost as possible to HMG: to make the cost of things to the army as cheap as possible: and finally to prevent starvation, riot and conditions generally which obliged us to keep more than the minimum number of troops in the country.[22]

The lira policy was summed up in succinct form by one of Rodd's deputies: 'Don't take in lira unless you have to: Don't pay it out if you take it in: Don't accumulate lira.'[23] The aim was as far as possible to avoid valorising the Italian currency in any form.

One reason for this approach was that the British did not have their own stocks of lire or a means of acquiring them. The British had been told prior to the occupation of Ethiopia that large note reserves of Italian lire had been destroyed – probably because the Italians imagined that the British would depend on using Italian currency. But there was uncertainty as to whether this had actually happened and over the quantity of surviving notes. The worry was, as Rodd explained to Auchinleck, that if larger denominations were accepted, there would be a tendency for all public money to be in the form of lire and all hoarding in the form of East African and other currencies. In this context, Rodd wanted a policy which only permitted the official use of four main currencies in Italian East Africa: rupees, Maria Theresa dollars, East African currency and Egyptian currency. Italian coinage and small notes were also permitted, but larger notes only in exceptional circumstances.[24] The policy of allowing for a gradual decline in the Italian financial system also applied to banks. Italian banks were allowed to reopen but on condition of them only permitting limited withdrawals. They were, moreover, prohibited from taking in money in non-lira currencies, except in Mogadishu. Concurrently, branches of Barclays Bank were opened in Asmara, Addis Ababa and elsewhere, where people could open accounts in non-lira currencies. The Italian banks were eventually closed down after Haile Selassie took over, with their staff and assets being transferred to Asmara.[25]

In practice, the currency policy was a cause of some division in OETA/OTA, particularly in connection with events in Eritrea. It also brought into focus questions around the extent of Rodd's remit. Rodd insisted that deputy controllers of banks in occupied territories were directly accountable to him rather than to his own deputies in the territories – the aim being to ensure that no discretion was permitted on matters relating to currency, banking and exchange. But in Eritrea, where the deputy CPO was Brian Kennedy-Cooke, this did not go down well. Rodd's policy was not adhered to in the weeks up until the end of June 1941, and lire continued to be used; higher-denomination

---

22. Rodd, draft letter to Stephen Longrigg, May 1942, 4, Rennell of Rodd Papers, BD, Box 72.
23. Brian Kennedy-Cooke, cited in Rodd, draft letter to Stephen Longrigg, May 1942, 11, Rennell of Rodd Papers, BD, Box 72.
24. Report of CFA (Rennell) to Auchinleck, until 15 September 1941, 4–8, CAB 106/357.
25. Report of CPO (Mitchell) to Auchinleck, until 15 September 1941, 26, CAB 106/356. Rennell, *British Military Administration in Africa 1941–43*, 9.

lire continued to be taken in and, in some cases, paid out.[26] Rodd officially attributed this to 'kindness of heart' on the part of the administration in Eritrea, but he was frustrated. He thought a tough approach to currency issues was vital because of the imperative to operate in the 'context of the whole': having different policies in different territories could only lead to destabilisation.[27] Mitchell was also concerned. He reported to Auchinleck that the failure to stick with the agreed policy had helped to stimulate inflation, which, in combination with the decline in the availability of consumer goods and the expenditure by British forces of large sums in Egyptian currency, had led to economic and financial problems of 'great difficulty'.[28]

Rodd remained worried about the situation in Eritrea well into 1942. In January 1942, he told P. J. Grigg, permanent undersecretary at the War Office, that there was 'no goodwill' in carrying out the financial policy as laid down, and a lack of effective financial oversight for enterprises in the colony.[29] In relation to the latter, Rodd's concerns were connected with the formation of what was called the 'Eritrean Projects Scheme'. This was an idea for making Eritrea a hub for commercial activity in the Middle East, which would bring together British and US enterprises. The scheme, originating in October 1941, was directed from March 1942 by an Eritrean Projects Board, which held 45 meetings in the first four months of its existence. Rodd thought the whole idea ill-conceived. In a typical trenchant manner, he explained his concerns in a paper titled 'The Eritrean Projects Scheme or Why Grow Bananas in Greenland if You Don't Have To'. Too much was envisaged for Eritrea, he declared. He also questioned the colony's suitability for the scheme in regard to water, food, climate and internal communications.[30]

Kennedy-Cooke was replaced as deputy chief political officer in Eritrea in summer 1942 by Stephen Longrigg, who had had experience of the same job in Cyrenaica. But ahead of this, in the winter of 1941–42, Kennedy-Cooke took his grievances about Rodd to Oliver Lyttelton in Cairo. An old friend of Churchill, Lyttelton had been made minister of state for the Middle East in June 1941 and appointed to the War Cabinet. Rodd picked up gossip that Lyttelton was hostile to him.[31] Part of the problem, according to Rodd, was that Kennedy-Cooke did not accept Mitchell's, and hence his own, authority and had been claiming to the Cairo office that the financial management of Eritrea from Nairobi – where Rodd was then based – had been unhelpful: 'The representations that were made in Cairo undoubtedly had the effect of suggesting that Nairobi in general and the CFA in particular were obstructive and tiresome people.' In recounting all this to Grigg, Rodd emphasised that, far from being too intrusive, Nairobi had in fact been too

---

26. Report of CFA (Rennell) to Auchinleck, until 15 September 1941, 2, CAB 106/357. See also Rodd to Grigg, summary of letter, 14 April 1941, WO 230/32.
27. Rodd, draft letter to Stephen Longrigg, May 1942, Rennell of Rodd Papers, BD, Box 72.
28. Rennell, *British Military Administration in Africa 1941–47*, 377. Report of CPO (Mitchell) to Auchinleck, until 15 September 1941, 20, CAB 106/356.
29. Rodd to Grigg, 1 January 1942, Rennell of Rodd Papers, BD, Box 69/2.
30. Rennell, 'The Eritrean Projects Scheme or Why Grow Bananas in Greenland if You Don't Have To', 24 March 1942, Rennell of Rodd Papers, BD, Box 69/2.
31. 'Buster' to Rodd, n.d., Rennell of Rodd Papers, BD, Box 69/2.

lenient. He exonerated Lyttelton himself, stating that there had been no particular reason why the statements against Rodd should not have been believed.[32] Nevertheless, he had doubts about Lyttelton's financial capabilities. He was not alone in having concerns about Lyttelton. When Lyttelton was appointed to his role, Mitchell recorded in his diary that he had been given a 'loose sort of commission to meddle, and probably muddle most things, especially OETA'. Similarly, later in the year, Haining told Rodd that Lyttelton was acting like an 'overgrown schoolboy' in the way he was intruding into issues.[33] In view of the challenges facing OETA/OTA, it was not surprising that there were sometimes differences between the central administration and the localities.

Rodd faced a different set of problems when dealing with Ethiopia. A key figure in Britain's complex negotiations with Addis Ababa was deputy CPO Maurice Lush, previously governor of the northern province of Sudan. Lush was responsible for the creation of a nucleus military administration for Ethiopia already prior to the fall of Addis Ababa. At one point, he complained to Rodd that he was trying to impose an artificial structure onto Ethiopia, stressing that the country posed a different set of problems from those of other territories:

> You cannot administratively, financially or politically hope to treat Ethiopia as an OETA proper where existing staff remain and a transitional stage only is required. Here you are trying to re-establish a Government, non-existent for 5 years and pretty inefficient before that [...] I think you have got to realise that the picture here is entirely different from that in the Somaliland or Eritrea, or in Cyrenaica when we occupied it. Do *not* for the sake of tidiness try to impose on us a system which won't work.[34]

Lush was essentially telling Rodd what Rodd himself believed – that, in setting up transitional governments, flexibility was needed.

Once Haile Selassie was back in Ethiopia, the central challenge was how to balance his desire to re-establish his rule in the country with the concerns of the commander-in-chief and the exigencies of war. The future management of Ethiopia proved the focus of a battle between the War Office and the Foreign Office. Emperor Haile Selassie returned to Addis Ababa on 5 May and immediately began pressing his claims for power to be transferred to him. For the War Office, maintaining stability in the country was paramount, especially in view of the threat posed to Egypt by forces led by German general Erwin Rommel. On the other hand, the Foreign Office was anxious to rebut potential charges of colonial intent.[35] In short, the War Office wanted to maintain some level of control in Ethiopia, pending the cessation of hostilities, while the Foreign Office wanted to accelerate the transfer of the country to the emperor.

---

32. Rodd to Grigg, 9 February 1942, Rennell of Rodd Papers, BD, Box 69/2.
33. Mitchell Diary, 14 July 1941, Philip Mitchell Papers, BD, Mss Afr.r. 101. Haining to Rodd, 31 December 1941, Rennell of Rodd Papers, BD, Box 69/2.
34. Lush to Rodd, 3 June 1941, Rennell of Rodd Papers, BD, Box 69/2.
35. Frost, *Enigmatic Proconsul*, 125.

Rodd's initial response to the fall of Ethiopia was to question whether it was right to transfer power to the emperor at all. Just a few days after the fall of Addis Ababa, he wrote to Haining making the case for keeping the defeated viceroy of Italian East Africa, Amedéo, duke of Aosta, in post. He was afraid that Haile Selassie would not be up to the job:

> We have destroyed the military power of the adversary. Having done that, have we not done enough without complicating life for ourselves and wasting our resources by trying to make Ethiopia fit for the Emperor to misgovern? [...] Why should we not now say to the Duke of Aosta: 'We are not going to stay at all. We are going to go home. On a certain day we are going to leave Addis Ababa with all our men and all our transport and you can carry on.'? I have tried out my idea on Mitchell and one or two others. They all think I am being funny. When I assure them I am serious they say it can't be done.[36]

Mitchell liked Aosta; he thought it a 'tragedy' that the British were at war with such a man. Moreover, Aosta was an anglophile who had warned the British about Mussolini even before the war. But Rodd's idea was clearly far-fetched. It reflected the fact that British administrators were somewhat daunted by some of the challenges of managing the takeover of Ethiopia.[37]

Rodd's thinking may have been influenced by the fact that the duke of Aosta and his wife were friends of his parents. Helen, duchess of Aosta, was godmother to one of Rodd's cousins, Christopher Emmet.[38] Rodd saw the duke in June 1941 and found him in a regretful frame of mind. Aosta said that before leaving for Ethiopia in April 1940, he had been told by his government that there was no danger of war between Britain and Italy in 1940 and probably not in 1941. He concluded that he had been misled and wanted Rodd's father to know this. He described the war as the 'greatest tragedy' that had ever happened to him. He thought that, as far as he and the opposing generals were concerned, it had been a 'clean war', adding that he 'forgave and understood' incidents that had taken place against him. He also warned that the expansion of the Somalis would be a problem for the British in managing Italian East Africa while offering to help sort out economic and financial difficulties. The following year, the duke died of tuberculosis in a Kenyan hospital. Rodd visited him a couple of weeks before he died. 'I am dreadfully sorry and sad', he told his mother about his death.[39]

Rodd's role meant he was closely involved in discussions about Ethiopia's future. He joined Mitchell, Wavell, Platt, Cunningham and others at a conference in Asmara on 25 and 26 June 1941, when the main lines of British policy towards Ethiopia were

---

36. Rodd to Haining, 14 April 1941, Rennell of Rodd Papers, BD, 69/2.
37. Mitchell Diary, 20 May 1941, Philip Mitchell Papers, BD, Mss Afr.r. 101. Anglim, 'MI(R), G(R) and British Covert Operations 1939–42', 636.
38. Edward W. Hanson, *The Wandering Princess: Princess Helene of France, Duchess of Aosta, 1871–1951* (Havertown: Fonthill Media, 2017), 265.
39. Rodd's notes on a conversation with Aosta, 11 June 1941, Rennell of Rodd Papers, BD, 69/2. Rodd to his mother, 4 March 1942, Rennell of Rodd Papers, BD, Box 32. Stuart-Wortley, *Life without Theory*, 150.

formulated. Their proposals involved allowing the British a major degree of control over the country pending the end of hostilities. The emperor was to be required to follow British advice or approval on matters relating to government, taxation and expenditure, and to permit continued British military operations, in return for Britain providing funding, advisors in the task of re-establishing the armed forces, and administration for the country. It was Rodd who took this framework of negotiation to Addis Ababa for further discussion.[40]

Initially, it was expected that differences between Britain and Ethiopia would be bridgeable. But the negotiations proved complicated. The British found Haile Selassie stubborn and difficult. 'The Emperor does *not* see that the *co* in co-operation applies to him and his people as much as to us', Lush remarked to Rodd.[41] The situation was made more complicated by the fact that some of Haile Selassie's confidantes, in particular his political advisor Daniel Sandford and the Foreign Office official Gilbert Mackereth, thought Mitchell wanted to create a British protectorate. Sandford and Mackereth, whose opinions were taken seriously in the Foreign Office, thought the Ethiopians well capable of managing themselves and took the side of Haile Selassie in pressing for a rapid transfer of power. The dispute came to a head at a meeting of the War Cabinet in London in November. Mitchell's line was overturned, and a swifter and more complete transfer of power endorsed. Mitchell resigned in reaction. This prompted an about-turn by the government, which changed its position to keep Mitchell on-board. Mitchell thought Eden was trying to bypass him and communicate with Ethiopia directly.[42]

Rodd was in London throughout these discussions, having returned to Britain at the end of October. He took his seat in the House of Lords for the first time on 11 November, after which he was known as Lord Rennell or Francis Rennell, rather than Francis Rodd. He was in these weeks fiercely critical of the government. In a diary entry for late November 1941, Dalton mentioned an episode in which Eden was 'indescribably rude' to Rodd, stating that this was 'most justifiable'; Rodd, he wrote, was going around London declaring that there was 'no government' in the country. Dalton went as far as to suggest that Rodd was 'an almost 18B case'. This was a reference to the defence ministry regulation '18B' permitting the internment of people suspected of being Nazi sympathisers.[43] This was clearly a melodramatic reaction. It reinforces the impression that there was an element of personal animosity between Dalton and Rodd.

The clash with Eden probably originated in the differences between the War Office and the Foreign Office over policy in the Horn. But a personal dimension cannot be ruled out in this case either. Rodd's father had previously been critical of Eden. In June 1935, as Italo–Ethiopian relations were deteriorating, Eden – who had just been made minister for League of Nations Affairs – flew to Rome to offer Italy territorial concessions in the

---

40. Rennell, *British Military Administration in Africa 1941–47*, 76.
41. Lush to Rodd, 18 September 1941, Rennell of Rodd Papers, BD, Box 69/2.
42. Frost, *Enigmatic Proconsul*, 133–35. Mitchell Diary, 19 November 1941, Philip Mitchell Papers, BD, Mss Afr.r. 101.
43. Pimlott (ed.), 28 November 1941, *The Second World War Diary of Hugh Dalton 1940–45*, 327.

Ogaden in exchange for giving Ethiopia a land corridor through British Somaliland to the port of Zeila. The idea behind this was to give Italy an inducement to stay in the League of Nations rather than become allied with Germany. But the talks did not go well, and Mussolini and Eden had a violent quarrel. Rennell Rodd, who thought the whole plan ill-conceived, told the House of Lords that there had been a lack of consultation with relevant experts about this, causing Eden to make 'errors of judgment'.[44] Just over a year later, with Eden now foreign secretary, Rennell Rodd told the House of Lords that a letter from Eden containing observations on a recent German request for negotiations had been poorly drafted in some of its details.[45] Suspicion of Eden was in the family. For his part, Eden was acutely sensitive to criticism.[46]

While in London, on 27 October 1941, Rodd was called to explain OTA policy towards Italian evacuees at an interdepartmental meeting. This was a potentially explosive issue because of the strong anti-Italian feeling in Ethiopia. In the end, some 32,000 Italians were evacuated, with frailer individuals, women and children being repatriated, but men interned in British East African territories.[47] Rodd subsequently called the evacuation process the 'largest organised evacuation under humane conditions which has been attempted during the war' and a 'complete success'.[48] He was also present at meetings of the War Cabinet Committee on Ethiopia on 5 and 21 November, at which British control over revenue and expenditure in Ethiopia was discussed. He came under pressure to justify expenditure estimates that he had put together with Lush and Sandford, which some thought excessive.[49] The conclusion reached was that, as a general principle, British grants were not to exceed what the Ethiopian government, once it was working properly, could reasonably be expected to collect on its own without a grant. In practice, this meant yearly grants on a diminishing scale from 1942 to 1945, from £1.5 million down to £250,000, with the underlying aim of bringing British responsibility for Ethiopian finance and administration to an end. Rodd was in Addis Ababa in January 1942 for the signing of the final Agreement and Military Convention, which led to the closing of the Italian banks and the transfer of Italian assets to designated Ethiopian officials.[50]

---

44. Lord Rennell, 22 July and 23 October 1935, House of Lords, Hansard. Rose, *The Cliveden Set*, 146. On this episode, see Mario Toscano, 'Eden's Mission to Rome on the Eve of the Italo–Ethiopian Conflict', in A. O. Sarkissian (ed.), *Studies in Diplomatic History and Historiography in Honour of G. P. Gooch* (London: Longmans, 1961), 126–52. Richard Lamb, *Mussolini and the British* (London: John Murray, 1997), 122–25.
45. Eden had requested elucidation on the matter of whether or not Germany was willing to abide by its treaty commitments. Rennell Rodd thought that the answer to this had already been given. Lord Rennell, 1 July 1936, House of Lords, Hansard.
46. David Dutton, 'Simon and Eden at the Foreign Office, 1931–1935', *Review of International Affairs* 20, no. 2 (1994): 35.
47. Rennell, in minutes of meeting, 27 October 1941, Rennell of Rodd Papers, BD, Box 69/2.
48. Rennell, *Listener*, 7 January 1943, 7. Rennell, *British Military Administration in Africa 1941–43*, 11.
49. See minutes of these meetings in Rennell of Rodd Papers, BD, Box 69/1. Rennell, 'Report on the Ethiopian Budget', 7 November 1941, Rennell of Rodd Papers, BD, 69/2.
50. Rennell, *British Military Administration in Africa 1941–47*, 76, 87, 91–94, 128.

Rodd was worried about the possibility of corruption in Ethiopia. In a post-war account of events, he drew attention to a particular phrase in the Agreement, which he thought too elastic to ensure adequate financial discipline: 'His Majesty the Emperor agrees that there shall be the closest co-operation between the Ethiopian authorities and his British Advisers [...] regarding public expenditure.' He remarked tersely: 'No effective control of expenditure was now envisaged.'[51] In early January 1942, he told Grigg that in all likelihood the emperor and his servants were financing themselves by 'blackmail or presents from clients seeking office or favours'. The financial and economic management of the country had been good when the British had been in charge, he said.[52] After the war, Rodd indicated that the final outcome had been a missed opportunity; Britain failed to impose a western-style financial system and left the country in the hands of a more traditional way of operating:

> An attempt to set up a western financial system by the organisation of provincial treasuries wherever British political officers were stationed in the provinces also failed since the Emperor from the outset preferred to collect whatever was possible by the older methods which had existed before the Italian occupation through local chiefs and officials without assistance from the British Military Administration.[53]

Another cause for disappointment in Rodd was the attitude of some of the Ethiopians to the British. It was, he said in one report, a matter of 'great regret' to the forces that liberated the country that so 'little gratitude' was shown to them by the Ethiopians who returned to power.[54]

Rodd was also closely involved in discussions about the so-called Reserved Areas of Ethiopia – territories which, for one reason or another, the British wanted to keep out of direct control by Addis Ababa. These were the Franco–Ethiopian railway from Addis Ababa to the French Somaliland border; a belt of Ethiopian territory 25 miles wide, adjacent to French Somaliland which was needed for the blockade of Vichy-controlled Djibouti; and the Somali-inhabited areas of eastern Ethiopia, the Haud and the Ogaden. There was considerable tension over the last of these, in particular, because of the disputed nature of the area. Haile Selassie wanted but failed to secure a British commitment to return the Haud and the Ogaden to Ethiopian rule at the end of the 1942 Agreement and Military Convention in 1944.[55] Trouble between Ethiopians and Somalis in the area to the north-east of Harar in spring 1942 was a reminder of the unstable nature of these disputed territories. A few months later, Haile Selassie pressed for the recognition of Ethiopian legal jurisdiction in the Reserved Areas. Rodd, for the sake of public order, wanted to avoid a situation in which the Ethiopians attempted to collect taxes from the Somalis. His innate pragmatism was evident in what

---

51. Ibid., 89.
52. Rodd to Grigg, 1 January 1942, Rennell of Rodd Papers, BD, Box 69/2.
53. Rennell, *British Military Administration in Africa 1941–43*, 10.
54. Rennell, *British Military Administration in Africa 1941–47*, 77.
55. Kelly, 'Desert Conquests', 1012.

ensued: 'I adopted the attitude that the theory underlying the administration of, and jurisdiction in, the Reserved Areas was less important than their practical application.' After taking legal advice, he agreed to recognise the emperor's authority in the area. But little changed in practice; the British administration continued to operate as before, and no Ethiopian forces entered the area.[56]

The British found that managing the Reserved Areas as a collective made it easier to deal with interterritorial disputes. This was facilitated by the fact that both British and Italian Somaliland came under the supervision of East Africa command. This made good sense administratively, as Rodd explained in one post-war account: 'Numerous trans-frontier problems affecting nomadic tribes transgressing former international boundaries have been treated more consistently and with greater benefit to the local population than has ever before been possible in this turbulent part of Africa.' As he also noted, the market at Jigjiga in the Reserved Areas became a meeting ground of Somalis from different places and one of the most important places in the Somali world.[57] In this context, it was not surprising that some policy-makers began to take seriously the idea of a Greater Somalia. This thought was given expression in London, from August 1943 onwards, by Viscount Hood of the Economic and Reconstruction Department.[58] Rodd was an early advocate of the idea. Moreover, he manoeuvred to make it possible. When he left East Africa, he expressed pride in the way he had protected the Reserved Areas of Ethiopia from being ruled directly from Addis Ababa. 'I succeeded in getting the reserved areas of Ethiopia consolidated so as to make possible a settlement on the basis of a Greater Somaliland', he wrote in his diary.[59] After the war, he lamented the splitting up of Somalia, remarking:

> For one brief period during the war the whole of Somaliland was under British administration [...] [But] the only large part of Africa which is radically homogeneous has again been split up into such three parts as made Caesar's Gaul the problem and the cockpit of Europe for the last two thousand years. And Somaliland will probably become a cockpit of East Africa.[60]

As well as wishing to protect the Reserved Areas from control by Addis Ababa, Rodd was opposed to the idea of Eritrea being incorporated into Ethiopia.[61]

---

56. Rennell, CPO report to Platt for 1 May–31 December 1942, 7, Maurice Lush Papers, Box 2, 5/2, IWM. See also Rennell, *British Military Administration in Africa 1941–43*, 12; *British Military Administration in Africa 1941–47*, 200.
57. Rennell, *British Military Administration in Africa 1941–43*, 16.
58. Kelly, 'Desert Conquests', 1015.
59. Rodd, Diary for 1943, 8, Rennell of Rodd Papers, BD, Box 111; *British Military Administration in Africa 1941–47*, ch. 9.
60. Gerald Reece, 'United Somalia', *Times*, 1 April 1967, 11. Reece suggests that Rodd made this point 15 years previously – that is, in 1952.
61. Rennell to the secretary of the Abyssinia Association, 2 April 1944, Rennell of Rodd Papers, BD, Box 151/3.

In addressing these issues, Rodd was consciously following in the footsteps of his father: Rennell Rodd had grappled with the same boundary questions in 1897. Rennell Rodd died on 26 July 1941, in a troubled state of mind over what appeared to be the collapse of his life's work in Italy and Greece.[62] On hearing of his father's passing, Rodd wrote to his mother: 'I am in some sense completing what he began out here and in the way he would have wanted it. The same lines I am trying to follow because taught in that school.'[63] After the war, he was eager to defend his father's legacy. Writing in the *Guardian* in 1955, he rejected suggestions that the Somalis had got a raw deal in the 1897 agreement by countering that in reality the British had prevented the Ethiopians from taking over Somali territory; he said that the British had remained true to their obligations to the Somalis. Rodd emphasised that the agreement had been made in opposition to the French attempt to gain a sphere of influence right across Africa.[64] Rodd's two brothers were also serving in Africa at this time. At the beginning of the war, Peter had joined the Welsh guards. But he then got involved in dealing with refugees in the Horn of Africa, in the role of evacuation officer in Asmara. In this he was building on work he had done before the war – looking after Spanish refugees in Perpignan. Taffy's wartime career involved a mixture of naval responsibilities and intelligence work, which led him to becoming head of the Cairo branch of the Combined Services Detailed Interrogation Service.[65] Rodd told his mother that his father would have been proud at having his three sons serving in Africa in and around the places he knew.[66]

The Foreign Office was fearful of Ethiopian reactions to any favours being granted to the Somalis. Not surprisingly, commentators aligned to the emperor were also suspicious. This is evident from the memoirs of John H. Spencer, a historian who had advised Haile Selassie during the Abyssinian crisis and who resumed the role in 1943. Writing after the war had ended, Spencer described Mitchell, Rodd and Lush as a 'colonial group' aiming to break up the area into three sections: Ethiopia, Eritrea and the Somalias; their policy, in his view, was a bid for a British-dominated Horn with the 'Greater Somaliland Project' a key part of it. He criticised their approach on the grounds that it assumed that all the territories conquered from Italy, except for British Somaliland, were enemy territory and had to be retained under British control until a peace settlement was signed. It was, he said, a 'strategic-colonialist policy'. The policy towards the Reserved Areas was a

---

62. When Rennell Rodd died, he was president of the Anglo–Hellenic League. *Times*, 27 October 1941, 6.
63. Rodd to Lilias, 29 July 1941, Rennell of Rodd Papers, BD, Box 32. Lilias to Rodd, 5 August 1941, Rennell of Rodd Papers, BD, Box 71/1. See also Rodd to Mary, 29 July and 5 August 1941, Rodd Family Papers, AC.
64. Rennell, 'Somalis and Ethiopia: 1. How 1897 Agreement Was Made', *Manchester Guardian*, 19 December 1955, 6, 2. 'The French and Fashoda', *Manchester Guardian*, 20 December 1955, 6.
65. Peter Rodd, 'Report on the Evacuation of Italian Civilians from Ethiopia', 30 June 1942, BD, Mss. British Empire, 5360. Adrian O'Sullivan, *Espionage and Counterintelligence in Occupied Persia (Iran)* (London: Macmillan, 2015), 143.
66. Rodd to Lilias, 29 July 1941, Rennell of Rodd Papers, BD, Box 32.

key aspect of this. The fact that the January 1942 agreement retained some measure of British control meant that it was essentially a military occupation, in Spencer's mind.[67]

The British were not well prepared for the collapse of Italian East Africa. In this context, it was not surprising that in the takeover of Italian territories they frequently resorted to the mechanism of indirect rule – not through local African institutions but already established European ones. This was very much Rodd's instinct – as his comments about the desirability of keeping the duke of Aosta in power indicated. In relation to Eritrea, he recalled after the war: 'No alternative was open when Asmara fell than to maintain as much of the Italian administration as remained.' If they had got rid of the Italian police force, chaos would have resulted, he observed. When Wavell met with Eden in Cairo in March 1941, Rodd wrote a memorandum for Mitchell to inform their discussions which illustrated his approach:

> If H.M.G. are to become responsible for the direct administration of the native *and* Italian populations [...] the cost will be onerous and the actual method of government difficult [...] The alternative and cheaper method is to secure the co-operation of the Italian authorities to continue their administration under our control in Eritrea and Somaliland [...] [We should] seek a *modus vivendi* with the Italian authorities in Italian East Africa before a complete collapse has occurred, or in other words, while there is still time to take over a running machine.[68]

In practice, different approaches to civil affairs were applied in different areas. For example, in Eritrea, military defeat meant that the Italian settlers lost much of their credibility. The result was that it was only in the major cities of Asmara and Massawa and their surrounding settlements, and the Hamasein Plateau, that the Italian administration was initially utilised, although the Offices of Political and Native Affairs were closed down and their work transferred to the British Administration Affairs secretariat. Elsewhere, it was felt better to have virtually no administration at all than to prop up a decaying Italian organisation. In the western plain province, however, a form of direct rule was adopted. In Italian Somaliland, no attempt was made to preserve the Italian framework of administration; a completely new administration was set up of a 'direct' nature, utilising some elements of Somali tribal machinery. But in Mogadishu, the local fascist podestà was retained for a while in his role as head of the municipality.[69] The dilemmas associated with the question of whether to retain or dismiss local fascist leaders would confront Rodd again with the invasion of Sicily.

The nature of Rodd's work meant that he did a huge amount of travelling; he did roughly 58,000 miles in 1941 alone. It reflected the fact that huge responsibilities fell on just a few people. The end of 1941 was particularly hectic. After his trip to Britain, Rodd returned to Nairobi on 22 December and then headed to Addis Ababa for Christmas.

---

67. John H. Spencer, *Ethiopia at Bay: A Personal Account of the Haile Selassie Years* (Hollywood: Tsehai, 2006), 94–98.
68. Rennell, *British Military Administration in Africa 1941–47*, 102–3, 111.
69. Rennell, *British Military Administration in Africa 1941–43*, 16; *British Military Administration in Africa 1941–47*, 101–4, 158.

On Christmas morning, he met with Mitchell, Lush, Hone and the deputy CFA Frank Stafford. Dinner was spent with Mitchell, his brother Peter and Major-General Samuel Butler. On 26 December, Rodd flew with Mitchell and Hone for a meeting with Lyttelton in Asmara, before returning with Mitchell to Addis Ababa on 28 December. He finally got back to Nairobi on 29 December. All this activity cemented his friendship with Mitchell. A few weeks earlier, in London, they had had dinner with Ralph Hamlyn, with the menu including oysters, partridges, Chablis and claret. They also attended performances of the review *Rise Above It*, starring Hermione Baddeley, and Noel Coward's *Blithe Spirit*; and they joined Platt for a showing of the documentary *Target for Tonight* at an MO11 film theatre. Occasionally, their social activities took in figures of political importance: some months later, when Rodd was based in Cairo – sharing a flat with Simon Elwes – Mitchell came to stay and met Sayyid Idris.[70]

Every so often, Rodd was reminded of his geographical interests. War threw up new opportunities for tourism. Whenever he could, he made a point of visiting some of the great historic sites, as well as places of archaeological interest. In early March 1942, he went to the temple complex of Karnak, near Luxor. 'The great temple is truly magnificent and some of the low relief surprisingly beautiful', he reported to Mary. A couple of weeks later, in Asmara, he visited an old Axamite site some 80 miles away, which he said was 'well worth digging'.[71] The plane flights themselves gave opportunities for contemplating spectacular scenery. In May 1941, on a trip to Cairo, the pilot took the plane over Ripon Falls at the north end of Lake Victoria, so that he could see big game.[72] Mitchell was also impressed with the landscape. Travelling with Rodd in late June 1941, on the way to the Asmara conference, he recorded that they flew over the 'most fantastic peaks and precipices'.[73]

For Rodd, the enjoyment was enhanced by the fact that his travels brought him into contact with leading political figures. In August 1941, he visited South Africa, where he met Prime Minister Jan Smuts, as well as the politician and intellectual Jan Hendrik Hofmeyr, who had overlapped with him at Balliol. He returned to Nairobi via Salisbury, where he took time out to see the Victoria Falls. 'I saw in the Falls the only great sight which is wholly un-disappointing', he said. A year later, he flew through Northern Rhodesia (Zambia) in the company of Smuts: 'We had the greatest view […] of Kilimanjaro and the Tanganyika volcanoes at dawn. [Smuts] said that he had never seen them all so clear and beautiful against the dawn sky.' Smuts' 'courage and faith' greatly impressed him; he told Mary that he was the 'most remarkable' person he had met in his life.[74]

Rodd was generally optimistic about the war. As early as September 1941, he told Lamont: 'I begin to see light for an end, but the post-war period is going to be hell.' He

---

70. Mitchell Diary, 27 October; 7, 13, 15, 19 November; 25 December 1941; 2, 13, 16 May 1942, Philip Mitchell Papers, BD, Mss Afr.r. 101.
71. Rodd to Mary, 3 and 12 March 1942, Rodd Family Papers, AC.
72. Rodd, Flight Log, 1940–43, Rennell of Rodd Papers, BD, Box 76.
73. Mitchell Diary, 25 June 1941, Philip Mitchell Papers, BD, Mss Afr.r. 101.
74. Rodd to Mary, 2 September 1941, 2 August 1942, Rodd Family Papers, AC. Rodd to Lamont, 8 August 1942, Thomas Lamont Papers, BK, Box 112/12.

was delighted when the United States came into the war following the Japanese attack on Pearl Harbour on 7 December. 'It is a wonderful thing that America and we should be fighting against the Hun and the Jap', he told Lamont. But a few months later, he was feeling jaded and frustrated. Africa – with the exception of Libya – suddenly seemed a 'bywater'. But he found it appealing at a deep psychological level. As he explained to Mary: 'I know a lot about a little in Africa, but I know I understand even more, much more than I know. It is sucked in through the pores of the skin.' In this context, he cited some lines from his father about Frank Rhodes's death in Cape Colony in 1905: 'Oh why did you feed that siren hand, / That drew you back to Lepas land.'[75]

In summer 1942, there was talk of Rodd becoming the governor of Southern Rhodesia, but that fell through. 'I don't know whether the role of a constitutional monarch would have suited me', he told Mary.[76] Instead, on 1 July, he was given Mitchell's job as chief political officer south, based in Nairobi – Mitchell had been appointed governor of Fiji. On the recommendation of Henry Monck-Mason Moore, governor of Kenya, he was also made a member of the East African Governors' Conference, the case for this being that he was in practice the representative of the military administrations of Somalia, British Somaliland and the Reserved Areas of Ethiopia. Rodd's new role was reconfigured to bring supply matters in East Africa under his remit. The idea was that he would be a channel of communication between the East African Supply Group and the Middle East Supply Centre. But this never really transpired. Rodd got increasingly involved in providing political and economic advice to Platt.[77] Rodd's promotion led to his elevation to the rank of major-general, although without the salary. This he found 'acutely embarrassing', he explained to Mary, while also noting that he and Mitchell had been the only major-generals in the army created out of nothing.[78] Churchill once criticised the tradition of giving military rank to civil affairs officers, on the grounds that it led to 'hordes of sham Major-Generals preening themselves in all directions'. Rodd later said he had much sympathy with this view, adding that he considered himself one of these 'primus inter pares'. But he also defended the practice, saying he could not have done his job in civil affairs without the rank and red adornments accompanying it.[79]

Rodd found his new responsibilities 'fun and awe-inspiring'. He relished the fact that he was in practice running territories under conditions and with responsibilities larger than most colonial governors. He compared himself to the hero of Rudyard Kipling's poem 'Song of Diego Valdez', the story of a man who rose to become a Spanish admiral.

---

75. Rodd to Lamont, 17 September and 30 December 1941, Thomas Lamont Papers, BK, Box 112/12. Rodd to Mary, 3 March 1942, Rodd Family Papers, AC.
76. Rodd to Mary, 2 August 1942, Rodd Family Papers, AC.
77. Hone to minister of state, 17 June 1942; notes from an interview between Hone and Moore, 16 June 1942; Rodd to Grigg, draft letter, 27 July 1942, Rennell of Rodd Papers, BD, Box 69/2. Rennell, *British Military Administration in Africa 1941–47*, 308.
78. Rodd to Mary, 29 June 1942, Rodd Family Papers, AC.
79. Churchill, cited in F. S. V. Donnison, *British Military Administration in the Far East, 1943–46* (London: HMSO, 1956), 48. Rennell, Memorandum to Secretary of State for War, 20 January 1944, Rennell of Rodd Papers, BD, Box 76/2, BD.

He also greatly valued the close connections with people thrown up by the war. He thought he was not always popular and thus was delighted when he sensed real camaraderie with people. As he explained to Mary in August 1942: 'I have made enemies and people dislike me as much as ever but I have made friends and I have people working for me with a devotion and loyalty that few can ever have had.' Rodd called the friendships created by war 'one of the few mitigations in a world of beastliness'. 'This life is very lonely', he told Mary.[80]

The solitary nature of wartime life had an effect on Rodd's personal life. While in East Africa, he became emotionally involved with a woman working as a secretary in the Colonial Office in Kenya, 'Peggy' Cavendish. During the war, pressure was sometimes placed on marriages when spouses were separated for long periods. Post-war, Cavendish was private secretary to Lilias for a time.[81]

The main focus of Rodd's work in late summer and early autumn 1942 was Madagascar. The takeover of the island in what was known as Operation Ironclad began with the seizure of the northern port city of Diego Suarez on 5 May 1942. But not until July was the city handed over to the formal authority of Platt and Rodd. Throughout the summer, Rodd was involved with the political challenges associated with the island's takeover. From May to September, the British had a dual policy of pursuing talks with Vichy leader Armand Annet – whom Rodd had met in Dahomey in 1940 – while preparing to march south to claim the whole island. Vichy forces surrendered in September. Annet left the capital, Tananarive, on 18 September, although he instructed the Vichy garrison to fight on. Tananarive was occupied on 23 September, after which proclamations were issued announcing military rule and the transfer of administrative responsibility to Platt. But the actual armistice was not signed until 6 November. Rodd and Platt arrived in Tananarive on 26 September and, two days later, set up their administrative headquarters there. Rodd was excited by the task ahead of him: he was the chief military administrator of the island, in effect the acting governor-general.[82]

In Rodd's mind, some of the problems he faced in Madagascar were connected with the unhelpful interference of the Foreign Office. He was annoyed that some of the negotiations were being run from London, with the Foreign Office taking the lead; in May, the Foreign Office had appointed its own man, Lawrence Grafftey-Smith, as CPO in the island. Rodd thought that negotiations with Annet could have been advanced more quickly if he himself or Lush, who had been redeployed to the Madagascar operation by the War Office, had been in charge of them. His anger boiled over in a letter he drafted to Grigg, by now Secretary of State for War. The letter was not, in the end, sent – Rodd found another way to communicate his concerns – but it illustrates the strength of

---

80. Rodd to Mary, 2 and 8 August 1942, Rodd Family Papers, AC.
81. Rodd's letters to Cavendish have not survived. But some of Cavendish's letters to Rodd can be found in Rennell of Rodd Papers, BD, Boxes 71/2, 72/1, 110.
82. Rodd to Mary, 7 November 1942, Rodd Family Papers, AC.

his feelings about the Foreign Office. He was scathing about much of what the Foreign Office had done in Africa since the summer of 1940:

> They have made a mess of everything they have tried to do for the last two years, except Turkey. The only two things in Africa that have been well done were the Belgian Congo by Hailey and French Equatorial Africa by Bourdillon, and both of these because the F. O. were kept out until it was too late to make a mess. Since then what have you: Egypt – a mess[:] W. Africa – quite apart from Dakar a mess: N. Africa – a howling mess: Syria – chaos: Jibuti – pretty dim: Madagascar – a miss and not even a near miss diplomatically: Ethiopia – Well, well![83]

Rodd got on well with Grigg – they were alike in being men with strong opinions. When Grigg was appointed Secretary of State, Rodd wrote to Mary: 'I like [Grigg] enormously. But he suffers fools very badly.' He and Rodd were alike in being sceptical about Eden's effectiveness as foreign secretary.[84]

The turf war between the Foreign Office and the military came to a head in September when Platt decided that Lush, rather than Grafftey-Smith, should have the primary role as CPO on the island. In this case, Rodd turned out to be good at smoothing relationships, in a way that suggests that he was sometimes more conciliatory in his approach to resolving problems than his fiery rhetoric would indicate. He simply worked out an arrangement whereby the two men had separate areas of responsibility under his own leadership.[85] In his memoirs, Grafftey-Smith paid tribute to Rodd's pragmatism in handling the problem, although in a post-war summary of the episode he also stated that Rodd exaggerated the extent of the Foreign Office's ambitions.[86]

The War Office and the Foreign Office had had different timetables for the transfer of power to the emperor in Ethiopia. A similar difference was now evident in the way they approached the situation in Madagascar. The Foreign Office was eager to transfer power to the Free French immediately after occupying the island, because it was sensitive to Gaullist irritability over the fact that Free French forces had been excluded from the planning for the invasion and the operation itself. But ongoing negotiations with de Gaulle made this impossible. In case a British military administration was needed in Madagascar, Rodd readied a team of officers for the work. But it was only on 16 September that he received instructions to set up a temporary British military administration on the island. A few weeks later, on 6 October, the Committee on Foreign (Allied) Resistance in London discussed the timetable for the British administration of Madagascar. Rodd advised that only a period of extended British occupation of the

---

83. Rodd to Grigg, draft letter, 27 July 1942, Rennell of Rodd Papers, BD, Box 69/2.
84. Rodd to Mary, 8 March 1942, Rodd Family Papers, AC. Max Hastings, *Finest Years: Churchill as Warlord 1940–45* (London: Harper, 2009), 126.
85. Rennell, *British Military Administration in Africa 1941–47*, 220, 228–29. See also Rennell, CPO report to Platt for 1 May–31 December 1942, 21–29, Maurice Lush Papers, IWM, Box 2, 5/2; see also Lush's notes in Box 2, 5/3.
86. Laurence Grafftey-Smith, *Hands to Play* (London: Routledge and Kegan Paul, 1975), 43, 60. Grafftey-Smith was referring to Rodd's book *British Military Administration in Africa, 1941–47*.

island would keep the settler population happy – to the irritation of the Foreign Office.[87] Rodd was forced to adjust to the Foreign Office's timetable. He was particularly keen to see the appointment of General Paul Legentilhomme as high commissioner, on account of his popularity. The final agreement over the transfer of the island to French rule was signed at the Foreign Office on 17 December by Eden and de Gaulle, in the presence of Legentilhomme and Rodd. The formal handover of the island, and the Island of Reunion, to Legentilhomme took place on 8 January 1943.[88]

Similar principles were evident in the British approach to Madagascar as in the Horn. Already after the fall of Diego Suarez, Lush had started using local French administrative staff, where they were willing to cooperate. Rodd adopted a similar approach. In a statement to the War Cabinet Committee of the French Resistance on 20 November – he was back in Britain by this time – Rodd emphasised that the successful transition of power from the French to the British had been based on observing French legal process: it appealed to the French love of 'matters of form'. Within three days of the British occupation, the whole machinery of the French administration was functioning satisfactorily, he declared.[89] British military administration during the transition period was carried out 'through the machinery of French local decrees and orders in correct French legal form', he said later. Rodd's thinking here echoed some remarks once made by Lord Cromer: Cromer thought that French administrative systems were characterised by 'elaborate detail', whereas the English preferred laying down rules on a few main points and leaving their application to individual discretion.[90]

The man chosen by Rodd to replace Annet, in the role of acting secretary-general, was M. Bech, director of economic affairs. Annet gave written authority for Bech to take over his position, and this helped to smooth the transition. As Grafftey-Smith recalled: 'To functionaries desperately anxious to find some excuse for reconciling their loyalty to the governor-general with the no less incumbent duty of retaining their jobs under any and every regime, it was precious comfort to know that M. Bech had, in some measure, received the holy oils, and that the legality of his succession was capable of demonstration.' With the provincial administration essentially accepting the British takeover, Rodd was able to use British administrative staff, small in number though they were, as liaison officers with the French departments rather than instructing them to run things themselves. It is worth noting, in view of similar issues arising in Italy, that Lush, who was given charge of policing, was accused by some of leaving too many 'equivocal personages' in posts of authority. Similar accusations were made against Legentilhomme after he took over. Tact was needed in managing enthusiastic Free French activists,

---

87. Rennell, CPO report to Platt for 1 May–31 December 1942, 23–24, Maurice Lush Papers, IWM, Box 2, 5/2. Thomas, *French Empire at War*, 14. Committee on French Resistance (42), 6 October 1942, 1, FO ADM 199/874.
88. Rennell, *British Military Administration in Africa 1941–47*, 232, 238.
89. Summary of War Cabinet discussion on 20 November, dated 23 November 1942, Rennell of Rodd Papers, BD, Box 73. See also Rennell's memorandum, 'Transfer of the administration of Madagascar to the Fighting French', 22 November 1942, Rennell of Rodd Papers, BD, Box 73
90. Rennell, *British Military Administration in Africa 1941–43*, 28. Cromer, cited in Said, *Orientalism*, 212.

pending negotiations with de Gaulle in London. One advantage of the fact that the transition took some weeks to implement was that it gave space for previously pro-Vichy officials to adjust their allegiances.[91]

Rodd's interests were not exclusively political; he was concerned equally with Madagascar's economic potential. He was always conscious of the strategic importance of economic questions. Earlier in the year, he wrote to I. N. Clayton at the Middle Eastern Intelligence Centre, explaining that the Allies and the enemy had a common problem in ensuring access to food supplies in their respective spheres. Many geopolitical and military policies had their roots in the struggle for food.[92] Supply issues relating to Madagascar were a major preoccupation for him throughout the summer. In the autumn, he was exercised by the question of which supply area Madagascar should fall into – India, the Middle Eastern Supply Centre, East Africa or South Africa. For various reasons, Rodd did not think any of these suitable and proposed that Madagascar be bracketed with Mauritius and Reunion in a new supply area, with a supply board in Mauritius, on the grounds that they were on the same shipping route.[93] Some of Rodd's thinking was evident in his statement to the War Cabinet. As well as looking at Madagascar from political, historical, constitutional and financial points of view, he summarised the island's communications and its economic potential in relation to its main products – graphite, mica, rock crystal, nickel and coal – as well as its secondary industries and gave space to matters pertaining to agriculture, trade, the population and labour.[94]

Rodd was chief military administrator in Madagascar until 22 October – at which point he returned to Nairobi for a week. He then left for London to report on events in the French colony. He was very pleased at his success in setting up an interim government. 'It was really rather an achievement', he told Mary. How emotionally involved in the island he became is questionable. As he explained to Mary, he did not really care for Madagascar itself except as an exercise in diplomacy and administration. But he called it a 'well-done thing', while also observing that Platt got the credit for the success.[95]

The record of Rodd's activities in Madagascar reinforces what was already evident from his work in the Horn, namely that he had a pragmatic approach to getting things done. His continued advocacy in Madagascar of a form of indirect rule – managing the country through French colonial institutions – reflected that. The origins of his thinking on this went back to well before the war. He had written positively about Lugard's thinking on indirect rule in *People of the Veil*. During the Second World War, he found himself working with two men who were keen advocates of the concept: Bourdillon and Mitchell.

---

91. Laurence Grafftey-Smith to Eden, 'Madagascar, May 1942–July 1943', 10–12, FO 371/36138 Z8719.
92. Rodd to Clayton, 30 March 1942, Rennell of Rodd Papers, BD, 69/2.
93. See Committee on French Resistance (42), 17th Meeting, 17 July 1942, FO ADM 199/874. Memorandum, 25 October 1942, Rennell of Rodd Papers, BD, Box 73.
94. Summary of War Cabinet discussion on 20 November, dated 23 November 1942, Rennell of Rodd Papers, BD, Box 73.
95. Rodd to Mary, 7 January 1942 and 10 January 1943, Rodd Family Papers, AC.

He liked the way these men approached administrative problems. 'I learnt my African administration from Bourdillon at Lagos and Mitchell', he told Mary.[96] Bourdillon was an advocate of indirect rule, although not in its most radical form; he saw it as a means to the longer-term end of creating parliamentary institutions in Nigeria.[97] Mitchell had become familiar with the concept while serving as secretary of native affairs in Tanganyika between 1929 and 1934. A gradualist in outlook, he was an idealistic supporter of the concept of 'trusteeship' in Africa. His thinking was influenced by Donald Cameron, governor-general of Tanganyika (1925–31). Cameron was himself influenced by Lugard, although he had a more interventionist philosophy than him.[98] These figures were associated with the 'Tropical Dependency' school of thought informed by Britain's experience in West Africa, Uganda and Tanganyika, which sought protection for Africans against western ownership of land and means of production.[99] The extent to which Rodd learnt his ideas about indirect rule specifically from Bourdillon and Mitchell is hard to measure, but their practical frame of mind and interest in African development would have appealed to him.

Rodd's link with Lord Hailey in 1940 brings in a different perspective. There was a combination of elements in Hailey's outlook. He was never an advocate of indirect rule as a doctrine, although he came to appreciate the more gradualist approach of men like Bourdillon and Mitchell. His *African Survey* (1938) came to be associated with a more activist conception of trusteeship in Africa and the replacement of the conception of indirect rule with the idea of 'partnership' – a tendency connected with the Colonial Development and Welfare Acts of 1940 and 1945. Back in Britain after his time in the Belgian Congo, Hailey chaired the Committee on Post-war Problems in the Colonies. In his *Native Administration and Political Development* (1944), he emphasised the need for the creation of an African political class capable of managing the modern state.[100] This would have appealed to Rodd; Rodd came to share Hailey's belief in the need actively to encourage African development. In July 1944, he proposed a motion in the House of Lords calling on the government to put more thought into the education and housing of

---

96. Rodd to Mary, 27 March 1943, Rodd Family Papers, AC.
97. C. Sylvester Whitaker, *The Politics of Tradition: Continuity and Change in Northern Nigeria, 1946–66* (Princeton: Princeton University Press, 1970), 52. Pearce, *Bernard Bourdillon*, 210–12, 216.
98. See Mitchell, *African Afterthoughts*, ch. 7. Frost, *Enigmatic Proconsul*, 266, 269. Pearce, *Turning Point*, 8. Lugard's most famous interpreter is Marjorie Perham; see in particular *Lugard, The Years of Authority 1898–1945* (London: Collins, 1960), chs 7 and 8. On indirect rule in Tanganyika, see John Iliffe, *A Modern History of Tanganyika* (Cambridge: Cambridge University Press, 1979), esp. ch. 10.
99. See John Cell, *Hailey: A Study in British Imperialism, 1872–1969* (Cambridge: Cambridge University Press, 1992), 217.
100. Ronald Hyam, *Britain's Declining Empire: The Road to Decolonisation 1918–1968* (Cambridge: Cambridge University Press, 2006), 90. Cell, *Hailey*, 246. John D. Hargreaves, *Decolonization in Africa* (London: Longman, 1988), 61. Pedler to Rodd, 30 July 1941, Rennell of Rodd Papers, BD, Box 69/2. Lord Hailey, *African Survey* (Oxford: Oxford University Press, 1938); *Native Administration and Political Development in British Tropical Africa. Report 1940–42* (London: HMSO, 1944).

Africans returning to civilian life after the war. One of his main points was that former African servicemen were likely to head for the cities after the war rather than back to employment in primitive agriculture. It was regrettable, he said, that during the war the army had had to address such issues when the civilian government ought to have been doing it over the previous decades. 'Plans must be drawn up now for their settlement in new walks of life', he declared. Rodd's motion was backed by Hailey, in the light of the need for Africans to take greater responsibility for their own social and economic development.[101]

Rodd did not think indirect rule offered long-term benefits for Africa. Speaking in the House of Lords in August 1944, he remarked that indirect rule was generally thought of as 'liberal', and direct rule as 'reactionary'; but he argued that direct rule did not always have to be reactionary and that native administrations could be 'extremely reactionary'. More specifically, he questioned the policy of extending indirect rule as applied in the northern parts of Nigeria and the Gold Coast to the south. A year later, in a speech prior to the general election, Rodd warned against 'enthusiastic anthropological administrators' trying to wrap the African up in 'cotton wool' to protect him from the outside world.[102] Such comments indicate that Rodd's enthusiasm for indirect rule in East Africa was essentially a practical response to a wartime need; he was more a pragmatic reformer than a traditionalist.

Rodd's wartime experience in Africa left him with the conviction that the empire more generally needed significant reform. This is evident in his thinking on organisational questions in the British colonies. His War Office work led him to believe that there needed to be greater integration in the empire. For example, he wanted Northern Rhodesia to be integrated into British plans for East Africa. He discussed his ideas in London in April 1943 with George Gater, permanent undersecretary for the colonies, and Arthur Dawe, head of the Colonial Office's Africa division, a man who took the view that indirect rule was an outmoded method of government. They found his ideas 'novel'. He also shared his thinking with the colonial secretary, Oliver Stanley.[103] In a debate in the House of Lords in late 1945, he complained that the administrative divisions existing in British East Africa and the Indian Ocean made little sense, and there needed to be a more cohesive plan for the area.[104]

More generally, Rodd's work in Africa in 1940–42 led him to formulate his own philosophy of decision-making. In a letter to Mary in November 1942, he explained: 'The process of letting things happen and letting decisions make themselves has become more deep-seated, inescapable and satisfactory. Even the major ones in my work of a political

---

101. *Times*, 20 July 1944, 8. Speeches by Rennell and Hailey, 19 July 1944, House of Lords, Hansard.
102. Rennell, 1 August 1944, House of Lords, Hansard. Rennell, 'Africa and the British Political Parties', *African Affairs* 44 (1945): 107.
103. Rodd, Diary for 1943, 6–7, Rennell of Rodd Papers, BD, Box 111. On Dawe's outlook, see Hyam, *Britain's Declining Empire*, 88.
104. Rennell, 29 November 1945, House of Lords, Hansard. See also Rennell, 'Development in Colonial Administration', *Fortnightly*, July 1945, 26.

and technical nature have made themselves – that is they reached a point at which no other decision really rationally presented itself as an alternative.'[105] In one letter to Mary, in which he reported a conversation with Daphne Moore, wife of the governor of Kenya, he even suggested that he never really made decisions:

> I told [Daphne] the last evening when I was giving a farewell party that I never made decisions myself. They were always made for me because when the time came there never seemed to me to be any room for doubt. She was intensively interested and somewhat sceptical but said that you had told her this too. It may take a very different form with me than with you [...] but the result is the same and derived from the same source.[106]

There was a hint here of a kind of providentialism in Rodd's outlook and an indication that he shared this with Mary in some ways; Rodd seems to have been saying that in any situation there was a right or sensible thing to do, but that this revealed itself through allowing events to take their course. His thinking here contained echoes of his father's approach to decision-making, as expressed in the First World War.

---

105. Rodd to Mary, 14 November 1942, Rodd Family Papers, AC.
106. Rodd to Mary, 7 November 1942, Rodd Family Papers, AC.

Chapter Eight

AMGOT (ALLIED MILITARY GOVERNMENT OF OCCUPIED TERRITORIES)

Rodd got back to Britain in mid-November 1942. In formal terms, he was still chief political officer in East Africa command. But he was uncertain about what to do next. He was also free of personal ambition on the matter – or so he claimed in a letter to Mary: 'I do not really care what I do and shall take no active steps to do one thing or another. In these two years […] I have ceased to have any ambition to do anything else than what I was doing.' Rodd even floated the idea with some of his friends that he might withdraw from his wartime work and go to live at the Rodd. This was met with some derision.[1] Rodd's reputation was high. Henry Monck-Mason Moore wrote Rodd a warm letter expressing appreciation for all his assistance while working in East Africa. Platt also wrote him a letter of appreciation while also telling a mutual friend that he found him 'sometimes encouraging, sometimes provocative, but always a stimulant'. Rodd thought it was a 'triumph' to be thanked by these two men, since they did not get on well together, and he had spent 'appreciable time' keeping the peace between them.[2]

Rodd was, in fact, full of ideas. There was often in his political thinking a desire to promote a degree of centralisation, as he explained to Mary in April: 'I am apprehensive, as I always have been, of the disintegration of central authority and the growth of local potentates who won't agree with their fellow potentates.'[3] This instinct now came out in a plan to bring order to the work of civil administration in East Africa and the Middle East. In early December, at a meeting in London called by Archibald Nye, vice chief of the Imperial General Staff, he suggested that there was a lack of coordination in the British management of civil affairs. He then produced a paper for the Directorate of Military Operations proposing the integration of the system under one person with the title of chief civil affairs officer (CCAO). This person would act as a liaison person between commanders-in-chief of different commands, and between them and the War Office on civil administration issues; a vice CCAO would be attached to each command.[4] The idea was initially accepted. The most obvious candidate for such an expanded role was Rodd himself. In early January

---

1. Rodd to Mary, 14 November 1942, 10 January 1943, Rodd Family Papers, AC.
2. Moore to Rodd, 13 March 1943, Rennell of Rodd Papers, BD, Box 69/2. Erica Bailey-Southwell to Rodd, 8 May 1943, Rennell of Rodd Papers, BD, Box 71/2, Folder 4. Rodd to Mary, 27 April 1943, Rodd Family Papers, AC.
3. Rodd to Mary, 27 April 1943, Rodd Family Papers, AC.
4. Meeting called by VCIGS, 4 December 1942; Rennell, note with attachment to director of military operations, 15 December 1942, Rennell of Rodd Papers, BD, 69/2.

1943, Grigg wrote to Harold Alexander, since August 1942 commander-in-chief of Middle East command, recommending Rodd as the person to fulfil this role, noting that his knowledge of Italy and the United States enhanced his suitability.[5] Rodd went back to Africa in early January to explore the possibility of assuming this role.

Even though he was the originator of the concept for the role, Rodd felt nervous about the size of its remit, as well as experiencing a slight sense of isolation. As he explained to Mary: 'For the first time I think I have a bit too much put on me. [...] I feel a little like I did in 1941 that I haven't enough chaps and not enough people to talk to.'[6] There was sufficient momentum around Rodd's idea for him to be formally appointed to the role in March 1943, with the title of inspector-general of OTA. But there remained doubts about the viability of the concept in Middle East command: Alexander thought the role might be too much for one man to fill; and Henry Wilson, the GOC Middle East command, was concerned about creating an additional source of authority between the commander-in-chief and the War Office.[7]

At this point, Rodd's most important wartime responsibility – as head of Allied Military Government of Occupied Territories (AMGOT) – suddenly opened up. In February, Eisenhower had been appointed commander of the North African theatre of operations. He wanted the invasion of Italy to be a joint operation to ensure it was not dominated by the British; and Churchill was forced to comply with this.[8] With the invasion of Italy pending, the question then arose as to who should oversee the administration of conquered territory. Rodd was first proposed for the role by Grigg in February. A possibility from the American side was the mayor of New York, Fiorello H. La Guardia, a reform-minded but authoritarian figure, to whom the British were not sympathetic. Eisenhower was also keen to avoid having La Guardia forced upon him, and he came to favour Rodd as a way to prevent that. There was opposition in Cabinet to Rodd's appointment from Lyttelton, now minister of production. Rodd got back to London at the end of March. He was appointed AMGOT senior planning officer on 30 March and moved to Algeria, the base for Allied planning for the forthcoming campaign. He stepped down from his role as chief political officer in East Africa on 26 April and, on 1 May, was formally made CCAO in AMGOT.[9] Churchill confirmed the appointment on 17 May, after consultation with Roosevelt.[10]

---

5. Grigg to Alexander, 1 January 1943, Rennell of Rodd Papers, BD, 69/2.
6. Rodd to Mary, 19 February 1942, Rodd Family Papers, AC.
7. Rennell to chief of general staff, 29 January 1943; Alexander to Grigg, 30 January 1943; Wilson to Grigg, 14 March 1943, Rennell of Rodd Papers, BD, Box 69/2.
8. Andrew Buchanan, *American Grand Strategy in the Mediterranean during World War II* (Cambridge: Cambridge University Press, 2014), 122.
9. Rennell, *British Military Administration in Africa 1941–47*, 609. Flint, 'The Development of British Civil Affairs', 138. Isobel Williams, *Allies and Italians under Occupation: Sicily and Southern Italy 1943–45* (Basingstoke: Palgrave Macmillan, 2013), 21. Dalton, 24 July 1943, cited in Ben Pimlott (ed.), *Second World War Diary of Hugh Dalton*, 621. Rodd, Diary for 1943, 2, Rennell of Rodd Papers, BD, Box 111. See also Duff, 'Civil Affairs in Italy (the Sicily Campaign)', Section 1, Part 2, CAB 44/171.
10. Telegram from Churchill to Grigg, 17 May 1943, CHAR 20/128/35, CCC.

Rodd was unsure of his own motives for swapping the inspector-general role for the AMGOT post. In late March, he confided in Mary:

> [I] would like to go on doing [African administration] but as things are they won't let me and so I am to start again on less African things and in surroundings which are not only new but very difficult. I must tell them in London that I am not the right person to do it. I have already told them by telegram but they won't listen.[11]

While worried that he was not the right person for the AMGOT role, Rodd wondered if the caution he felt about taking it on was rooted in fear of a new challenge: 'What I cannot make out at the moment is how far in telling them I am not the right person, I am really trying to run away to what I know I can do, or trying to refuse to do what I am more doubtful about.' He concluded his letter by citing a prayer associated with Elizabethan explorer Francis Drake: 'Grant us to know that it is not the beginning but the continuation of the same till it is thoroughly finished which findeth the true glory.'[12] Rodd's uncertainty was again evident in another letter to Mary written some weeks later. He explained that he felt he had had no choice about taking on the AMGOT role, even though he would like to have continued his African work: 'So much pressure was put on me in London to come here and here to stay both by the British as well as the American authorities that I could not refuse.' But he now felt a sense of destiny about the job: 'I realise that the work I am doing and that which I have done is precisely the work for which the training and experience I have had suit me for.'[13]

AMGOT was set up with a somewhat tortuous system of accountability designed to please all parties, but leave ultimate power with the American military. Rodd was answerable to Alexander, head of 15th Army Group – which, in the invasion of Sicily, was composed of the British 8th and the US 7th armies. Alexander had helped to nominate Rodd for his role. Alexander reported to Eisenhower, but through the medium of the American colonel Julius Holmes, who was head of the Military Government Section (MGS) at the Allied Force Headquarters (AFHQ).[14] The American Brigadier-General F. J. McSherry was made Rodd's deputy. Right from the outset, Rodd was worried about the structure; even before the role was confirmed, he expressed an anxiety that he would be an 'executive organ for conflicting policies with no access to the fountain heads'. Fear of the Foreign Office was one of his worries: 'I am pretty satisfied that one of the complications is the desire […] of the F. O. to run things behind the scenes without any responsibility for the administrative side for which W. O. and myself will get all the kicks.' On the other hand, he was drawn to the role because it was a way of contributing to Anglo–American unity. He also thought that if he did the job, he might end up as governor of Rome – which appealed to him.[15]

---

11. Rodd to Mary, 27 March 1943, Rodd Family Papers, AC.
12. Ibid.
13. Rodd to Mary, 27 April 1943, Rodd Family Papers, AC.
14. Buchanan, *American Grand Strategy*, 123.
15. Rodd, 20 April, Diary for 1943, Rennell of Rodd Papers, BD, Box 111.

Ahead of Operation Husky, a programme for planning and education was set up at Chrea, south of Algiers. Chrea was a resort in a cedar forest in the Atlas Mountains. Rodd found it beautiful. Moreover, the desert was alluringly close. 'I can see from my window [...] 40 miles to the south across the ranges of hills to a long line of mountains on the skyline, beyond which the desert begins', he reported to Mary.[16] Two courses of instruction, each lasting 21 days, were completed before the start of the invasion. Italian language teaching was part of the programme. Much of the input came from officers who had been involved with civil affairs in Africa over the previous three years. Rodd himself gave talks on behavioural issues and Anglo–American relations. Developing good relationships between the British and Americans was a particular challenge, as Rodd explained in a speech at Chatham House in early 1944, after he had returned to Britain: '[At Chrea] we collected 400 officers, 200 British, 200 Americans, and put them to sleep together in houses and made them mess together for six weeks. They complained horribly but ended by being good friends.'[17] The emphasis on Allied integration was such that the nominal rolls of AMGOT did not show a distinction between British or American officers, although at the senior level a more concerted attempt at attaining balance was made.[18] Initially, Rodd was dismissive of the talents of some of the Americans. He called the American police officers 'college men with no training as soldiers', and McSherry 'a nice old thing with no conception of what it is all about'. But he was impressed with McSherry's handling of General George Patton, commander of the US 7th Army, who he called a 'difficult customer'.[19] He warmed to his American colleagues. In August, he reported that the American officers in AMGOT had done 'very well', showing 'enterprise, ingenuity and tremendous keenness'; they were 'exceeding expectations'. Later he remarked that the 'Anglo–American fusion' in the administration of AMGOT had been 'outstandingly successful and complete'.[20]

One of Rodd's biggest challenges ahead of the invasion was finding enough civil affairs personnel – as he explained to one of his former colleagues in OTA after the invasion: 'The material difficulty of collecting people from Civil commands and two armies and sorting them out over 3,000 miles of North African coast from Casablanca to Suez and as far afield as the United Kingdom in order to embark them for the enterprise was a nightmare.'[21] In the end, in addition to the 400 officers, there were 1,400 men of other ranks, although not all were in readiness at the time of the actual invasion.

Prior to the invasion of Sicily, in mid-June, the islands of Pantelleria and Lampedusa were taken over and Allied administration introduced. Operation Husky itself was launched on 9–10 July 1943. The terms of the occupation were explained in what was

---

16. Rodd to Mary, 3 May 1943, Rodd Family Papers, AC.
17. Rennell, 'Allied Military Government in Occupied Territory', *International Affairs*, July 1944, 311.
18. Rennell, Address to MPs, 29 October 1943, 1–3, J. R. M. Butler Papers, TCC.
19. Rodd, Dairy for 1943, 48, Rennell of Rodd Papers, BD, Box 111.
20. Extracts from letter from Rennell to French, 3 August 1943, WO 220/312, 2. Rennell, 'Allied Military Government in Occupied Territory', 311.
21. Rodd to Adshead, 9 August 1943, Rennell of Rodd Papers, BD, Box 69/2.

known as Proclamation Number 1, issued in Alexander's name. This was followed in due course by a series of other proclamations concerning matters such as criminality, the law courts, currency policy and agriculture. On 17 July, there was a formal announcement about the setting up of AMGOT, with Alexander as military governor and Rodd as CCAO.[22] About 60 AMGOT officers were assigned to the initial invasion force along with clerks, drivers and orderlies, a number increased to 150 by 19 July. Ferrying people across to Sicily and giving them instructions at the same time as liaising with the British and US war establishments, with their different scales of equipment and vehicles, was a complicated process.[23]

Rodd was not part of the initial invasion force. He was ferried over to Syracuse on 22 July in an invasion ship, accompanied by his personal assistant Douglas Pirie, two cars and chauffeurs, a batman and his baggage. His first task was to set up an advanced AMGOT headquarters in Syracuse.[24] By the end of the month, the main parts of the island, apart from some parts of Palermo, had been placed directly under his administration. He moved to the Sicilian capital on 7 August. An element of glamour was attached to his offices – at 9 via Bari – through the fact that they were guarded by carabinieri (local police) wearing swords, white gloves and bandoliers, and 'Napoleon' cocked hats with the red, white and green tricolour.[25] In practice, the AMGOT operation did not start functioning properly until the second half of August. There was a lot of coming and going, as staff were sent out into the provinces or had to be replaced. It took until 17 August for the Germans to be finally driven off the island.[26]

The practical details for the administration of Sicily and southern Italy were initially formulated by Charles Spofford, an American lieutenant who became Rodd's chief of staff. These were based in part on a study of British military administration. When Rodd took charge of AMGOT, he approved the Spofford Plan, with some amendments. The Plan involved attaching civil affairs officers to advancing army units so that they could take immediate charge of conquered areas.[27] Arriving in an occupied town, civil affairs officers were usually confronted with a multitude of problems: the town in ruins and lacking municipal government, abandoned houses and streets, a collapse in the water supply, no electric lights and a large number of corpses.[28] Gerald Wellesley – who was for some weeks senior civil affairs officer (SCAO) in Catania – where the fighting was heavy – was confronted with 12,000 people living in underground shelters and 20,000

---

22. Coles and Weinberg, *Civil Affairs*, 190; Harris, *Allied Military Administration of Italy 1943–1945*, appendix 1. Rennell, *British Military Administration in Africa 1941–47*, 612.
23. Rennell to Platt, 19 July and 9 August 1943, Rennell of Rodd Papers, BD, Box 69/2.
24. Rodd to Mary, 22 July 1943, Rodd Family Papers, AC. Coles and Weinberg, *Civil Affairs*, 189.
25. G. R. Gayre, *Italy in Transition. Extracts from the Private Journal of G. R. Gayre, etc.* (London: Faber and Faber, 1946), 36.
26. Coles and Weinberg, *Civil Affairs*, 200. Woodward, *British Foreign Policy in the Second World War*, vol. 2, 466. On AMGOT administration, see also Charles Spofford, 'Allied Military Government [in] Sicily and Southern Italy 1943–44', Rennell of Rodd Papers, BD, Box 86.
27. Buchanan, *American Grand Strategy*, 121. Harris, *Allied Military Administration of Italy 1943–1945*, 3.
28. Rennell, 'Allied Military Government of Occupied Territory', 311–12.

Figure 8.1 British soldiers in Catania. 5 August 1943. Imperial War Museum.

uninhabitable houses. Horse-carts were the only means of getting 50 tonnes of grain into the town.[29]

From the outset, a major difference between British and American planners was over how to deal with local officials. Washington took the view that prefects and mayors should be removed. Rodd, drawing on his experience in East Africa, wanted to utilise already existing administrative structures and personnel. He particularly had in mind the experience of the Madagascan campaign, which he thought was the 'nearest analogy' to what AMGOT did.[30] Rodd played a central role in persuading Alexander and Eisenhower of the merits of indirect rule. But it took a long time; he and Spofford spent many hours explaining to Eisenhower's chief of staff, Walter Bedell Smith, the difference between the Allies ruling themselves and organising indirect rule. In the end, he and Spofford simply went ahead and formulated their plans on the basis of indirect rule, because they did not have the personnel to do it differently. Alexander told them: 'Do whatever you think

---

29. Gerald Wellesley, *The Collected Works of Gerald 7th Duke of Wellington* (privately printed, 1970), 25.
30. Rennell to Alexander, 29 January 1944, Rennell of Rodd Papers, BD, Box 111.

right: don't ask for any decisions.'³¹ It was only at the end of June that AMGOT was freed from the requirement automatically to dismiss mayors and prefects of important communities. Rodd stressed the importance of the issue in a summary of events he wrote for Alexander in January 1944:

> On the basis of the rulings I had received from the commander-in-chief about indirect rule, I made an estimate of the staff required on the supposition that the Italian administrative machine would be kept in existence subject to early removal of dangerous Fascists and the progressive, but not immediate removal of all Fascists which I did not regard as practical.³²

More details about Rodd's thinking about indirect rule were evident from a memorandum he wrote in April, in which he argued that Allied administrators should not replace local prefects but sit alongside them and explain AMGOT objectives; prefects would then issue orders to their subordinates in their own names. The aim was to avoid giving the impression that the Allies were establishing a government of their own or annexing the territory. Rodd emphasised that indirect rule brought with it many advantages. It required fewer officers, created a culture in which local officials were more likely to remain obedient to their superiors, meant fewer language difficulties and gave people an incentive to remain at work since there was a possibility of them filling the posts of their superiors. There was less danger of a general strike under indirect rule; administrative breakdowns were less likely to be attributed to the Allies; and education of the local administrative machine was more likely when there were fewer dismissals. Rodd also thought indirect rule less complicated from a budgetary point of view, since it protected AMGOT from having to absorb local personnel onto its payroll because a local treasury system would be maintained.³³

There was a wider issue at stake here, relating to the extent to which a military government was expected to have a political agenda. Rodd was critical of the 'reformer spirit' of some of his US colleagues. Many of them, he observed, thought in terms of 'recasting' the Italian social and governmental structure: even at Chrea, they were discussing social security plans and the future fiscal system for Italy. To Rodd, this failed to take into account that the role of the military government was to manage the country on a 'maintenance basis', before giving way either to a national administration under an Armistice Commission or a more formal Allied civil administration. For this to happen, it was necessary to keep in existence as much as possible of the local administrative machinery. This, he insisted, was the rationale behind his emphasis on indirect rule. His concerns about reformism seem to have fallen on deaf ears: 'In vain I pointed out that this was not a function of military government and was a concern of the Italian people

---

31. Harris, *Allied Military Administration of Italy 1943–1945*, 3. Rennell to Spofford, 10 December 1948, Rennell of Rodd Papers, BD, Box 86.
32. Rennell to Alexander, 29 January 1944, Rennell of Rodd Papers, BD, Box 111, Section 16. Harris, *Allied Military Administration of Italy 1943–1945*, 4.
33. Rennell, Memorandum, 18 April 1943, 1–3, National Archives and Records Administration (NARA), ACC, 10000/100/604; Coles and Weinberg, *Civil Affairs*, 171–72.

themselves under a government of their own choice, which liberated nations had been promised under the Atlantic charter.'[34]

While American planners were instinctively more drawn to direct rule, they were aware of the need to take account of local sensitivities. The United States' *Field Manual 27–5* (1940), which formed the basis for the School of Military Government set up in Charlottesville in Virginia in 1942, stressed that military government should take account of local laws, customs and institutions. It also stated that local governmental institutions in occupied areas should be permitted to continue, unless military necessity or some other cogent reasons required otherwise. This principle was evident in the planning for Operation Torch – the invasion of French North Africa in November 1942 – when directives were issued stating that French civilian administration should, as far as possible, be kept intact. Yet, there was suspicion of British imperialism on the American side; some saw their own history of military government as more benign than European examples of it.[35]

Rodd's gradualism and localism were evident in a report of 2 August 1943. He explained here that initial arrests were few in the first two weeks owing to a lack of information and a desire to do nothing which would cause a breakdown in the administration, while AMGOT officers were trying to get the whole operation running. In his view, it was the 'right course' to weed out 'undesirables' week by week, rather than to embark on wholesale arrests with 'insufficient information', which, in some cases, might have to be reversed.[36] Rodd was mindful, too, that some fascists had vital practical skills and that not all anti-fascists were law-abiding citizens.[37] Another factor was that 40 per cent of the adult Sicilian population was illiterate, so it was sometimes hard to find people with sufficient education to take on administrative roles, especially in the rural areas. Sicily was also the least fascist part of Italy.[38] A distinction was made between the Fascist party itself, which was to be suppressed immediately, and institutions operating within the fascist system, which could have some continuing use. Nevertheless, leading fascists were removed relatively quickly, as Rodd explained in his report for August: 'There are now no prefects of pre-occupation days; the last of these in Enna was an old civil servant without pronounced leanings towards Fascism: he was removed for incompetence.' By the end of August, all prefects from the pre-occupation period had been removed, but in most places, deputy mayors were permitted to remain. In all, just over 1,500 fascists were arrested and interned.[39] Geography could be an impediment to swift action. In October 1943, with the 8th Army on the mainland, Rodd told Alexander that

---

34. Rennell to Alexander, 29 January 1944, 36, Rennell of Rodd Papers, BD, Box 111.
35. William M. Hudson, *Army Diplomacy: American Military Occupation and Diplomacy after World War II* (Lexington: University Press of Kentucky, 2015), 80, 130, 149–51. Coles and Weinberg, *Civil Affairs*, 32–33, 68–69, 77.
36. Coles and Weinberg, *Civil Affairs*, 195.
37. Rennell, Foreword to Gayre, *Italy in Transition*, 12–13.
38. Rennell, Address to MPs, 29 October 1943, 3–4, J. R. M. Butler Papers, TCC.
39. Rennell, Monthly Report for August 1943, CAB 122/442, 9. Coles and Weinberg, *Civil Affairs*, 202. Harris, *Allied Military Administration of Italy 1943–1945*, 10, 41, 48–49.

because parts of Calabria had been difficult to reach, some fascist elements had yet to be purged.[40]

Rodd stressed the importance of drawing local society into provincial administration, as he explained in a directive of 6 September: 'I think it is desirable that [...] a small council be set up in each commune to assist the mayor, take some of the responsibility off his shoulders and explain the necessity of unpopular measures to their constituents.' He went on to suggest that these councils should include representatives from different classes and interests, including local farmers, and that priests, doctors and schoolmasters could be useful in building links with the community. In consequence, there emerged what David Ellwood has called a '*de facto* alliance' between Allied authorities in the provinces and the most prominent local citizens.[41] In his August report, Rodd also explained that when seeking to fill vacant posts, local opinion was consulted and a 'limited number of better class Sicilians' were co-opted for administrative work. But finding citizens ready to take responsibility was often difficult. Rodd's brother, Peter, who had been appointed SCAO in the central Sicilian province of Enna, observed that Italian officials had become so accustomed to shelving responsibility that it was sometimes necessary to force them to assume it. Furthermore, some were fearful that there would be a reversal of fortunes in the war.[42] Even so, indirect rule was never fully established. Arriving in Sicily, the Allies found little in the way of central government, since many of the island's provinces had been run from Rome. 'We had to compromise between direct and indirect policy', Rodd told a group of MPs in late October.[43] Post-war, some commentators suggested that the emphasis on indirect rule had not been thought through adequately: in some areas, Italians had been in need of training and greater supervision from the Allies, whereas, in others, Allied involvement was over-intrusive.[44]

Rodd found the church 'neutrally helpful', in the sense that it preached acceptance and cooperation with the Allies. He heard two sermons to large congregations exhorting the people to obey and accept the Allied military government coupled with invective against the fascist regime. But he found some churchmen ambivalent about denouncing the mafia or prominent fascists. Cardinal Lavitrano in Palermo, for example, was prone to encouraging Allied authorities to release interned fascists and let them move on from the past. Not all local interests were encouraged. For example, Rodd was keen to prevent any signs of Sicilian separatism: An inter-provincial meeting that separatists tried to organise in August was forbidden.[45]

---

40. Rennell to Alexander, 10 October 1943, Frank J. McSherry Papers, USAH, Box 27.
41. Coles and Weinberg, *Civil Affairs*, 284. Ellwood, *Italy 1943–1945*, 58.
42. Rennell, Monthly Report for August 1943, CAB 122/442, 9. Coles and Weinberg, *Civil Affairs*, 202, 279.
43. Rennell, Address to MPs, 29 October 1943, J. R. M. Butler Papers, TCC.
44. George C. Benson and Maurice Neufeld, 'American Military Government in Italy', in Carl J. Friedrich (ed.), *American Experiences in Military Government* (New York: Reinhart, 1948), 121–22.
45. Rennell to Alexander, 29 January 1944, 32, Rennell of Rodd Papers, BD, Box 111. Rennell, cited in Ellwood, *Italy 1943–1945*, 58. Harris, *Allied Military Administration of Italy 1943–1945*, 59, 61.

AMGOT used the carabinieri to maintain civil order. On arrival in Sicily, Rodd found little in the way of a functioning police system in operation, and the number of Allied policemen needed to enforce order was too great to countenance. This meant he was compelled to make use of local carabinieri. Some British policemen were sent. In May, Rodd made an urgent request to the career police officer Eric St Johnston, who was involved in the planning of the Allied invasion, for police officers to be sent to North Africa. A meeting on the issue took place in the Home Office.[46] But this was never enough to cover all needs. Already on 8 August 1943, Rodd explained that the practice of retaining carabinieri as the nucleus of local police forces had been successful: The carabinieri had been very cooperative and worked with 'dignity' and a 'sense of duty'. Petty criminality in the first few days after the invasion had been countered by arrests from the carabinieri.[47]

Rodd thought the carabinieri important for controlling the mafia. 'In a country like Sicily where the Mafia is far from dead, it requires an intimate local knowledge which is only possessed by the carabinieri to keep Mafia activities in bounds', he said in early August.[48] Already at Chrea, Rodd warned of the dangers of the mafia. Seeing it as 'less a secret society than an attitude of mind', he was conscious that no Italian government had succeeded in stamping it out completely – even taking into account the efforts of prefect Cesare Mori in the late 1920s.[49] He saw it as a 'racket organisation', but one which had acquired considerable political influence. Already in mid-August, he reported a growth in mafia activity. Part of the problem, he observed, was simply that war itself and the breakdown of authority accompanying it provided a good 'culture ground for the virus'.[50] 'Unruly elements' often took advantage of the relative chaos that followed the Allied occupation of an area.[51] A case can be made for saying that indirect rule was not well suited to dealing with the criminal possibilities in this situation. C. R. S. Harris, who wrote the official history of the Allied administration of Italy, argued that indirect rule was a 'definite failure' in suppressing the black market, although he conceded that direct rule might not have been much better. He blamed the black market on the Agents of Public Safety – those responsible for criminal investigation – suggesting that they had been corrupted by fascism.[52]

---

46. Williams, *Allies and Italians under Occupation*, 21. Eric St Johnston, *One Policeman's Story* (London: Rose, 1978), 93. The Home Office meeting was attended by Johnston and Frank Brook.
47. Coles and Weinberg, *Civil Affairs*, 196.
48. Rennell, notes in reply to Commons debate on 3 August 1943, F. J. Rennell Papers, Folder 7, NCO.
49. Prefect of Palermo, Cesare Mori, was known as the 'Iron prefect' for his campaigns against the Mafia.
50. Rennell, report to general commanding in chief, 15th Army Group, 18 August 1943, NARA, ACC, 10000/100/688.
51. Rennell, notes in response to House of Commons debate of 3 August 1943, 1, F. J. Rennell Papers, NCO.
52. Harris, *Allied Military Administration of Italy 1943–1945*, 53.

One sign of mafia activity was murder cases about which it proved impossible to find any evidence. Rodd tried to be tough; he wanted to suppress the mafia altogether rather than just keep it under control. When a local landowner, Baron Genuardo, was murdered, he had the suspects – who were mafiosi – tried in a military court rather than by local jury, in order to ensure that death sentences were given and carried out immediately.[53] But distinguishing members of the mafia was not easy, as he explained: 'With the people clamouring to be rid of a Fascist *Podestà*, many of my officers fell into the trap of selecting the most forthcoming self-advertiser [...] The choices in more than one instance fell on the local "Mafia" boss or his shadow, who in one or two cases had graduated in an American gangster environment.'[54] Speaking to MPs in late October, he explained that in Palermo province, six people had been appointed as local mayors who had turned out to be local mafia bosses. Subsequently dismissed though they were, he thought there were a lot more.[55] Although conscious that some imprisoned mafiosi were genuinely anti-fascist, Rodd warned that they were not people to whom clemency could be extended on the grounds that they were political prisoners.[56] He later blamed the Americans for releasing some anti-fascist prisoners who were mafiosi. There is nothing in Rodd's writings during or after the war to support the idea that some Allied intelligence organisations enlisted the support of the mafia during the Sicilian campaign. If he suspected that something like this had happened, he did not say so. He strongly rejected suggestions that the Allies encouraged a recrudescence of the mafia for the purpose of fighting the Germans.[57] His interpretation of how organised crime re-emerged under AMGOT is essentially in line with the view of writer Tim Newark that it was through 'misunderstanding and administrative overstretch', and 'by mistake', that AMGOT created space for the mafia.[58]

More personally, one historian has speculated that Rodd's aristocratic background may have blinded him to the fact that some of Sicily's landed families had mafia connections, citing as evidence for this AMGOT's appointment as mayor of Palermo of the landowner Lucio Tasca Bordonaro, a man from a separatist family with mafia links.[59] This is not impossible, for, in his report for August 1943, Rodd remarked that the Tasca

---

53. Rennell, response to questions, 29 October 1943, 6, J. R. M. Butler Papers, TCC. Tim Newark, *Mafia Allies: The True Story of America's Secret Alliance with the Mob in World War II* (St Paul: Zenith, 2007), 195.
54. Rennell to Alexander, 29 January 1944, 32–33, Rennell of Rodd Papers, BD, Box 111. Harris, *Allied Military Administration of Italy 1943–1945*, 63. Manoela Patti, *La Sicilia e gli Alleati: Tra Occupazione e Liberazione* (Rome: Donzelli, 2013), 108.
55. Rennell, Address to MPs, 29 October 1943, 4, J. R. M. Butler Papers, TCC.
56. Rennell, report to general commanding in chief, 15th Army Group, 18 August 1943, NARA, ACC, 10000/100/688.
57. Rodd to Joanna Rodd, 6 March 1963, Rodd Family Papers, AC.
58. Newark, *Mafia Allies*, 195. Salvatore Lupo also dismisses conspiracy theories about the re-emergence of the Mafia; see 'The Allies and the Mafia', *Journal of Modern Italian Studies* 2, no. 1 (1997): 29. For more on this, including the links between the US Navy and the New York Mafia, see Carlo W. D'Este, *Bitter Victory: The Battle for Sicily, 1943* (Harper Perennial, 1991), 622–33.
59. John Dickie, *Mafia Brotherhoods: The Rise of the Italian Mafias* (London: Sceptre, 2012), 353–56.

family was 'commendably cooperating' on straightforward administrative questions. On the other hand, he was not blind to the allegiances of the Tasca family; he was conscious of its connection to separatism, for example. Furthermore, he could see that some local dignitaries wanted to curry favour with him. In one report, he remarked that Finocchiaro Aprile, another separatist leader from a liberal ruling family, was trying to take up certain issues with him with the view to securing his recognition as a local leader.[60]

As a possible conduit for mafia influence, Newark points the finger at Charles Poletti, an Italian-American who had briefly been governor of New York and was SCAO in Palermo. Poletti was responsible for appointing Tasca; he claimed that Tasca's appointment had produced a 'wave of confidence' in the methods of Allied military government.[61] Poletti was privately damning about Rodd. In September, he wrote to John McCloy, American assistant secretary of war, stating that Rodd would be better off abandoning military government and devoting himself to grouse shooting. He did not know what 'hard work at a desk' really meant, knew nothing of governmental administration and was 'superficial' in his analysis of problems. He added that he was not the kind of person who would promote liberal government.[62] For his part, Rodd was critical of Poletti's 'appetite for press publicity' and warned against his appointment to a senior role in the Allied Control Commission set up in November.[63]

In Rodd's mind, endemic corruption was one of the causes of the serious food supply problems under AMGOT, as he explained in his report for August: 'Twenty years of corrupt management have ingrained hoarding and black market practices to an extent which it will take more than a few months of Allied Military Administration to change.' A lot of food from North Africa, especially flour, was held up in the ports. Rodd wanted to store grain or flour at strategic points on the island, in order to 'break the black market and make the producers disgorge grain', thereby building up a reserve. The more immediate background problem under AMGOT was that transportation, including that of food, remained in the hands of the military.[64]

As in Italian Africa, currency management was another important issue. On this, the main lines of policy were formulated at the beginning of June by the Combined Chiefs of Staff. The system reflected in some ways the principles Rodd had held to in East Africa, in the sense that there was a priority to avoid chaos and ensure that the occupying power was in ultimate control. To ensure financial stability in the area of occupation, the Allies brought with them 'Allied Military lire', an initial shipment of which (to the tune

---

60. Rennell, Monthly Report for August 1943, 3, CAB 122/442. Rennell, Report of 20 August 1943, 3, WO 221/312. Harris, *Allied Military Administration of Italy 1943–1945*, 59.
61. Charles Poletti, page of comments on Tasca, 24 October 1943, Frank J. McSherry Papers, USAH, Box 27.
62. Poletti to McCloy, 27 September 1943, cited in Matthew Jones, *Britain, the United States and the Mediterranean War 1942–44* (London: Macmillan, 1996), 94.
63. Rennell to Alexander, 29 January 1944, 12, Rennell of Rodd Papers, BD, Box 111. Newark, *Mafia Allies*, 218–19.
64. Rennell, Report for August, CCAC for Information No. 5. Coles and Weinberg, *Civil Affairs*, 203–4.

of 2.2 billion lire) was brought into the country in late July. But pending the establishment of this, two 'spearhead' currencies were used as substitutes: yellow-seal dollars for American forces, and British Military Administration notes for the British. Metropolitan lire were also permitted to circulate, but people were not allowed to exchange them for either the spearhead currencies or Allied military lire. In early August, an Allied Military Financial Agency was set up to oversee the management of Allied military lire, operating, where necessary, through the bank of Sicily, which was under AMGOT control. To prevent panic withdrawals, all banks were closed and remained so for a couple of months. When they reopened in September, withdrawals were restricted to 5,000 lire from existing accounts. This worked well, because there were immediate deposits in new accounts. The restrictions were lifted by mid-October.[65]

On 3 September 1943, fighting moved to the mainland, with the British 8th Army's attack on Calabria. The first British and American flags hoisted in occupied Europe were raised from the prefecture in Reggio that evening, with the Union Jack being sent on to Churchill a month later.[66] The Mussolini regime itself had fallen some weeks earlier: on 24 July, the Fascist Grand Council gave the king command of the Italian armed forces; and a day later, Mussolini was arrested. But not until 8 September did Italy surrender to the Allies – one day before the American 5th Army under General Mark Clark landed at Salerno to face a strong German counterattack. On 13 September, the king of Italy and Marshal Badoglio established a new Italian government in Brindisi. Following negotiations with the Allies, headed by General Noel Mason-MacFarlane representing Eisenhower, it was agreed that the four provinces of Apulia would remain under Italian control, with AMGOT representatives acting as liaison officers. Although Rodd was not directly involved in these negotiations, he and Holmes came to Brindisi to work out some of the details. In his memoirs, Badoglio described Rodd as heading up the 'financial experts', noting that he was well known and popular in Rome because of his father.[67] A month later, on 13 October, the Italian king declared war on Germany, and the Allies reciprocated by bestowing on Italy co-belligerency status. Italy was not exactly an ally, since it remained subject to Allied terms, but it had, nevertheless, aligned itself with the Allies.

Naples fell to the 5th Army on 1 October. Rodd flew to the city with Alexander on 5 October. His initial assessment of the situation was cautiously positive: he reported to Spofford that they would soon be 'out of the woods' in addressing food supply problems in the city, although he warned of a lack of water and electricity.[68] But a few weeks later, in a summary of events to Alexander, he explained that on entering the city the

---

65. Frank Southard, *The Finances of European Liberation* (New York: King's Crown, 1946), 22–23, 90–93. Harris, *Allied Military Administration of Italy 1943–1945*, 11–13.
66. Rennell to Churchill, 5 October 1943, CHAR 2/463, CCC. Rennell to Alexander, 10 October 1943, Frank J. McSherry Papers, USAH, Box 27.
67. Pietro Badoglio, *Italy in the Second World War: Memories and Documents* (Westport: Greenwood, 1976), 94. Harris, *Allied Military Administration of Italy 1943–1945*, 74–75.
68. Rennell to Spofford, 6 October 1943, NARA, ACC, 10000/100/1075.

Allies had faced an 'almost overwhelming' challenge: there had been roughly 750,000 people in the city – out of a total of 1.1 million – but the urban environment was badly damaged and there were problems with the power supply and a lack of water and food. But gradually things fell into place. Rodd partly attributed this to the good working relationship between Clark and Edgar Hume, the man responsible for civil affairs in the 5th Army. Rodd highlighted the priority given to re-establishing the Serino water supply – which took three weeks, and the work of the United States Base Organisation in restoring quay accommodation sufficient to bring 200 tonnes of wheat a day into the city. But he acknowledged a number of negatives, including the fact that British troops had used the main infectious diseases hospital as quarters, damaged the Royal Palace, and committed a 'gross act of sacrilege' in the historic Castello Nuovo.[69] Another potential flashpoint was the city of Foggia, which fell to the 8th Army on 27 September. With much of the city destroyed or in a dysfunctional state, the swift return of evacuees into the city, competing for space with US Air Force personnel, made for a chaotic situation. Attempts to find an alternative administrative centre for the area proved unsuccessful. Following a visit to the area in early November, Rodd warned Alexander that there was continuing unrest in the villages. He thought this might have been attributable to communist agitation or enemy subversion.[70]

The invasion of the mainland threw up several major administrative challenges for AMGOT. Rodd saw that it would be hard for him to oversee developments in Palermo while remaining attached to the army in mainland Italy; and he wanted to forestall the possibility of AFHQ consolidating its hold on Sicily in such a way as to encourage Sicilian separatism. At one point, he told Alexander that he would be willing to become regional administrator of Sicily, but he warned that this would only work if he had direct contact with London and Washington, as opposed to operating through the MGS at AFHQ.[71] In the end, on 24 September, he proposed to Alexander and Eisenhower splitting AMGOT into Forward and Rear sections – a suggestion to which they agreed. On 26 September, Rodd left Palermo – leaving McSherry in charge – travelling northwards through Sicily and southern Italy to establish his new headquarters near Bari on 3 October. After the trip, he gave Alexander a positive assessment of the situation while reporting to Spofford that Calabria was 'less unhappy' than he had expected. On the other hand, at roughly the same time, his brother Peter, who had now moved to Calabria, reported a 'growing sense of disappointment' in the local population that the Armistice had not yet brought about the 'Golden Age'.[72] The formal division of AMGOT took place on 10 October,

---

69. Rennell's despatch to Alexander, cited in Duff, 'Civil Affairs in Italy', Section II, 109–11, CAB 44/172.
70. Rennell to Alexander, 17 November 1943, WO 220/312. See also Duff, 'Civil Affairs in Italy', Section II, 208–13, CAB 44/172.
71. Rennell to Alexander, 3 September 1943, Rennell of Rodd Papers, Box 111, BD.
72. Rennell to Alexander, 10 October, Frank J. McSherry Papers, USAH, Box 27. Rennell to Spofford, 6 October 1943, NARA, ACC, 10000/100/1075. Peter Rodd, 5 October 1943, cited in Coles and Weinberg, *Civil Affairs*, 436.

with the Forward part, AMG 15th Army Group, responsible for territory within the areas occupied by the 5th and 8th Armies.

Although Alexander remained responsible for both Forward and Rear sections, the new structure immediately created fresh problems. They were serious enough for Rodd later to suggest that the separation had been a mistake.[73] Importantly, it created two potentially competing centres of authority. There was now an ambiguity about the extent of McSherry's remit, since McSherry was now called chief of headquarters, AMG, and was accountable to AFHQ for the administration of Sicily and parts of southern Italy. It also removed Rodd from the centre of discussions about the creation of the ACC, the body created to replace AMGOT. When the ACC came into being on 11 November, it added to the confusion, for it was a body that, according to one historian, turned into a 'large, military bureaucracy'.[74] When it was formed, it was assumed that it would amalgamate with AMG Rear and come to administer its territories before handing them back to Italy. But to begin with, there was uncertainty about how far its remit extended. Rodd himself was unhappy with the fact that it was created and trained separately in Algiers, and not on the basis of AMGOT. This meant that when it came into being, its officers often found themselves superior in rank and inferior in experience to those whose work they took over. Rodd was also worried about the size of the ACC: 'The number of officers, and in many cases their training and background, leave me in doubt whether the Italian Government would ever survive being overlaid by such a nursery governess. The authority of the Prefectorial Government in the provinces will never survive so numerous a staff.'[75]

In Rodd's mind, the ACC as constituted pointed more in the direction of direct rather than indirect rule and so ran counter to the political strategy he had been strongly promoting. As he observed: 'The more men available in the field the more direct administration they will try to undertake.' His concerns were shared by the Soviet representative on the Allied Advisory Council for Italy, Andrei Vyshinsky. In general, Rodd thought that the existence of a 'nomadic' ACC administration added to the problems connected with managing the Forward and Rear sections of AMGOT. He went as far as to blame the ACC for some of the economic and civil supply problems that emerged in Naples and beyond.[76]

Rodd attributed many of these problems to the MGS. He had originally hoped the MGS would be a channel of communication between AMGOT and AFHQ, but, already in June, was concerned that it was starting to become a policy-making body in its own right. To his frustration, it turned into the main channel of communication

---

73. Rennell, 'Memorandum on AMG and ACC', 30 December 1943, 1; Rennell to Alexander, 29 January 1944, 44–45, Rennell of Rodd Papers, BD, Box 111. Duff, 'Civil Affairs in Italy', Section II, 225–26, CAB 44/172. Harris, *Allied Military Administration of Italy 1943–1945*, 95–96.
74. Ellwood, *Italy 1943–1945*, 55.
75. Rennell to Alexander, 29 January 1944, 54, Rennell of Rodd Papers, BD, Box 111. Harris, *Allied Military Administration of Italy 1943–1945*, 108, 113.
76. Rennell, 'Memorandum on AMG and ACC', 30 December 1943, 4, 6. Rennell to Alexander, 29 January 1944, 34–35, 55, Rennell of Rodd Papers, BD, Box 111.

with Washington and London on matters relating to AMGOT and the ACC, with him and Alexander being kept out of the loop. He was particularly unhappy about being excluded from discussions about the future government in Rome; he was informed by the MGS that he would not be involved in the Armistice Commission, nor in any Allied organisation in Rome, in the event that there was no Italian government.[77] He also felt the MGS was disingenuous; it presented its plans as emanating from the Combined Chiefs of Staff in Washington, when in fact the combined chiefs had simply approved the plans submitted to them. Rodd was particularly concerned with the leadership of the MGS. He was suspicious of Holmes's ambition and lack of administrative experience. He also thought his British deputy, Colonel Terence Maxwell, lacked governmental experience. Maxwell was frequently engaged in trying to 'drive my car from the back seat', he observed. More broadly, he thought the Combined Chiefs of Staff, and their civil affairs committees, were too distant from events and too much like a post office for the departments of the different governments to be really effective.[78]

Post-war, Rodd's frustrations with the ACC found their way into Harris's history of the Allied administration of Italy. Harris and Rodd collaborated to some extent in the writing of the book; as Harris explained in his preface, Rodd personally revised the first four chapters – those dealing with the AMGOT period. Some details in the book came from Rodd's overview of AMGOT written in January 1944.[79] Harris's account carried the imprint of Rodd's perspective on the administrative confusion of the time: 'The [...] chaos will be remembered by those who took part in it as an administrative nightmare, of successive and often contradictory policies, the details of which were circulated (or more often failed to circulate) between five headquarters and two continents.' Harris also exonerated Rodd over food supply issues; according to Harris's account, it was AFHQ in Algiers, rather than Rodd or the Advanced Echelon of AFHQ in Naples, that was responsible for food shortages in the winter of 1943–44.[80] On the other hand, Harris made some positive remarks about the ACC; he noted that it brought about a simplification in the structure through unifying the Forward and Rear sections of Allied military government – AMGOT became known as 'Allied military government' in October 1943. He also observed that Rodd's initial concept for the MGS – which was for it to be a kind of 'post office' for transmitting information – was 'perhaps not really practical'.[81] In the light of Rodd's influence on Harris, these thoughts may point to a subsequent evolution in Rodd's own views, reflecting a realisation that the takeover of Italy inevitably

---

77. Rennell, 26 June 1943; 'Memorandum on AMG and ACC', 30 December 1943, 2, 6, Rennell of Rodd Papers, BD, Box 111. Harris, *Allied Military Administration of Italy 1943–1945*, 9.
78. Rennell to Alexander, 29 January 1944, 34–38, 56, Rennell of Rodd Papers, Box 111, BD.
79. Harris, *Allied Military Administration of Italy 1943–1945*, ix, xi. The quotations from Rennell on pp. 63 and 113 of Harris's *Allied Military Administration* come from Rennell's letter to Alexander, 29 January 1944, 33 and 54, Rennell of Rodd Papers, BD, Box 111.
80. As the 'five headquarters', Harris had in mind AFHQ at Algiers and its advanced Echelon in Naples, 5th Army Group at Bari, AMG/ACC at Palermo and the headquarters of the ACC in Brindisi. Harris, *Allied Military Administration of Italy 1943–1945*, 98, 113.
81. Harris, *Allied Military Administration of Italy 1943–1945*, 47, 85–88, 112–14, 121.

brought with it a growth of bureaucracy. Not all readers found Harris's book convincing: one American reviewer complained of a pro-British bias in the text, citing, for example, criticisms in it of AFHQ and the ACC – criticisms which were in the chapters revised by Rodd.[82]

The administrative tensions affected Rodd's mood. Although he experienced moments of optimism, he often reverted to a gloomy frame of mind. In mid-September, writing from 15th Army Group headquarters, he told a friend that the AMGOT administration there was 'lousy and untidy'.[83] Writing to Grigg a few weeks later, he described Allied initiatives in Italy as 'operations Dogsbreakfast and Catshit'; and he said that military personnel at AFHQ had 'committed a MFU'. He also sensed that he was not popular at AFHQ. 'They do not want me here and will be very thankful to see the last of me', he declared.[84] He was also tired. Occasionally he had some time out: after the Salerno landings, he flew over to the area and was able to fit in a couple of yachting trips during the visit. But he was often on edge. This was not a new development. Even before the invasion had begun, he had told Mary he was in a 'dissatisfied' frame of mind and needed a rest and that he wanted to be relieved of his job.[85] He now made a similar point to Grigg, stating that he was 'very tired mentally' and 'ripe to make a first class mess soon'. He attributed his state of mind to the absence of time off during the war. Back in London in late October, he had discussions at the War Office, in which he proposed being replaced by someone whose sole responsibility was to work with 15th Army Group. This was agreed. He returned to Italy with instructions to manage the handover.[86]

Rodd was increasingly eager to leave Italy altogether. He turned down the offer of being made British vice-president of the Economic and Administrative Section of the ACC on the grounds that he did not approve of how it was constituted. The job went instead to William Wedgwood Benn, the 1st Viscount Stansgate. Rodd firmly told Eric Speed, one of the permanent undersecretaries at the War Office, that he did not want this or any role which might require him to work outside of a military framework.[87] The man who replaced Rodd at 15th Army Group – on Rodd's recommendation – was Lush. After his work in Madagascar, Lush had been re-deployed to Tripolitania. He had originally been nominated for Rodd's own job with AMGOT by the British section at AFHQ, but had not received War Office backing.[88] After Lush and Stansgate arrived on 21 and 22 November, Rodd, in a melodramatic flourish, reminded Grigg of his desire to leave by referring to a verse from the Gospel of Luke: 'Now lettest thou thy servant depart in peace, according to thy word.' In the event, Alexander was reluctant to let go of Rodd

---

82. Lynn M. Case, *Journal of Modern History* 31, no. 1 (1959): 67–68.
83. Rodd to Travers, 16 September 1943, Rennell of Rodd Papers, BD, Box 69/2.
84. Rodd to Grigg, 30 October and 5 November 1943, PJGG 9/7/27 & 29, CCC.
85. Rodd to Mary, 7 July 1943, Rodd Family Papers, AC.
86. Rodd to Grigg, 30 October 1943, PJGG 9/7/29, CCC. Duff, 'Civil Affairs in Italy', Section II, 182–86, CAB 44/172.
87. Rodd to Speed, 25 September 1943, Rennell of Rodd Papers, Box 111, BD.
88. Rennell to Alexander, 29 January 1944, 2, Rennell to P.U.S., 25 October 1943, Rennell of Rodd Papers, BD, Box 111.

immediately. He remained in his post until mid-December, but still in a dissatisfied state. He told Lush that Lush was taking over an 'untidy show'. The formal handover was 'most unsatisfactory', Lush recalled; Rodd told him very little.[89]

Rodd and Lush visited Naples together before Rodd handed over his responsibilities on 12 December. He left Bari on 16 December and flew to Algiers, where he saw Bedell Smith and Harold Macmillan, chief British advisor to Eisenhower. He also had a long talk with Eisenhower about food supply problems and personnel issues. In the latter case, he raised concerns he had about the American general chosen to head the ACC, Kenyon Joyce; Rodd was worried that there was a tendency under Joyce to 'Americanise' the culture at ACC headquarters. Rodd and Douglas Pirie flew back to London on 21 December.[90]

On the eve of his return to Britain, while he was still formally CCAO, Rodd sent a message to all civil affairs personnel in Italy, one reflective of his thinking both about AMGOT specifically and about the nature of administration generally. In this, he stressed what he saw as AMGOT's success in creating a 'fused Anglo–American organisation'; and he paid tribute to the officers at Chrea who had made this possible, expressing the hope that it would flourish in 'other theatres of war and peace'. In addition, he said that the war could not be won by one nation alone, nor Europe rebuilt; Allied military government, which he described as the 'first necessary stage in reconstruction' in the wake of battle, was a 'joint responsibility and enterprise'. He stressed that idle criticism of members of other forces was to be avoided.[91]

In this final statement, Rodd included some lines from the widely distributed *AMGOT Plan* – lines he had written himself – about the qualities needed in any good administrator:

> You will administer to the best of your ability with a sense of impartiality and justice, without fear or favour. In administration, and especially administration of justice, all men and women must be equal to you. You must learn to disregard the nationality of the people who you are administering, if you are going to be a good administrator. The principles of good administration are the same in all countries and for all people. They are the preservation of law, order and justice, the prevention of disease and distress, the removal of fear, and the creation of economic well-being.

Rodd added that in the case of a military government, there was the additional requirement to do this in the context of the needs of the high command.[92] Pragmatist though

---

89. Duff, 'Civil Affairs in Italy', Section II, 246, CAB 44/172. A. J. M. Lush (ed.), *A Life of Service: The Memoirs of Maurice Lush* (London: A. J. M. Lush, 1992), 171–72.
90. Rennell, 'Memorandum on AMG and ACC', 30 December 1943, 4, 6; Rodd to Alexander, 29 January 1944, 34–35, 55, Rennell of Rodd Papers, BD, Box 111. Flint, 'The Development of British Civil Affairs', 157.
91. Statement of 18 December 1943, F. J. Rennell Papers, Folder 7, NCO. Duff, 'Civil Affairs in Italy', Section II, 248–50, CAB 44/172.
92. Statement of 18 December 1943, F. J. Rennell Papers, Folder 7, NCO. Duff, 'Civil Affairs in Italy', Section II, 248–50, CAB 44/172. These lines came from General Administrative Instruction No. 1 and were subsequently included in *A.M.G.O.T. Plans, Proclamations and Instructions* (Palermo, 1943), 80.

he was, there was an element of idealism here. Good administration, he believed, was about building foundations for the future, whether in AMGOT or any other area of life. Writing to Mary in late 1942, in connection with his involvement in the family-owned Guthrie Trust, Rodd said:

> If you lay the foundations well and on good principles the troubles that do occur are always less fearsome than one had thought. In spite of all my absences the many trusts that I look after are all in pretty good shape and running smoothly. That is rather one of the interesting sides and amusements of administration if one is patient enough to watch the developments over the years. The catch is that one does not see the results except over years and most people are not patient enough to do so.[93]

Back in Britain, Rodd's role with AMGOT put him in the public eye. After the invasion of Sicily, the *Illustrated London News* made him one of their personalities of the week.[94] But he also provoked hostile reactions on the left. The author of an unsigned article in *New Statesman and Nation* on 24 July argued that he was not a suitable person to be running AMGOT: '[Our choice to be running AMGOT] has fallen on a financier, Lord Rodd, Oxford Grouper and former friend of Volpi, Big Business backers of Italian fascism.' Implying that Rodd's Italian links were primarily with the fascist elite, the author went on to ask: 'Will it be easy for groups which might organise a popular mass movement […] to deal with him?' A few days later, the magazine returned to the attack with a warning that the post-war world could end up by being run by a 'Supreme Council of Lord Rennells'.[95] The attacks had a ripple effect. The *New York Times* cited the controversy on 25 July, apparently prompted by the first of the *New Statesman and Nation* articles. A few weeks later, the author of an article in the *Daily Worker* suggested that there was 'less trade union liberty and far more security and authority' in Allied-occupied Italy than in the area of the country ruled by Badoglio.[96] Even after the war, the idea that Rodd was in some way pro-fascist survived. The Nazi hunter, Curt Reiss, suggested that, as a friend of industrialists like Schacht and Pirelli, Rodd did everything he could to see that the fascist regime remained in power.[97]

It is not clear who wrote the *New Statesman and Nation* articles. One possibility was left-wing Labour MP and journalist Tom Driberg. The citing of Rodd's association with the Oxford Group (OG) in one of the articles may be an indication that Driberg was its author – Driberg was an outspoken critic of the OG. Driberg attacked Rodd in parliament at this time. Speaking in the Commons on 3 August 1943, he expressed concern that AMGOT as constituted would always tend to leave 'more of the official Fascist functionaries than we would wish left in office'. In the same debate, the deputy leader

---

93. Rodd to Mary, 19 November 1942, Rodd Family Papers, AC.
94. *Illustrated London News*, 24 July 1943, 91.
95. 'Policy and Aims in Sicily', *New Statesman and Nation*, 24 July 1943, 1. 'The Road to Cosmopolis', *New Statesman and Nation*, 7 August 1943, 2.
96. *New York Times*, 25 July 1943, E1. *Daily Worker*, 7 September 1943, 1.
97. Curt Reiss, *The Nazis Go Underground* (Fonthill Media, 2013), 65.

of the Labour party, Arthur Greenwood, expressed a concern as to whether Rodd and his associates would have the interests of the workers and peasants of Sicily at heart. His colleague, Ivor Thomas, then complained that there were too many bankers in AMGOT; alongside Rodd, the regional administrator in AMGOT, C. E. Benson, and chief finance officer, A. P. Grafftey-Smith, had banking experience. A couple of days later, in the House of Lords, Lord Cranborne (Cecil) came to Rodd's defence, stating that his previous involvement in the Foreign Office, expert knowledge of Italy and experience in civil affairs were reasons why he was a good person for the role.[98]

The controversy continued the following month. On 21 September, Ivor Thomas suggested that there was little difference between rule by AMGOT and what had gone on before. His colleague Richard Stokes then declared that AMGOT represented the 'most reactionary' elements, suggesting that Rodd was a 'diehard tory' – although he retracted this. A day later, the Labour MP John Dugdale encouraged AMGOT to hold elections as soon as possible; he was afraid that military expediency was being used as a reason for maintaining military rule.[99] In response and in a lengthy statement, Eden insisted that AMGOT was doing a 'very fine work' in addressing practical issues, while also noting that the fascist leaders of all the nine Sicilian prefectures had been arrested or had fled. He went on to distinguish the carabinieri from the Italian secret police, the Ovra, noting that if use had not been made of the former, at least 10,000 British troops would have been required to do the job. 'We discussed all this before we went into Sicily and I am absolutely certain that our system is right', he insisted. He defended restrictions against political activities in Sicily, while countering that freedom of the press had been permitted.[100] Eden, then, came to the defence of all the main policies Rodd was associated with. However, he did not defend Rodd himself. Rodd subsequently complained that the Foreign Office had failed to give AMGOT adequate support, and Eden's failure to support him personally was a key reason for this.

Back in Britain in late October, Rodd gave a talk to a group of MPs at the Civil Affairs Staff Centre in Wimbledon, followed later in the day by an off-the-record press conference at the War Office. At the start of the first of these, Rodd referred to himself as 'Daniel in the Lion's Den'. The meeting went some way to improving AMGOT's image. Ivor Thomas, with whom he had a 'frank talk' over lunch, wrote him a conciliatory letter afterwards, thanking him for the courtesy shown to the visitors and remarking on the 'vitally important work' he was doing.[101] But the sense that Rodd was insufficiently anti-fascist persisted in some left-wing circles. Writing from New York in early December, Luigi

---

98. Tom Driberg, Arthur Greenwood, Ivor Thomas, 3 August 1943, House of Commons, Hansard. Lord Cranbourne, 5 August 1943, House of Lords, Hansard. *Times*, 30 July 1943, 4.
99. Ivor Thomas, Richard Stokes, 21 September 1943, John Dugdale, 22 September 1943, House of Commons, Hansard.
100. Anthony Eden, 22 September 1943, House of Commons, Hansard.
101. Rennell, Address to MPs, 29 October 1943, 1, J. R. M. Butler Papers, TCC. War Office press conference, 29 January 1943; Thomas to Rodd, 29 October 1943, Rennell of Rodd Papers, Box 111, BD. See also Rodd to Grigg, 30 October 1943, PJGG, CCC.

Sturzo, co-founder of the Italian People's Party, criticised him for failing adequately to promote democratic elements and showing a lack of imagination.[102]

AMGOT had an image problem. As Edward Flint explains, civil affairs gained a reputation for attracting elderly gentleman from public school backgrounds. Work in civil affairs seemed to lack the dynamism and excitement associated with battle. Some joked that OETA stood for 'Old Etonians Touring Association', and AMGOT for 'Ancient Military Gentlemen on Tour'.[103] The comic associations were accentuated when Nazi sympathiser William Joyce ('Lord Haw Haw') suggested that 'AMGOT' meant 'dung' in Turkish. Churchill asked Alexander Cadogan, permanent undersecretary at the Foreign Office, to find out if this was true. When Rodd was in Britain in late October, he explained to MPs that the Turkish word in question was not AMGOT but 'OTBOK'.[104]

The exploits of Rodd's own family also became a source of humour. As AMGOT's reputation waned, someone combined the term 'AMGOT' with the title of Wagner's opera, *Götterdämmerung* – 'The Twilight of the Gods', in English – to make the comic-sounding word 'AMGOTterdämmerung'. This was then turned into 'Rotterdämmerung' – 'The Twilight of the Rodds'. A journalist at the *Sunday Times* thought this one of the cleverest quips of the war.[105] One man responsible for publicising the 'Rotterdämmerung' phrase, indeed the probable author of it, was Peter Clarke, a British civil affairs officer attached to the 8th Army with a flair for writing satirical verses. One of them, the so-called AMGOT hymn, written in August 1943, was titled 'Amgot Strafe Italy'. This was an allusion to a German propaganda slogan of the First World War, 'Gott strafe England' – 'May God punish England'.[106] The 'hymn' included lines parodying Rodd or AMGOT, such as 'We are Lord Rennell's Army, who never fire a shot. / When danger's o'er we come ashore to set up our AMGOT'; 'Hand-picked by "Monty" (Norman), our chiefs are Bankers all. / The proud elite of Lombard Street, Cornhill and London Wall. / They know the "Price" of Freedom, are "Liberal" with their loans'; 'So hail Lord Rennell's Army, and "Hands across the sea!" / Somewhere in war-torn Europe, there's peace for you and me.'[107]

Peter Rodd was also a target of Clarke's humour. Clarke's 'The Lay of the Lost Administrator' from 'Rotterdämmerung' poked particular fun at his activities in Calabria: 'Alas, Calabria – spurned and wild – / neath Colonel Rodd's regime reviled, / land of olive and the mud, / and home of many an Amgot dud.'[108] Post-war, a number

---

102. Luigi Sturzo, *New Leader*, 11 December 1943, 5.
103. Flint, 'The Development of British Civil Affairs', 158.
104. H. L. Mencken, 'War Words in England', *American Speech* 19, no. 1 (1944): 6. Churchill, cited in Jones, *Britain, the United States and the Mediterranean War 1942–44*, 94. Rennell, Address, 29 October 1943, J. R. M. Butler Papers, TCC.
105. Hastings, *Nancy Mitford*, 140. Atticus, *Sunday Times*, 23 March 1947, 5.
106. Matthew Stibbe, *German Anglophobia and the Great War, 1914–1918* (Cambridge: Cambridge University Press, 2001), 18.
107. Peter Clarke, 'Amgothic Lines and Other Outbursts of an Uncivil Affairs Officer', Sicily August 43–Romagna January 45, manuscript, 53–54. This was composed at Taormina. For a slightly different version, see James Carr Grizzard, *The War Was More Than the Cannon's Roar: A Story of the Allied Occupation of Italy* (Atlanta: Swan Arts, 2000), 60.
108. 'Amgothic Lines and Other Outbursts of an Uncivil Affairs Officer', manuscript, 9.

of colourful stories circulated in the Rodd family about Peter's activities with AMGOT – doubtless involving some embellishment. According to one of them, he once had to deal with a case of two hooligans who had been arrested for shouting 'Viva Mussolini'. His response was to require them to write out 'Viva Mussolini' a thousand times on bits of paper and have these distributed as loo paper in the public toilets.[109] In another, recounted by Nancy Mitford, he was supposed to have run a pirate fleet under the Rodd family ensign (three clubs), plundering German fuel supplies.[110]

Rodd (Francis) had a reputation for upper-class eccentricity among US personnel. The American serviceman Stephen Mavis was struck by the fact that he had a habit of taking snuff. He also mistakenly thought he was a Scotsman:

> The general was an impressive Scottish gentleman who usually wore a military jacket or a kilt. He had a noticeable habit of gracefully indulging in a piece of snuff taken from a silver snuff box. He remained a continuing source of curiosity to the Americans. One would never meet his kind either on Broadway or the main streets of the Midwest.[111]

Rodd also made an appearance in US fiction. Lord Runcin, a snuff-taking AMGOT leader in John Hersey's Pulitzer Prize-winning novel, *A Bell for Adano* (1944), was evidently modelled on him; Runcin, Hersey's novel suggested, was a man with a 'purely colonial point of view towards the Italians'. Another character in the novel, Joppolo, was widely held to be the model for Poletti.[112]

The way in which Rodd was seen by his peers was varied. Harold Macmillan, who saw a lot of him in the second half of 1943, was impressed by his ability, while thinking that his ambition got the better of him. In August, he wrote in his diary: 'Francis (with occasional lapses into prima donna mood) is really awfully good at his job. He is quick, intelligent and persistent. His chief fault is that he is sometimes impulsive and makes decisions too rapidly.' In November, however, he called him a 'great prima donna and prime intriguer', suggesting that he was determined to resign from AMGOT if he could not be head of the new Allied Control Commission. People like Rodd and Kenyon Joyce were 'plotting and worrying' about their jobs, he remarked.[113] Rodd has his own opinions on Macmillan. When they met in April, he expressed frustration over what he saw as a lack of understanding in people like Macmillan over what was involved in administration.[114] Lush was another person who thought Rodd temperamental: in his view, Rodd tended to make 'heavy weather over ordinary problems' and lacked experience in

---

109. Recollections of Mary Daniell, November 2014.
110. Hastings, *Mitford*, 140.
111. Stephen Mavis, unpublished manuscript, 'Reminiscences of Allied Military Government under Two Flags in Sicily–Italy (1943–47)', 47.
112. John Hersey, *A Bell for Adano* (New York: Alfred A. Knopf, 1944), 128–35. Buchanan, *American Grand Strategy*, 127.
113. Harold Macmillan, *War Diaries: Politics and War in the Mediterranean January 1943–May 1945* (London: Macmillan, 1984), 190, 280.
114. Rodd, Diary for 1943, 20, Rennell of Rodd Papers, BD, Box 111.

military government.[115] General Bernard Montgomery – in charge of the 8th Army – was also critical of Rodd. He found Rodd 'pompous' when they met in the early autumn; Rodd 'resented any criticism of his show', he observed. Coming from a man known for his self-confidence, this was somewhat ironic. In this case, Montgomery was almost certainly personalising what were at root some practical differences between the two men. Montgomery thought the way civil affairs staff operated in Italy was sometimes an impediment to military operations. For his part, Rodd thought the needs of civil affairs officers were not addressed adequately by the 8th Army – he attributed tensions with Montgomery to transport and supply issues.[116]

Rodd also inspired much loyalty. An educationalist who worked under him for AMGOT, G. R. Gayre, wrote in his diary in October 1943 that Rodd had two outstanding qualities. The first of them was his ability to choose staff. 'Never have I met a staff of like proportions', he declared. He mentioned, in particular, D. G. Cheyne, director of public health; A. P. Grafftey-Smith; Mason Hammond, advisor on monuments and fine arts; C. R. S. Harris; Frank Southard, later a director of the International Monetary Fund; and Charles Spofford. Gayre reported at the time: 'The spirit of the headquarters is good – perhaps because Rennell's staff has excluded mediocrity to such a degree that all jockeying for position which one so often finds in bad organizations, is not so apparent.' Second, Gayre praised Rodd for having confidence in his staff:

> Having chosen a staff, he reposes confidence in it. Furthermore, there is no question of rank or "channels" here. He is ready of access and it is a question of a direct approach between head of a division and the general, or General McSherry, or the chief of staff, whichever might be most readily accessible. The result is that there is both freedom and rapidity of action and decision.[117]

There was an element of informality in Rodd's style of leadership – in spite of his somewhat patrician demeanour. This suggests that the pattern of running things evident in OETA/OTA under Mitchell was replicated in AMGOT. Gayre attributed this leadership style to the fact that Rodd was himself a civilian rather than a military man by mentality. When AMGOT came to an end, he lamented the loss of this: 'Here, anyway, passes away the Rennell régime which has always kept a strong informal civilian touch about it, and its replacement by a body of officers, many of them high-ranking, who whether drawn from the regular army or not, tend to have in their ranks an unduly large proportion who think more of "channels" than getting the job done.' Military government of Rodd's kind was efficient because it was informal, he said. Gayre's admiration for Rodd seems to have been strengthened by the fact that they had a joint love of mead, an alcoholic drink created from fermenting honey: 'Lord Rennell appears to be as keen

---

115. Lush, *A Life of Service*, 146.
116. Flint, 'The Development of British Civil Affairs', 157–58. Rennell to Spofford, 10 September 1948, Rennell of Rodd Papers, BD, Box 86. Montgomery to Grigg, 14 October 1943, PJGG 9/8/3, CCC.
117. Gayre, *Italy in Transition*, 79.

upon mead as I am. He tried to make it recently, but it did not come out rightly. I think he was using some of those *Metheglin* recipes, some of which are very poor.'[118]

Gayre's remarks hint at the fact that some of the tensions in AMGOT were not simply about whether the British or Americans should have predominance, but also about the culture of the US military and the extent of its control. This had been a source of tension in Washington itself. When the School of Military Government was set up, there was suspicion among some of Roosevelt's staff that it could prove a vehicle for conservative military ideas. It took some persuasion by Henry Stimson, Secretary of State for War, to persuade Roosevelt of the soundness of the school's vision. The US military was always insistent that its control of military operations in the field should be unhindered. Eisenhower, for example, insisted that the State Department representative on his staff, Robert Murphy, was not independently accountable to Washington. When, in 1943, the Combined Civil Affairs Committee was set up in Washington to advise the Combined Chiefs of Staff, it was organised in such a way as to leave the ultimate authority with the military.[119]

---

118. Gayre, *Italy in Transition*, 47, 84, 190.
119. Hudson, *Army Diplomacy*, 117, 130, 149–51. Coles and Weinberg, *Civil Affairs*, 119–25.

Chapter Nine

'JACK OF MANY TRADES'

In summer 1943, with Rodd engrossed in AMGOT, Mary decided to return to Britain. Leaving Philadelphia in August, she brought the family back across the Atlantic on a Portuguese liner, in what was a harrowing crossing: a cyclone forced the ship to turn south towards the Azores before it finally docked in Portugal in late September.[1] Rodd got news of their safe arrival on 9 October and saw them briefly in Lisbon at the end of the month. He was keen to alert Mary to the nature of the situation she was returning to, including the scarcity of food in the cities. He had already told her that, post-war, she would have to make some adjustments to her lifestyle. Her priority, he suggested, needed to be the re-establishment of family life in Herefordshire. But this was going to be a challenge: 'The position roughly is that if you have servants you will have to work in a factory, or you can do the work yourself instead.' But he sought to reassure her that he had not been able to detect any criticism of her for having been away from Britain.[2] Mary knew of Rodd's desire to settle down at the Rodd after the war. But she was unsure that this would suit him. In the summer of 1942, she told him that any desire he had to live quietly in Herefordshire for the rest of his life was a 'nostalgic' dream; he was meant to get involved in the running of the country in some way, rather than be a country squire or farmer.[3]

Rodd warned Mary about the attacks on him in parliament and the press:

> I have come in for a good deal of slanging in parliament and in the press. I think I have done a good deal to clear things up. But it has been hard work. Keep out of the press as much as you can and don't see newspaper men. You will almost certainly be assailed on arrival. My life seems to have become a subject of interest unfortunately.[4]

The whole process had been 'very unpleasant', he declared, adding that any thoughts he had had of being a colonial governor had been set back by this publicity and criticism.[5] Rodd was proud of the fact that his daughters had been schooled in the United States – he wanted his children to identify with America as much as with their own country. A few weeks after being reunited with his family, he wrote to Lamont thanking him for his daughters' time in North America. Noting that if he had had a son, he would have

---

1. The ship was the *Serpa Pinto*. For more on the crossing, see Shirley Williams, *Climbing the Bookshelves: The Autobiography of Shirley Williams* (London: Virago, 2010), ch. 3.
2. Rodd to Mary, 13 January, 3 October, 10 October 1943, Rodd Family Papers, AC.
3. Mary to Rodd, 15 July 1942, Rennell of Rodd Papers, BD, Box 71/2.
4. Rodd to Mary, 30 October 1943, Rodd Family Papers, AC.
5. Ibid.

tried to get him an Anglo–American education, he said that he had not been ambitious enough to dream of one for his daughters. But he was thrilled at what they had gained from their American experience. He went on to liken the AMGOT experience to that of his family. While noting that the AMGOT experiment had become 'ragged' and that there was an 'atmosphere of Fin de Siecle' about it, he stressed the importance of the 'Anglo–American community of effort, equality of status and responsibility' which had underpinned it. He then compared this to what had happened to his family: 'I rather think that thanks to all of you in America the same has been achieved in my family. I am well satisfied.'[6]

On his return to Britain, Rodd was exhausted. Early in 1944 he was reported in the *Times* as being on sick leave. He spent much of the time in the ensuing months at the Rodd, trying to recover his energy. He wrote to Mary in February stating that he had been 'very near breaking', but was 'gradually getting fitter' and starting to sleep better. At this time, he was doing 8–9 hours of manual work a day. The desire to work with his hands had been with him for some time. 'What I would like most of all to do is to go into the wilderness for three months as a farm labourer', he wrote in November 1942. Now, in early 1944, he found working with his hands therapeutic: 'I have found great peace here alone doing things with the hand instead of with the head', and he talked of the 'peace that the land brings'. He was uncertain about his future: 'I am unrepentant at my long holiday when all others are working.' Rodd also had a reaction against the internal politics that had been a feature of his experience in the previous year: 'I regard with horror the shambles of talk, intrigue and wire-pulling that I know is going on in London. I regard with dread being one day called back [...] I told you a long time ago that I no longer had any ambition. I am indulging that lack now and further I don't want to compete anymore with anyone who wants a job – especially mine.'[7]

In fact, Rodd was conflicted. Back in the autumn, he had told Grigg that he was thinking of leaving the War Office; he had indicated that he might be able to do more for him not from within the War Office but in his 'old black coat and trousers'. He had also signalled to Lamont a wish to return to banking.[8] In terms of his rank and responsibility, he remained CCAO in 15th Army Group until 14 February 1944. But he knew he would not be returning to Italy; he asked for his kit to be sent home on 22 January. He had returned to Britain as a high-profile figure in civil affairs: he gave talks about AMGOT at the Civil Affairs Staff Centre on 21 January and at Chatham House on 1 February.[9] At this point, Grigg made a concerted effort to get him another major position, but quickly

---

6. Rodd to Lamont, 8 August 1942, Thomas Lamont Papers, BK, Box 112/12. Rodd to Lamont, 10 December 1943, Thomas Lamont Papers, BK, Box 127/9.
7. *Times*, 18 January 1944, 2. Rodd to Mary, 19 November 1942, 25 February, 14 March 1944, Rodd Family Papers, AC.
8. Rodd to Grigg, 30 October 1943, PJGG, CCC. Rodd to Lamont, 10 December 1943, Thomas Lamont Papers, BK, Box 127/9.
9. Rennell, talk at Civil Affairs Staff Centre, 21 January 1944, Rennell of Rodd Papers, BD, Box 76/1. Talk at Chatham House was published as 'Allied Military Government in Occupied Territory', 307–16.

encountered opposition to the idea. As he explained to him: 'I have done my damnedest to get you fixed in a job commensurate with your great experience [and] ability & in the process of trying have fought two members of the War Cabinet who for differing reasons did not want you about the place.' Doubtless, Rodd's differences with men like Dalton, Eden and Lyttelton – all former Etonians – were at the root of this. Grigg was disappointed, but he was also frustrated with Rodd himself, because he noted that he had not always made it clear what he actually wanted.[10]

The possibility of having a major role in the Normandy campaign was almost certainly in Rodd's mind. Just under a year earlier, in May 1943, he had talked with Lieutenant-General Frederick Morgan about the desirability of having a civil affairs organisation within COSSAC (Chief of Staff to the Supreme Allied Commander) and, since then, had contributed to discussions about the forthcoming campaign.[11] But no job at the Supreme Headquarters Allied Expeditionary Force (SHAEF) became available. Grigg was embarrassed: 'I can only say that I realise how silly it is that you are not being used.' He persisted in trying to keep Rodd's name in the public mind. In March, he told parliament that some of AMGOT's successes were down to Rodd himself: 'The executive head of [AMGOT] was Lord Rennell, and though he is always concerned to emphasise the work of his co-adjutors, both American and British, I am sure that a great part of the credit, both for making [AMGOT's] plans and carrying them into effect, must be given to him personally.'[12] Back in July 1943, he had been given the award of Commander of the Bath – for being a 'good boy' in East Africa, he told Mary. Now he was awarded a KBE (Knight Commander of the British Empire) for his services.[13]

A wider problem for Rodd was that AMGOT was seen by some as flawed. It had a bad reputation in 21st Army Group, which had a leading role in Europe after D-Day. Montgomery, who returned to Britain in January 1944 to take up the leadership of 21st Army Group, had clashed with Rodd in the autumn. A. E. Hodgkin, a senior civil affairs officer in 21st Army Group, blamed Rodd for some of the problems in Italy. These men were worried about civil affairs interfering with their primary purpose – winning battles – and eager to ensure that the management of civil affairs was properly integrated into the chain of command. Ironically, Rodd himself was eager to ensure that commanders had a free hand. He thought of military government as an 'absolute government'; it had the merit of allowing the commander-in-chief to do whatever he liked.[14] He had also promoted the idea of civil affairs officers working within formation headquarters. But there were some who questioned the very idea of military government. The senior civil affairs planner at COSSAC and SHAEF, Major-General Roger Lumley, helped to persuade opinion away from using a military government of the AMGOT type in the

---

10. Grigg to Rodd, 3 February 1944, Rennell of Rodd Papers, BD, Box 76/2.
11. *History of COSSAC, Chief of Staff to the Supreme Allied Commander, 1943–44*, prepared by Historical Sub-section, Office of Secretary General Staff, SHAEF, May 1944, 9. DCA conference minutes, 23 October 1943, Rennell of Rodd Papers, BD, Box 111.
12. Flint, 'The Development of British Civil Affairs', 155. Grigg, 2 March 1944, House of Commons, Hansard.
13. Rodd to Mary, 22 July 1943, Rodd Family Papers, AC. *Times*, 24 March 1944, 2.
14. Rennell, 'Allied Military Government of Occupied Territory', 308.

Normandy campaign. The Foreign Office was also sceptical about deploying a military government approach.[15] Some thought that military government in Italy should have been assigned to civilians responsible to a civilian theatre commander, rather than the army itself.

Rodd's continuing good standing in the War Office resulted, in early summer 1944, in his being offered the job of director of civil affairs – MO11 had been retitled the Directorate of Civil Affairs (DCA). Rodd had long regarded the DCA as having an important role – indeed, a year earlier he had pressed for the Directorate's creation.[16] It was thus reasonable for people in the War Office to believe he might have found the job attractive. But he rejected it, in part because he thought it conflicted with work for Morgan Grenfell, which he had again taken up.[17] But another reason was that he felt a lack of backing from the Foreign Office. He told Grigg that Eden had failed adequately to defend AMGOT in parliament the previous September, and that he lacked sufficient backing outside the War Office to take up such a post:

> From all these circumstances and the undeniable fact that in the future Civil Affairs are likely to come more rather than less under the limelight, I can only come to the conclusion that I, at any rate, am not sufficiently persona grata to be able to count on support or help outside the War Office to fulfil the functions properly which you wish me to assume.[18]

Rodd was pressed by Bovenschen to reconsider, but declined.[19] The role was taken instead by Major-General Alexander Anderson. There were still some occasions when Rodd's expertise was called upon. In November 1944, he accompanied a group of generals on a visit to Caserta to meet the Italian resistance leader Alfredo Pizzoni. Rodd, who had befriended Pizzoni in 1918 while working in Palestine, was present to reassure them of Pizzoni's reliability.[20]

The fact that Rodd was now a peer meant that the House of Lords offered him an alternative platform for making a contribution to British political or public life. He gave his maiden speech on 9 May 1944 on the subject of economic warfare, arguing that the natural home for the MEW after the war was the Foreign Office.[21] Post-war reconstruction was a subject that particularly interested him. Speaking on this at the end of 1944, he insisted that the work of reconstructing conquered territories could not be hurried: 'It is not the material things that have been broken down there that matter; it is that the fabric of society has broken down, and that is not a thing that can be mended in a few

---

15. Flint, 'The Development of British Civil Affairs', 155–58, 195–98.
16. Maurice F. Neufeld, 'The Failure of AMG in Italy', *Public Administration Review* 6, no. 2 (1946): 139.
17. Rodd to S. W. Kirby, 24 August 1943, Rennell of Rodd Papers, BD, Box 111.
18. Rodd to Grigg, 16 June 1944, Rennell of Rodd Papers, BD, Box 151/3.
19. Rodd to Mary, 12 July 1944, Rodd Family Papers, AC. See also Rodd, Diary, 1943, 2, Rennell of Rodd Papers, BD, Box 111.
20. Tomasso Piffer, *Il Banchiera della Resistenza* (Milan: Mondadori, 2005), 23–24.
21. Rennell, 9 May 1944, House of Lords, Hansard. *Times*, 19 May 1944, 8.

weeks or, indeed, in a few months.'²² In his view, material reconstruction was easier to achieve than psychological renewal. In early 1945, he told Lamont that the distinction between Germans and Nazis was a spurious one; the majority of Germans were Nazis and the challenge was to convert them from their former mentality to a more Christian and socially possible frame of mind. This would not be easy. 'I wish I knew how to do that!', he declared. Rodd was defensive of the part played by the Italian monarchy in recent Italian history. He described as 'nonsense' complaints by anti-fascist politician Carlo Sforza and others that the king could have done more to oppose Mussolini; the king could only have gone against the regime when the population wished it, he believed; and in his opinion, the population had been broadly fascist in its sympathies.[23]

Rodd often addressed economic questions in his speeches in the House of Lords. In March 1947, he introduced a motion condemning what he saw as a lack of coherence in British economic policy, urging the government to hold fast to its policy of balancing the budget. The motion was carried by the margin of 119-to-30. He made a good impression: a commentator in the *Sunday Times* reported that people thought Rodd's performance one of 'superlative merit'.[24] In some ways, the speech marked a renewal of hostilities with Hugh Dalton – Dalton was at that time chancellor of the exchequer. Dalton was enduringly suspicious of men like Rodd. Three years earlier, when he was president of the Board of Trade, Dalton had met Rodd and some other bankers for a dinner that seems not to have been a great success. Dalton was privately critical of the bankers, suggesting in his diary that their dealings involved getting 'commissions and rake-offs' corresponding to 'no indispensable service'. He also hinted that they had failed to stand up to Hitler: 'They lent large sums of money to Germany and lost the greater part – serve them right!'[25]

Rodd was increasingly hostile to the socialist agenda. When he took his seat in the House of Lords in 1941, he had chosen to sit on the opposition – Liberal – benches rather than with the Conservatives. This was a break with family tradition; his father had been Conservative MP for Marylebone between 1928 and 1932. In May 1944, he defended his Liberal affiliation to Mary by stating that the Liberals and the Conservatives in the House of Lords were 'pretty mixed up together', and that he did not care much for the wartime government and what it stood for. He also said that he was not concerned with getting office.[26] He did not consider the socialist benches an option. He was wary of communism while being conscious of its historical significance; he once called the Bolshevik revolution the most important date in the history of the world for centuries.[27] His commitment to the Liberals was not permanent. In spring 1950, he and another Liberal peer, Lord Reading, switched to the Conservatives, explaining to the leading Liberal Lord Samuel that the Conservatives were the only party capable of offering

---

22. Rennell, 29 November 1944, House of Lords, Hansard.
23. Rodd to Lamont, 3 January 1945, Thomas Lamont Papers, BK, Box 112/13.
24. *Times*, 20 March 1947, 4; 21 March 1947, 4. Atticus, *Sunday Times*, 23 March 1947, 5.
25. Pimlott, *Second World War Diary of Hugh Dalton*, 762.
26. Rodd to Mary, 1 May 1944, Rodd Family Papers, AC.
27. Rodd, 'Life and Reflections', 1950, Section 1, Rodd Family Papers, AC.

'effective resistance to socialism' – the threat of socialism being, in their view, the most pressing challenge of the day. They were also of the view that the decision of the Liberal party to fight the recent election on the widest possible front had been disastrous.[28]

Rodd inherited from his parents an instinct for public service – a sense of social responsibility present in many of Britain's upper-class families.[29] Nor was it just him: his sister, Evelyn (1899–1980), also had a strong civic consciousness. She was one of the most successful Conservative women of her generation. Married to artist Thomas Emmet, who died in 1934, she lived most of her adult life at Amberley Castle in Sussex. Initially her career was connected with responsibilities in Sussex; for example, from 1935 to 1944, she was chair of the children's court and matrimonial court in the county. Like her older brother, she had an imposing personality – on seeing her in early 1941, Rodd called her 'more Queen of West Sussex than ever'.[30] Post-war, she served as a British delegate to the United Nations General Assembly (1952–53), before working as a Conservative MP (1955–64). After the 1964 election, she joined the House of Lords as a life peer under the name Baroness Emmet of Amberley. Between 1968 and 1977, she was a deputy speaker in the House of Lords – the first Conservative woman to perform the formal functions of speaker. She devoted much of her time to issues surrounding women's equality.[31]

Soon after the war ended, Rodd set to work to write up the story of wartime administration in Africa. This started out in the form of a short work on British military administration in Africa during the period 1941–43. But Rodd expanded it, drawing on his own experience and papers, along with official documents, to produce a more ambitious study, *British Military Administration of Occupied Territories in Africa, 1941–1947*, which came out in 1948. The book covered British rule in Ethiopia, Eritrea, British and Italian Somaliland, Madagascar, Cyrenaica, Tripolitania and the Dodecanese Islands. In its structure and narrative detail, the volume had the character of a reference book. Moreover, it had a semi-official feel to it. But, as Rodd explained in the preface, it was not an official record – even though it was written with the 'permission' of the Army Council; it was written 'in anticipation' of any official history that might have been produced at a later date.[32] In reality, the book was a defence of British wartime administration in Africa and of Rodd's own activities. The underlying principles of British military government, as Rodd saw them, were evident in the volume: pragmatism, adaptability and respect for locality. The book demonstrated how the British had sometimes deployed the doctrine of indirect rule out of expediency, because of the lack of alternative options. One reviewer, Major-General Charles Gwynn, accurately summarised the thrust of the book when he suggested that British military governments in Africa had been 'improvisations'. Another reviewer explained that the book presented the established principle of British colonial

---

28. 'Two Peers Leave Liberal Party', *Times*, 15 April 1950, 6.
29. Laura Trevelyan, *A Very British Family: The Trevelyans and Their World* (London: I.B. Tauris, 2006), 2.
30. Rodd to Mary, 19 January 1941, Rodd Family Papers, PC.
31. G. E. Maguire, 'Emmet, Evelyn Violet Elizabeth, Baroness Emmet of Amberley (1899–1980)', *Oxford Dictionary of National Biography* (Oxford: Oxford University Press, 2011).
32. Rennell, *British Military Administration in Africa, 1941–1947*, vii.

Figure 9.1 Evelyn Emmet, 1958. Photograph by Walter Bird. National Portrait Gallery.

administration, namely that the use of troops to enforce administrative measures was inadvisable.[33]

Some of Rodd's reading at this time reflected this political philosophy. One of his favourite books was *Lydia Bailey*, a historical novel by American writer Kenneth Roberts that came out in 1947. This was a love story set against the backdrop of anti-French unrest in Haiti in 1802 and William Eaton's mission to Libya a couple of years later. It is obvious why Rodd liked it. From the first page, the book preached the importance of flexibility in ways Rodd would have endorsed: 'Any nation that cannot or will not avoid the dreadful pitfalls of consistency will be one of the dead empires whose crumbling monuments studded our battlegrounds in Haiti and in Africa.' Roberts depicted Eaton as a leader with a great idea destroyed by small-minded superiors, a narrative that would have appealed to a man who liked blaming the Foreign Office for some of Britain's mistakes. Rodd would also have enjoyed some of the references to Africa in the novel: 'There is fatigue and endless struggle in traveling under the African sun; yet it seems the only life, the only true life.'[34]

African affairs were central to many of Rodd's speeches in the House of Lords. The Gold Coast featured in a number of his interventions. In 1952, he expressed concern about what he saw as Prime Minister Kwame Nkrumah's intolerance of political

---

33. Charles Gwynn, 'Improvisation in Occupied Africa', *Fortnightly*, October 1948, 260. T. H. Vail Motter, *Military Affairs* 13, no. 4 (1949): 251–52. For a summary of the book, see H. B. T., *Geographical Journal* 113 (January–June 1949): 113–15.
34. Kenneth Roberts, *Lydia Bailey* (New York: Doubleday, 1947), 1, 453.

opposition and tendency to inflame opinion against ex-patriot officials. When Ghana did gain its independence, he was keen to ensure the creation of a second chamber to provide proper constitutional safeguards.[35] In 1957, an opportunity opened up for him to take on the kind of big job that he had always hoped would come his way: Harold Macmillan, now British prime minister, invited him to be the first governor-general of Ghana. He agreed and was endorsed by Nkrumah. But before this could happen, Nkrumah took over Christiansborg Castle in Accra – the home designated for the governor-general – and Rodd and Mary decided they would not go after all. His change of mind might have been down to pique over the accommodation. But he may also have been relieved not to add yet another responsibility to an already crowded life. He discussed the matter with chairman of the Cotton Board, Raymond Streat, who recalled: '[Rodd] appeared partly relieved and partly sorry by the decision NOT to go.' The Australian international administrator, Robert Jackson, and his wife, Barbara Ward, were then in Ghana in connection with the Volta River Project, and Rodd told Streat that the three of them 'might have been able to guide [the Ghanaians] during the first vital stages'.[36] There was an element of paternalism in Rodd's outlook here.

Rodd also monitored developments in Egypt. In parliament he was associated with right-wing 'Suez Group', the group of backbenchers who, in the years before the Suez crisis, tried to pressurise the government into maintaining its Suez Canal base and into using force during the Suez crisis itself. In the House of Lords, he was allied in this with such figures as lords Hankey, Killearn and Vansittart.[37] On 7 October 1953, he joined a group of what one historian has called 'imperialist stalwarts' backing a letter from Julian Amery to Churchill opposing military evacuation of the Suez Canal.[38] A couple of months later, he introduced a debate in the House of Lords on the subject, 'In any new arrangements with Egypt, it is essential for this country to maintain a position that is consistent with our commitments and responsibilities'. He thought that anti-British feeling in Egypt did not reflect the true attitudes of the people there. He wanted the government to maintain the status quo in the canal, pending a cooling of emotions that would make agreement more likely. Clearing out and leaving the region did not seem right to him. Lord Hankey supported him, warning against 'appeasement'.[39]

Speaking in the House of Lords in December 1956 during the Suez crisis, Rodd defended British intervention in Egypt on the grounds that it had helped prevent the crisis spreading beyond the region. He also expressed concern over the fact that the crisis had endangered relations with the United States. Echoing his wartime enthusiasm for transatlantic cooperation, he declared that rebuilding the Anglo–American alliance was essential for western civilisation. He condemned President Nasser's dream of creating

---

35. *Times*, 25 January 1957, 11; 25 July 1952, 2.
36. Raymond Streat, *Lancashire and Whitehall: The Diary of Sir Raymond Streat*, vol. 2, ed. M. Dupree (Manchester: Manchester University Press, 1987), 925.
37. Sue Onslow, 'Suez Group', *Oxford Dictionary of National Biography* (Oxford: Oxford University Press, 2005).
38. Julian Amery to Winston Churchill, 7 October 1953, FO 371 102766 JE1052/148.
39. *Times*, 17 December 1953, 6.

a pan-Islamic movement as unrealistic. Here there were echoes of the paper he had written for the Foreign Office in 1924 warning of the possibility of an anti-western Islamic uprising. In his speech in the House of Lords, he cited Lawrence in support of his thinking; he called Lawrence 'one of the greatest friends of the Arabs' that Britain had produced, although without mentioning his name.[40]

Rodd also evinced a tough attitude to the Mau Mau rebellion in Kenya. Speaking in the House of Lords in late 1952, Rodd stated that the Mau Mau uprising was the 'nastiest, filthiest movement' seen in modern history, and that mass movements of this kind required a tough response. Areas where unrest occurred needed to be isolated from the rest of society, Rodd insisted: 'Where outbreaks have taken place in an area, that area should be treated as practically on a war footing; it should be cordoned off and [...] transit in and out should be regulated by passes, as happens in time of war in a war zone.' In the case of this not working, Rodd pressed for the 'inevitable and distasteful necessity of collective punishment' even while acknowledging that the innocent would sometimes suffer as well as the guilty. Here, Rodd warned, the innocent sometimes suffered the consequences of failing to denounce people who had committed crimes, on account of fear or misplaced loyalty.[41] In these remarks and in his comments on the Suez crisis, Rodd showed less imaginative sympathy for the subjects of empire than he had demonstrated in the 1920s; whereas he had shown a respect for Tuareg radicalism, he found less to appreciate in Egyptian or Kenyan nationalism in the 1950s. His readiness to support decolonisation as a principle suggests that he saw imperial retreat as inevitable. But he wanted to see a gradualist approach to it. In 1956, he voted against the abolition of the death penalty – another example of him taking a tough line.[42]

Although Rodd was a regular contributor in the House of Lords, banking remained his primary activity. Morgan Grenfell came out of the war in a good state. While the first two years of the war were difficult for the bank, things began to improve by the end of 1942, mainly because of growing profit in the bond account and also because of a growth in private transactions. Post-war, the bank had some of the largest companies in Britain as clients. Its status led to it being chosen as the bank to manage the nationalisation and then denationalisation of British Steel. It also had connections with many other institutions through personal links: Catto, for example, became governor of the Bank of England in 1944, and Harcourt was in the mid-1950s seconded to work in Washington with the World Bank and the International Monetary Fund. Yet, while Morgan Grenfell was influential and internationally active, it lacked dynamism. According to Kathleen Burk, the early 1950s at the bank were 'staid and dull'. Its leadership, drawn from a narrow social circle, was ageing. Lord Bicester remained chairman until his death in 1956, when he was 89. He was succeeded by Rufus, then aged 58. Rodd himself was no longer a young man. But, if this was a problem at Morgan Grenfell, it was also an issue for

---

40. Rennell, 11 December 1956, House of Lords, Hansard.
41. Rennell, 26 November 1952, House of Lords, Hansard.
42. *Times*, 11 July 1956, 7.

many of the other merchant banks. The work ethic was also relaxed; the hours in which directors of the bank were present were generally between 11 and 4. The ongoing family involvement in the bank was reflected in the fact that Rufus's son-in-law, J. E. H. ('Tim') Collins, became a managing director in 1957. Rodd's nephew, J. A. T. ('Tremayne') Rodd (1935–2006) – who inherited Rodd's peerage when he died – also worked at the bank.[43]

Rodd was a managing director at the bank until 1961, although he remained on the Board until 1967. His work in finance went well beyond the bank itself. His position with Morgan Grenfell meant he was invited to take on responsibilities with other companies organisations. In 1945, he was elected to the boards of Sun Insurance Office Limited and the Sun Life Assurance Society; he was made vice-chairman of the former in 1953 and deputy chairman in 1963 – when he also became deputy chairman of the latter. He remained on the boards of these two companies until 1965. He was also for a time the English representative on the National Bank of Australasia; he joined the London Board of Advice to the bank in 1951 and became its chairman in 1961. He also joined the board of the Australia-based Anglo–Australian Corporation, when it was founded in September 1949 – which was the first issuing house in Australia, and Morgan Grenfell's first overseas venture. It was a joint project with the merchant bank Lazards, in collaboration with the Consolidated Zinc Company. Its first managing director, Eric Speed, resigned his role at the War Office to take up the post. The company became the Australian United Company in 1963. For a time, Rodd was also a member of the Trust Corporation of the Bahamas.[44]

In a sense, Rodd's career reflected the argument, promoted by Peter Cain and A. G. Hopkins, that the post-war era saw the survival of the 'gentleman capitalist'; Rodd belonged to the set of 'gentlemanly directors' of the clearing and merchant banks who were 'key intermediaries' in the system because of the wide range of important directorships they held. He was a good networker in an environment that largely functioned through relationships.[45] But if, in the interwar period, he had been a fierce, self-confident figure with an instinct for promoting modernisation, he was now more obviously a defender of a ruling class. He was arguably part of a neocolonial elite eager to promote its business interests abroad.[46] Not surprisingly, he saw things differently. In his opinion, the City of London was founded on honesty and fairness. This was evident from an article he wrote in 1955 in which, after summarising the City's history and

---

43. Burk, *Morgan Grenfell 1838–1988*, 157, 166–69, 186–88. Chernow, *House of Morgan*, 431. Rob Cole, obituary of Tremayne Rodd (son of Taffy), *Independent*, 23 December 2006, 36.
44. *Times*, 26 October 1945, 9; 10 January 1963, 17; 1 March 1963, 17; 18 June 1965, 22; 2 October 1969, 22. *Manchester Guardian*, 14 September 1949, 7; 20 February 1963, 12. *Daily Telegraph*, 15 September 1949, 5. Burk, *Morgan Grenfell 1838–1988*, 226, 229. See also dive Jenkins, 'Retreat: The Labour Party and the Public Corporations', *Universities and Left Review* 3 (Winter 1958): 42–60.
45. P. J. Cain and A. G. Hopkins, *British Imperialism: 1688–2000* (Harlow: Pearson, 2002), 621. Chernow, *House of Morgan*, 521.
46. See Robert L. Tignor, 'Decolonization and Business: The Case of Egypt', *Journal of Modern History* 59, no. 3 (1987): 495–66.

activities, he concluded that the City was a model of 'fair dealing and competence in a changing pattern of life'. He called it a 'living and conscious community' in which the 'bondage of good faith' was more highly valued than the 'freedom of expediency'.[47] It was an affirmation of solid, traditional values. Rodd's thinking about the place of government in the economy was evident from a speech he gave in the House of Lords in 1951 on the Colonial Development Corporation, in which he criticised government plans as a 'tropical all sorts' suffering from a lack of preliminary investigation. The right approach when there was a lack of private finance, he suggested, was to support small-scale ventures, which could be written off without disastrous losses if they did not work. Government's role was to finance initiatives, not run them.[48]

Another of Rodd's post-war interests was civil aviation. Signs of a passion for aviation were already evident during the Second World War when, during his extensive journeys in Africa, he recorded the details of every plane he travelled on.[49] In the late 1940s, he spoke a number of times in the House of Lords on matters relating to aviation. In the following decades, this interest expressed itself through his being a part-time member of the board of the British Overseas Airways Corporation (BOAC) from 1954 to 1964. During this time, he served as BOAC's part-time deputy chairman from November 1955 to April 1956, succeeding Whitney Straight in the role. He was also for a time deputy chairman and, for a couple of weeks, acting chairman of BOAC Associated Companies, as well as a director of Air Finance; and in October 1961, he was made chair of the board of governors of the College of Air Training, which had come into being a couple of years previously. He also served for a time on the boards of the Malayan, Hong Kong and Borneo Airways. In 1958, he was made one of two BOAC representatives on the board of Ghana Airways when it was set up.[50]

Through his involvement in aviation, Rodd experienced first-hand the complicated relationships that often existed between the nationalised industries and government. A particular challenge was the matter of deciding where the authority for making big decisions lay. In April 1956, with the imminent retirement of BOAC chairman Miles Thomas – and in the context of financial problems at BOAC – the minister of transport and civil aviation, Harold Watkinson, announced the appointment of a new part-time chairman, Gerard D'Erlanger, and chief executive, George Cribbett, who was the minister's deputy secretary. Rodd promptly resigned from his role in protest at this; using a military metaphor, he suggested that it did not work to have a part-time colonel commanding troops, with an adjutant in the orderly room all the time and in charge of troops.[51] There was an additional problem in that the minister was not, according to the rules, permitted to appoint a chief executive. Rodd's resignation prompted a rethink by

---

47. Rennell, 'A Square Mile of Finance, Commerce and Good Faith', *Optima*, March 1955, 23.
48. *Manchester Guardian*, 14 June 1951, 6.
49. Rodd, Flight Log, 1940–43, Rennell of Rodd Papers, BD, Box 76.
50. *Times*, 2 May 1956, 10; 5 July 1958, 5; 14 May 1960, 10; 28 September 1960, 19; 19 October 1961, 5. Rennell, Memorandum, 'I Had Six Days in Tokyo', Rennell of Rodd Papers, BD, Box 102.
51. Rennell's views as reported by Lord Ogmore, 15 May 1956, House of Lords, Hansard.

Figure 9.2 Rodd speaking at the Douglas Aircraft Company, Santa Monica, California, November 1956. The plane is a DC 7C. Mary is seated to Rodd's right, second from left facing the camera. Rodd Family Papers.

the minister; he gave Cribbett the role of deputy chairman – in place of Rodd – while the board gave the managing director role to the financial controller Basil Smallpiece. Rodd then agreed to resume his place on the board at the request of the minister.[52]

Flight had its moment of danger. In 1955, Rodd went to Japan for a week as a representative of BOAC. During a subsequent flight from Tokyo to Minneapolis – across Alaska and the Aleutians – the plane got into trouble over the Arctic and the passengers were told they should 'prepare to ditch'. In the end, this proved unnecessary, but Rodd was impressed by the fearless and unhysterical attitude of the passengers and discipline of the crew. On his return, he summarised his conclusions about the trip for some of his Morgan Grenfell colleagues, emphasising the opportunities Japan offered for investment, but warning that it remained a precarious place to do business which was still dependent

---

52. Robin Higham, *Speedbird: The Complete History of BOAC* (London: I.B. Tauris, 2015), 167. See ch. X for details of another BOAC Board dispute, involving Rodd, in 1963. See also Julian Amery, 2 December 1963, House of Lords, Hansard; *Times*, 2 December 1963, 10.

on American help.⁵³ He was back in the country three years later, for a visit in which he stressed the airline's intention to open up a trans-Pacific service between San Francisco and Tokyo, via Honolulu, utilising the Britannia Jet-Prop airliners. This was intended to be complementary to the Qantas round-the-world service. BOAC, he stressed, wished to maintain its lead in international aviation while also noting that it was continuing with a programme of research into polar flight.⁵⁴ In a sense, aviation was a field in which Rodd's commercial and geographical instincts converged.

Geography remained one of Rodd's central interests in the post-war era. From 1945 to 1948, he was president of the RGS. In 1971, he was made an honorary member. The post-war revival of the organisation owed a lot to his administrative skills. He oversaw the appointment of archaeologist Laurence Kirwan as the new secretary in place of Hinks. Lord Catto was made honorary treasurer – he served in this role from 1946 to 1953. The RGS was not in a strong financial position, and its membership had fallen considerably. Rodd worked on building up its reserves and investments, and he also raised money through renting out rooms at the society for kindred groups. He had a vision for making the RGS's premises a centre for use by other like-minded organisations, thereby contributing to the 'better advantage of geography as a whole'. One result of this was that the Institute of Navigation, formed in 1947, came to be housed in the RGS. When Rodd died in 1978, Kirwan wrote in an obituary that Rodd created the foundations for the society to embark on a new era of research, education and scientific exploration. Then secretary, John Hemming, told Mary that Rodd had effectively 'recreated' the Society after the war.⁵⁵

Refining the RGS's post-war mission was one of Rodd's priorities. From its inception in 1830, the RGS had functioned as a kind of 'imperial information exchange' even while it was also quite heterogeneous in its makeup.⁵⁶ It still had something of this character in the interwar period. But, post-war, it needed rethinking and relaunching. There was a similarity between how Rodd saw the RGS developing and the vision articulated by Rivet and Rivière for the Musée d'Ethnographie in Paris before the war. Rodd wanted the RGS to have a broad educational and public purpose, rather than a narrow academic agenda. He told a council meeting in December 1945 that the RGS's Research Committee should not limit its activities to overseeing the reading and publication of papers, but engage in work with an educational relevance and make plans for geographical research. As RGS president, he supported the creation of a new Education Committee, as well as a separate Research Committee composed mainly of geography teachers. In May 1946, it was agreed to allow a limited number of school children to become members of the RGS, provided they were recommended by appropriate directors of education.⁵⁷

---

53. Memorandum beginning 'I Had Always Wanted', Rennell of Rodd Papers, BD, Box 102.
54. *Shipping Gazette*, 31 March 1958, 68.
55. Obituary of Lord Rennell (by L. P. Kirwan), *Geographical Journal* 144, no. 2 (1978): 392–93. John Hemming to Mary, 17 May 1978, Rodd Family Papers, AC.
56. Driver, *Geography Militant*, 27.
57. Rennell, 'The Functions of Committees of Council: Memorandum by the President of Council', RGS, Council Minutes, vol. 16, 12 December 1945, 2. *Guardian*, 13 May 1946, 6.

Rodd saw geography as implicitly interdisciplinary. Reviewing a book by botanist and explorer F. Kingdon-Ward in 1945, he commended the author for his belief that geography was a discipline touching all branches of science.[58] 'Every definition of geography that I have seen connotes some relationship with one or more other branches of science', he said the following year at the RGS's annual general meeting. This meant embracing human geography, botanical and zoological geography, and social, economic, political and historical geography. It also meant broadening the scope of lectures at the RGS. Rodd promoted the use of documentary films, the publication of memoirs and the revival of map-making. Exhibitions were put on, with the aim of demonstrating the relevance of geography, and the RGS itself, to wider topics of interest. In spring 1947, an exhibition on the 'World in Focus' attracted 13,000 visitors. Later in the year, there was an exhibition on civil aviation, which brought in more than 7,000 people. Activities of a more specialist educational nature were also promoted. For example, a syllabus for a diploma in surveying was created. Rodd also promoted the use of smaller grants to encourage specialised research; the RGS did not have the capacity to finance major projects or expeditions.[59]

Rodd remained committed to supporting the RGS's tradition of exploration. He welcomed Swedish geographer Hans Ahlmann's proposal for a Norwegian–British–Swedish Antarctic Expedition – which came to fruition in 1949–52; and it was during his term as president that discussions took place with the Alpine Club about a renewed attempt on Mount Everest, which led eventually to the successful mission of 1953. Rodd was alive to the way such events could function as propaganda for geography. In July 1952, he was invited to open an Everest exhibition in London's Regent Street, which included a scale model of Everest with the North Col and western routes to the summit marked. Success in the impending 1953 expedition, and a possible subsequent one in 1955, would depend on adopting a new scientific approach to the problems involved, Rodd insisted.[60] Rodd's position meant he was seen by other geographers as an important conduit of information. Wilfred Thesiger was one such. Like Rodd, Thesiger had been involved in military intelligence during the war. He was attached to G(R) in Cairo for a time, before being recruited to serve as a political officer in Orde Wingate's Ethiopian unit. Post-war, after he made his journey across the Empty Quarter, he wrote to his mother: 'You can tell Francis (Rodd) where I have been, for now that I have done it, it is no longer necessary to keep it secret.' In October 1947, Rodd was in the chair when Thesiger gave a paper about his journey, with Bagnold and the Saudi Arabian chargé d'affairs in attendance.[61]

---

58. Review of F. Kingdon-Ward, *Exploring Up To Date*, Sunday Times, 17 June 1945, 3.
59. Rennell, addresses at AGMs, 24 June 1946, *Geographical Journal* 107, no. 3/5 (1946): 83, 88, 89; 16 June 1947, *Geographical Journal* 109, no. 4/6 (1947): 162–63; June 1948, *Geographical Journal* 111, no. 4/6 (1948): 156.
60. *Times*, 1 July 1952, 3.
61. Anglim, *Orde Wingate and the British Army*, 107. Alexander Maitland, *Wilfred Thesiger: The Life of the Great Explorer* (London: HarperCollins, 1985), 280. Rennell et al., 'The Empty Quarter: A Discussion', *Geographical Journal* 111, no. 1/3 (1948): 19–21.

Rodd used the RGS as a vehicle for demonstrating what geographers could contribute to contemporary political or military questions. High-profile speakers were brought in for this purpose, with distinguished guests invited to attend. In May 1946, Rodd introduced a lecture on geographical influences on American history by Dexter Perkins, with American ambassador in London, Averell Harriman, in the audience.[62] Later in the year, Viscount Mountbatten was present when F. Spencer Chapman presented a paper on his experiences operating behind enemy lines in Malaya.[63] In May 1948, Rodd chaired a paper on 'Geography and War Strategy' by Cyril Falls, professor of military history at Oxford, in which Falls emphasised world geography's importance to commanders and staff officers and the relevance of Halford Mackinder's ideas on historical geography. Montgomery, now chief of the Imperial General Staff, and Gerald Templar, vice chief, were in attendance. At the end of the evening, Montgomery said that he was a firm believer in the link between geography and war. He also stated that he had learned that every situation needed to be tackled as a wholly new problem, for which there was a new answer. Rodd would have thoroughly concurred. Rodd concluded the evening by saying: 'We are all grateful to [Montgomery] for having reminded us of those essential things without which no battle can be fought either in war or peace: the sharp weapon, the desire to win, the necessity to exist. These are the very things of which Field Marshall Montgomery is the great exemplar of our age.'[64] If the two men had not developed much of a rapport in 1943, it seems that, at least outwardly, there was now greater mutual respect.

Rodd's interests in geography extended to its wider role in education and science. He was for a time president of the 'Geography' section of the British Association for the Advancement of Science, and the Association's treasurer; the Association had a long history of promoting geography as a science relevant to empire and the world.[65] In an address to the organisation's geographers in 1948, he expressed a hope that geography be included in all curricula for school and higher certificates, and that social geographers might help the West European nations to rationalise the mess they had made in Africa. As a result of his work with the Association, he was awarded the honorary degree of LLD by Manchester University in 1962. From 1947 to 1959, he was a visiting fellow of Nuffield College, Oxford, which had been founded in 1937 with a remit to focus on the social sciences.[66]

---

62. Rennell (with Averell Harriman), 'Geographical Influences in American History: Discussion', *Geographical Journal* 109, no. 1/3 (1947): 37–38.
63. Rennell (with Viscount Mountbatten), 'Travels in Japanese-Occupied Malaya: Discussion', *Geographical Journal* 110, no. 1/3 (1947): 36–37.
64. Rennell (with Lord Montgomery), 'Geography and War Strategy: Discussion', *Geographical Journal* 112, no. 1/3 (1948): 18. Cyril Falls, 'Geography and War Strategy', *Geographical Journal* 112, no. 1/3 (1948): 4.
65. See on this Charles W. J. Withers, *Geography and Science, 1831–1939: A Study of the British Association for the Advancement of Science* (Manchester: Manchester University Press, 2010).
66. *Times*, 11 September 1948, 6. *Times*, 30 August 1962, 10. Post-war, Rodd was also for a time a member of the Board of the British School in Rome.

An insight into Rodd's thinking about science can be gained from an address he gave in 1961 on the 'function' of the British Association for the Advancement of Science in people's everyday lives. Speaking at the Birmingham and Midland Institute, he suggested that the 'right or liberty to think for oneself' was a central thread in British national life. He also suggested that the British tradition for invention could have been put to better practical use. Another topic he raised was the relationship between science and the humanities. A couple of years earlier, scientist and novelist C. P. Snow had famously addressed this question at a lecture in Cambridge, 'The Two Cultures and the Scientific Revolution'. Snow criticised what he saw as an unfortunate division in Britain between the sciences and humanities, suggesting that representatives of the humanities were ignorant of the world of science. This prompted a lively debate in the United States and Britain, to which Rodd's talk was clearly intended to contribute. Rodd insisted that it was a 'fallacy' to think that the humanities and science ran on parallel lines and could never meet; the humanist and the natural scientist had a 'common ideal' in having a 'passion for truth'. Rodd's sympathies lay more with the scientists: 'Scientists today are playing an effective part, and I think a more effective part than the humanists, in bending the two lines towards each other and in bridging gaps, even if the lines have not, as yet, met.'[67]

Alongside his involvement with geography and science, Rodd remained academically interested in Africa. In 1947, he was made chairman of the International African Institute (IAI), an organisation founded in 1926 by Lord Lugard under the title of the International Institute of African Languages and Cultures. Lugard was chairman of the organisation until 1945, when he was replaced by Lord Hailey. In July 1947, Lord Hailey stepped down from the position, nominating Rodd in his place for his linguistic qualifications, contacts in Europe and African experience. Rodd agreed to take on the role. He remained in post until a meeting of the IAI's Executive Council in March 1949, when he resigned on the grounds of busyness. His approach to science was in evidence at this meeting, when he stated that in a scientific study the mind needed to be free from all national or personal prejudice. Echoing his thinking about geography, he also stressed the importance of the practical application of scientific knowledge – the link between science and humanism. He also expressed a hope that the Institute might be able to play a role in bridging the worlds of administration and science – he saw a clear link between politics and the academic study of Africa. The meeting was opened by Robert Delavignette, director of political affairs in the Ministry for Overseas France.[68]

Rodd continued to follow the latest research on North Africa. In 1957, he chaired a discussion at the RGS on Barth's exploration of the western Sudan, and he later gave

---

67. Rennell, presidential address, *The Function of the British Association for the Advancement of Science in our Everyday Lives* (Birmingham: Birmingham and Midland Institute, 1961), 8, 10, 15, 16. C. P. Snow, *The Two Cultures and the Scientific Revolution* (Cambridge: Cambridge University Press, 1959).
68. Minutes of IAI Executive Council, 2 July 1947, 21 March 1949, IAI/1/27. *Africa: Journal of the International African Institute*, 17 (1947): 270. The day-to-day management of the IAI was done by administrative secretary Daryll Forde.

an illustrated talk on Barth to the society.[69] East Africa was another sphere of interest. From 1964 to 1975, he was on the Council of the British Institute of Eastern Africa. Here he played an important role in initiating its Bantu Studies research project. The aim of this was to do research on the origins and migration of the Bantu-speaking peoples. In the event, this proved difficult, and the focus shifted to Iron Age archaeology in East Africa more generally. According to one of its directors, Robert Soper, the project was conceived by Rodd himself and made possible by the fact that Rodd was a trustee of the Waldorf Astor Foundation; he arranged for a grant of $10,000 over three years to be given to support this work from 1965.[70]

Australia was another focus of Rodd's post-war activities. The interplay between his financial, agricultural and geographical interests was evident in a series of visits he made to the country, particularly Western Australia. His first visit to Australia was in February 1950 to work with Eric Speed. He came first to Perth, where he was welcomed with a civic reception in honour of the fact that he was descended from James Stirling, the founder of the city in 1829. Rodd and Speed met a number of people working in finance and business, some of them involved with agriculture. They also flew over to the goldfields at Kalgoorlie, on the invitation of the Western Mining Corporation. The landscape there reminded Rodd of Africa: 'The bush is like so much African orchard and Savannah bush on the same red earth, gently undulating but featureless except from the air when the landscape is chequered by vast dry salt lakes shimmering in the sun.' The two men flew on for further meetings on the east coast. The aim of the trip was to find ways of boosting British–Australian commercial relations.[71] Rodd returned regularly over the next two decades, visiting over 20 times.

Rodd's mind was stimulated by the fact that a combination of scientific research and geographical knowledge was needed to make best use of the commercial opportunities in Western Australia. On one visit, he was the guest of West Australian Petroleum Pty Ltd (WAPET), a company drilling for oil in the Exmouth Gulf area; WAPET combined a boring programme with geological work along the Australian coast.[72] Beef production was another sphere of interest. In 1952, his journey took him to the remote Mount House station in the Kimberley district, managed by cattle farmer Gordon Blythe. Here he was much impressed by what he called an 'important experiment' in cattle farming, operated by the company 'Air Beef'. This involved slaughtering cattle on farms before flying the carcasses and offal to freezing plants in the coastal town of Wyndham – the enterprise

---

69. Rennell (with E. W. Bovill), 'Heinrich Barth and the Western Sudan: Discussion', *Geographical Journal* 124, no. 3 (1958): 338–39; and Rennell, 'Heinrich Barth and the Opening Up of Central Africa', *Geographical Journal*, 132, no. 1 (1966): 72–73.
70. Robert Soper, 'The Bantu Studies Research Project', *Azania: Journal of the British Institute in Eastern Africa* 6 (1971): 1–4. L. P. Kirwan, obituary of Lord Rennell, *Azania: Journal of the British Institute in Eastern Africa* 13 (1978): vii.
71. 'First Visit to Australia', 7, Rennell of Rodd Papers, BD, Box 102. Rodd to Mary, 7 February 1950, Rodd Family Papers, AC. *Kalgoorlie Miner*, 9 February 1950, 4.
72. Rennell, 'The Sand Dunes Areas of the North-West and Kimberley Divisions of Western Australia', *Geographical Journal*, 121, no. 4 (1955): 544.

was supported by Australian National Airways – from where they were shipped overseas on refrigerated steamers. The commercial opportunities associated with this method of food production were 'not a negligible factor to Great Britain', he wrote in the *Times*. Later in the year, he talked of the agricultural potential of the Kimberley region in a talk at the RGS.[73] Occasionally, he expressed himself with a certain tough-talking swagger. 'Anyone who does not have investments in West Australian mining is a bloody fool', he declared in 1968.[74] In 1964, his youngest daughter, Rachel, married Gordon Blythe's son, Richard, a factor consolidating the family's link with Western Australia.

The empty, desert landscape of north-western Australia caught Rodd's imagination in the same way that the Sahara had done in the interwar period. But it was now the aeroplane, rather than the camel, that enabled him to access its remoter corners. He came to the conclusion that air transport was the answer to the communication problems presented by the vastness of Western Australia. He loved the extent of the place: he was struck by the fact that his home county, Herefordshire, was in expanse only about a third of a single one-million-acre cattle station in the Kimberley area.[75] On one of his early visits, he noticed the consolidated parallel dunes in the area to the south-east of the coastal city of Broome. He was especially intrigued by the wide spacing of the flat bottoms between the dune crests. He turned some of his thoughts on this into an article.[76] There was a tradition here. Barth mentioned the dunes of the Sahara in his journals. Sand waves featured as an object of study in English geographer Vaughan Cornish's *Waves of Sand and Snow and the Eddies Which Make Them*, published in 1914. Rodd was aware of this. He referenced Cornish's book in *People of the Veil*, in connection with the dunes of the Tagedufat valley in the arid Azawagh region. These dunes, he remarked, were 'small crescentic dunes of very fine white sand' overlying the heavier buff-coloured sand of the surface.[77] During the Second World War, Bagnold published a famous text on the subject, *The Physics of Blown Sand and Desert Dunes* (1941). Rodd's discussion of the dunes of Western Australia was a new manifestation of an older conversation.

The border area in which the Rodd estate was located was another focus for Rodd's post-war interests. He liked the feeling of being attached to the land. In 1942, he told Mary that he wished he was at the Rodd. He had just read Henry Williamson's *Story of a Norfolk Farm* (1941), an account of how the author had set out to transform the fortunes of a piece of derelict farmland. On reading it, Rodd found his passion for the land 'worse

---

73. Special Correspondent, 'Beef by Air', *Times*, 15 May 1952, 7. Rennell, Memorandum starting 'An Experiment of Far-Reaching Importance', Rennell of Rodd Papers, BD, Box 102. Rennell, 'The Kimberley Division of Western Australia', *Geographical Journal* 119, no. 3 (1953): 306–14.
74. Rennell, cited in newspaper clipping, 'Banker Sees Great Future in W. A.', 1968, Rodd Family Papers, AC.
75. Rennell, 'The Kimberley Division of Western Australia', 308.
76. Rennell, 'The Sand Dune Areas of the North-West and Kimberley Divisions of Western Australia', 342–44.
77. Rodd, *People of the Veil*, 66–67. Vaughan Cornish, *Waves of Sand and Snow and the Eddies Which Make Them* (London: T. Fisher Unwin, 1914).

than ever'.[78] He saw the Rodd as a long-term base for the family. In his view, the experience of connection with the land was in some way an antidote to divisiveness. As he explained to Mary at the end of 1942:

> I think there is a good reason for [the children] to live and grow up in Rodd and be able to farm it and run it. That small piece of land seems to have become an anchor of stability in a very curious world here. The political divisions are becoming more and more obscene and imponderable but I believe people wish and ought to live on and farm the land they own.[79]

He added, unexpectedly in view of his political views, that the valley in which the Rodd estate was situated would make a 'very good collective farm'. The appeal of the locality was also partly aesthetic. In the last years of his life, he enjoyed being driven around the area and drinking in the scenery.[80]

The Rodd was located in a valley through which a small river, the Hindwell, passed before joining the River Lugg in west Herefordshire. The Hindwell Valley became a particular source of fascination for Rodd. This was evident as early as 1944, when he published an article in the local *Radnorshire Society Transactions* on the local manors of Rodd, Nash and Little Brampton and their identification in Domesday Book in 1086.[81] Further research on the history of the valley resulted in a book, *Valley on the March*, subtitled 'A History of a Group of Manors on the Herefordshire March of Wales', published in 1958. This was a history of the Hindwell Valley, with particular reference to the period between the publication of Domesday Book and the reign of Queen Anne (1702/7–1714). Rodd started out with the idea of writing an introduction to the subject for family and friends; but – not surprisingly, in view of his love of research – it expanded into a more detailed study. In his introduction to the book, he touched on the way in which the locality gave him a sense of belonging: 'I always yearn when I am away to return to the home of my ancestors in this quiet valley on the March where the purpose and continuity of human life on the land for a thousand years are so pleasant and rewarding.'[82]

Although different in focus from *People of the Veil*, *Valley on the March* reflected Rodd's interest in landscapes, roads and pathways, along with the construction of maps. In a chapter titled 'Tracks and Fields', Rodd explained that maps are 'provocative inquisitors': 'They are always asking you if you know the reasons for their statements, and when you think you have found the reason they put another question.' The book included a number of air photographs, highlighting the topography of the area. As in *People of the Veil*, Rodd was alive to the military dimensions of the terrain. One of his arguments was to suggest there were two branches – 'alignments' – of the seventh-century Offa's Dyke

---

78. Rodd to Mary, 23 September 1942, Rodd Family Papers, AC.
79. Rodd to Mary, 29 November 1942, Rodd Family Papers, AC.
80. Rodd to Mary, 29 November 1942, Rodd Family Papers, AC. Brian Boobbyer, *Like a Cork Out of a Bottle* (Arundel: John Faber, 2004), 47.
81. Rennell, 'The Manors of Rodd, Nash and Little Brampton, Near Presteigne: A Note on Possible Domesday Book Identification', *Radnorshire Society Transactions* 14 (1944), 24–29.
82. Lord Rennell of Rodd, *Valley on the March: A History of a Group of Manors on the Herefordshire March of Wales* (London: Oxford University Press, 1958), xiv.

Figure 9.3 Rodd, c. late 1950s. Rodd Family Papers.

in the area, with the second, eastern branch of the dyke running from the local 'Rushock' hill to the nearby Wapley hill-fort and incorporating a dyke called Rowe Ditch.[83] Unfortunately, this did not convince archaeologist Cyril Fox, the premier authority on Offa's Dyke; in a review of the book, Fox called Rodd's argument a 'failure'.[84] But Rodd would not be deterred. He returned to the issue in a short article for *Radnorshire Society Transactions* in 1961, in which he insisted that, while the building of Rowe Ditch made no sense if conceived as a self-contained military work, it was fully comprehensible if seen as linking the dyke with the Wapley hill-fort; the banks of the ditch were 'rational' from the point of view of a fighting force operating from Wapley.[85] It was an example of how Rodd applied some of the thinking he had learned in military intelligence to local geography.

Cyril Fox was not the only scholar with reservations about *Valley on the March*. The book's reception in academic circles was mixed. Rodd was praised for identifying all 76 places mentioned in Domesday Book for that part of Herefordshire in which the Hindwell Valley was located, as well as for his use of field names, local pathways and boundaries. He was also commended for reconstructing the original nucleus of arable cultivation in the oldest settlements of the Hindwell Valley.[86] But Marxist historian

---

83. Ibid., 21–22, 84.
84. Cyril Fox, 'Review of *Valley on the March*', *Antiquaries Journal* 39, no, 1–2 (1959): 125–26.
85. Rennell, 'Note on Rowe Ditch and a "Second Alignment" of Offa's Dyke in the Pembridge–Wapley–Herrock Area', *Radnorshire Society Transactions* 30 (1960): 31–33.
86. Edmund B. Fryde, *Journal of Economic History* 22, no. 1 (1962): 132–34. H. P. R. Finberg, *English Historical Review* 75, no. 295 (1960): 328–29.

Rodney Hilton complained that, after looking at the pre-Conquest and Domesday topography, Rodd failed to maintain the agrarian focus of the book, while church historian David Walker thought the book interesting but not authoritative.[87] The fact that Rodd had not brought his task to completion was hardly surprising, considering the range of his other activities. Much of the writing took place while Rodd was travelling: he began writing it while on a tramp steamer in the North Atlantic and finished it during a flight over the northern Pacific.[88]

Rodd's interest in history was expressed in other ways. While he was president of the RGS, he arranged for the thirteenth-century Hereford map, known as the 'Mappa Mundi', to be brought to the map room at the British Museum for cleaning and repairing; the map was then put on show at the RGS. Nearly a decade later, he spent time disproving a theory that a tapestry in the Anglican church in Presteigne originated with a series that had been completed in Aix-en-Provence in the early sixteenth century. He did this by obtaining a complete set of photographs of the original series, enabling people to differentiate the Presteigne tapestry from the Aix originals. Rodd also built up a large library in his home. Roughly 450 of his books were donated to the RGS on his death, including many volumes collected by James Rennell.[89] In 1968, he supported the publication of the translation of the will of a wealthy woman landowner in the tenth century, *The Will of Aethelgifu: A Tenth Century Anglo-Saxon Manuscript*. This was published by the Roxburghe Club, a society of bibliophiles that required its members to produce a book at their own expense for the benefit of the members.[90]

Sometimes Rodd's love of local history spilt over into politics. In 1972, he opposed a plan to keep some of the land around Offa's Dyke in Herefordshire rather than be absorbed into the newly created Welsh county of Powys. His combative character was evident here: in declaring himself ready to fight the administrative change, Rodd noted that his ancestors had fought for the land in the area for more than 600 years. He differed in his stance from some of the local villagers, who voted to support the change.[91] Rodd was deputy lieutenant of Herefordshire in 1948 and vice-lieutenant in 1957–73, and he was also a justice of the peace.

Much of Rodd's post-war energy was invested in developing the Rodd estate itself. He modernised the cottages lived in by farm labourers, installing electricity and running water. He brought in some of the latest farm machinery; even in the 1940s, much of the arable land was still being worked by horses. Although somewhat patrician in his

---

87. R. H. H. Hilton, *Agricultural History Review* 7, no. 2 (1959): 124–32. David Walker's review of *Valley on the March*, *Welsh History Review* 1, no. 2 (1960): 246–47.
88. Rennell, *Valley on the March*, xiv.
89. *Times*, 9 July 1948, 3. *Illustrated London News*, 24 July 1948, 95. W. H. Howse, 'Flemish Tapestry in Presteigne Church', *Radnorshire Society Transactions* 27 (1957): 33. Johnson, 'The Rennell Collection', 138–42.
90. *The Will of Aethelgifu: A Tenth Century Anglo-Saxon Manuscript*, translated and examined by Dorothy Whitelock, with a note on the document by Neal Ker and analyses of the property, livestock and chattels concerned by Lord Rennell (Oxford: Roxburghe Club, 1968).
91. John Cunningham, *Guardian*, 7 February 1972, 7.

manner, Rodd made efforts to develop a sense of community, for example, by instituting a yearly harvest supper. The farm itself was run by a manager from the locality. Rodd encouraged sheep farming. He was for a time chairman of the British Sheep Society, an organisation linked to the Sheep Development Association which had as its purpose the improvement of sheep health and breeding. Rodd kept pedigree flocks of Clun and Kerry Hill sheep, which were regularly shown at local shows. He became passionate about the improvement of wool clip quality – an example of his tendency to throw himself into new projects and interests. He experimented with crossing Merino sheep – which were central in Australian wool production – with Kerry Hills with the aim of increasing fleece weight. The experiment was overseen by Harold Carter, an Australian scientist who had worked for the Commonwealth Scientific and Industrial Research Organisation, in cooperation with Leeds University. Carter lent Rodd two British full-bred Merino rams descended from an original strain imported from Tasmania. The findings – 'surprisingly satisfactory' in the first instance – were written up in pamphlets published in 1970 and 1971.[92]

Rodd had in common with Mary a love of landscape. Like her husband, Mary was drawn to the countryside of the English–Welsh border; the landscape and rural life of the area provided the inspiration for many of her post-war paintings and drawings (see Figure 9.4). She also shared Rodd's interest in Australia and painted a number of pictures of the Australian bushland. After she died, in 1981, the main house on the Rodd estate was sold to Australian artist Sidney Nolan, another painter fascinated by landscape. Alongside some shared interests, Rodd and Mary sometimes found it hard to communicate. In autumn 1948, Rodd suggested that they had 'gone [their] several ways too much'. 'We are both to blame in this, each trying perhaps to push the other too much in their own way', he said.[93] In particular, they continued to diverge in their approaches to religion. Following a visit to Rome in 1950, Mary announced her intention to convert to Catholicism and, two years later, went through the formal process of joining the Roman church. She was attracted by what she saw as the universality of the Catholic faith and the capacity of the Catholic catechism to give a structure to people's beliefs. She was also drawn to the experience of devotion to the Sacrament: praying before the Blessed Sacrament, she found 'peace and quietness of mind'. Over the next decades, the Catholic Church became increasingly central to her social life. She was closely involved with a Carmelite convent in Presteigne. She was also a member of the Order of St Benedict; she was attached to a Benedictine community of nuns at Stanbrook Abbey in Worcestershire.[94]

---

92. *Merino–Kerry Hill Cross Bred Sheep at the Rodd Farm: An Interim Report on Four Seasons' Experiment*; *Merino–Kerry Hill Cross Bred Sheep at the Rodd Farm: A Second Interim Report on Five Seasons' Experiment* (Herefordshire: Rodd Farm, 1970 and 1971). *Times*, 8 July 1963, 5. Interview with George Mills, 22 June 2020.
93. Rodd to Mary, 3 October 1948, Rodd Family Papers, AC.
94. Pollen, 'Mary Rennell', 17–19. Paper of responses to Archbishop Roberts and 'Somebody Asked Me', c. 1952–53, Rodd Family Papers, AC.

Figure 9.4 The Boy Jesus and the Shepherd, 1974. Etching in Chinese ink by Mary Rodd/Rennell.

Rodd, who remained an Anglican, was unhappy at Mary's decision to become a Catholic. He was suspicious of Catholicism and often referred to it in a dismissive way; he had absorbed many of the anti-Catholic attitudes widespread in British society.[95] In what was a tense stand-off, he invited the Catholic priest Ronald Knox, whom he had first met during his year at Balliol, to help mediate between them. Knox was himself an Anglican convert to Catholicism, with a strong sacramental spirituality. Rodd made a concerted effort to set out his concerns to Mary. A key issue for him was that he associated Catholicism with 'fixed dogmas', which he feared ran counter to his tendency to keep an 'open mind' in life. He was also concerned that Mary's religious life was too often driven by emotion. Emotionalism was not wrong, he told her, except when it governed mind and spirit and when a person mistook the 'entering in of the Spirit' for a 'surge of Emotion'. But Rodd was eager not to give the impression of being anti-emotional. He complained that Mary often thought of him as an 'intellectual [...] with a spicing of emotions which he keeps rigidly in check'. This was far from being the case, he said.[96]

---

95. Interview with Margaret Fowler-Wright, 7 September 2020.
96. Rodd, 'Life and Reflections', 1950, Section 4, 5 and 8, 3 Rodd Family Papers, AC.

Rodd emphasised to Mary that while his interests were less religious than hers, spiritual questions did occasionally impinge on his life with intensity. In setting out his ideas, he stated that the intellect itself was 'God given'. But in his view, God's Spirit brought a further quality; it gave people the capacity not just to make judgments but also to make choices: 'If the intellect provided men with knowledge of good and evil [...] the Spirit gave men the capacity to prefer and select – and perhaps even to reject [...] good to evil.'[97] Rodd did not see good and evil as entirely relative things, although he had a personalistic slant on ethical questions. Before the war, he suggested that a 'good motive' was 'absolute' while suggesting that the final judge of whether a motive was good or bad was the individual conscience.[98]

It is revealing of Rodd's practical mentality that a sermon he gave in January 1952, while travelling by ship to Australia, was about the ethic of 'unselfishness'. Using a couple of verses from the hymn by Cecil Spring-Rice, 'I Vow to Thee My Country', he declared that many of the world's troubles were rooted in selfishness, and that the essence of Christian teaching lay in the ethic of love and sacrifice: 'The sacrifice involved in being unselfish, in loving your neighbour in the doing of something for him that costs you something – that is what is meant by unselfishness and true love.' In the same sermon, he cited a line coming from biologist Thomas Huxley: 'A man's worst difficulties begin when he is able to do what he likes.'[99] In a post-war review of a book on Charles de Foucauld, Rodd emphasised Foucauld's refusal to proselytise among the people with whom he lived, and his openness to talk to anyone who wanted to talk with him – attributes he admired.[100] Spiritual themes even impinged to a degree on his thinking on geographical issues. In 1946, he declared: 'The modern danger is that material equipment is catching up and forging ahead; spiritual equipment is lagging far behind.'[101]

Mary ceased her involvement in Moral Re-Armament (MRA) when she became a Catholic. But Rodd's eldest two daughters were active in the movement. As a result, Rodd attended some of its events in the early 1950s. He also occasionally corresponded with Buchman – for whom he had considerable respect. After 1945, MRA devoted many of its activities to peace-building in Europe and Asia. In 1952, Rodd sent a commendation about Buchman to the Nobel Prize Committee, when Buchman was (unsuccessfully) nominated for the Nobel Peace Prize. In this, he expressed support for MRA's attempts at encouraging post-war reconciliation. It is revealing of his approach to spiritual questions that he praised MRA for the fact that it embraced people of different faiths. He wondered if this reflected a well-known maxim originating in the Book of Esdras – 'magna est veritas, et praevalebit' ('great is truth and it will prevail').[102] The value Rodd placed here

---

97. Ibid., Section 1, 1; 4, 3 and 6; 5, 7, Rodd Family Papers, AC. Pollen, 'Mary Rennell', 19.
98. Rodd to William Sanderson, 1 June 1933, Rennell of Rodd Papers, BD, Box 56.
99. Sermon on SS Strathmore, 13 January 1952, Rennell of Rodd Papers, BD, Box 102.
100. Review of Anne Fremantle's *Desert Calling*, *Sunday Times*, 16 July 1950, 3.
101. Review of F. Kingdon-Ward's *About This Earth*, *Sunday Times*, 27 October 1946, 4.
102. Rodd, 'Life and Reflections', 1950, Section 1, 5, Rodd Family Papers, AC. Rodd to Buchman, letter and memo, 29 January 1953, Oxford Group Papers, BD, 3/125. This line comes from Latin Vulgate version of 1. Esdras 4.41. The original version is slightly different: 'Magna est veritas et praevalet' – 'Great is truth and it prevails'.

on 'truth' foreshadowed the emphasis he gave to truth in his speech to the Birmingham Midland Institute in 1961. He ended his 1961 talk by citing the same quotation from the Book of Esdras as he cited here. He saw science and religion as originating in a joint love of truth – 'truth' for him was a unifying concept.

For all their differences, Mary was often a sounding board for Rodd's private thoughts. He was sometimes troubled about how his career had unfolded since returning from Italy in 1943. He was only 48 when he stepped down from AMGOT. After that, he was twice offered roles of military or political significance – as head of the DCA in 1944 and as governor-general of Ghana in 1957 – and he turned down both for different reasons. But at times he hankered after a role commensurate with his former responsibilities. In autumn 1948, he told Mary that he would like to 'do something worth doing in public life again'. A couple of years later, he expressed a sense of frustration that a bigger job had not come his way: '[After the war, I] went back to my pre-war life in which no ambition was any longer really there. I saw things slipping past me, and other people doing and being things which I ought and could have been and done, and I was sad.' All this suggests that he found it hard to find a sense of direction in the post-war world. Behind a life of constant activity, he was insecure in himself and uncertain about where to put his energy.[103] Conversely, Rodd defended his post-war career trajectory, stating that he had an 'underlying curiosity' about the world, which made it hard to focus on one thing alone. As he explained to Mary: 'If I have been a jack of many trades and master of none, as so many people say of me, I have had a good life which I cannot find it in me to regret [...] If I have not made a first class job of anything, there is no reason to feel that I would have done better if I had concentrated on only one thing.'[104]

'Versatility' was a phrase sometimes used about Rodd. After one of his speeches in the House of Lords, one commentator acclaimed him for his 'versatility', adding that this very quality was a possible reason why he had not had a more substantial post-war career.[105] The *Financial Times* once called him a 'versatile banker'.[106] There was a family tradition here, for 'versatility' was a quality his father admired. In his book on Raleigh, Rennell Rodd described the Elizabethan explorer as a man 'compounded with many elements and endowed with a versatility which amounted to genius'.[107] In effect, Rodd embraced an ideal of versatility as a way of explaining his post-war career.

Rodd tried to make sense of his life by thinking of himself as an adventurer. In his library at the Rodd, he had framed a verse from a poem called 'The Ship of Fools' (1907) reflecting this: 'We are those fools who could not rest/In the dull earth we left behind, / But burned with passion for the West / And drank a frenzy from its wind; / The

---

103. Rodd to Mary, 3 October 1948, Rodd Family Papers, AC. Rodd, 'Life and Reflections', 1950, Section 5, 14, Rodd Family Papers, AC.
104. Rodd, 'Life and Reflections', 1950, Section 1, 1–2, Rodd Family Papers, AC.
105. Atticus, *Sunday Times*, 23 March 1947, 5.
106. *Financial Times*, 28 June 1961, 10.
107. Rennell Rodd, *Sir Walter Raleigh*, 2. Talk of Raleigh's 'versatility' was not new. Rennell Rodd was drawing on an earlier account of his life in which his 'versatility' was emphasised: see *Edinburgh Review* 71 (1840): 73.

world where small men live at ease/Fades from our unregretful eyes, / And blind across uncharted seas / We stagger on our enterprise.'[108] Rodd attributed the poem to novelist John Buchan, but it was in fact written by poet St John Lucas. The 'ship of fools' trope, originating with German humanist Sebastian Brant, was well known in European culture; it had inspired artists like Hieronymous Bosch and Albrecht Dürer. Antarctic explorer Ernest Shackleton loved St John Lucas's poem; in his version of it, he replaced the word 'West' with 'South'.[109] For Rodd, the lines obviously encapsulated how he wanted to think of himself – a man operating in the tradition of earlier transatlantic explorers. His admiration for the poem suggests that he saw himself as a man slightly above the ordinary.

There was, doubtless, an element of rationalisation in all this. By identifying himself as an adventurer breaking into uncharted seas – in other words, a person constantly exploring and following new interests – Rodd could account for why he had not been more successful in any one branch of his life and why a bigger role had not come his way after the war. The image was a comfort to him when he was restless. At the same time, the 'ship of fools' image corresponded to a real feature of his character. He did have many interests and was genuinely curious about the world. People noticed this. Towards the end of his life, after Rodd gave a talk on the Libyan desert to the Oxford University Exploration Club, the student secretary Roger Chapman reported that what he was not interested in could be written on a 'postage stamp'.[110]

---

108. *Spectator*, 7 December 1907, 31.
109. *New York Times*, 19 March 2006, section 9, 15.
110. E-mail message from Roger Chapman to author, 24 February 2015. Rodd's talk took place in the early 1970s.

CONCLUSION

Rodd died at the Rodd on 16 March 1978 and was buried in Presteigne cemetery. At the top of his gravestone – which was designed by letter-cutter David Kindersley[1] – there is an image of the 'Agadez cross'. This is a prominent Tuareg image which, according to Rodd, probably originated with the 'Ankh', an Egyptian hieroglyphic symbol. Further down there is a Tamasheq word written in traditional Tifinagh script, '‖ ∷ O ⫶ ⊙'. Pronounced 'Al-har-as', this was (and remains) a greeting meaning something like 'Peace to you'. Rodd translated it as 'Naught but good'. This word had been embossed in gold on the front cover of *People of the Veil*.[2] The references to Tuareg culture on the gravestone were clearly intended to convey the idea that, although Rodd was buried in Wales, a remote section of the central Sahara remained in his heart: he was a man whose interests and emotions straddled different continents. This was undoubtedly true. The landscape of Aïr was always before him. In his bedroom at home, he kept a framed photo of Agellal village and mountains (see Figure 3.4) – an area to the south-west of Iferuan. At the same time, while his interests extended to many countries, geography in some ways pulled him in different directions: it fed both his desire to see the world (through his trips to Africa and Australia, for example) and his wish to settle down (to life on the English–Welsh border).

Throughout his life, Rodd was in a kind of dialogue with the landscapes he encountered. If, as David Livingstone notes, agency can be understood as not solely connected to human intentionality, it opens up the possibility of the natural, non-human world having some element of agency.[3] Rodd's experience illustrates this possibility. Landscapes conveyed a variety of messages to him. He was a restless person, and there is a case for saying that empty or beautiful places suggested to him the existence of a stable, harmonious environment – they hinted at an answer to his restlessness. In this, they provoked an existential response from him. But they also appealed to the aspiring scientist in him. The Enlightenment project of subjecting the world to a rational analysis appealed to his enduring desire to impose order over chaos and be systematic in his thinking. The landscapes of central North Africa also spoke to him about the military history of the region, prompting thoughts of how they might be relevant to the conflicts

---

1. Lottie Hoare, 'Kindersley, David Guy Barnabas 1915–95', *Oxford Dictionary of National Biography* (Oxford: Oxford University Press, 2004).
2. Rodd, *People of the Veil*, 184–85. I am indebted to Henrietta Butler for her advice about Tuareg symbols on the gravestone.
3. David Livingstone, 'Landscapes of Knowledge', in Peter Meusburger, David N. Livingstone and Heike Jöns (eds), *Geographies of Science* (London: Springer, 2010), 10.

Figure C.1 Rodd's gravestone, designed by David Kindersley. Photograph by Henrietta Butler.

of the twentieth century. Rodd's dialogue with landscape was made more complicated by the fact that he sometimes felt uncertain about his career choices. There were different vocational impulses competing within him, and each of those responded to the landscape in a different way: geographer, historian, Foreign Office official, banker, intelligence officer, military administrator, farmer, and so on. Landscapes appealed to a range of instincts within him, while at the same time reminding him of an unresolved problem about his own identity.

Rodd's career in geography was made up of a number of elements and went through different phases. At one level, he can be seen as a gentlemanly or aristocratic adventurer. His trips to Africa in the 1920s were a reflection of that. An academic instinct was layered onto this. He wanted to be a serious scholar of the central Sahara rather than a mere travel-writer. Rodd was not a professional academic; he once described himself as a 'European amateur geographer'.[4] But there was a systematic quality about some of his writings and map-making that went beyond the level of the amateur. In the 1920s, he made a significant contribution to Tuareg studies and the cartography of Aïr; and in the 1930s, he was influential as a networker. But, with his career built around banking, he did not have the time to sustain this. During the Second World War, his North African expertise fed into his roles in military intelligence and civil affairs. Post-war, it was as an administrator that he influenced the world of geography: he had an

---

4. Rodd, 'A Journey in Aïr', 98.

eye for demonstrating the subject's interdisciplinary character, as well as for giving the RGS a mission and institutional presence in post-war Britain. Near his home, he became fascinated by local history and topography, while in Australia, an instinct for geography fed into his business activities. Camels, in the interwar period, and then aeroplanes were preferred vehicles for seeing the world.

In the years immediately after the Second World War, the defeat of Nazism made it relatively easy to see Britain's role in the world as essentially benign. But increased scrutiny of the British empire has made the picture much more complicated.[5] Recent scholarship has highlighted the complicity of German geographers in Nazism. If the British empire is seen as flawed, then questions about complicity can also be asked about the relationship between British geography and empire – after all, empire gave British geographers the infrastructure for their work.[6] While this is a point that is easy to make in a general sense, history, on close scrutiny, often turns out to be more complicated than it first appears. It can be hard to make definitive moral judgments about people caught up in larger historical and cultural processes. Clearly, Rodd's story demonstrates a truth that has often been made about the history of geography – namely that geographers often operate in a political context. His knowledge of North Africa informed his work at the Foreign Office and helped shape his military career during the Second World War. He was like others in this respect – Bagnold being a good example. For good or ill, the British exploration and study of the Sahara, in which the RGS played a central role, contributed to the advancement of British power and interests. But it would be simplistic to see politics alone as driving men like Rodd.

Rodd's friendship with men like Lawrence and Hogarth might suggest that he deserves classification among those whom Said has termed 'Orientalists-*cum*-imperial agents'.[7] Rodd can certainly be seen as belonging to the same social and intellectual current as these men. But, as this book demonstrates, Rodd tended to project not so much an orientalist 'other' onto his North African friends as British social hierarchies; he saw in Hasssanein and Ahmed examples of English gentlemen. Furthermore, his inclusion in *People of the Veil* of the photograph of T'ekhmedin and himself standing alongside each other suggests that he wanted to see the Tuareg guide as his moral equal. It is best to see men like Rodd as human beings with a variety of motives, as opposed to as abstract representatives of a system or spokespeople for a particular discourse. With people like

---

5. See, for example, David Anderson, *Histories of the Hanged: Britain's Dirty War in Kenya and the End of Empire* (London: Weidenfeld and Nicolson, 2005); and Caroline Elkins, *Britain's Gulag: The Brutal End of Empire in Kenya* (London: Jonathon Cape, 2005).
6. Trevor J. Barnes and Christian Abrahamsson, 'Tangled Complicities and Moral Struggles: The Haushofers, Father and Son, and the Spaces of Nazi Geopolitics', *Journal of Historical Geography* 47 (2015): 64–73. Stephen Legg, 'Decolonialism', *Transactions of the Institute of British Geographers* 42, no. 3 (2017): 345–48. Driver, *Geography Militant*, 37–39.
7. Said includes in this group, in addition to Lawrence and Hogarth, Edward Henry Palmer, Gertrude Bell, Ronald Storrs, St John Philiby and William Gifford Palgrave; Said, *Orientalism*, 196–97. For a critique of Said's arguments, see Robert Irwin, *The Lust for Knowing: The Orientalists and Their Enemies* (London: Penguin, 2006), 277–309. See also Jonathon Crush, 'Post-colonialism, De-colonization and Geography', in Anne Godlewska and Neil Smith (eds), *Geography and Empire* (Oxford: Blackwell, 1994), 334–39.

Hassanein and T'ekhmedin, Rodd made genuine friends. There was a class dimension to this: in these cases, he was befriending people from similar positions in their social hierarchies to his own. In the case of T'ekhmedin, there was also an anthropological dimension: T'ekhmedin was a person from another race requiring some analysis. Alongside these elements, Rodd was working to further the political interests of Britain abroad. Some of these elements could be seen as contradictory. But these diverse tendencies should not surprise us. Humanitarian, scientific and political instincts are often present in geographers and explorers, and they can be hard to distinguish from each other. There was also a commercial agenda at work in Rodd's visits to Australia.

It was not only landscapes with which Rodd was in dialogue, it was also people. Just as landscapes hinted to Rodd at different versions of himself, so too did family members, colleagues and friends. For example, his father (diplomat), T. E. Lawrence (soldier-adventurer), Montagu Norman (banker with an international vision) and Philip Mitchell (pragmatic administrator) can be seen as representing different vocational ideals or fields of activity of the kind he found appealing. Some of his role models were people from the past; Heinrich Barth was an example to him of what a geographer should be like. Rodd was also in a kind of ongoing dialogue with the organisations and institutions he was involved with. Sometimes he spoke with different voices, depending on his audience. To academic geographers, for example, he tried to speak in the 'objective' language of reason and science, while with British diplomats, he used the vocabulary of British national interest. The ideal of the 'Elizabethan adventurer', depicted in St John Lucas's 'Ship of Fools' poem, arguably offered him a way of making sense of his life-long enthusiasm for doing new things, as well as his geographical expeditions. At the same time, amidst the diversity of his interests, we should not forget that Rodd had much in common educationally and socially with the wider British establishment and ruling elite. It is striking how often he found himself working alongside people who, like him, had had an 'Eton and Oxbridge' education.

Although Rodd performed a variety of roles in his life, there were certain skills or features of character that kept appearing across his different activities. He brought a 'problem-solving' mentality to a variety of situations, as well as confidence in his own judgment and ability to manage events in such a way as to get to a desired outcome. This was evident in the Austrian banking crisis of 1931, as well as in the way he worked with Lamont to find an international way of dealing with Austrian debt in 1938. It was also evident in his work for the MEW. Here he overestimated the capacity of economic incentives to pull Italy out of Germany's orbit. But his self-confidence and strategic awareness enabled him to make a significant contribution to the work of MI(R) in West Africa and fed into the application of motorised transport to the desert war. It is not surprising that he was able to thrive in the fluid environment of the Second World War. It was a time when Britain's resources were stretched, and people with Rodd's abilities in short supply. For men like him, the war threw up opportunities they would not otherwise have had. Many from his background were influential at that time.[8]

---

8. David Cannadine, *Decline and Fall of the British Aristocracy* (New Haven: Yale University Press, 1990), ch. 13.

Rodd exuded an air of authority and was capable of taking a strong stance on issues. But qualities helpful in one context are not always good in another. His tendency to be outspoken made him enemies and was probably one reason why a larger role did not come his way after the war. Although temperamental by nature, his frustrations should not be solely attributed to his personality. Psychological explanations of behaviour have their place, but are not on their own sufficient.[9] Rodd's moodiness sometimes came from being trapped in situations beyond his control. He did not find institutional weaknesses and rivalries easy to deal with. There are a number of examples of this. During the Second World War, he got frustrated with the MEW for what he saw as its slowness to act; the Foreign Office for trying to bypass OETA/OTA; and the MGS at AFHQ for conspiring behind his back. More generally, it is clear that Rodd was a person with strong emotions, sometimes hidden from others. While these emotions sometimes came out in the form of anger, there was a softer side to his nature as well. This was a point remarked on by Kirwan in his obituary of Rodd: behind Rodd's shyness, reserve and sometimes 'formidable' manner, Kirwan suggested, there lay a deep capacity for friendship and sense of family ties. Kirwan also suggested that Rodd was more a nineteenth- than a twentieth-century figure, perhaps alluding to his aristocratic demeanour and the variety of his enthusiasms.[10] Rodd was more insecure in himself and self-reflective than others realised.

Occupiers always face the problem of whether to replace or to build upon existing systems of authority. The problem with eradicating a power structure, as Henry Kissinger noted, is that in practice 'naked power' is needed to enforce an alternative.[11] A challenge facing OETA and AMGOT was that they simply did not have the personnel to run conquered territories at the local level. They could not, in practice, have enforced their rule, even if they had wanted to. The result was a kind of halfway house. Senior fascist or Vichy leaders were replaced, but other more junior figures left in post. The appeal of the doctrine of indirect rule was that it gave legitimacy to this approach. It would be wrong to see Rodd as a deep thinker about indirect rule. He was a practical man, responding to certain wartime emergencies. His readiness to adapt the terminology of direct and indirect rule to different contexts reinforces the idea that indirect rule was more a set of attitudes than a clearly defined doctrine.[12] Rodd was also conscious that indirect rule had limitations: like Lord Hailey, he saw a need for a greater level of modernisation in the empire. In some ways, the challenges confronting the Allies were similar to those facing the European empires managing their colonies. Colonial governments were often enfeebled by their lack of staff and resources; and in that context, indirect rule was a

---

9. For a helpful discussion of this subject, see Ronald Grigor Suny, 'Beyond Psychohistory: The Young Stalin in Georgia', *Slavic Review* 50, no. 1 (1991): 48–58.
10. (L. P. Kirwan), obituary of Lord Rennell, *Geographical Journal* 144, no. 2 (1978): 393.
11. Henry Kissinger, *Diplomacy* (New York: Simon and Schuster, 1994), 655.
12. Christopher Prior takes this view of indirect rule; see his *Exporting Empire: Africa, Colonial Officials and the Construction of the Imperial State, c. 1900–39* (Manchester: Manchester University Press, 2013), 43.

convenient excuse for inaction.¹³ In much the same way, wartime military administration was run with a minimum of resources.

Rodd's enthusiasm for indirect rule was connected with his belief that military government needed to be transitional. In Italy, this meant arguing for a minimum of Allied interference, pending an Italian rather than an Allied decision about the country's future. In effect, he was promoting the idea that AMGOT had a duty to be non-political. Whether this was realistic can be doubted. As Colin Newbury has observed, one of the problems with indirect rule as an administrative typology is that it misses the political character of colonial government.¹⁴ The same could be said of Allied military government, even while it was temporary in character. By their very nature, Allied administrations in Africa and Italy were rooted in assumptions about what good government should look like. At a personal level, Rodd's ideas about government contained a combination of instincts arising out of his experience in different spheres of life. There was a respect for locality in his thinking, coming from his father's philosophy and his exposure to different cultures. This made him wary of artificially imposing Anglo–American systems of government on occupied territories. By contrast, a different approach was evident in his approach to financial questions. In OETA, he stressed that – with occasional exceptions – all local administrations needed to adopt the same currency policy, or chaos would ensue. He was also worried about the possibility of corruption in Ethiopia after power had been handed back to Haile Selassie. Here, Rodd's perspectives implicitly favoured a more international than local approach, even if we can see that this 'international' dimension was western in its character.

An instinctive pragmatism was present in many of Rodd's dealings. This was evident in his work with the MEW; it made sense to him to establish an understanding with fascist Italy in order to prevent an Italian alliance with Germany. He saw Italian fascism as more benign than Nazism. Exposure to Italian life through family links and business trips made him feel that the Italian people were not in favour of war, and he sought to capitalise on this. The British war trade negotiations, associated with Halifax, Loraine, Greene and Rodd, can be seen as a form of appeasement – although this depends on how appeasement is defined. But there is also a case for seeing Rodd's work for the MEW in the context of his father's activities as ambassador in Rome; both he and his father sought to manage Italian behaviour in such a way as to favour British interests. Rodd's adherence to the doctrine of indirect rule also reflected a pragmatic mindset; for reasons of expediency, he and other civil affairs officers were attracted by the idea of building British military rule on top of Italian or French structures.

Rodd defies easy categorisation. There are moments in his career that suggest an element of complacency about the threat of far-right regimes. His membership of the January Club, even if not in itself indicative of fascist sympathies, might suggest that. His very optimism about the possibility of keeping Italy neutral would be another. But it is hard to be definite about this. The evidence also points in a different direction. Rodd was

---

13. John Darwin, *The End of the British Empire: The Historical Debate* (Oxford: Blackwell, 1991), 93.
14. Colin Newbury, *Patrons, Clients and Empire: Chieftancy and Overrule in Asia, Africa and the Pacific* (Oxford: Oxford University Press, 2003), 12.

perceptive about the growing radicalisation of the Nazi regime in the 1930s – more so than his father. His eagerness to organise paramilitary activity in North Africa, evident from early 1939, suggests that he was well aware of the seriousness of the situation facing Britain in the late 1930s. He was an idealist as well as a pragmatist: he was enthusiastic about political causes like the Free French movement and the Greater Somalia Project and an advocate for the virtues of good administration. The way in which he tried to prevent the resurgence of the Italian mafia in 1943 was indicative of a firm belief in the rule of law. He can be seen as a kind of liberal conservative, with these two tendencies being reflected in the fact that he sat with both the Liberals and the Conservatives in the House of Lords. He supported decolonisation, if in a gradualist form and on British terms. He was fearful of radical African nationalism. There were patrician or authoritarian attitudes present in his responses to the Suez crisis and the Mau Mau rebellion.

Rodd was interested in the very nature of decision-making. It is obvious why this was so. A variety of institutions and individuals made demands of him, and he of them. His life was embedded in a number of different worlds, each with its own perspectives and values. Those closest to him had different approaches to making decisions: his father had a philosophy that was a kind of secular providentialism; his mother prioritised the advancement of the family's interests; and Mary looked to inspiration from her faith for finding her way through life. In the face of all this, and the challenges confronting him through his work, Rodd had to make choices. During the Second World War, he arrived at a philosophy that meant, when a decision was needed, letting events take their course until such time as the right way forward seemed obvious and inevitable. It was his own brand of providentialism. But if there was an element of passivity here, it was counterbalanced by a headstrong and impulsive quality in his nature and a recurring enthusiasm for taking on new projects.

Rodd's dialogues with Mary about the nature of religion should be seen in a broader context: they were an example of a wider British conversation taking place in the twentieth century about how Christianity should respond to Enlightenment values and the reality of a globalised world. Mary died in 1981 and was buried in the same grave as Rodd. An inscription was then added to the gravestone referring to her membership of the Order of St Benedict. It was as if the two of them, even after death, were still discussing the nature of religion.[15] Rodd was a Christian with a belief in a personal God, even if his faith was somewhat hesitant. There was in him an instinct to find a middle way between opposing tendencies. His religious beliefs were more ethical and ecumenical than dogmatic and denominational; he was drawn to beliefs he thought capable of reconciling differences. Truth was for him a concept capable of bridging the worlds of religion, science and the humanities. Although more a man of action than a thinker, he was in search of a unifying philosophy of life. Like many of his contemporaries, he was a man trying to make sense of an interconnected world and find his place in it.

---

15. The inscription for Mary around the edge of the gravestone reads: 'Mary the painter secular oblate of the abbey of the blessed Virgin Mary of consolation at Stanbrook OSB of the English congregation 5th November 1901–31st May 1981'.

SOURCES AND BIBLIOGRAPHY

Manuscript Sources

Papers of Francis Rodd

F. J. Rennell Papers, Nuffield College, Oxford (NCO).
Rennell of Rodd Papers, Bodleian Library (BD).
The Rodd Collection, Royal Geographical Society (RGS).
Rodd Family Papers, Author's Collection (AC).

Other Private Papers

J. G. C. Allen, Bodleian Library (BD).
Julian Amery, Churchill College, Cambridge (CCC).
Ralph Bagnold, Churchill College, Cambridge (CCC).
Winston Churchill, Churchill College, Cambridge (CCC).
P. J. Grigg, Churchill College, Cambridge (CCC).
Lord Hailey, Bodleian Library (BD).
Charles Hardinge, Cambridge University Library (CUL).
Teresa Hulton, Shropshire County Council (SCC).
Cynthia Jebb, Lady Gladwyn, Churchill College Cambridge (CCC).
Thomas W. Lamont, Baker Library, Harvard Business School (BK).
Irene Lawley/Forbes Adam, Hull University Archives (HUA).
T. E. Lawrence, Bodleian Library (BD).
Maurice Lush, Imperial War Museum (IWM).
H. W. Luttman-Johnson, Imperial War Museum (IWM).
Frank J. McSherry, US Army Heritage and Education Center (USAH).
Philip Mitchell, Bodleian Library (BD).
Frederick Pedler, Bodleian Library (BD).

Official Records and Papers

Balliol College Rowing Club.
Bank of England (BE).
Bank for International Settlements, Basle (BIS).
Cabinet Office, National Archives (CAB).
Eton College.
Forces War Records, Army, UK.
Foreign Office, National Archives, UK (FO).
International African Institute, London School of Economics Library (LSE).
Morgan Grenfell & Co., Deutsche Bank Business Administration Records (DBBAR).
Morgan Grenfell & Co. (Kathleen Burk), London Metropolitan Archives (LMA).
National Archives and Records Administration, Maryland (NARA).
Oxford Group, Bodleian Library (BD).

Pitt Rivers Museum, Oxford.
Treasury, National Archives, UK (T).
War Office, National Archives, UK (WO).

Newspapers and Magazines

Christian Science Monitor
The Daily Mirror
The Daily Telegraph
The Field
The Financial Times
Geographical Magazine
The Independent
Kalgoorlie Miner
Manchester Guardian
New Leader
New Statesman and Nation
The New York Times
The Spectator
The Sunday Times
The Times

Online Sources

Hansard: https://api.parliament.uk/historic-hansard/index.html
T. E. Lawrence Studies: http://www.telstudies.org/writings/writings_introduction.shtml

Interviews/Conversations

Juliet Boobbyer, Mary Daniell, Margaret Fowler-Wright, George Mills, David Preece.

Works by Francis Rodd/Lord Rennell

1922 *Report on the Commercial & Financial Situation in Bulgaria*. London: HMSO.
1923 'A Journey in Aïr', *Geographical Journal* 62, no. 2, 81–101.
1924 'Across the Libyan Desert: Hassanein Bey's Great Journey', *Field*, May 1924.
1924 'Review of René Bazin, *Charles de Foucauld: Hermit and Explorer*', *Geographical Journal* 63, no. 1, 78–79.
1924 'Review of Edward Freiherr von Callot, bearbeitet von F. Bieber, *Reise durch Kusch und Habesch*', *Geographical Journal* 64, no. 3, 254–55.
1924 'Review of Captain R. S. Rattray, *Ashanti*', *Geographical Journal* 64, no. 4, 339–40.
1924 'Review of Lady Dorothy Mills, *The Road to Timbuktu*', *Geographical Journal* 64, no. 4, 340–41.
1925 'Kahena: Queen of the Berbers: A Sketch of the Arab Invasion of Ifrikiya in the First Century of the Hijra', *Bulletin of the School of Oriental Studies* 3, no. 4, 729–46.
1925 'Notes on Mr Newbold's Desert Odyssey', *Sudan Notes and Records* VIII, 233–35.
1925 'Early British Stones in Cornwall', *Times*, 21 August, 11.
1925 'Review of Douglas Jardine, *The Mad Mullah of Somaliland*', *Geographical Journal* 65, no. 1, 70–71.
1925 'Review of F. A. Donnithorne, *Wonderful Africa* and E. F. Gautier, *La Sahara*', *Geographical Journal* 66, no. 3, 268–69.

1925 'Reviews of Henry Walton, *Livingstone: Fifty Years After* and Frank Savile, *The River of the Giraffe*', *Geographical Journal* 66, no. 4, 364.
1925 'Review of W. Harding King, *Mysteries of the Libyan Desert*', *Geographical Journal* 65, no. 6, 538–39.
1925 'Review of William M. Sloane, *Greater France in Africa*', *Geographical Journal* 65, no. 6, 539.
1926 *People of the Veil: Being an Account of the Habits, Organisation and History of the Wandering Tuareg Tribes Which Inhabit the Mountains of Aïr or Asben in the Central Sahara*. London: Macmillan.
1926 'The Deferred Payments System in the United States', *Economic Journal* 36, no. 142, 204–14.
1926 'The Origin of the Tuareg', *Geographical Journal* 67, no. 1, 27–47.
1926 'The Origin of the Tuareg: Discussion', *Geographical Journal* 67, no. 1, 47–52; discussion led by D. G. Hogarth, with Rodd's comments, 50–51.
1926 'The Tuareg Veil', comments by R. H. Palmer with a response from Francis Rodd, *Geographical Journal* 68, 412–18; Rodd's comments, 416–18.
1926 'Review, "Three Maps of the Sahara" (*Sahara Occidental et Central*) by A. Meunier, *Carte du Sahara* by Delinguette, *Croquis du Sahara au 1,000,000 me*', *Geographical Journal* 67, no. 3, 252–53.
1927 'Positions in Aïr', *Geographical Journal* 69, no. 1, 94–95.
1927 (with D. G. Hogarth et al.) 'Some Contrasts in Nigeria: Discussion', *Geographical Journal* 69, no. 6, 511–16.
1927 'Review of H. H. Princess Marie Louise, *Letters from the Gold Coast*', *Geographical Journal* 69, no. 2, 172–73.
1928 'People of the Veil', *Times*, 20 March, 17.
1928 'French West Africa', *Times*, 11 July, 17.
1928 'French West Africa', *Times*, 20 July, 15.
1928 'A Journey across the Sahara from Kano to Ouarghla: Discussion', *Geographical Journal* 71, no. 6, 560.
1928 'Review of Douglas Frazier, *Through the Congo Basin*, and C. V. A. Peel, *Through the Length of Africa*', *Geographical Journal* 72, no. 5, 481–82.
1929 *The Meteorological Results of Journeys in the Southern Sahara, 1922 and 1927* (*Geophysical Memoirs*, No. 48), discussion by C. E. P. Brooks. London: HMSO.
1929 'A Second Journey among the Southern Tuareg', *Geographical Journal* 73, no. 1, 1–18.
1930 'Major James Rennell', *Geographical Journal* 75, no. 4, 289–99.
1933 *General William Eaton: The Failure of an Idea*. London: George Routledge and Sons.
1933 'A Reconnaissance of the Gilf Kebir by the Late Robert Clayton–East–Clayton', *Geographical Journal* 81, no. 3, 249–54.
1933 (with William Goodenough and K. S. Sandford) 'Further Journey through the Libyan Desert: Discussion', *Geographical Journal* 82, no. 2, 128.
1935 'The Forgotten of God: The Veiled Tuareg of the Sahara', *Geographical Magazine*, 2 November, 23–28.
1935 'Rennell's Comments on the Journeys of Park and Laing to the Niger', *Geographical Journal* 86, no. 1, 28–31.
1935 'Colonel Warrington', *Times*, 19 January, 8.
1935 'Comments on A. J. Arkell, "Some Tuareg Ornaments and Their Connections with India"', *Journal of the Royal Anthropological Institute* 65, July–December, 304–6.
1935 'Review of E. W. Bovill, *Caravans of the Old Sahara: An Introduction to the History of the Western Sudan*', *Antiquity* 9, no. 35, September, 377–78.
1935 'Review of L. di Caporiacco, *Nel Cuore del Deserto Libico, A Cufra, El-Auenàt ed oltre, Con la Spedizione Marchesi*', *Geographical Journal* 85, no. 1, 87–88.
1935 'Review of Arnold Heim, *Negro Sahara: von der Guineaküste zum Mittelmeer*', *Geographical Journal* 85, no. 5, 475.
1935 (with Percy Cox and R. A. Bagnold) 'Explorations Sahariennes: A Discussion', *Geographical Journal* 86, no. 1, 25–28.

1936 (with E. W. Bovill) 'A Fezzani Military Expedition to Kanem and Bagirmi', *Journal of the Royal African Society* 35, no. 139, 153–68.
1936 'Review of Emilio Scarin, *Le Oasi del Fezzàn: ricerche e osservazioni di geografia umana*', *Geographical Journal* 88, no. 2, 175.
1937 'Camels', in E. A. Reeves (ed.), *Hints to Travellers: Organization and Equipment Scientific Observation, Health, Sickness, and Injury*, vol. 2. London: Royal Geographical Society, 146–49.
1938 'Some Rock Drawings from Aïr in the Southern Sahara', *Journal of the Royal Anthropological Institute of Great Britain and Ireland* 68, January–June, 99–111.
1938 Letter on 'The Sahara', *Geographical Journal* 91, no. 4, 354–55.
1939 'Foreword', in Leonard Waight, *The History and Mechanism of the Exchange and Equalisation Account*. Cambridge: Cambridge University Press, vii–viii.
1943 'How Italians Were Repatriated from Ethiopia', *Listener*, 7 January, 7.
1944 'Allied Military Government in Occupied Territory', *International Affairs*, July, 307–16.
1944 'The Manors of Rodd, Nash and Little Brampton, Near Presteigne: A Note on Possible Domesday Book Identification', *Radnorshire Society Transactions* 14, 24–29.
1944 'Foreword', in W. H. Howse, *Radnor: Old and New*. Hereford: Jakemans, 5–6.
1945 'Africa and the British Political Parties', *African Affairs* 44, 107.
1945 *British Military Administration of Occupied Territories in Africa During the Years 1941–43*. London: HMSO.
1945 'Development in Colonial Administration', *Fortnightly*, July, 23–27.
1945 'Review of F. Kingdon-Ward, *Exploring Up to Date*', *Sunday Times*, 17 June, 3.
1946 'Foreword', in *Italy in Transition: Extracts from the Private Journal of G. R. Gayre*. London: Faber, 7–16.
1946 Obituary of Ahmed Hassanein, *Geographical Journal* 107, no. 1/2, 77–78.
1946 Address at AGM of RGS, *Geographical Journal* 107, no. 3/5, 81–89.
1946 'Review of F. Kingdon-Ward, *Beyond this Earth*', *Sunday Times*, 27 October, 4.
1946 (with Leonard Brooks et al.) 'High Latitude Flying by Coastal Command in Support of Convoys to North Russia: Discussion', *Geographical Journal* 108, no. 1/3, 21–23.
1947 (with Averell Harriman) 'Geographical Influences in American History: Discussion', *Geographical Journal* 109, no. 1/3, 37–38.
1947 (with G. W. Rowley) 'Exercise Muskox: Discussion', *Geographical Journal* 109, no. 4/6, 184–85.
1947 Address at AGM of RGS, *Geographical Journal* 109, no. 4/6, 161–64.
1947 (with Viscount Mountbatten) 'Travels in Japanese Occupied Malaya: Discussion', *Geographical Journal* 110, no. 1/3, 36–37.
1948 *British Military Administration of Occupied Territories in Africa During the Years 1941–47*. London: HMSO.
1948 Address at AGM of RGS, *Geographical Journal* 111, no. 4/6, 153–57.
1948 (with B. P. Uvarov and Wilfred Thesiger) 'Across the Empty Quarter: Discussion', *Geographical Journal* 111, no. 1/3, 19–21.
1948 (with J. A. Beasley and Henry M. Adams) 'Australia's Frontier Province: Discussion', *Geographical Journal* 111, no. 1/3, 31–32.
1948 (with Lord Montgomery) 'Geography and War Strategy', *Geographical Journal* 112, no. 1/3, 15–18.
1950 'Review of Lt-Col. J. H. Williams, *The Elephant Man*', *Sunday Times*, 7 May, 3.
1950 'Review of Anne Fremantle, *Desert Calling: The Story of Charles de Foucauld*', *Sunday Times*, 16 July, 3.
1951 'Review of B. Rivlin, *Italian Colonies*', *Africa: Journal of the International African Institute* 21, no. 3, 244–45.
1951 'Review of *Report of United Nations Commission for Eritrea*', *Africa: Journal of the International African Institute* 21, no. 3, 245–46.
1951 'Review of A. Desio, *Le Vie della Sete*', *Geographical Journal* 117, no. 2, 231.
1952 'Beef by Air', *Times*, 15 May, 7.

1953 'The Kimberley Division of Western Australia', *Geographical Journal* 119, no. 3, 306–11, followed by discussion, 311–14.
1954 'Aids to the Domesday Geography of North-West Hereford', *Geographical Journal* 120, no. 4, 458–67.
1955 'The Sand Dune Areas of the North-West and Kimberley Divisions of Western Australia', *Geographical Journal* 121, no. 4, 442–43.
1955 'A Square Mile of Finance, Commerce and Good Faith', *Optima: A Quarterly Review Published in the Interests of Mining, Industrial, Scientific and Economic Progress* 5, no. 1, 20–23.
1955 'Somalis and Ethiopia: 1. How 1897 Agreement Was Made', *Guardian*, 19 December, 6.
1955 'Somalia and Ethiopia: 2. The French and Fashoda', *Guardian*, 20 December, 6.
1958 *Valley on the March: A History of a Group of Manors on the Herefordshire March of Wales*. London: Oxford University Press.
1958 (with E. W. Bovill) 'Heinrich Barth and the Western Sudan: Discussion', *Geographical Journal* 124, no. 3, 338–39.
1960 'The Boundaries of the Saxon Manor of Staunton-on-Arrow in a Charter of King Edgar of 958 A.D.', *Transactions of the Woolhope Club* 36 (1958–60), 79–90.
1960 'Note on Rowe Ditch and a "Second Alignment" of Offa's Dyke in the Pembridge–Wapley–Herrock area', *Radnorshire Society Transactions* 30, 31–33.
1961 *The Function of the British Association for the Advancement of Science in Our Everyday Lives*. Birmingham and Midland Institute, 1961.
1961 'Review of L. Briggs, *Tribes of the Sahara*', *Geographical Journal* 127, no. 1, 103–4.
1962 'Bernoldune and Barland', *Radnorshire Society Transactions* 32, 42–43.
1962 'Review of N. Bodington, *The Awakening Sahara*, and E. Migliorini, *L'Esplorazione del Sahara*', *Geographical Journal* 128, no. 1, 90.
1962 'Review of G. Gardel, *Les Touareg Ajjer*', *Geographical Journal* 129, no. 2, 216–17.
1962 'Review of R. Mauny, *Tableau Géographique de l'Ouest Africain au Moyen Age*', *Geographical Journal* 128, no. 2, 219–20.
1964 'A Note on "Hech" in the Domesday Book', *Radnorshire Society Transactions* 34, 63–64.
1965 'The Montagu Norman Controversy: The Obverse of the Coin', *Sunday Times*, 30 May, 8.
1965 'Review of E. W. Bovill (ed.), *Missions to the Niger. 1. The Journal of Friedrich Hornemann's Travels from Cairo to Murzuk in the Years 1797–98; The Letters of Major Alexander Gordon Laing 1824–6*', *Geographical Journal* 131, no. 2, 278–79.
1966 'Heinrich Barth and the Opening Up of Central Africa', *Geographical Journal* 132, no. 1, 72–73.
1968 *The Will of Aethelgifu: A Tenth Century Anglo–Saxon Manuscript*, translated and examined by Dorothy Whitelock, with a note on the document by Neal Ker and analyses of the property, livestock, and chattels concerned by Lord Rennell. Oxford: Roxburghe Club.
1970 *Merino-Kerry Hill Cross Bred Sheep at the Rodd Farm: An Interim Report on Four Seasons' Experiment*. Herefordshire: Rodd Farm.
1971 *Merino-Kerry Hill Cross Bred Sheep at the Rodd Farm: A Second Interim Report on Five Seasons' Experiment*. Herefordshire: Rodd Farm.

Selected Speeches in the House of Lords (from Hansard)

Economic Warfare, 9 May 1944; Trade with Russia, 24 May 1944; Education, 29 June 1944; Housing for African Servicemen, 19 July 1944; Post-war Civil Aviation, 12 October 1944; Relief Problems, 14 December 1944; Gold Coast Legislature, 20 December 1944; Mining in British Colonies, 15 May 1945; Government of Burma, 17 June 1945; UN Charter, 23 August 1945; Colonial Government, 29 November 1945; Anglo–American Finance Agreement, 18 December 1945; Administration of Colonial Affairs, 27 February 1946; Future of Defence Services, 27 March 1946; Economic Position, 8 May 1946; Coinage Bill, 24 October 1946; Organisation of Western Europe, 3 December 1946; Food Situation, 8 May 1947; Agriculture,

11 December 1947; Economic Situation, 23 February1948; World Food Situation, 16 June 1948; Gas Bill, 7 July 1948; British West Africa and Cocoa, 15 September 1948; Forest Bill, 9 December 1948; Exports, 24 February 1949; West African Colonies, 17 March 1949; Iron and Steel Bill, 29 January 1949; Economic Situation, 24 May 1950; European Payments Union, 30 November 1950; Government Accounts, 12 December 1950; Colonial Development, 13 June 1951; Finance Bill, 17 July 1951; Wye and Usk River Board, 27 November 1951; Gold Coast, 24 July 24, 1952; Collective Punishment in Kenya, 26 November 1952; Economic Situation, 29 April 1953; Finance Bill, 21 July 1953; Britain and Egypt, 17 December 1953; Gold Coast, 1 April 1954; Finance Bill, 21 July 1954; Colonial Territories, 6 July1955; Suez Crisis, 11 December 1956; Ghana Independence Bill, 31 January 1957; The Economic Situation, 9 February 1966; Local Government Bill, 11 September 1972.

Manuscripts

Budden, Michael John, 'British Policy towards Fascist Italy in the Early Stages of the Second World War', PhD thesis, King's College London, 1999.
Clarke, Peter, 'Amgothic Lines and Other Outbursts of an UnCivil Affairs Officer', Sicily August 43–Romagna January 45, possession of Peter Clarke.
Duff, D. S., 'Civil Affairs in Italy (Narrative)', Section 1, chs 1–3, Planning the Sicily. 'Campaign/ The Consolidation of AMGOT', 1943; Section II, ch. IV, Southern Italy. September to December 1943, Prepared by the Historical Section of the Cabinet. Sources: CAB 44/171 & 172; Rennell of Rodd Papers, BD, Boxes 62 and 63.
Flint, Edward R., 'The Development of British Civil Affairs and Its Employment in the British Sector of Allied Military Operations during the Battle of Normandy, June to August 1944', PhD thesis, Cranfield Defence and Security School, 2008.
Hansen, Per H., 'Sensemaking and Financial Crises: Central Banks and the Austrian Crisis of 1931', unpublished paper, 2017.
Hoar, A. S. G., 'ASG Hoar – Bank of England Memories', n.d., author's copy.
Mavis, Stephen F. O., 'Reminiscences of Allied Military Government under Two Flags in Sicily–Italy (1943–47)', n.d., possession of Peter Clarke.
Millen, Raymond A., '"Bury the Dead, Feed the Living": The History of Civil Affairs/Military Government in the Mediterranean and European Theaters of Operation during World War II', US Army Peacekeeping and Stability Operations Institute, 2019.
Rodd, Gustav (Taffy), *Where I Trodd*, unpublished memoir, c. 1971, possession of Phyllis Rodd.
Seddon, Jack A., 'Between Collapse and Decline: The Dissolution of International Monetary Systems in Comparative Historical Perspective', DPhil, Oxford University, 2015.
Spicer, Charles, '"Ambulant Amateurs": The Rise and Fade of the Anglo–German Fellowship', PhD thesis, School of Advanced Study, University of London, 2018.

Published Works

Acton, Harold, *Nancy Mitford: A Memoir*. London: Gibson Square, 2004.
Aguado, Iago Gil, 'The Creditanstalt Crisis of 1931 and the Failure of the Austro–German Customs Union Project', *Historical Journal* 44, no. 1 (2001): 199–221.
A.M.G.O.T. Plan, Proclamations and Instructions. Palermo, 1943.
Andersen, C. and Cohen, A. (eds), *The Government and Administration of Africa 1880–1939*, vol. 1. London: Pickering and Chatto, 2013.
Anderson, Major General A. V., 'Administration of Occupied and Liberated Territories during the 1939–45 War', *RUSI Journal* 92, no. 565 (1947): 51–58.
Anderson, David, *Histories of the Hanged: Britain's Dirty War in Kenya and the End of Empire*. London: Weidenfeld and Nicolson, 2005.

Anglim, Simon, 'MI(R), G(R) and British Covert Operations 1939–42', *Intelligence and National Security* 20, no. 4 (2005): 631–53.
———, *Orde Wingate and the British Army 1922–44*. London: Routledge, 2010.
Audoin-Rouzeau, Stéphane, '1915: Stalemate', in Jay Winter (ed.), *The Cambridge History of the First World War*, vol. 1. Cambridge: Cambridge University Press, 2014, 65–88.
Badoglio, Pietro, *Italy in the Second World War: Memories and Documents*. Westport: Greenwood Press, 1976.
Bagnold, Ralph, 'Early Days of the Long Range Desert Group', *Geographical Journal* 105, no. 1 (1945): 30–42.
———, 'A Further Journey through the Libyan Desert', *Geographical Journal* 82, no. 2 (1933): 103–26.
———, *Libyan Sands: Travels in a Dead World*. London: Eland, [1935] 2010.
———, *Sand, Wind and War: Memoirs of a Desert Explorer*. Tuscon: University of Arizona Press, 1990.
Baker, J. N. L., *The History of Geography*. New York: Barnes & Noble, 1963.
Balchin, W. G. V., 'United Kingdom Geographers in the Second World War', *Geographical Journal* 153, no. 2 (1987): 159–80.
Baldoli, Claudia, *Exporting Fascism: Italian Fascists and Britain's Italians in the 1930s*. Oxford: Berg, 2003.
Barnes, Trevor J., 'American Geographers and World War II: Spies Teachers and Occupiers', *Annals of the American Association of Geographers* 106, no. 3 (2016): 543–50.
Barnes, Trevor J. and Christian Abrahamsson, 'Tangled Complicities and Moral Struggles: The Haushofers, Father and Son, and the Spaces of Nazi Geopolitics', *Journal of Historical Geography* 47 (2015): 64–73.
Barth, Heinrich, *Travels and Discoveries in North and Central Africa*. London: Longman, 1857.
Bates, Oric, *The Eastern Libyans*. London: Macmillan, 1914.
Bell, P. M. H., *A Certain Eventuality: Britain and the Fall of France*. Farnborough: Saxon House, 1974.
Bennett, Gill, *Churchill's Man of Mystery: Desmond Morton and the World of Intelligence*. London: Routledge, 2007.
Benson, George C. S. and Maurice Neufeld, 'American Military Government in Italy', in Carl J. Friedrich (ed.), *American Experiences in Military Government*. New York: Reinhart, 1948, 111–47.
Berdine, Michael, D., *Redrawing the Middle East: Sir Mark Sykes, Imperialism and the Sykes–Picot Agreement*. London: I.B. Tauris, 2018.
Bergman, Jay, *Meeting the Demands of Reason: The Life and Thought of Andrei Sakharov*. Ithaca: Cornell University Press, 2009.
Bernasek, Lisa, 'Colonial, Popular and Scientific? The *Exposition du Sahara* (1934) and the Formation of the Musée de l'Homme', *Museum Anthropology* 42, no. 2 (2019): 89–108.
Berretta, Alfio, *Amedeo d'Aosta: Il Prigioniero del Kenia*. Milano: Eli, 1956.
Boobbyer, Brian, *Like a Cork Out of a Bottle*. Arundel: John Faber, 2004.
Boobbyer, Philip, 'Francis Rodd', in Hayden Lorimer and Charles W. J. Withers (eds), *Geographers: Biobibliographical Studies* 35 (2016): 9–31.
———, 'Lord Rennell, Chief of AMGOT: A Study of His Approach to Politics and Military Government (c. 1940–1943)', *War in History* 25, no. 3 (2018): 304–27.
———, 'Moral Judgements and Moral Realism in History', *Totalitarian Movements and Political Religions* 3, no. 2 (2002): 83–112.
———, *The Spiritual Vision of Frank Buchman*. University Park: Pennsylvania State University Press, 2013.
Bosworth, R. J. B., *Italy, the Least of the Great Powers: Italian Foreign Policy before the First World War*. London: Cambridge University Press, 1979.
Bovill, E. W., *Caravans of the Old Sahara: An Introduction to the History of Western Sudan*. London: Oxford University Press, 1933.
Boyle, Andrew, *Montagu Norman*. London: Cassell, 1967.
Bruce, James, '"A Shadowy Entity": M.I.1 (b) and British Communications Intelligence, 1914–1922', *Intelligence and National Security* 32, no. 3 (2017): 313–32.

Buchanan, Andrew, *American Grand Strategy in the Mediterranean during World War II*. Cambridge: Cambridge University Press, 2014.

Buchanan, Angus, *Out of the World – North of Nigeria*. London: John Murray, 1921.

Burk, Kathleen, 'Grenfell, Edward Charles, First Baron St Just, 1870–1941', *Oxford Dictionary of National Biography*. Oxford: Oxford University Press, 2004.

———, *Morgan Grenfell, 1838–1988: The Biography of a Merchant Bank*. Oxford: Oxford University Press, 1989.

———, 'Rodd, Francis James Rennell, Second Baron Rennell (1895–1978), Merchant Banker and Geographer', *Oxford Dictionary of National Biography*. Oxford: Oxford University Press, 2004.

Butler, Henrietta (ed.), *The Tuareg or Kel Tamasheq and a History of the Sahara*, introduction by Robin Hanbury-Tenison. London: Unicorn Press, 2015.

Cain, P. J. and A. G. Hopkins, *British Imperialism: 1688–2000*. Harlow: Pearson, 2002.

Cameron, D. R. G., 'A Journey across the Sahara from Kano to Ouarghla', *Geographical Journal* 71, no. 6 (1928): 538–59.

Campbell, J. L., 'Fraser, Marjory Kennedy (1857–1930), Folklorist', *Oxford Dictionary of National Biography*. Oxford: Oxford University Press, 2004.

Cannadine, David, *The Decline and Fall of the British Aristocracy*. New Haven: Yale University Press, 1990.

———, *Ornamentalism*. Oxford: Oxford University Press, 2002.

Card, Tim, *Eton Renewed: A History from 1860 to the Present Day*. London: John Murray, 1994.

Case, Lynn M., 'Review of C. R. S. Harris, *Allied Administration of Italy 1943–45*', *Journal of Modern History* 31, no. 1 (1959): 67–68.

Cassels, Alan, *Mussolini's Early Diplomacy*. Princeton: Princeton University Press, 1970.

Cell, John W., 'Colonial Rule', in J. D. Brown and W. R. Louis (eds), *The Oxford History of the British Empire*. Oxford: Oxford University Press, 1999, 237–43.

———, *Hailey: A Study in British Imperialism, 1872–1969*. Cambridge: Cambridge University Press, 1992.

Chapman, F. Spencer, 'Travels in Japanese Occupied Malaya', *Geographical Journal* 110, no. 1/3 (1947): 17–36.

Chernow, Ron, *House of Morgan: The American Banking Dynasty and the Rise of Modern Finance*. New York: Simon and Schuster, 1991.

Clavin, Patricia, *The Failure of Economic Diplomacy: Britain: German, France and the United States, 1931–1936*. London: Macmillan, 1996.

———, '"The Fetishes of So-Called International Bankers": Central Bank Co-operation for the World Economic Conference, 1932–33', *Contemporary European History* 1, no. 3 (1992): 281–311.

Clay, Henry, *Lord Norman*. London: Macmillan, 1957.

Clayton, Daniel and Trevor J. Barnes, 'Continental European Geographers and World War II', *Journal of Historical Geography* 47 (2015): 11–15.

Cloake, John, *Templer, Tiger of Malaya: The Life of Field Marshall Sir Gerald Templer*. London: Harrap, 1985.

Clout, Hugh, 'French Geographers during Wartime and German Occupation', *Journal of Historical Geography* 47 (2015): 16–28.

Coles, Harry L. and Albert K. Weinberg, *Civil Affairs: Soldiers Become Governors*. Washington, DC: United States Army Centre of Military History, 1992.

Collier, Peter, 'Aerial Photography in Geography and Exploration', in Fraser Macdonald and Charles W. J. Withers (eds), *Geography, Technology and Instruments of Exploration*. Abingdon: Routledge, 2016, 179–98.

Connell, John, *Wavell: Scholar and Soldier*. London: Collins, 1964.

Connolly, Mark and David R. Wilcox, 'Are You Tough Enough? The Image of the Special Forces in British Popular Culture, 1939–2004', *Historical Journal of Film, Radio and Television* 25, no. 1 (2005): 1–25.

Cook, Andrew S., 'Maps by James Rennell in Lord Rennell's Bequest', *Geographical Journal* 144, no. 3 (1978): 515–17.
———, 'Rennell, James (1742–1830)', *Oxford Dictionary of National Biography*. Oxford: Oxford University Press, 2004.
Cornish, Vaughan, *Waves of Sand and Snow and the Eddies Which Make Them*. London: T. Fisher Unwin, 1914.
Courtauld, Augustine, *Man the Ropes*. London: Hodder and Stoughton, 1957.
——— (with Charles Close and Peter Rodd), 'A Second Journey among the Southern Tuareg: Discussion', *Geographical Journal* 73, no. 1 (1929): 18–19.
Crosswell, D. K. R., *Beetle: The Life of General Walter Bedell Smith*. Lexington: University Press of Kentucky, 2012.
Crush, Jonathon, 'Post-colonialism, De-colonization, Geography', in Anne Godlewska and Neil Smith (eds), *Geography and Empire*. Oxford: Blackwell, 1994, 333–50.
Darwin, John, *The End of the British Empire: The Historical Debate*. Oxford: Blackwell, 1991.
Davenport, Nicholas, *Memoirs of a City Radical*. London: Weidenfeld and Nicolson, 1974.
Davenport-Hines, Richard, 'Smith, Vivian Hugh, First Baron Bicester, 1867–1956', *Oxford Dictionary of National Biography*. Oxford: Oxford University Press, 2004.
Davis, Wade, *The Great War, Mallory and the Conquest of Everest*. London: Vintage, 2012.
Dawson, Graham, *Soldier Heroes: British Adventure, Empire and the Imagining of Masculinities*. London: Routledge, 1994.
Dickie, John, *Mafia Brotherhoods: The Rise of the Italian Mafias*. London: Sceptre, 2012.
Dietz, Bernhard, *Neo-Tories: The Revolt of British Conservatives against Democracy and Political Modernity (1929–1939)*. London: Bloomsbury Academic, 2018.
Dixon, Thomas, *Weeping Britannia: Portrait of a Nation in Tears*. Oxford: Oxford University Press, 2015.
Dolev, Eran, Yigal Shelly and Haim Goren (eds), *Palestine and World War I: Grand Strategy, Military Tactics and Culture in War*. London: I.B. Tauris, 2014.
Donnison, F. S. V., *British Military Administration in the Far East, 1943–46*. London: HMSO, 1956.
———, *Civil Affairs and Military Government: Organisation and Planning*. London: HMSO, 1966.
Doria, Andrea, *Cento Uno Viaggi*. Milan: Hoepli, 2006.
Drew, Pamela Statham, *James Stirling: Admiral and Founding Governor of Western Australia*. Crawley: University of Western Australia Press, 2003.
Driver, Felix, *Geography Militant: Cultures of Exploration in the Age of Empire*. Oxford: Blackwell, 2001.
Dutton, David, *Neville Chamberlain*. London: Arnold, 2001.
———, 'Simon and Eden at the Foreign Office 1931–1935', *Review of International Studies* 20, no. 1 (1994): 35–52.
D'Este, Carlo W., *Bitter Victory: The Battle for Sicily, 1943*. New York: Harper Perennial, 1991.
Elkins, Caroline, *Britain's Gulag: The Brutal End of Empire in Kenya*. London: Jonathon Cape, 2005.
Elliott, Ivo (ed.), *The Balliol College Register 1900–1950* (3rd ed.). Oxford: Charles Batey at the University Press, 1953.
Ellwood, David W., *Italy 1943–1945*. Leicester: Leicester University Press, 1985.
Evans-Pritchard, E. E., *The Sanusi of Cyrenaica*. Oxford: Oxford University Press, 1954.
Farndale, Martin, *History of the Royal Regiment of Artillery*. London: Royal Artillery Institution, 1987.
Falls, Cyril, 'Geography and War Strategy', *Geographical Journal* 112, no. 1/3 (1948): 4–15.
Fethney, Michael, *The Absurd and the Brave: CORB – The True Account of the British Government's Evacuation of Children Overseas*. Sussex: Book Guild, 1990.
Fetter, Bruce, 'Changing War Aims: Central Africa's Role, 1940–41, as Seen from Léopoldville', *African Affairs* 87, no. 348 (1988): 377–92.
Finberg, H. P. R., 'Review of *Valley on the March*', *English Historical Review* 75, no. 295 (1960): 328–29.
Finkelstein, Monte S., *Separatism, the Allies and the Mafia: The Struggle for Sicilian Independence 1943–48*. London: London University Presses, 1998.

Fisher, Thomas R., 'Allied Military Government in Italy', *Annals of the American Academy of Political and Social Science* 267 (1950): 114–22.
Fitzpatrick, Sheila, *Mischka's War: A Story of Survival from War-Torn Europe to New York*. London: I.B. Tauris, 2017.
Foliard, Daniel, *Dislocating the Orient: British Maps and the Making of the Middle East 1854– 1921*. Chicago: Chicago University Press, 2017.
Forbes, Neil, *Doing Business with the Nazis: Britain's Economic and Financial Relations with Germany 1931– 39*. Southgate: Frank Cass, 2001.
———, 'London Banks, the German Standstill Agreements, and "Economic Appeasement" in the 1930', *Economic History Review* 40, no. 4 (1987): 571–87.
Forbes, Rosita, *The Secret of the Sahara, Kufara*. London: Cassell, 1921.
———, *Unconducted Wanderers*. London: John Lane, 1919.
Forsyth, Isla, 'Desert Journeys: From Exploration to Covert Operations', *Geographical Journal* 182, no. 3 (2016): 226–35.
———, 'Piracy on the High Sands: Covert Military Mobilities in the Libyan Desert, 1940–43', *Journal of Historical Geography* 58 (2017): 61–70.
Fox, Cyril, 'Review of *Valley on the March*', *Antiquaries Journal* 39, no. 1–2 (1959): 125–26.
Frost, Richard, *Enigmatic Proconsul: Sir Philip Mitchell and the Twilight of Empire*. London: Radcliffe Press, 1992.
Fryde, Edmund, 'Review of *Valley on the March*', *Journal of Economic History* 22, no. 1 (1962): 132–34.
Fuglestad, Finn, *A History of Niger 1850–1960*. Cambridge: Cambridge University Press, 1983.
Fulbrook, Mary and Ulinka Rublack, 'In Relation: The "Social Self" and Ego-Documents', *German History* 28, no. 3 (2010): 263–72.
Fussell, Paul, *The Great War and Modern Memory*. New York: Oxford University Press, 2013.
Gaulle, Charles de, *War Memoirs: The Call to Honour, 1940–42. Documents*, vol. 1. London: Collins, 1955.
Gautier, E. F., *Exposition du Sahara, 15 mai–28 oct 1934. Guide illustré*. Paris: Museé de l'Homme, 1934.
———, 'Review of *People of the Veil*', *Geographical Review*, 18, no. 3 (1928): 478–84.
Gayre, G. R., *Italy in Transition. Extracts from the Private Journal of G. R. Gayre, etc.* London: Faber and Faber, 1946.
Gleichen, Count, *With the Mission to Menelik*. London: Edward Arnold, 1898.
Goldstein, Erik, 'Neville Chamberlain, the British Official Mind and the Munich Crisis', in Igor Lukes and Erik Goldstein (eds), *The Munich Crisis, 1938: Prelude to World War II*. London: Routledge, 1999, 276–92.
Goodman, Michael S., *The Official History of the Joint Intelligence Committee. Vol 1: From the Approach of the Second World War to the Suez Crisis*. London: Routledge, 2014.
Gottlieb, Julie V., *Feminine Fascism: Women in Britain's Fascist Movement*. London: I.B. Tauris, 2003.
Grafftey-Smith, Laurence, *Bright Levant*. London: John Murray, 1970.
———, *Hands to Play*. London: Routledge and Kegan Paul, 1975.
Gregory, Adrian, 'Beliefs and Religion', in Jay Winter (ed.), *The Cambridge History of the First World War*, vol. 3. Cambridge: Cambridge University, 2014, 418–44.
———, *The Last Great War: British Society and the First World War*. Cambridge: Cambridge University Press, 2008.
Gregory, John Walter and Currie, Ethel Dobbie (et al.), 'The Geological Collection from the South Central Sahara made by Mr Francis R. Rodd', *Quarterly Journal of the Geological Society* 86 (1 March 1930): 399–414.
Griffiths, Richard, *Fellow Travellers of the Right: British Enthusiasts for Nazi Germany 1933–9*. London: Constable, 1980.
Grizzard, James Carr, *The War Was More Than the Cannon's Roar: A Story of the Allied Occupation of Italy*. Atlanta: Swan Arts, 2000.
Gubbins, Colin, *The Art of Guerilla Warfare*. London: MI(R), 1939.
———, *The Partisan Leader's Handbook*. London: MI(R), 1939.

Gwynn, Charles, 'Improvisation in Occupied Africa', *Fortnightly*, October 1948, 256–60.
Hanson, Edward W., *The Wandering Princess: Princess Helene of France, Duchess of Aosta, 1871–1951*. Stroud: Fonthill Media, 2017.
Hargreaves, John D., *Decolonization in Africa*. London: Longman, 1988.
Harris, C. R. S., *Allied Military Administration of Italy 1943–45*. London: HMSO, 1957.
Harvey, John (ed.), *The Diplomatic Diaries of Oliver Harvey 1937–40*. London: Collins, 1970.
Haslam, Nicky, *Redeeming Features: A Memoir*. London: Cape, 2009.
Hastings, Max, *Finest Years: Churchill as Warlord 1940–45*. London: Harper Press, 2009.
Hassanein Bey, Ahmed, *The Lost Oases*, with an introduction by Sir Rennell Rodd. London: Butterworth, 1925.
———, *The Lost Oases*, with an introduction by Michael Haag. Cairo: American University of Cairo Press, 2005.
Hassanein Bey, A. M., 'Through Kufra to Darfur', *Geographical Journal* 64, no. 4 (1924): 273–91, and 64, no. 5 (1924): 353–63.
Hastings, Selina, *Nancy Mitford*. London: Hamish Hamilton, 1985.
Heffernan, Michael, 'Cartography and Military Intelligence: The Royal Geographical Society and the First World War', *Transactions of the Institute of British Geographers* 21, no. 3 (1996): 504–33.
———, 'The Limits of Utopia: Henri Duveyrier and the Exploration of the Sahara in the Nineteenth Century', *Geographical Journal* 155, no. 3 (1989): 342–52.
———, 'The Spoils of War: the Société de Géographie de Paris and the French empire, 1914–1919', in M. Bell, R. Butlin and M. Heffernan (eds), *Geography and Imperialism 1820– 1940*. Manchester: Manchester University Press, 1995, 221–64.
Hersey, John, *A Bell for Adano*. New York: Alfred A. Knopf, 1944.
Hess, Robert, L., 'Italy and Africa: Colonial Ambitions in Africa', *Journal of African History* 4, no. 1 (1963): 105–26.
Higham, Robin, *Speedbird: The Complete History of BOAC*. London: I.B. Tauris, 2013.
Hilton, R. H. H., 'Review of *Valley on the March*', *Agricultural History Review* 7, no. 2 (1959): 124–25.
History of COSSAC, Chief of Staff to the Supreme Allied Commander, 1943–44, prepared by Historical Subsection, Office of Secretary General Staff, SHAEF, May 1944.
Hoare, Lottie, 'Kindersley, David Guy Barnabas 1915–95', *Oxford Dictionary of National Biography*. Oxford: Oxford University Press, 2004.
Horn, Martin, 'J. P. Morgan & Co., the House of Morgan and Europe, 1933–39', *Contemporary European History* 14, no. 4 (2005): 519–38.
Horne, Alistair, *Macmillan: 1894–1956*. London: Macmillan, 1956.
Howse, W. H., 'Flemish Tapestry in Presteigne Church', *Radnorshire Society Transactions* 27 (1957): 33–35.
Hudson, W. H., *Army Diplomacy: American Military Occupation and Diplomacy after World War II*. Lexington: University Press of Kentucky, 2015.
Hurewitz, J. C., *The Middle East and Africa in World Politics: A Documentary Record – British–French Supremacy 1914–1945*. New Haven: Yale University Press, 1979.
Hyam, R., *Britain's Declining Empire: The Road to Decolonisation 1918–1968*. Cambridge: Cambridge University Press, 2006.
Iliffe, John, *A Modern History of Tanganyika*. Cambridge: Cambridge University Press, 1979.
Irwin, Robert, *For Lust of Knowing: The Orientalists and their Enemies*. London: Penguin, 2006.
Jackson, John Brinkerhoff, *Discovering the Vernacular*. New Haven: Yale University Press, 1984.
Jackson, Julian, *A Certain Idea of France: The Life of Charles de Gaulle*. London: Penguin, 2019.
Jenkins, dive, 'Retreat: The Labour Party and the Public Corporations', *Universities and Left Review* 3 (Winter 1958): 42–60.
Jennings, E. T., *French Africa in World War II*. Cambridge: Cambridge University Press, 2015.
Johnson, Alison M., 'The Rennell Collection', *Geographical Journal*, 148, no. 1 (1982): 38–42.
Jones, Matthew, *Britain, the United States and the Mediterranean War, 1942–44*. London: Macmillan, 1996.

Jones, Tony, *The Sacred War: Spiritual Practices for Everyday Life*. Grand Rapids: Zondervan, 2005.

Kelly, Saul, 'Desert Conquests: Early British Planning on the Future of the Italian Colonies, June 1940–September 1943', *Middle Eastern Studies* 50, no. 6 (2014): 1006–26.

———, *The Hunt for Zerzura: The Lost Oasis and the Desert War*. London: John Murray, 2002.

Kemper, Steve, *A Labyrinth of Kingdoms: 10,000 Miles through Islamic Africa*. New York: W.W. Norton, 2012.

Kilian, Conrad, 'Explorations Sahariennes', *Geographical Journal* 86, no. 1 (1935): 17–25.

Kirwan, L. P., 'Obituary of Lord Rennell', *Azania: Journal of the British Institute in Eastern Africa* 13 (1978): vii.

(Kirwan, L. P.), 'Obituary of Lord Rennell', *Geographical Journal* 144, no. 2 (1978): 392–93.

Kissinger, Henry, *Diplomacy*. New York: Simon and Schuster, 1994.

Kitchen, James E., *The British Imperial Army in the Middle East: Morale and Military Identity in the Sinai and Palestine Campaigns, 1916–18*. London: Bloomsbury Academic, 2014.

Knightly, Philip and Colin Simpson, *The Secret Lives of Lawrence of Arabia*. London: Nelson, 1969.

Knox, M., *Mussolini Unleashed: Politics and Strategy in Fascist Italy's Last War*. Cambridge: Cambridge University Press, 1981.

Kynaston, David, *The City of London: Illusions of Gold 1914–1945*, vol. 3. London: Pimlico, 2000.

Laithwaite, Gilbert, 'Obituary of E. W. Bovill', *Geographical Journal* 133, no. 2 (1967): 280–81.

Lamb, Richard, *Mussolini and the British*. London: John Murray, 1997.

Lavin, Deborah, *From Empire to International Commonwealth: A Biography of Lionel Curtis*. Oxford: Clarendon Press, 1995.

Lawrence, T. E., *Seven Pillars of Wisdom*. Global Grey, [1926] 2018.

Lean, Garth, *Frank Buchman: A Life*. London: Constable, 1985.

Legg, Stephen, 'Decolonialism', *Transactions of the Institute of British Geographers* 42, no. 3 (2017): 345–48.

Leith-Ross, Frederick, *Money Talks: Fifty Years of International Finance*. London: Hutchinson, 1968.

Livingstone, David N., 'Landscapes of Knowledge', in Peter Meusburger, David N. Livingstone and Heike Jöns (eds), *Geographies of Science*. London: Springer, 2010, 3–22.

Loraine, Percy and Alan Campbell, 'Rodd, James Rennell, First Baron Rennell (1858–1941), Diplomatist and Classical Scholar', *Oxford Dictionary of National Biography*. Oxford: Oxford University Press, 2004.

'Lord Rennell', obituary, *Times*, 16 March 1978, 20.

Lugard, F. D., *The Dual Mandate in Tropical Africa*. Edinburgh: William Blackwood and Sons, 1922.

Lupo, Salvatore, 'The Allies and the Mafia', *Journal of Modern Italian Studies* 2, no. 1 (1997): 21–33.

Lush, A. J. M. (ed.), *A Life of Service: The Memoirs of Maurice Lush*. London: A. J. M. Lush, 1992.

Machiavelli, Niccolò, *The Ruler*, trans. Peter Rodd. London: Bodley Head, 1954.

Mack, John E., *A Prince of Our Disorder: The Life of T. E. Lawrence*. London: Weidenfeld and Nicolson, 1976.

Macmillan, Harold, *War Diaries: Politics and War in the Mediterranean January 1943–May 1945*. London: Macmillan, 1984.

Maguire, G. E., 'Emmet, Evelyn Violet Elizabeth, Baroness Emmet of Amberley (1899–1980)', *Oxford Dictionary of National Biography*. Oxford: Oxford University Press, 2004.

———, *Conservative Women: A History of Women and the Conservative Party, 1874–1997*. London: Palgrave Macmillan, 1998.

Maitland, Alexander, *Wilfred Thesiger: The Life of the Great Explorer*. London: HarperCollins, 1985.

Mallett, Robert, 'The Anglo-Italian War Trade Negotiations: Contraband Control and the Failure to Appease Mussolini, 1939–40', *Diplomacy and Statecraft* 8, no. 1 (1997): 137–67.

———, *Mussolini and the Origins of the Second World War, 1933–1940*. Basingstoke: Palgrave Macmillan, 2003.

Marcus, Nathan, *Austrian Reconstruction and the Collapse of Global Finance*. Cambridge: Harvard University Press, 2018.

Markham, C. R., *Major James Rennell and the Rise of Modern English Geography*. London: Cassell, 1895.
Markus, Harold G., 'The Rodd Mission of 1897', *Journal of Ethiopian Studies* 3, no. 2 (1965): 25–35.
Marsden, Ben and Crosbie Smith, *Engineering Empires: A Cultural History of Technology in Nineteenth-Century Britain*. London: Palgrave Macmillan, 2005.
Martinelli, Chiara and David Ronneburg, 'The Rodds in Italy', *Mitford Society Annual* 2 (22 October 2014): 73–78.
Massey, Doreen and Nigel Thrift, 'The Passion of Place', in Ron Johnson and Michael Williams (eds), *A Century of British Geography*. Oxford: Oxford University Press, 2003, 275–99.
May, Alex, 'Curtis, Lionel George (1872–1955), Writer and Public Servant', *Oxford Dictionary of National Biography*. Oxford: Oxford University Press, 2004.
McCarthy, Helen, *Women of the World: The Rise of the Female Diplomat*. London: Bloomsbury, 2014.
McGrath, Arthur (Rosita Forbes) et al., 'From Kufra to Darfur: A Discussion', *Geographical Journal* 64, no. 5 (1924): 363–66.
Medlicott, W. N., *The Economic Blockade*, 2 vols. London: HMSO, 1952, 1959.
Meinertzhagen, Richard, *Army Diary: 1899–1926*. Edinburgh: Oliver and Boyd, 1960.
Mencken, H. L., 'War Words in England', *American Speech* 19, no. 1 (1944): 3–15.
Mills, William C., 'The Nyon Conference: Neville Chamberlain, Anthony Eden and the Appeasement of Italy in 1937', *International History Review* 15, no.1 (1993): 1–22.
Mitchell, Philip, *African Afterthoughts*. London: Hutchinson, 1954.
Mitford, Nancy, *The Complete Novels*. London: Penguin, 2015.
———, *Pigeon Pie*. London: Hamish Hamilton, 1976.
Moggridge, Donald Edward, *Maynard Keynes: An Economist's Biography*. London: Routledge, 1992.
Mohs, Polly A., *Military Intelligence and the Arab Revolt: The First Modern Intelligence War*. London: Routledge, 2008.
Mosley, Charlotte (ed.), *Love from Nancy: The Letters of Nancy Mitford*. London: Hodder and Stoughton, 1993.
Myers, Margaret G., 'The League Loans', *Political Science Quarterly* 60, no. 4 (1945): 492–526.
Neufeld, Maurice F., 'The Failure of AMG in Italy', *Public Administration Review* 6, no. 2 (1946): 137–48.
Neville, Peter, 'The Appointment of Sir Nevile Henderson, 1937 – Design or Blunder?', *Journal of Contemporary History* 33, no. 4 (1998): 609–19.
Newark, Tim, *Mafia Allies: The True Story of America's Secret Alliance with the Mob in World War II*. St Paul, MN: Zenith Press, 2007.
Newbold, Douglas, 'Desert Odyssey of a Thousand Miles', *Sudan Notes and Records* 7 (1924): 43–92.
Newbury, Colin, *Patrons, Clients and Empire: Chieftancy and Over-Rule in Asia, Africa and the Pacific*. Oxford: Oxford University Press, 2003.
Onslow, Sue, 'Suez Group (*Act.* 1953–1957)', *Oxford Dictionary of National Biography*. Oxford: Oxford University Press, 2005.
Orlans, Harold, *T. E. Lawrence: Biography of a Broken Hero*. Jefferson: McFarland, 2002.
Otte, Thomas G., *The Foreign Office Mind: The Making of British Foreign Policy 1865–1914*. Cambridge: Cambridge University Press, 2011.
O'Sullivan, Adrian, *Espionage and Counterintelligence in Occupied Persia (Iran)*. London: Macmillan, 2015.
Palmer, H. R., 'The Tuareg of the Sahara. 1', *Journal of the Royal African Society* 31, no. 123 (1932): 153–66.
Pankhurst, Sylvia E., *The Home Front: A Mirror to Life in England during the World War*. London: Hutchinson, 1932.
———, *The Suffragette Movement*. London: Virago, 1972.
Paris, Timothy J., *In Defence of Britain's Middle Eastern Empire: A Life of Sir Gilbert Clayton*. Brighton: Sussex Academic Press, 2016.
Parker, Linda, *Ice, Steel and Fire: British Explorers in Peace and War, 1921–45*. Solihull: Helion, 2013.

Passerini, Luisa, *Europe in Love, Love in Europe: Imagination and Politics in Britain between the Wars*. London: I.B. Tauris, 1999.
Pateman, John, *T. E. Lawrence in Lincolnshire*. Sleaford: Pateran Press, 2012.
Patti, Manoela, *La Sicilia e gli Alleati: Tra Occupazione e Liberazione*. Rome: Donzelli, 2013.
Pattinson, Juliette, 'Fantasies of the "Soldier Hero": Frustrations of the Jedburghs', in Linsey Robb and Juliette Pattinson (eds), *Men, Masculinities and Male Culture in the Second World War*. London: Palgrave Macmillan, 2018, 25–46.
Pearce, Robert D., *Sir Bernard Bourdillon: The Biography of a Twentieth Century Colonialist*. Oxford: Kensal Press, 1987.
———, *The Turning Point in Africa: British Colonial Policy 1938–48*. London: Frank Cass, 1982.
Perham, Marjorie, *Lugard, The Years of Authority, 1898–1945*. London: Collins, 1960.
Petrie, Charles, *A Historian Looks at His world*. London: Sidgwick and Jackson, 1972.
Piffer, Tomasso, *Il Banchiera della Resistenza: Alfredo Pizzoni, Il Protagonista Cancellato dalla Guerra di Liberazione*. Milan: Mondadori, 2005.
Pimlott, Ben (ed.), *The Second World War Diary of Hugh Dalton 1940–45*. London: Jonathon Cape in Association with the London School of Economics, 1986.
Pollard, John F., *Money and the Rise of the Modern Papacy: Financing the Vatican 1850–1950*. Cambridge: Cambridge University Press, 2005.
Pollen, Daphne, 'Mary Rennell', *Paintings and Drawings of Mary Rennell*. Tenbury Wells: Fowler Wright Books, 1976, 11–23.
Prior, Christopher, *Exporting Empire: Africa, Colonial Officials and the Construction of the Imperial State, c. 1900–39*. Manchester: Manchester University Press, 2013.
Pugh, Martin, *Hurrah for the Blackshirts!: Fascists and Fascism in Britain between the Wars*. London: Pimlico, 2006.
Rae, Eugene, Catherine Souch and Charles W. J. Withers, 'The Life and Liveliness of Instruments of British Geographical Exploration, c. 1860–1930', in Fraser Macdonald and Charles W. J. Withers (eds), *Geography, Technology and Instruments of Exploration*. Abingdon: Routledge, 2016, 139–60.
Reiss, Curt, *The Nazis Go Underground*. Stroud: Fonthill Media, 2013.
Rennell Rodd, James, *Ballads of the Fleet and Other Poems*. London: Edward Arnold, 1897.
———, *Diplomacy*. London: Ernest Benn, 1929.
———, *Frederick, Crown Prince and Emperor: A Biographical Sketch Dedicated to His Memory*. London: D. Stott, 1888.
———, *Love, Worship and Death*. London: Edward Arnold, 1916.
———, 'Memoir', in Sir Gerald Portal (ed.), *The British Mission to Uganda in 1893*. London, 1894, xxv–xlvi.
———, *Newdigate Prize Poem: Raleigh*. Oxford: T. Shrimpton and Son, 1880.
———, *Rome of the Renaissance and of Today*. London: Macmillan, 1932.
———, *Sir Walter Raleigh*. London: Macmillan, 1904.
———, *Social and Diplomatic Memories*, 3 vols. London: Edward Arnold, 1922–25.
———, *Trentaremi and Other Moods*. London: Edward Arnold, 1923.
———, *War Poems with Some Others*. London: Edward Arnold, 1940.
Richardson, Adam, 'Sir Percy Loraine and British Relations with Italy, 1939–40', *Diplomacy & Statecraft* 31, no. 2 (2020): 257–77.
Ripsman, Norrin M. and Jack S. Levy, 'Wishful Thinking or Buying Time: The Logic of British Appeasement in the 1930s', *International Security* 33, no. 2 (2008): 148–81.
Roberts, Kenneth, *Lydia Bailey*. New York: Doubleday, 1947.
Rose, Norman, *The Cliveden Set: Portrait of an Exclusive Fraternity*. London: Jonathon Cape, 2000.
Rudwick, Martin J. S., *The Great Devonian Controversy*. Chicago: University of Chicago Press, 1985.
Ryan, James R., *Picturing Empire: Photography and the Visualisation of the British Empire*. London: Reaktion, 1997.
Sadler, Jonathon, *Ghost Patrol: A History of the Long Range Desert Group, 1940–45*. Oxford: Casemate, 2015.

Said, Edward W., *Orientalism*. New York: Vintage, 2003.
Sayers, R. S., *The Bank of England, 1891–1944*, 2 vols. Cambridge: Cambridge University Press, 1976.
Savile, R. A., 'Notes on the Account of Commandant Tilho's Journey', *Geographical Journal* 52, no. 6 (1918): 401.
Sbacchi, A., 'Haile Selassie and the Italians', *African Studies Review* 22, no. 1 (1979): 25–42.
Schama, Simon, *Landscape and Memory*. London: HarperCollins, 1995.
Seton-Watson, Christopher, 'Britain and Italy, 1914–1915', in Alessandro Migliazza and Enrico Declava (eds), *Diplomazia e Storia delle Relazioni: Studi in Onore de Enrico Serra*. Milan: Giuffrè, 1991, 216–29.
Sharp, Alan, 'Adapting to a New World? British Foreign Policy in the 1920s', in Gaynor Johnson (ed.), *Foreign Policy and British Diplomacy in the Twentieth Century*. London: Routledge, 2005, 74–86.
———, 'The Foreign Office in Eclipse, 1919–1922', *History* 61, no. 292 (1976): 198–218.
Sharwood Smith, Bryan, *'But Always as Friends': Northern Nigeria and the Cameroons, 1921–1957*. London: George, Allen and Unwin, 1969.
Sheffy, Yigal, *British Military Intelligence in the Palestine Campaign 1914–1918*. London: Frank Cass, 1998.
Skidelsky, Robert, *John Maynard Keynes: The Economist as Saviour 1920–1937*. London: Macmillan, 1992.
Slight, John, 'British Understandings of the Sanussiyya Sufi Order's Jihad against Egypt, 1915–17', *Round Table* 103, no. 2 (2014): 233–42.
Slinn, Judy, 'Falk, Oswald Toynbee (1879–1972)', *Oxford Dictionary of National Biography*. Oxford: Oxford University Press, 2004.
Smith, Neil, *American Empire: Roosevelt's Geographer and the Prelude to Globalization*. Berkeley: University of California Press, 2004.
Snow, C. P., *The Two Cultures and the Scientific Revolution*. Cambridge: Cambridge University Press, 1959.
Soper, Robert, 'The Bantu Studies Research Project', *Azania: Journal of the British Institute in Eastern Africa* 6, no. 1 (1971): 1–4.
Southard, Frank, A., *The Finances of European Liberation with Special Reference to Italy*. New York: King's Crown, 1946.
Spencer, John H., *Ethiopia at Bay: A Personal Account of the Haile Selassie Years*. Hollywood: Tsehai, 2006.
St Johnston, Eric, *One Policeman's Story*. London: Rose, 1978.
Stibbe, Matthew, *German Anglophobia and the Great War, 1914–1918*. Cambridge: Cambridge University Press, 2001.
Storrs, Ronald, *The Memoirs of Sir Ronald Storrs*. New York: G. P. Putnam's Sons, 1937.
Strachey, Lytton, *Eminent Victorians*. Oxford: Oxford University Press, 2003.
Streat, Sir Raymond, *Lancashire and Whitehall: The Diary of Sir Raymond Streat*, ed. M. Dupree. Manchester: Manchester University Press, 1987.
Stuart-Wortley, Violet, *Life without Theory: An Autobiography*. London: Hutchinson, 1946.
Suny, Ronald Grigor, 'Beyond Psychohistory: The Young Stalin in Georgia', *Slavic Review* 50, no. 1 (1991): 48–58.
Syrett, David, *The Eyes of the Desert Rats: British Long Range Reconnaissance Operations in the North African Desert 1940–43*. Solihull: Helion, 2014.
Talbot, Colonel Milo G., 'Libya in the Last War: The Talbot Mission and the Agreements of 1917', *Journal of the Royal African Society* 40, no. 159 (1941): 128–31.
Thesiger, Wilfred, *Arabian Sands*. London: Penguin, 2007.
Thomas, Martin, *The French Empire at War*. Manchester: Manchester University Press, 1998.
———, 'Imperial Backwater or Strategic Outpost? The British Takeover of Vichy Madagascar, 1942', *Historical Journal* 39, no. 4 (1996): 1049–74.
Thomas, Nicola J. and Jude Hill, 'Explorations in the Libyan Desert: William J. Harding King', in Simon Naylor and James R. Ryan (eds), *New Spaces of Exploration: Geographies of Discovery in the Twentieth Century*. London: I.B. Tauris, 2010, 78–104.

Thompson, Paul, 'The Pyrrhic Victory of Gentlemanly Capitalism: The Financial Elite of the City of London, 1945–90', *Journal of Contemporary History* 32, no. 3 (1997): 283–304.
Tignor, Robert, L., 'Decolonization and Business: The Case of Egypt', *Journal of Modern History* 59, no. 3 (1987): 479–505.
Tilley, John and Stephen Gaselee, *The Foreign Office*. London: G. P. Putnam's Sons, 1933.
Toniolo, Gianni (with Pierre Clement), *Central Bank Cooperation at the Bank for International Settlements*. Cambridge: Cambridge University Press, 2005.
Toscano, Mario, 'Eden's Mission to Rome on the Eve of the Italo–Ethiopian Conflict', in A. O. Sarkissian (ed.), *Studies in Diplomatic History and Historiography in Honour of G. P. Gooch*. London: Longmans, 1961, 126–52.
Toye, Richard, *The Roar of the Lion: The Untold Story of Churchill's World War II Speeches*. Oxford: Oxford University Press, 2013.
Trevelyan, Laura, *A Very British Family: The Trevelyans and Their World*. London: I.B. Tauris, 2006.
Vail Motter, T. H., 'Review of Lord Rennell, *British Military Administration of Occupied Territories*', *Military Affairs* 13, no. 4 (1949): 251–52.
Walker, David, 'Review of *Valley on the March*', *Welsh History Review* 1, no. 2 (1960): 246–47.
Waterfield, Gordon, *Professional Diplomat: Sir Percy Lorraine of Kirkharle Bt. 1880–1961*. London: John Murray, 1973.
Waugh, Evelyn, *Black Mischief*. London: Chapman and Hall, 1932.
———, *Put Out More Flags*. London: Chapman and Hall, 1942.
Wellesley, Gerald, 'September 1943', *The Collected Works of Gerald 7th Duke of Wellington*. Privately printed, 1970, 23–28.
Wellesley, Jane, *Wellington: A Journey through My Family*. London: Weidenfeld and Nicolson, 2015.
Westrate, Bruce, *The Arab Bureau: British Policy in the Middle East, 1916–1920*. University Park: Pennsylvania University Press, 2004.
Whitaker, C. S., *The Politics of Tradition: Continuity and Change in Northern Nigeria, 1946–66*. Princeton: Princeton University Press, 1970.
Wilkinson, Peter and Joan Bright Astley, *Gubbins and SOE*. Barnsley: Pen and Sword Military, 2010.
Williams, Isobel, *Allies and Italians under Occupation: Sicily and Southern Italy 1943–45*. Basingstoke: Palgrave Macmillan, 2013.
Williams, Shirley, *Climbing the Bookshelves: The Autobiography of Shirley Williams*. London: Virago, 2010.
Wise, M. J., 'Rodd, Francis James Rennell', *Dictionary of National Biography, 1971–1980*, ed. Lord Blake and C. S. Nicholls. Oxford: Oxford University Press, 1986, 732–33.
Withers, Charles W. J., 'Afterword: Geographers, Historical Geographies, War', *Journal of Historical Geography* 47 (2015): 89–93.
———, *Geography and Science, 1831–1939: A Study of the British Association for the Advancement of Science*. Manchester: Manchester University Press, 2010.
———, 'Mapping the Niger, 1798–1832: Trust, Testimony and "Ocular Demonstration" in the Late Enlightenment', *Imago Mundi* 56, no. 2 (2004): 170–93.
Wollaston, Nicholas, *The Man on the Ice Cap: The Life of August Courtauld*. London: Constable, 1980.
Woodward, E. L., *British Foreign Policy in the Second World War*, 5 vols. London: HMSO, 1970–76.
Wright, John, *Libya, Chad and the Central Sahara*. London: C. Hurst, 1989.
Wynter, H. W., 'The History of the Long Range Desert Group (June 1940–March 1943)', *Special Forces in the Desert War 1940–1943*. London: National Archives, 2008, 1–232.
Yeats, W. B., *The Land of Heart's Desire; The Countess Cathleen*. London: T. Fisher Unwin, 1925.
Yivisaker, Marguerite, 'On the Origins and Development of the Witu Sultanate', *International Journal of African Historical Studies* 11, no. 4 (1978): 669–88.
Young, Robert J., 'Spokesmen for Economic Warfare: The Industrial Intelligence Centre in the 1930s', *European Studies Review* 6, no. 5 (1976): 473–89.
Younghusband, Francis, *India and Tibet*. London: John Murray, 2010.

INDEX

Abd el Galil en Nasr 127–28
ACC. *See* Allied Control Commission (ACC)
Acton, Harold 8
Addis Ababa 10, 143, 145–50, 152–53
Adshead, P. W. 139
aerial photography 46
AFHQ. *See* Allied Force Headquarters (AFHQ)
Africa 3, 7, 10, 33, 68, 70–71, 76, 95, 113–15, 117, 119, 121, 124–26, 129–30, 137, 151, 154, 156, 159–60, 164, 166, 192–93, 197, 201–3, 214, 218. *See also* East Africa; West Africa
African Association 7
African Survey 159
Agadez 50, 51, 53, 56, 59, 67, 70, 72
Agnesa, Giacomo 31–32
Ahlmann, Hans 200
Ahmed 65, 215
Ahmed, Sayyid 31
Ahmed Seif en Nasr 127
Ahodu 51, 61
Air Beef company 203
Air 1, 48–51, 53–56, 58–60, 64–65, 70, 72, 213, 214
Aix originals 207
Alexander, Harold 4, 164–65, 167–70, 175–79
Ali, Seyyid 9
Allen, J. G. C. 124
Allenby, Edmund 36–37, 137
Allied Control Commission (ACC), 174–80, 184
Allied Force Headquarters (AFHQ) 165, 176–79, 217
Allied Military Financial Agency 175
Allied military government 138, 171, 174, 178, 180, 218
Allied Military Government of Occupied Territories (AMGOT) 1, 4–5, 163–86, 176–77
  ACC and 177–78
  administration of 166
  Allied military government 178

Allied administrators in 169
American military and 165
Anglo–American fusion 166
culture of US military and control 186
currency management 174
division of 176
food supply problems in 174
freed from dismissing mayors and prefects 169
functioning of 167
fused Anglo–American organization 180
headquarters at 167
image problem 183
invasion of Sicily 166
local police to maintain order 172
mafia activity 173–74
major administrative challenges 176
most reactionary elements 182
power with American military 165
prefects issuing orders 169
removal of fascists 170
setting up of 167
tortuous system of accountability 165
transportation problem 174
Allied Military lire 174–75
Amery, Julian 194
AMGOT. *See* Allied Military Government of Occupied Territories (AMGOT)
ANB. *See* Austrian National Bank (ANB)
Anderson, Alexander 190
Anglican Church 18
Anglo-Australian Corporation 196
Anglo-Canadian Telephones 128
Anglo-German Naval Agreement 94
Anglo-German Payments Agreement 92
Anglo-Italian agreement 109
Anglo-Italian economic relations 109
Anglo-Italian Joint Standing Committee 104–6
Anglo-Italian Protocol of 1894 10
Anglo-Sanusi conflict 120
Annet, Armand 123, 155, 157
Antiquity 70

appeasement 3, 103, 111–12, 194, 218
Aprile, Finocchiaro 174
Arabian Sands 72
Ardath 14
Armistice Commission 169, 178
Arragorn, Alan 96
Art of Guerilla Warfare 119, 122
Ashton, Dorothy. *See* Wellesley, Dorothy ('Dottie')
Asmara 143, 146, 151, 152–53
Asquith, Herbert 87
Astor, Lady 94
Astor, Waldorf 94
Auchinleck, Claude 139, 143–44
Auderas 50–51, 53–54, 62, 64–65
Australia 1, 203–4
Australian National Airways 204
Australian United Company 196
Austrian National Bank (ANB) 80
Austro-German Customs Union 81

Baddeley, Hermione 153
Badoglio, Marshal 175
Bagehot, Walter 83, 99
Bagnold, Ralph 3, 45, 71–72, 126–27, 200, 204, 215
Balfour, A. J. 33
Balfour, Henry 56
Balliol College, Oxford 8, 9, 11, 18, 19, 31, 42, 47, 65, 66, 153, 209
Balliol Roundtable 19, 42, 120
Balliol Rowing Club 42
Bank for International Settlements (BIS) 2, 79–80, 92
Bank of England 2, 49, 77–79, 81–84, 87, 93, 97–98, 101, 136, 142, 195
Banque Afrique Orientale 135
Barth, Heinrich 50, 67
Bastianini, Giovanni 109
Bates, Oric 59
Beaumont-Nesbitt, Frederick 119–21, 129, 132
Bech, M. 157
Bedouin tribes 30
Belgian Congo 125
A Bell for Adano 184
Bell, Gertrude 43
Benn, William Wedgwood 179
Benson, C. E. 182
Berliner Tageblatt 13
Bernasek, Lisa 69
Bertie, Francis 12–13
Beyen, J. W. 92

Bicester Lord. *See* Smith, Vivian Hugh
Bingham, Cecil Edward 8, 10
Bingham, Cecilia 119
Bingham, David Cecil 42
Birmingham and Midland Institute 202, 211
BIS. *See* Bank for International Settlements (BIS)
Black Diamond system 106
black market 172, 174
Black Mischief 65
Blessing, Karl 90
Blithe Spirit 153
Blythe, Gordon 203
BOAC. *See* British Overseas Airways Corporation (BOAC)
Boisson, Pierre 130
Bolshevik revolution 191
Booker, R. P. L. 17–18, 20
Bordonaro, Lucio Tasca 173–74
Borneo Airways 197
Bosch, Hieronymous 212
Bourdillon, Bernard 121, 123, 126, 128–29, 131–33, 140, 158–59
Bovenschen, Frederick 137, 190
Bovill, E. W. 70
Bowman, Isaiah 4–5, 43
Bowyer-Smith, P. 104
Brant, Sebastian 212
Britannia Jet-Prop airliners 199
British 2, 4–5, 11, 13, 19, 25–26, 29, 35–36, 38, 40–42, 46–48, 50, 54, 57, 67–68, 71–73, 77–78, 82, 84, 91–93, 97, 101–17
  agency in Zanzibar 8
  agreement with Italy 31
  Anglo–Sanusi conflict 120
  anti-British propaganda 131
  approach to military government 140
  Arab government under 42
  aristocratic and gentleman hero-adventurers 48
  attacks on French 123
  borders imposed by 11
  desire for control 136
  exploration in the eastern Sahara 71
  fears of an Ethiopian expansion 10
  involvement in Witu expedition 9
  Italian empire falls to 3
  on Madagascar 157
  management of civil affairs 163
  military strategy 36
  mission in Libya 30
  occupation of Syria 41

penetration of the Sahara 1
purchases in Italy 102
in south Palestine 40
transfer of power to Free French 4
use of gas 25
world view assuming British superiority 10
British Association for the Advancement of Science 201–2
British East Africa Company 9
British empire 19, 47, 96
British Institute of East Africa 203
British-Italian Banking Corporation 77
British-Italian League 77
British military administration 156–57
British Military Administration of Occupied Territories in Africa 192
British Mission to Uganda 9
British Overseas Airways Corporation (BOAC) 197
British School of Archaeology and the Arts 15
British Sheep Society 208
British Somaliland 137–40, 148, 151, 154
British Union of Fascists (BUF) 89
Bruins, Gijsbert 81
Buchan, John 212
Buchanan, Angus 49–51
Buchman, Frank 113–14, 210
BUF. *See* British Union of Fascists (BUF)
Burk, Kathleen 195
Burne-Jones, Edward 8
Butler, Samuel 153
Byron, Robert 114

CA. See Credit-Anstalt (CA)
Cadogan, Alexander 183
Cain, Peter 196
Cairo 3, 15, 30–32, 34–36, 39–40, 48, 58, 71, 121, 127, 138–39, 142, 144, 151–53, 200
camels 8, 10, 50, 53, 62–65, 72, 126, 132, 215
Cameron, D. G. R. 70
Cameron, Donald 159
Cannadine, David 47
carabinieri 172
Caravans of the Old Sahara 70
Carter, Harold 208
Catania 167–68
Catholicism 66, 208–9
Catto, Tom 87, 94–97, 115, 123, 195, 199
Cavendish, 'Peggy' 155
CCAO. *See* chief civil affairs officer (CCAO)

Chad 69, 124–25, 127, 129–32, 134
Chamberlain, Austen 84, 86
Chamberlain, Basil 19
Chamberlain, Neville 91, 111
Chapman, F. Spencer 201
Chapman, Roger 212
Charles, Noel 104
Cheyne, D. G. 185
chief civil affairs officer (CCAO) 1, 138, 163
Chief of Staff to the Supreme Allied Commander (COSSAC) 189
Children's Overseas Reception Board (CORB) 115
Chrea 166, 169, 172, 180
Christian Science Monitor 61
Christianity 18, 59, 219
Churchill, Winston 91, 111, 112–13, 125, 134, 144, 154, 164, 175, 183, 194
Ciano, Galeazzo 105–7
Civil Affairs Staff Centre 182, 185, 188
Civitas Dei: The Commonwealth of God 120
Clark, Mark 175
Clarke, Peter 183
Clauson, Gerard 39, 129
Clay, Henry 79
Clayton, Gilbert 31, 40
Clayton, I. N. 158
Clayton, Patrick ('Pat') 71–72, 127
Clifford, Hugh 57
Close, Charles 43, 68
College of Air Training 197
Collins, J. E. H. 196
Colonial Development and Welfare Acts 159
Colonial Development Corporation 197
Colonial Office 39, 123, 129, 137, 155
Colosimo, Gaspare 32
Combined Chiefs of Staff 174, 178, 186
Combined Civil Affairs Committee 186
Combined Services Detailed Interrogation Service 151
Committee of Imperial Defence 101
Committee on Foreign (Allied) Resistance 156
Commonwealth Scientific and Industrial Research Organisation 208
Confessions 18
Conrad, Joseph 121
Conservatives 89, 191, 219
Consolidated Zinc Company 196

CORB. *See* Children's Overseas Reception Board (CORB)
Cornish, Vaughan 204
Cornwallis, Kinahan 40–41
Cortier geographical mission 54
COSSAC. *See* Chief of Staff to the Supreme Allied Commander (COSSAC)
Coupland, Reginald 19
Courtauld, Augustine 18, 62–64, 99
Courtauld, Samuel 99
Coward, Noel 153
Cox, Percy 69, 126
Cranborne, Lord 182
Credit-Anstalt (CA) 80–82
Cribbett, George 197–98
Cromer, Lord 10, 16, 40, 126, 157
Cross, Ronald 101
Crowe, Eyre 45
cryptanalysis 39
Cunningham, Alan 140
Curtis, Lionel 19, 58, 120
Curzon, Lord 11
Cuthbert Peek Medal 68
Cyrenaica 30–32, 45, 137–39, 144, 192

D'Agostino, Major Francesco 34, 36–38
D'Erlanger, Gerard 197
d'Ornano, Colonel Camille 125
Daily Telegraph 61, 99
Daily Worker 181
Dakar-Djibouti expedition 69
Dalton, Hugh 110–11, 113, 147, 189, 191
Davis, Wade 43
Davison, Harry 117
Dawe, Arthur 79, 89–90, 92–93
Dawson, Geoffrey 112
DCA. *See* Directorate of Civil Affairs (DCA)
de Gaulle, Charles 1, 124–25, 128–29, 131–36, 156–58
de Larminat, Edgard 124, 128–36
Deedes, Wyndham 34
Delmé-Radcliffe, Charles 29
Dering, Herbert 48
Dill, John 138
direct rule 152, 160, 169–70, 172
Directorate of Civil Affairs (DCA) 190
Directorate of Military Intelligence 121–23
Directorate of Military Operations 119, 137, 163
Dirksen, Herbert von 96

Domesday Book 206–7
Drake, Francis 165
Driberg, Tom 181
Driver, Felix 50
dual mandate 4
Dugdale, John 182
Dunkirk speech 112, 120
Dürer, Albrecht 212
Duveyrier, Henri 50

East Africa 137–61
East African currency 143
East African Supply Group 154
East India Company 7–8
Eaton, William 68, 193
Eboué, Felix 124, 135
Economic and Reconstruction Department 150
Eden, Anthony 1, 91, 93, 112, 147–48, 152, 157, 182, 189–90
Edward VII, King 17
Edwardian culture 16, 19
EEF. *See* Egyptian Expeditionary Force (EEF)
Egypt 31–32, 34, 45, 47, 71, 103, 126, 137, 145, 194
Egyptian Expeditionary Force (EEF) 35
Eisenhower, Dwight 4, 164–65, 168, 175–76, 180, 186
el Sanusi, Muhammad Ibn Ali 30
Elizabethan principle 49
Ellwood, David 171
Elwes, Simon 62, 95, 153
Eminent Victorians 10
Emmanuel III, King Victor 13
Emmet. Baroness. *See* Emmet, Evelyn
Emmet, Christopher 146
Emmet, Evelyn (Baroness Emmet) 192–93
Emmet, Thomas 192
emotions/emotional 8, 16, 20, 62, 130, 209, 214, 217
'English Men of Action' series 8
Eritrea 71, 105, 137, 139–40, 143–44, 150–52, 192
Esdras, Book of 210–11
Ethiopia 4, 10–11, 91, 94, 96, 108, 121, 137–40, 143, 145–51, 154, 156, 192, 218
Eton College 17–18
Everest exhibition 200
Exploration du Sahara: Les Touareg du Nord 50

INDEX

Falk, Oswald 76–77
Falls, Cyril 201
Farinacci, Roberto 78
Faringdon, Lord 62
fascism 77, 87, 89, 104, 170, 172, 218
Fascist Grand Council 175
Faysal, King 40
Fellowes, Rupert 42
Fernando Po 124
Fezzani military expedition of 1821 70
The Field 47
Field Manual 27–5 170
The Financial Times 211
First Barbary War (1801–5) 68
First World War 1–2, 18–19, 21, 23–26, 30, 43, 45–46, 57–58, 64, 71–72, 85–86, 98, 101–3, 108, 112, 115, 120, 137, 161, 183
Flint, Edward 183
Forbes, Rosita 46
Foreign Office 8, 12–13, 40, 42, 45, 57, 94–95, 101–2, 109–10, 122, 135, 137, 145, 147, 151, 155–57, 165, 182–83, 190, 193, 195, 214–15, 217
Forgan, Robert 88
Foucauld, Charles de 59, 66, 210
Founder's Medal 1, 68, 72
Foureau–Lamy mission 50, 54
Fox, Cyril 206
France 8, 24, 29, 37, 41, 83, 85, 89, 95, 107, 131, 134, 202
Fraser, Leon 79
Frederick, Crown Prince 8
Free French rule in Brazzaville 130
French Camel Corps unit 132
French Equatorial Africa 3, 124, 126, 128–29, 131–33, 135–36, 156
French–Italian committee 104
Fripp, Alfred 17
Fummi, Giovanni 94, 109

G(R) 121–23, 125, 200. *See also* MI(R)
Gabriel, Edmund Vivian 29
Gater, George 160
Gautier, E. F. 61
Gayre, G. R. 185–86
Genuardo, Baron 173
Geographical Journal 58
Geographical Magazine 73
German economic structure 90

Germany 2, 13, 45, 84, 87–89, 90–92, 94–96, 102–9, 111–12, 114, 148, 175, 191, 216, 218
Ghana Airways 197
Giannini, Amadeo 104–5, 107
Giannini, M. 102
Giffard, George 122–23
Giolitti, Giovanni 13
Glover, T. A. 49, 51, 71
Gold Coast 119–21, 160, 193
Gold Standard 80, 83–85, 98
Gold Standard in Theory and Practice 83
Gordon, General 10
Grafftey-Smith, A. P. 182, 185
Grafftey-Smith, Laurence 76, 155–57
Gramain, Henri 51
Graves, Robert 48
Greene, Wilfrid 104
Greenwood, Arthur 182
Grenfell, Edward 85, 87, 97
Grey, Earl 87
Grey, Edward 13
Grey, Louisa 87
Grigg, P. J. 144, 149, 155–56, 164, 179, 188–90
Guardian 61, 151
Gubbins, Colin 119, 121–22
Guillebon, Captain de 125
Gunston, C. A. 84
Guthrie Trust 181
Guthrie, Lilias Georgina. *See* Rodd, Lilias Georgina
Guthrie, James Alexander 7
Gwynn, Charles 192

Hague Convention of 1907 137
Hailey, Lord 125, 128, 131–36, 159–60, 202, 217
Haining, Robert 138, 145–46
Halifax, Lord 94, 101, 103, 107, 109, 218
Hall, Noel 113
Hamlyn, Ralph 73, 153
Hammond, Mason 185
Hankey, Lord 194
Hansen, Per 80
Harcourt, William 87
Hardinge, Charles 13, 45
Hardy, Thomas 28
Harriman, Averell 201
Harris, C. R. S. 172, 178–79, 185

INDEX

Harvey, Oliver 91
Haslam, William ('Bill') 30–31, 119
Hassan, Sultan 34
Hassanein, Ahmed 31, 46–47
Hawtrey, R. G. 83
Hedin, Sven 13
Heffernan, Michael 71
Hemming, John 199
Henderson, Nevile 91
Hereford map. *See* Mappa Mundi
Herefordshire 115, 187, 204
Hersey, John 184
Hilaire, Colonel 34
Hilton, Rodney 207
Hindwell valley 205–6
Hinks, Arthur, 43, 58, 64
Hints to Travellers 63
Hitler 3, 87, 89–90, 102, 109, 114, 132, 192
Hodgkin, A. E. 189
Hofmeyr, Jan Hendrik 153
Hogarth, D. G. 58–59, 215
Holland, J. C. F. 119
Holmes, Julius 165
Hone, Ralph 139–41, 153
Hood, Viscount 150
Hopkins, A. G. 196
Horn, Martin 97, 147, 151, 157–58
Hornemann, Friedrich 69
House Debate Society 17
House of Lords 95–96, 147–48, 159–60, 182, 190–95, 197, 211, 219
Hudson, Arnold 119
Hülse, Ernst 79
Hulton, Teresa 35
Hume, Edgar 176
Huxley, Aldous 19
Huxley, Michael 73
Huxley, Thomas 210

IAI. *See* International African Institute (IAI)
Idris, Sayyid 31–33, 127, 153
Iferuan 54–55, 65
Illustrated London News 181
Imitation of Christ 18
Imperial General Staff 138, 163, 201
indirect rule 4–5, 60, 152, 158–60, 168–9, 171–72, 177, 192, 217–18
Industrial Intelligence Centre 101
Ingram, Maurice 75, 95
International African Institute (IAI) 202
International Monetary Fund 185, 195

Iron Age archaeology 203
Irvine, Andrew 43
Islam 59, 61, 66
Italian East Africa 137, 143, 146, 152
Italian fascism 89
Italian Palestine Detachment 34, 36, 38
Italian Somaliland 140
Italo-German agreement 109
Italy 1–5, 13, 29–31, 34, 77–79, 89, 94–96, 101–17, 126, 137–38, 146–48, 151, 157, 164, 170, 172–73, 175–83, 185, 188–90, 211, 216, 218

Jacks, L. P. 72
Jackson, J. B. 130
Jackson, Robert 194
January Club 88–89, 218
Jay, Dean 96
Jean, Lieutenant C. 50
Jebb, Gladwyn 111
Jennings, Eric 130
Jerusalem 38
Jones, G. I. 72
J. P. Morgan & Co. 84–86, 91, 93–94, 96–97, 113, 117
Jowett, Benjamin 8, 66
Joyce, Kenyon 180, 183–84
Joyce, William 183

Kamel, Hussein 34
Kano intelligence centre 124
Kaocen Ag Muhammad 54
Karamnelli, Hamet 68
Katsina, emir of 124
KBE. *See* Knight Commander of the British Empire (KBE)
Keats-Shelley Association 15
Keats, John 15
Kempis, Thomas à 18
Kennard, Howard 46
Kennedy-Cooke, Brian 143–44
Kennedy-Fraser, Marjory 130
Kerry Hill sheep 208
Kershaw, R. N. 79
Keynes, John Maynard 76, 84, 142
Kilian, Conrad 69
Kindersley, David 213
King, W. Harding 57
Kingdon-Ward, F. 200
Knight Commander of the British Empire (KBE) 189

INDEX 243

Kipling, Rudyard 154
Kirwan, L. P. 199, 217
Kissinger, Henry 217
Knox, Ronald 209

La Guardia, Fiorello H. 164
Labour Party 110
Laing, Alexander Gordon 69
Lamont, Thomas S. 117
Lamont, Thomas W. 85–86, 90–94, 97–98, 117, 140, 153–54, 187–88, 191, 216
landscape 28, 43–45, 65–67, 130, 153, 203–5, 208, 213–14
Langtry, Lily 23
Lateran Treaty 95
Laval, Pierre 69
Lavitrano, Cardinal 171
Lawley, Irene 20, 26–28, 32, 34, 45–46, 48, 86
Lawrence, T. E. 1, 40–41, 43, 48–49, 58–59, 66, 68, 119, 155, 195, 215–16
League Loans Committee 83, 86
Leclerc, Philippe 124
Legentilhomme, Paul 157
Leith-Ross, Frederick 91, 101, 109, 113
Leone, Sierra 121
Lhote, Henri 70
Liberals 191, 219
Libya 3, 30, 33, 45, 50, 59, 71, 120, 126–27, 129–32, 137, 154, 193
Libyan Sands 72–73
lira policy 142–43
Little Flowers of St Francis 18
Livingstone, David 213
Loder, John de Vere 36, 76
Lombard Street: A Description of the Money Market 83
Long Range Desert Group (LRDG) 3
Long Range Patrol 126
Loos, Battle of 24
Loraine, Percy 71, 103, 106–8, 111–12
Lost Oases 47
Love in a Cold Climate 114
LRDG. *See* Long Range Desert Group (LRDG)
Lucas, St John 212
Lugard, Frederick 4, 60
Lumley, Roger 189
Lush, Maurice 145, 147–48, 151, 153, 155–57, 179–80, 184
Lyautey, Hubert 126
Lydia Bailey 193

Lynden-Bell, Arthur 36
Lyttelton, Edward, 17
Lyttelton, Oliver 144–45, 153, 164, 189

Macdonald, Ramsay 85
Mackereth, Gilbert 147
Mackinder, Halford 201
Macmillan, Harold 18, 25, 180, 184, 194
Madagascar 3–4, 155–58, 179, 192
Mafia 5, 171–74, 219
Makonnen, Ras 11
Malcolm, Jeanne 23
Malet, Edward 8, 12
Mallett, Robert 112
Mallory, George 43
Mappa Mundi 207
maps 2, 7, 43, 51, 54, 64, 69, 120, 205
Marcus, Nathan 82
Maria Theresa dollars 143
Markham, Clements 7
Masi, M. 104, 110
Mason-MacFarlane, Noel 175
Mathews, Lloyd 9
Mavis, Stephen 184
Maxwell, Colonel Terence 178
McCloy, John 174
McDonnell, William 87
McGarrah, Gates W. 79
McSherry, F. J. 165–66
Medlicott, W. N. 106
Meinertzhagen, Amorei 46
Meinertzhagen, Richard 37
Menelik, Emperor 10–12
Mercier, Sub-Lieutenant 34
Merino sheep 208
Metropolitan lire 175
MEW. *See* Ministry of Economic Warfare (MEW)
MGS. *See* Military Government Section (MGS)
MI(R). *See* Military Intelligence Research (MI(R))
Middle East Supply Centre 154
Middle Eastern Intelligence Centre 158
Military Government Section (MGS) 165, 176–78
Military Handbook on Palestine 34
Military Intelligence Research (MI(R)) 3, 119–22, 129–30, 216
Mill, John Stuart 60
Milner, Lord 19

Ministry of Economic Warfare (MEW) 2–3, 101–3, 105–6, 110, 190
Mitchell, Philip 138–47, 151–54, 159, 185, 216
Mitford, Nancy 1, 89–90, 99, 114, 184
Monod, Théodore 70
Montagu-Stuart-Wortley, Edward 8
Montgomery, Bernard 185
Moore, Daphne 161
Moore, Henry Monck-Mason 154, 163
Moral Re-Armament (MRA) 113, 210
Morgan, Frederick 189
Morgan Grenfell & Co. 2, 84–87, 91–95, 97–98, 101, 113, 123, 190, 195–96, 198
Morgan, J. P. ('Jack') 84–86, 94, 98, 123
Mori, Cesare 172
Morton, Desmond 101, 125
Mosley, Oswald 89
Mountbatten, Viscount 201
MRA. *See* Moral Re-Armament (MRA)
Munich Agreement 96
Murphy, Robert 185
Murray, Archibald 35
Murray, John 57
Mussolini, Benito 1, 3, 77–78, 89, 91, 94–95, 101–7, 109–12, 146, 148, 175, 184, 191
Mysteries of the Libyan Desert 57

Nafi, Oqba ibn 54
Naples 77, 175, 177, 178
Nasser, President 154
National Bank of Australasia 196
National Geographic 73
Native Administration and Political Development 159
Nazi party 87–90
Nazism 104, 215, 218
New Statesman and Nation 181
New York Times 86, 181
Newark, Tim 173
Newbold, Douglas 70
Nicholls, J. W. 110
Nicolson, Harold 75
Niemeyer, Otto 79
Niger 1, 50, 57, 62, 70, 123–25, 127–28, 130
Nigeria 3, 54–55, 57, 60, 62, 70, 115, 119–24, 126, 129, 132, 159–60
Nigerian Defence Force 120
Nile expedition of 1898 9
Nkrumah, Kwame 193–94
Nobel Prize Committee 210
Nogara, Bernardino 94–95

Nolan, Sidney 208
Norman, Montagu 49, 77–80, 84–85
Normandy campaign 189–90
Nosworthy, Richard 103
Nugent, Walter 34–35
Nuovo, Castello 176
Nye, Archibald 163

Occupied Enemy Territory Administration (OETA) 3–4, 40, 138–43, 145, 183, 185, 217–18. *See also* OTA
Occupied Territory Administration (OTA) 138, 141–43, 145, 148, 164, 166, 185, 217
Oceanography 7
Odyssey 20
OETA. *See* Occupied Enemy Territory Administration (OETA)
Offa's Dyke 205–6
Officers' Emergency Reserve 119
OG. *See* Oxford Group (OG)
Ogaden 148–49
Operation Husky 4, 166
Operation Ironclad 4, 155
Operation Torch 170
Orientalism 10, 215
OTA. *See* Occupied Territory Administration (OTA)
Otte, Thomas 13
Out of the World – North of Nigeria 49
Overweg, Adolf 50
Owen, Roddy 9
Oxford Group (OG) 113, 181

Palmer, H. R. 62, 68
'Para-Military Activity' paper 122
Paris Peace Conference in 1919 5, 43, 85
Park, Mungo 7
Parr, Robert 134, 136
Partisan Leader's Handbook 119
partnership, 4, 159
Patton, George 166
Pedler, Frederick 128, 135
People of the Veil 1, 48, 51, 58–62, 65–66, 68, 158, 204–5
Perkins, Dexter 201
Perrone, Signor 95
Peterson, Maurice 71
Petrie, Charles 12
Peyton, William 31
Physics of Blown Sand and Desert Dunes 204

INDEX 245

Picot, François Georges 38
Piépape, Colonel de 38
Pietromarchi, Count 107
Pigeon Pie 114
Pirelli, Alberto 108
Pirie, Douglas 167, 180
Pitt Rivers Museum 56
Pizzoni, Alfredo 190
Platt, William 141, 146, 153–58, 163
Playfair, Edward 103–4, 110
Pleven, René 126, 128, 131, 134, 135
Poletti, Charles 174
Portal, Gerald 35
Portal, Maurice 35
Portal, Raymond 9
Presteigne tapestry 207
Proclamation Number 1 167
Progress Report 104
Pursuit of Love 114
Put Out More Flags 65

Quesnay, Pierre 82

Radnorshire Society Transactions 205–6
Ralegh Club 19
Raleigh, Walter 8
Raven-Hart, Rowland 39
Ravenhill, F. T. 24
Reading, Lord 191
Reeves, E. A. 63
Reiss, Curt 181
Rennell, Francis. *See* Rodd, Francis James Rennell
Rennell, James 7, 68, 69, 207
Rennell, Lord (1st Baron Rennell). *See* Rodd, James Rennell
Rennell, Lord (2nd Baron Rennell). *See* Rodd, Francis James Rennell
Rennell, Mary (Lady). *See* Rodd, Mary Constance Vivian
Reserved Areas 149–51, 154
Revolt against Mechanism 72
RFA. *See* Royal Field Artillery (RFA)
RGS. *See* Royal Geographical Society (RGS)
Rhodes, Cecil 9
Rhodes, Frank 9, 154
Ribbentrop, Joachim von 91
Richardson, James 50
Rise Above It 153
Rivet, Paul 68
Rivière, Georges Henri 68

Roberts, Kenneth 193
Rodd, Francis James Rennell
  acquired 'the Rodd' 115
  administrative tension 179
  adventurer 211–12
  advisor in French Equatorial Africa 136
  African education 119–20
  air transport of Western Australia 204
  ancestral lineage 7–8
  appearance in US fiction 184
  assisting the adjutant in war 24
  attacks from parliament and press 187
  aware of Free French movement 130, 135
  in Bank of England 84
  banking background 129
  Bantu Studies research project 203
  birth of 7
  Boden-Credit-Anstalt, problems in 80–82
  boosting British–Australian commercial relations 203
  Bourdillon's advisor 121
  as brigade orderly officer 23
  British–Italian Bank, problems in 77–79
  British military strategy, aspects of 36
  brothers of 151
  caravan routes of Sahara 130
  on Catholicism 209
  chief military administrator in Madagascar 158
  chief political officer 154
  civil aviation and 197
  class consciousness in British society 35–36
  on corrupt management 174
  course on classical history 19
  criticism of Harding King book 57–58
  currency policy issues 142–43
  Dakar raid 125
  daughters' schooling 187
  dealing with Ethiopia 145–46
  degree of centralisation 163
  detailed geological and meteorological calculations 54
  developing good relations between British and Americans 165
  differences with Etonians 189
  director of Air Finance 197
  discussion of the dunes of Western Australia 204
  educated by governesses 16
  engrossed in AMGOT 187
  enlisting in war 23

246 INDEX

Rodd, Francis James Rennell (*cont.*)
  on ethic of unselfishness 210
  to Eton 17
  evacuation process 148
  events in Niger 125
  experience of battle 26
  experiment in cattle farming 203
  father's death 151
  fear of Foreign Office 165
  financial advisor 141
  finding civil affairs personnel 166
  First World War 23–43
  flight experience 198–99
  focus on Australia 203
  Franciscan ideals 66
  gentlemanly director 196
  good administration according to 180–81
  Great Depression 83
  head of AMGOT 164
  honorary degree of LLD to 201
  idea of a Greater Somalia 150
  idea on integration in empire 160
  ideas on irregular warfare 120–21
  ill-health of 16–17
  importance of carabinieri 172
  impressions of Bardia 33
  indirect rule 160, 168–69
  instinct for public service 192
  interest in history 207
  interest in camels 63, 132
  interest in geography 2, 28, 153, 200–201
  international banker 75–100
  Italian Order of St Maurice and Lazarus 42
  Italian presence in Libya 33
  joined Buckmaster and Moore 76
  joined the Foreign Office 45
  journey into mountains of Aïr 49
  KBE 189
  knickname 'Babban Bature' 65
  on 'Land of Heart's Desire' 130
  leadership style is civilian 185
  learning the local language 51
  leaving the Western Front 28–29
  in Legation in Sofia 48
  letters to father on physical danger 26
  as liaison officer 34
  life at the front 27–28
  local society into provincial administration 171
  long standing interest in caravan routes 120
  meeting Mussolini 78
  military government approach 188–90
  in military intelligence 119
  military mission in Italy 28–29
  modifications to local maps 54
  monitored developments in Egypt 194
  moved to Arab Bureau 40
  negotiating with Italy 101–18
  offering medical help to natives 53
  officer of the Intelligence Corps 39
  OTA policy 148
  outstanding qualities of 184–85
  overview of AMGOT 178
  at Oxford 19–20
  passion for land 204–5
  philosophy of decision-making 160–61
  photographs during the expedition 51–52
  ports of Libya, reports on 33
  post-war interests 203–4
  post-war reconstruction 190–91
  president of RGS 199–201
  privileged upbringing 21
  problems with MGS 177–78
  as a problem-solver 79
  to public attention 1
  rapport with native peoples 53
  reason to leave Foreign Office 75
  reconnaissance expedition to Ottoman railway base 36
  religious thinking of 18
  Rennell's legacy 7
  research in Africa 202–3
  respect for Tuareg radicalism 195
  rowing, involvement in 17
  into the Sahara 45–74
  science and humanities 202
  second expedition to Aïr 53
  self-evaluation in 27
  sheep farming 208
  Shoeburyness, gunnery course at 23
  situation in Eritrea 144
  size of ACC 177
  spirit of self-reliance 16
  staff captain in Hijaz operation 42
  stepped down from AMGOT 211
  story of wartime administration 192
  studying astronomy and topography 62
  on Suez crisis 194–95
  support to RGS 200
  suppress mafia 173
  Talbot mission 30
  threat to British rule in West Africa 57
  tough attitude to Mau Mau 195

training intelligence corps 119
travelling 152–53
trip to Fort Lamy 128
under fire for the first time 27
unpleasant slur on 133
upset by D'Agostino 36
versatile banker 211
view on Arab 62
view on God's Spirit 210
Western Front to Italy, relocating from 34
work as adjutant 24
work under Gabriel 29
Rodd, Gustaf (Taffy) 15
Rodd, J. A. T. 196
Rodd, James Rennell 2, 7–15, 68–69, 151, 207, 211
ambassador in Italy 13–14
being under fire 9
in Berlin 8
biography of Raleigh 8
British agency, assigned to 8
education of 8
embassy in Cairo, work in 10
emperor of Ethiopia, agreement with 10–11
expedition to Addis Ababa 10
into Foreign Office 8
human relation, emphasis on 12
impressions of Lawrence 48
minister in the British Legation, role of 13
in Zanzibar 8–9
Rodd, Major James Rennell 8
Rodd, Lilias Georgina 7–8, 14, 130
Rodd, Mary Constance Vivian 2, 5, 66, 86, 103–4, 107, 113–15, 117, 120–24, 127–30, 132, 136, 140–41, 153–56, 158–61, 163–66, 179, 181, 187–89, 191, 194, 199, 204–5, 208–11, 219
Rodd, Peter 15, 65, 89, 114–15, 183
Roman civilisation 59
Rome 8, 12–13, 15, 20, 29–30, 32, 34, 45–46, 49, 66, 77, 94, 97, 103, 105, 107–11, 147, 165, 171, 175, 178, 208, 218
Rommel, Erwin 145
Rosebery, Lord 9, 14
Rousseau, Jean-Jacques 60
Round Table 19
Royal Field Artillery (RFA) 23
Royal Geographical Society (RGS) 1, 7, 43, 47, 53, 56, 58, 62, 63, 67–69, 71–73, 126, 199–200, 201–2, 204, 207, 215
Runcin, Lord 184

Sabatier, Paul 18
Sacerdoti, Cesare 110
Sahara 1–2, 43, 45–74, 120, 130, 204
French occupation of Aïr 54
map-making of 64
map of Aïr 55
map of trade roads of Sahara 56
military significance of the roads of 54
road systems 54
Said, Edward 10
Salandra, Antonio 13
Samuel, Lord 191
Sandford, Daniel 147
Sanusi 30–32, 57, 127
Sayers, R. S. 79
SCAO. *See* senior civil affairs officer (SCAO)
Scarin, Emilio 70
Schacht, Hjalmar 79
Schleicher, Kurt von 87
School of Military Government 170, 186
'Scragged' slang expression 129
Second World War 1–3, 30, 68, 76, 95, 97–98, 158, 197, 204, 214–17, 219
Secret of the Sahara, Kufara 47
Selassie, Haile 4, 137, 143, 145–49, 151–52, 218
Seven Pillars of Wisdom 48, 66, 119
Sforza, Carlo 191
Shackleton, Ernest 212
SHAEF. *See* Supreme Headquarters Allied Expeditionary Force (SHAEF)
Shaw, W. B. ('Bill') Kennedy 66, 70
Sheep Development Association 208
'ship of fools' image 211–12
Sicily 4, 32, 152, 165–67, 170–72, 175–77, 181–82
Siepmann, Harry 79
Simms, William Philip 112
Simon, Hans 80
Simpson, Adrian 121, 126–27, 131
Smallpiece, Basil 198
Smith, Bryan Sharwood 124–25
Smith, Hugh Colin 87
Smith, Mary Constance Vivian. *See* Rodd, Mary Constance Vivian
Smith, Randall Hugh Vivian ('Rufus') 87, 195
Smith, Vivian Hugh (Lord Bicester) 87, 94, 113, 115
Smith, W. H. 12
Smith, Walter Bedell 168
Smuts, Jan 153

248 INDEX

Snow, C. P. 202
SOE. *See* Special Operations Executive (SOE)
Somalia 137, 150, 154, 219
'Song of Diego Valdez' poem 154
Sonnino, Sidney 13
Soper, Robert 203
Southard, Frank 185
Spears, Edward 125, 134
Special Operations Executive (SOE) 119
Speed, Eric 179, 196, 203
Spencer, John H. 151
Spinoza, Baruch 6
Spofford, Charles 167–68, 175–76, 185
Spring-Rice, Cecil 210
St Aubyn's Preparatory School 16
St Johnston, Eric 172
Stafford, Frank 153
Stanford, Charles 16
Stanley, Oliver 160
Stephenson, D. C. 24
Stewart, Walter 79
Stimson, Henry 185–86
Stirling, Edward 8
Stirling, James 7, 203
Stirling, W. F. 40–41
Stokes, Richard 182
Stoneman, Walter 14
Story of a Norfolk Farm 204
Strachey, Lytton 10
Straight, Whitney 197
Stuart-Wortley, Louise 15
Sturzo, Luigi 182
Suez Group 194
Suliman, El Haj 60
Sun Insurance Office Limited 196
Sun Life Assurance Society 196
Sunday Times 84, 183
Supreme Headquarters Allied Expeditionary Force (SHAEF) 189
Sykes-Picot Agreement 40–41, 58
Sykes, Mark 33

T'ekhmedin 51–53, 64, 124, 215–16
Talbot, Colonel Milo 30–31, 33, 46
Tananarive 155
Tanganyika 159
Tarazit mountains 65
Target for Tonight 153
Taylor, Reginald 123
Tempest 14
Templer, Gerald 119

Termit mountains 50, 51, 70
Thesiger, Wilfred 67, 72, 200
Thomas, Ivor 182
Thomas, Miles 197
Thwain, Hamed bin 9
Tilho, Jean 70
Timbuktu 46, 65, 69
Times 9, 47, 68, 95–96, 112, 114, 141, 188, 204
Tonks, Henry 86
Toye, Richard 112
transatlantic alliance 120
Travels and Discoveries in North and Central Africa 50
Treaty of London 13
Trebartha Hall 8
Tripolitania 127
'Tropical Dependency' school of thought 159
Trust Corporation of the Bahamas 196
trusteeship, 4, 159
Tuareg 1, 40–52, 56–66, 68–70, 73, 75, 126, 195
Tuesday Club, 76, 128
Turkish currency 142
'Two Cultures and the Scientific Revolution' 202

Unconducted Wanderers 46
United Nations General Assembly 192
United States Base Organisation 176

Valley on the March 205–6
Vansittart, Robert 80
Versailles Settlement 120
Via Sacra 38
Volpi, Giuseppe 111
Volta River Project 194
Vyshinsky, Andrei 177

Waldorf Astor Foundation 203
Waley, David 134
Walker, David 207
Wallenburg, Markus 98
WAPET. *See* West Australian Petroleum Pty Ltd (WAPET)
Wapley hill-fort 206
War Cabinet 101, 103–4, 109, 137, 144, 147–48, 157–58, 189
War Office 3–4, 27, 37, 43, 119–21, 123, 126, 137–38, 141–42, 144–45, 147, 155–56, 160, 163–64, 179, 182, 188, 190, 196

INDEX

Ward, Barbara 194
Watkinson, Harold 197
Waugh, Evelyn 65
Wavell, Archibald 112, 126, 137–39, 146, 152
Wellesley, Dorothy ('Dottie') 20–21, 76, 86
Wellesley, Gerald 20, 86, 167
Wellesley, Victor 88
West Africa 54, 57, 70, 119–36
West Australian Petroleum Pty Ltd (WAPET) 203
Western Mining Corporation 203
western Sudan 70
Wethered, Hugh 39
Whistler, John 8
White, Hale 17
Wigs on the Green 90

Wilde, Oscar 8
Williams, Colonel 134, 136
Williamson, Henry 204
Wilson, Henry 164
Wilson, Woodrow 5, 85
Wingate, Orde 121
Wingate, Reginald 10, 30, 33–34
Witu expedition 9
World Economic Conference 84–85
'World in Focus' exhibition 200

Yeats, W. B. 20, 130
Young Plan 79–80
Younghusband, Francis 67

Zerzura oasis 71
Zola, Emile 28

www.ingramcontent.com/pod-product-compliance
Lightning Source LLC
Chambersburg PA
CBHW021822300426
44114CB00009BA/289